Global Issues

New to this edition, please find a Facebook page for *Global Issues*, which features updates on many of the subjects discussed in this book. Please feel welcome to visit, like, comment, and share:
https://www.facebook.com/GlobalIssuesHiteSeitz

Global Issues
An Introduction

FIFTH EDITION

Kristen A. Hite and John L. Seitz

WILEY Blackwell

This fifth edition first published 2016
© 2016 John Wiley & Sons Ltd

Edition History: Blackwell Publishers Ltd (1e, 1995); Blackwell Publishing Ltd (2e, 2002 and 3e, 2008); John Wiley & Sons Ltd (4e, 2012)

Registered Office
John Wiley & Sons Ltd, The Atrium, Southern Gate, Chichester, West Sussex, PO19 8SQ, UK

Editorial Offices
350 Main Street, Malden, MA 02148-5020, USA
9600 Garsington Road, Oxford, OX4 2DQ, UK
The Atrium, Southern Gate, Chichester, West Sussex, PO19 8SQ, UK

For details of our global editorial offices, for customer services, and for information about how to apply for permission to reuse the copyright material in this book please see our website at www.wiley.com/wiley-blackwell.

The right of Kristen A. Hite and John L. Seitz to be identified as the authors of this work has been asserted in accordance with the UK Copyright, Designs and Patents Act 1988.

Library of Congress Cataloging-in-Publication Data is available for this title

pbk. 9781118968857

A catalogue record for this book is available from the British Library.

Cover image: © Martin Barraud / Getty Images

Set in 10.5/13pt Minion by Aptara Inc., New Delhi, India
Printed and bound in Malaysia by Vivar Printing Sdn Bhd

1   2016

To those who serve the needs of others – humans, animals, and plants,
all essential parts of our lovely but endangered planet

Contents

List of Plates   xii
List of Figures, Maps, and Tables   xiv
Acknowledgments   xvi
Foreword   xvii

Introduction   **1**
The Creation of Global Issues   1
Developing toward What?   2
Notes   5

1 Population   **7**
The Changing Population of the World   8
Causes of the Population Explosion   17
How Population Growth Affects Development   20
   Rapid growth   21
   Slow growth   22
   An aging population and low birth rates   22
   International conferences on population   24
How Development Affects Population Growth   26
   Demographic transition   26
   Factors lowering birth rates   28
Governmental Population Policies   31
   Controlling growth   31
   Promoting growth   36
The Future   38
   The growth of the world's population   38
   The carrying capacity of the Earth   39
   Optimum size of the Earth's population   42
   Population-related problems in our future   43

Conclusions	44
Notes	46
Further Reading	49

2 Wealth and Poverty — **51**

Wave of Hope: The Millennium Development Goals	55
A Pessimistic View: The Persistence of Poverty	57
Development Assistance and Foreign Aid	59
A Market Approach	63
The State as Economic Actor	67
A Blended Approach	70
Geography and Wealth, Geography and Poverty	72
Globalization	73
Positive aspects	75
Negative aspects	76
An evaluation	77
Conclusions	78
Notes	80
Further Reading	83

3 Food — **85**

World Food Production	86
How Many Are Hungry?	87
Causes of World Hunger	89
How Food Affects Development	91
How Development Affects Food	93
The production of food	93
The loss of food	97
The type of food	100
The "Green" Revolution	105
Fertilizers	106
Pesticides	106
Irrigation	107
The future	107
Governmental Food Policies	108
Future Food Supplies	111
Climate	111
Arable land	112
Energy costs	114
Traditional/sustainable/organic agriculture	114
Biotechnology	115
Fishing and aquaculture	117
Future food production	119

Conclusions 120
Notes 121
Further Reading 127

4 Energy **129**
The Energy-Climate Crisis 130
    Energy and security 132
Government Responses to the Energy-Climate Crisis 133
    The United States 134
    Western Europe 136
    Japan 136
    China 138
The Effect of the Energy-Climate Crisis on Countries' Development
Plans 140
The Relationship between Energy Use and Development 141
    A shift in types of energy 141
    Increased use 142
    The decoupling of energy consumption and economic growth 142
The Energy Transition 147
    Nonrenewable energy sources 147
    Renewable energy sources 148
    Conservation/energy efficiency 155
Nuclear Power: A Case Study 157
    The potential and the peril 158
    The choice 161
Conclusions 164
Notes 165
Further Reading 169

5 Climate Change **170**
The Evidence and Impacts 172
    Warmer temperatures 172
    Food and water 174
    Extreme weather 174
    Sea level rise 175
    Coral reefs 176
    Air pollution 178
    Infectious diseases 178
    Agriculture 178
    Disruption of natural ecosystems 179
    Regional impacts 179
Uncertainties 180
What Is Being Done at Present? 181
What More Can Be Done? 182
Conclusion 185

	Notes	185
	Further Reading	187
6	**The Environment: Part I**	**189**
	The Awakening	190
	The Air	192
	Smog	192
	Airborne lead	196
	Ozone depletion	198
	Acid rain	200
	Climate change (global warming)	202
	The Water	203
	Water quantity	203
	Water quality	203
	The Land	206
	Minerals	206
	Deforestation	207
	The Extinction of Species	211
	The Extinction of Cultures	215
	The Yanomami	216
	Notes	218
7	**The Environment: Part II**	**224**
	The Workplace and the Home	224
	Cancer	224
	Chemicals	225
	Pesticides	226
	Managing Waste	228
	Solid wastes	228
	Toxic wastes	230
	Governmental and industrial responses to the waste problem	232
	Responsible Use	233
	Resource efficiency	233
	Recycling	234
	Substitution	235
	Reducing needs	236
	Environmental Politics	236
	Overdevelopment	238
	Conclusions	238
	Notes	239
	Further Reading	242

8 Technology **244**

Benefits of Technology 245

Unanticipated Consequences of the Use of Technology 245

    DDT 247

    Factory farms 248

Inappropriate Uses of Technology 250

Limits to the "Technological Fix" 253

War 255

The Threat of Nuclear Weapons: A Case Study 257

    The threat 258

    New dangers 260

Conclusions 264

Notes 264

Further Reading 266

9 Alternative Futures **268**

Development Pathways: Evaluating Our Current Situation 269

Current Outlook: Business as Usual 270

Collapse and Sustainable Development 272

Choices 274

    Improve production 275

    Reduce demand 275

Governance: Deciding How to Act on the Choices We Make 276

    Governing the commons 276

    Inclusive governance and the role of civil society 278

Conclusion 282

Notes 284

Further Reading 287

Appendix 1: Studying and Teaching Global Issues 289

Appendix 2: Relevant Videos 297

Appendix 3: Relevant Internet Websites 308

Appendix 4: The United Nations 2030 Agenda for Sustainable
        Development 314

Glossary 317

Index 323

Plates

1.1	Rural migrants often settle in urban slums in developing nations	12
1.2	Growing cities in less developed nations often have a mixture of modern and substandard housing	16
1.3	Children take care of children in many places, as this girl is doing in Mexico	20
1.4	Breast-feeding delays a woman's ability to conceive and provides the most healthful food for a baby	30
1.5	Advertisement for contraceptives in Costa Rica	32
1.6	Family planning class	34
1.7	A more frequent picture in the future? A crowded train in Bangladesh	44
2.1	Poverty in Indonesia	56
2.2	The weight of poverty falls heavily on children in less developed nations	57
2.3	Street children in Nepal	60
2.4	The market approach is followed on the streets in many countries	64
2.5	The state approach to development struggles to survive the collapse of communist regimes in Europe, as can be seen in the posters of a Communist Party conference in Nepal	69
3.1	Starvation in Somalia	89
3.2	The bloated belly is a sign of malnutrition, a major cause of stunting and death in children worldwide	92
3.3	Street vendors sell food to many urban dwellers	100
3.4	Tropical rainforests are being cut down to clear land to raise beef cattle for the US fast-food market – the so-called "hamburger connection"	101
3.5	Much of the food in Africa is grown and prepared by women	112
4.1	Shortage of wood is a part of the energy crisis, since many urban dwellers in developing nations rely on wood as their major source of fuel	134

4.2	The replacing of human-powered vehicles with oil-fueled vehicles in poor and crowded countries, such as Bangladesh, will be difficult	141
4.3	Wind turbines in Altamont Pass, California	150
4.4	Solar thermal power plant, California	152
4.5	Solar energy provides power for a water pump in Morocco	153
4.6	Geothermal power plant, California	154
6.1	Vehicles, such as this truck/bus, provide a lot of air pollution in the cities of the developing countries	197
6.2	Deforestation in Mexico	210
7.1	Water pollution in the United States is partly caused by large amounts of pesticides, herbicides, and fertilizers, which run off from fields during storms	229
8.1	Without modern technology to help, necessary tasks can be difficult. A woman in Nepal breaks up clumps of soil to prepare the land for planting	246
8.2	Underground nuclear weapons testing site in the United States	258

Figures, Maps, and Tables

Figures

1.1	Population growth from 8000 BCE to 2011 CE	9
1.2	Economic differences in population growth, 1950–2005 (projected)	10
1.3	World population projections to 2050: three scenarios	11
1.4	Population by age and sex in different groups of countries, 2010 (projected)	12
1.5	Urban and rural population by development group, 1950–2050	16
1.6	The classic stages of demographic transitions	27
1.7	Demographic transition in Sweden and Mexico	28
1.8	Fertility decline in world regions, 1950–1955, 2000–2005	31
1.9	Increases in modern contraceptive use in selected countries	33
1.10	A growing population and carrying capacity	40
2.1	Global extreme poverty rate	53
2.2	Fewer people in extreme poverty: people living on less than $1 a day, 1981, 1990, 2001	54
2.3	Reduction in extreme poverty in China and India, 1981–2001	55
2.4	Percentage of the population and number of people living in extreme poverty (less than $1.25 a day) in South Asia and Sub-Saharan Africa	59
2.5	World trade: merchandise exports, 1950–1998	74
2.6	World trade: goods exports, 2001–2009	74
3.1	Per capita consumption of major food items in developing countries, 1961–2005	87
3.2	Contribution of agriculture to Gross Domestic Product, 2012	95
3.3	Number of Earths required to sustain global population, 1960–2008 and 2008–2050 (scenarios)	113
4.1	Global energy consumption, 1850–2000	143
4.2	Global energy supply	144

4.3	Global nuclear production from 1971 to 2012	161
5.1	Global carbon dioxide emissions from human activity	171
5.2	Globally averaged combined land and ocean surface temperature anomaly	173
5.3	Climate impacts to agricultural production, by region and crop	175
8.1	Countries with nuclear weapons capacity	261

Maps

1.1	India	18
2.1	Brazil	61
3.1	The Mediterranean	104
4.1	Iraq	132
6.1	China	195
8.1	Borneo and Indonesia	247
8.2	Africa	252

Tables

1.1	Time taken to add each billion to the world population, 1800–2046 (projection)	8
1.2	Ten largest cities in the world, 1990, 2014, and 2030 (projection)	13
1.3	Regional trends in aging: percentage of total population 65 years or older, 2000, 2015 (projection), 2030 (projection)	23
2.1	The wealth of tropical, desert, highland, and temperate regions	72
3.1	Number and size of US farms, 1940–2010	96
3.2	Percentage of adults overweight and obese (various countries)	102
4.1	US gasoline prices, 1950–2009	131
4.2	Top world oil producers, 2013	135
4.3	Per capita and total electricity consumption by region of the world, 2012	145

Acknowledgments

This edition benefited from the substantial research contributions of Whitney Hayes (particularly the population, wealth and poverty, environment, and technology chapters), Cody Samet-Shaw (food, wealth and poverty chapters), and Liz Schmitt (energy and climate chapters), who also provided timely proofreading support.

We would like to thank the following reviewers who made useful suggestions for improving this edition: David Williams, Queen Mary University of London and Scott Anderson, State University of New York, Cortland.

We would also like to thank Wofford College, both for providing author Seitz with an office and for supporting the development and teaching of Global Issues as a semester-long course, which enabled author Hite to take the class from Seitz in the late 1990s and informed her orientation toward the subject.

Foreword

In the 1950s and 1960s I (Seitz) went as an employee of the US government to Iran, Brazil, Liberia, and Pakistan to help them develop. A common belief in those decades was that poverty causes people to turn to communism. As an idealistic young person, I was pleased to work in a program that had the objective of helping poor nations raise their living standards. After World War II the United States was the richest and most powerful country in the world. Many countries welcomed US assistance since it was widely believed that the United States could show others how to escape from poverty.

Disillusionment came as I realized that we did not really know how to help these countries relieve their widespread poverty. The problem was much more complex and difficult than we had imagined. Also, one of the main political objectives of our foreign aid program – to help friendly, noncommunist governments stay in power – often dominated our concerns.

And more disillusionment came when I looked at my own country and realized that it had many problems of its own that had not been solved. It was called "developed" but faced major problems that had accompanied its industrialization – urban sprawl and squalor, pollution, crime, materialism, and ugliness, among others. So, I asked myself, what is development? Is it good or bad? If there are good features in it, as many people in the world believe, how do you achieve them, and how do you control or prevent the harmful features? It was questions such as these that led me to a deeper study of development and to the writing of this book.

I came to recognize that development is a concept that allows us to examine and make some sense out of the complex issues the world faces today. Many of these issues are increasingly seen as being global issues. Because the capacity human beings have to change the world – for better or for worse – is constantly growing, an understanding of global issues has become essential. The front pages of our newspapers and the evening TV news programs remind us nearly daily that we live in an age of increasing interdependence. (The Introduction explains the creation of global issues.)

This book is an introduction to a number of complicated issues. It is only a beginning; there is much more to learn. Readers who are intrigued by a subject or point made and want to learn more about it should consult the relevant note. The note will either give some additional information or will give the source of the fact we present. Consulting this source is a good place for the reader to start his or her investigation. After each chapter a list of readings gives inquisitive readers further suggestions for articles and books that will allow them to probe more deeply. Appendix 1 gives the student some help in organizing the material the book covers and the teacher some suggestions for teaching this material. Appendix 2 offers suggestions of relevant video tapes and disks, an important and interesting resource for those who want to understand these issues more deeply. Appendix 3 gives internet sources. Many organizations on the internet now have a large amount of information related to many of the issues covered in this book. The glossary contains a definition of many of the uncommon terms used in the book.

The world is changing rapidly and significant developments have taken place in many of the topics covered in this book since the fourth edition was prepared. Climate change has become so central to development considerations that it now has its own chapter. An expanded discussion on governance reflects the increasingly apparent challenges that, even as the world increasingly understands the technical basis of global problems, make responsible choices and effective decision-making ever more important across political and temporal scales. This edition also offers new insights into the global implications of the collective impacts of consumer choices, in part through the concept of environmental footprints in an effort to link global issues with individual choices a reader can make.

Global issues can be a depressing subject as the reader learns of the many serious problems the world faces. To help counter this depression without "sugar coating" the issues, a highlighted box of an example of a positive action the reader can take will be presented in most chapters.

John L. Seitz

Introduction

The Creation of Global Issues

What causes an issue to become a "global issue"? Are "global issues" the same as international affairs – the interactions that governments, private organizations, and peoples from different countries have with each other? Or is something new happening in the world? Are there now concerns and issues that are increasingly being recognized as global in nature? It is the thesis of this book that something new is indeed happening in the world as nations become more interdependent. While their well-being is still largely dependent upon how they run their internal affairs, increasingly nations are facing issues that they alone cannot solve, issues that are so important that the failure to solve them will adversely affect the lives of many people on this planet. In fact, some of these issues are so important that they can affect how suitable this planet will be in the future for supporting life.

The issues dramatize our increasing interdependence. The communications and transportation revolutions that we are experiencing are giving people knowledge of many new parts of the globe. We see that what is happening in far-off places can affect, or is affecting, our lives. For example, instability in the oil-rich Middle East affects the price of oil around the world and since many countries are dependent on oil as their main source of energy, the politics of oil becomes a global concern.

Many nations in the world are now dependent on other nations to buy their products and supply the natural resources and goods they need to purchase in order to maintain a certain standard of living. An economic downturn in any part of the world that affects the supply and demand for products will affect the economic status of many other nations. This is an important part of globalization that will be discussed in Chapter 2.

Global Issues: An Introduction, Fifth Edition. Kristen A. Hite and John L. Seitz
© 2016 John Wiley & Sons, Ltd. Published 2016 by John Wiley & Sons, Ltd.

Even a global issue such as world hunger illustrates our increasing interdependence. A person might say that starving or malnourished people in Africa don't affect people in the rich countries, but even here there is a dependency. Our very nature and character depend on how we respond to human suffering. Some rich nations such as the Scandinavian nations in northern Europe give a significantly higher portion of their national wealth to poor nations for development purposes than do other rich nations such as the United States and Japan.

Global issues are often seen as being interrelated. One issue affects other issues. For example, climate change (an environmental issue) is related to an energy issue (our reliance on fossil fuels), the population issue (more people produce more greenhouse gases), the wealth and poverty issue (wealthy countries produce the most gases that cause climate change), the technology issue (technology can help us create alternative energy sources that produce less or no greenhouse gases), and the future issue (will the changes we are making in the Earth's climate seriously harm life on this planet?). As we recognize these interrelationships, we realize that usually there are no simple solutions.

Interdisciplinary knowledge is required to successfully deal with the issues. The student or adult learner reading this book will be receiving information from multiple disciplines such as biology, economics, political science, environmental science, chemistry, and others. Neither the social sciences nor the physical sciences have the answers on their own. Feel good about yourself, reader, because you are engaged in the noble task of trying to understand how the world really works. Complicated? Yes, of course. Impossible to discover? Certainly not. Just read seriously and carefully. It takes effort and you can keep learning throughout your life.

Perhaps, global issues were born on the day, several decades ago, when the Earth, for the first time, had its picture taken. The first photograph of Earth, which was transmitted by a spacecraft, showed our planet surrounded by a sea of blackness. Many people seeing that photograph realized that the blackness was a hostile environment, devoid of life, and that life on Earth was vulnerable and precious. No national boundaries could be seen from space. That photograph showed us our home – one world – and called for us to have a global perspective in addition to our natural, and desirable, more local and national perspectives.

This book discusses *some* of the main current global issues of our time. The reader can probably identify others. During the reader's lifetime, humanity will have to face new global issues that will continue to surface. It is a characteristic of the world in which we live. Maybe our growing ability to identify such issues, and our increasing knowledge of how to deal with them, will enable us to handle the new issues better than we are doing with the present ones.

Developing toward What?

When we talk about global issues, "development" can be a confusing term. Development, as used in this book, is the ways in which economies progress through their societies to improve well-being. This requires us to consider how to measure progress as a society at the global level. But cultures across the world have very different ideas of how to define progress. Many define it by material wealth. But not all, by any means. Bhutan, for example, has a national happiness indicator in addition to measuring national wealth by the more conventional means of domestic production (gross domestic product – GDP). The definition of development we use in this book is a "neutral" one – it does not convey a sense of good or bad, of what is desirable or undesirable. We have chosen this definition because there is no widespread agreement on what these desirable and undesirable features are. This inevitably causes us to wonder what we are developing *toward*.

The United Nations now defines human development as the enlarging of human capabilities and choices; in a yearly publication it ranks nations on a human development index, which tries to measure national differences of income, educational attainment, and life expectancy.[1] The United Nations has suggested that the purpose of development to be the creation of an environment in which people can lead long, healthy, and creative lives. Economists have traditionally used gross national product (GNP) or a country's average per capita income as the measures of economic development. This book combines both the economic and the social components into the concept of development. We use the neutral and expanded definition of development because economic development alone has sometimes led to negative social and environmental consequences that rival in scale the economic benefits generated.[2]

For roughly the past century, "development" has been viewed primarily through the lens of economic growth plus the social changes caused by or accompanying that economic growth.[3] With those advancements, which included major improvements in health conditions for many and the overall lowering of the death rate, came a population explosion. So at first development solved a huge human problem through its advancements in medicine: the early death of many by disease was ended. But this great success helped create a dangerous long-term problem – the population explosion, an explosion of the numbers of humans on the planet that we are facing today, with significant impacts for how rapidly humans deplete the Earth's resources, especially when combined with the growth of consumption. We will explore all of these dimensions in the coming chapters.

From 1950 to 2000, nations generally took one of two approaches to development. The first approach was to develop government policies focused on creating jobs and providing social services to meet basic needs.[4] In the 1950s and 1960s, it was common to think of development only in economic terms. It was, of course, economic growth with the agricultural and industrial revolutions that created the increased food and higher standard of living that permitted more human beings to inhabit the planet. For many economists, political scientists, and government officials, the conventional notion of "development" meant an increase in a country's average per capita income or an increase in its GNP, the total value of goods and services produced. Development and economic development were considered to be synonymous.

The other approach to development, encouraged by international development institutions like the World Bank, reevaluated the role of government in economic development and focused on minimizing government influence on market prices by gearing public policies away from regulation, encouraging the private sector to provide social services (also known as "market-based solutions").[5] This approach became known as the "Washington Consensus," focusing on economic efficiency and fiscal discipline. The Washington Consensus led on one hand to increases in the GDPs of many countries but also to cuts in social spending – and as a result some of the poorest became even worse off.[6] Both approaches were predicated on the assumption that economic growth was functionally synonymous with "development"; they simply differed in the political pathway to achieve it.

In the 1970s an awareness grew – in both the "less developed" nations and the "developed" industrialized nations – that some of the social and environmental changes which were coming with economic growth were undesirable.[7] More people were coming to understand that for economic development to result in happier human beings, attention would have to be paid to the effects that economic growth was having on social factors. Were an adequate number of satisfying and challenging jobs being created? Were adequate housing, healthcare, and education available? Were people living and working in a healthy and pleasant environment? Did people have enough nutritious food to eat? Every country is deficient in some of these factors and thus is in the process of developing.

As concerns mounted about the social and environmental implications of more and more countries following a development model based on ever increasing rates of production and consumption, the concept of "sustainable development" emerged. This said that improving well-being requires considering social and environmental conditions in addition to economic growth. The United Nations environmental conference in Rio de Janeiro in 1992 made the term "sustainable development" widely known around the world. At first, the concept of "sustainability" was mostly a popular buzzword for those who wanted to be seen as pro-environmental but who did not really intend to change their behavior. It became a public relations term, an attempt to be seen as abreast with the latest thinking of what we must do to save our planet from widespread harm.

Within a decade or so, some governments, industries, educational institutions, and organizations started to incorporate "sustainable development" in a more serious manner. In the United States a number of large corporations appointed a vice president for sustainability. Not only were these officials interested in how their companies could profit by producing "green" products, but they were often given the task of making the company more efficient by reducing wastes and pollution and by reducing its carbon emissions. Many colleges and universities adopted sustainability as a legitimate academic subject and something to be practiced by the institution. Many nonprofit organizations added the promotion of sustainability to their agendas.

Meanwhile, the "Washington Consensus" began to erode. In 2000 many nations adopted the United Nations Millennium Declaration and launched a set of Millennium Development Goals, which refocused development on the "basic needs" approach, recognizing that market-based solutions alone could not solve widespread poverty and that governments needed to support effective social policies such as healthcare and education to avoid marginalizing the poor.[8] Between 2000 and 2010, natural resource shortages contributed significantly to food and energy crises, in turn challenging traditional notions of economic development based on the once dominant Washington Consensus model.[9] Nancy Birdsall and Francis Fukuyama of the Center for Global Development argue that the global recession driven by the United States at the end of the first decade of the twentieth century changed the model for global development and that now the focus is much more on the ability of government to help the poor and provide social protections.[10] They predict that many mid- and lower-income countries will reject the free-market approach and will more likely adopt a basic needs approach while increasing domestic industrial production. "In fact," they explain, "development has never been something that the rich bestowed on the poor but rather something the poor achieved for themselves."[11]

In the second decade of the twenty-first century, countries began developing a broad set of "sustainable development goals" intended to help the United Nations develop new targets after the Millennium Development Goals had run their course by 2015. By integrating these sustainable development goals with conventional, high-level development discussions at the UN, countries made it clear that the concept of sustainability is fundamental to development. Now sustainable development is more integrated and global development goals are increasingly focused on the social and environmental basis of well-being in addition to conventional economic indicators.

In this book we will look at some of the most important current issues related to development. The well-being of people depends on how governments and individuals deal with these issues. We will first look at the issue of population, then move on to issues related to wealth and poverty, food, energy, climate change, the environment, and technology, and conclude with a consideration of the future. As you read this book, consider for yourself: If the goal is "development," what are we developing toward? And how do we manage the interdependent relationships between societies, the environment, and a globalized economy? The way we answer these question informs how we address global issues.

Notes

1 United Nations Development Programme (UNDP), *Human Development Report 2004* (New York: UNDP, 2004), p. 127.
2 For a criticism of the Western concept of development see Ivan Illich, "Outwitting the 'Developed' Countries," in Charles K. Wilber (ed.), *The Political Economy of Development and Underdevelopment*, 2nd edn (New York: Random House, 1979), pp. 436–44. See also Lloyd Timberlake, "The Dangers of 'Development,'" in *Only One Earth: Living for the Future* (New York: Sterling, 1987), pp. 13–22.
3 See, generally, Wolfgang Sachs, *The Development Dictionary: A Guide to Knowledge as Power* (Johannesburg: Witwatersrand University Press, 2003).

4   United Nations Department of Economic and Social Affairs (UN DESA), *World Economic and Social Survey 2010: Retooling Global Development* (New York: United Nations, 2010).

5   Ibid.

6   Nancy Birdsall and Francis Fukuyama, "The Post-Washington Consensus: Development after the Crisis," *Foreign Affairs* (March/April 2011); UN DESA, *World Economic and Social Survey 2010*.

7   The term "developing country" is based on the economic-focused definition of development and refers to a relatively poor nation in which agriculture or mineral resources have a large role in the economy while manufacturing and services have a lesser role. (Some of these countries are highly developed in culture and many such regions of the world had ancient civilizations with architecture, religion, and philosophy that we still admire.) The infrastructure (transportation, education, health, and other social services) of these countries is usually inadequate for their needs. These are the conditions for the vast majority of the world's inhabitants, and economists have focused on increasing economic growth as an opportunity to generate more resources with the expectation that doing so will improve livelihoods. Since many of the less (economically) developed nations are in the southern hemisphere, they are at times referred to as "the South." During the Cold War these nations were often called the "Third World." Because countries which were early adopters of intensive manufacturing amassed large amounts of wealth that lifted many of their citizens out of poverty, economists referred to these "industrialized" nations as "developed" nations. Most of them are located in the northern hemisphere, so they are also sometimes called "the North." Some organizations such as the World Bank also divide countries according to their level of income. The Bank considers low- and middle-income countries to be "developing" and high-income countries to be "developed."

8   Birdsall and Fukuyama, "The Post-Washington Consensus."

9   Ibid. ("The global food, energy and financial crises that exposed the systemic flaws inherent in the functioning of deregulated global markets required governments to step in to address those crises – and in ways that dealt a blow to the conventional wisdom underpinning the Washington Consensus.")

10   Ibid.

11   Ibid.

Chapter 1

Population

The Changing Population of the World	8
Causes of the Population Explosion	17
How Population Growth Affects Development	20
Rapid growth	21
Slow growth	22
An aging population and low birth rates	22
International conferences on population	24
How Development Affects Population Growth	26
Demographic transition	26
Factors lowering birth rates	28
Governmental Population Policies	31
Controlling growth	31
Promoting growth	36
The Future	38
The growth of the world's population	38
The carrying capacity of the Earth	39
Optimum size of the Earth's population	42
Population-related problems in our future	43
Conclusions	44
Notes	46
Further Reading	49

Prudent men should judge of future events by what has taken place in the past, and what is taking place in the present.
Miguel de Cervantes (1547–1616), *Persiles and Sigismunda*

Global Issues: An Introduction, Fifth Edition. Kristen A. Hite and John L. Seitz.
© 2016 John Wiley & Sons, Ltd. Published 2016 by John Wiley & Sons, Ltd.

The Changing Population of the World

The population of the world is growing. No one will be startled by that sentence, but what is startling is the rate of growth, and the fact that the present growth of population is unprecedented in human history. The best historical evidence we have today indicates that there were about 5 million people in the world in about 8000 BCE. By 1 CE there were about 200 million, and by 1650 the population had grown to about 500 million. The world reached its first billion people in about 1800. While it took thousands of years for the global population to reach 1 billion, it only took a little over a century for the population to reach the next billion: the second billion came about 1930. The third billion was reached about 1960, the fourth about 1974, and the fifth about 1987. The sixth came in 1999 and the seventh in 2011. The eighth billion is expected by 2024.[1] These figures indicate how rapidly the population is increasing. Table 1.1 shows how long it took the world to add each billion of its total population. A projection is also given for the next billion.

How can we explain this dramatic increase in population growth? Development gains over the last two centuries have seen major improvements in health conditions for many and the overall lowering of the death rate, dramatically and rapidly reducing rates of early death by disease. With this great success came a population explosion, the rapid increase of the number of humans on the planet that we are facing today, with significant impacts for the Earth's resources. While population growth rates are starting to stabilize in many places, the total number of people on the planet continues to increase while natural resources continue to decline. This chapter explores the complex situation of the global population in the context of development, and later chapters explore the relationships between population, wealth, food, energy, climate, and the environment.

Table 1.1　Time taken to add each billion to the world population, 1800–2046 (projection)

Date	Estimated world population (billions)	Years to add 1 billion people
1800	1	2,000,000
1930	2	130
1960	3	30
1974	4	14
1987	5	13
1999	6	12
2011	7	12
2024 (projected)	8	13
2046 (projected)	9	22

Source: Data from UN Department of Economic and Social Affairs, Population Division, *World Population Prospects: The 2012 Revision*.

There is another way to look at population growth, one that helps us understand the uniqueness of our situation and its staggering possibilities for harm to life on this planet. Because most people born can have children of their own, the human population can – until certain limits are reached – grow exponentially: 1 to 2; 2 to 4; 4 to 8; 8 to 16; 16 to 32; 32 to 64; 64 to 128; and so on. When something grows exponentially, there is hardly discernible growth in the early stages and then the numbers shoot up. The French have a riddle they use to help teach the nature of exponential growth to children. It goes like this: if you have a pond with one lily in it that doubles its size every day, and which will completely cover the pond in 30 days, on what day will the lily cover half the pond? The answer is the twenty-ninth day. What this riddle tells you is that if you wait until the lily covers half the pond before cutting it back, you will have only one day to do this – the twenty-ninth day – because it will cover the whole pond the next day.

If you plot on a graph anything that has an exponential growth, you get a J-curve. For a long time there is not much growth but when the bend of the curve in the J is reached, the growth becomes dramatic. Figure 1.1 shows what Earth's population growth curve looks like.

The growth of the Earth's population has been compared to a long fuse on a bomb: once the fuse is lit, it sputters along for a long while and then suddenly the bomb explodes. This is what is meant by the phrases "population explosion" and "population bomb." The analogy is not a bad one. The world's population has passed the bend of the J-curve and is now rapidly expanding. The United Nations estimates that the world's population reached 7 billion in 2011, adding 5 billion people in less than one century. But recent estimates indicate that while the population will grow substantially – especially in Africa – over the coming decades, the population

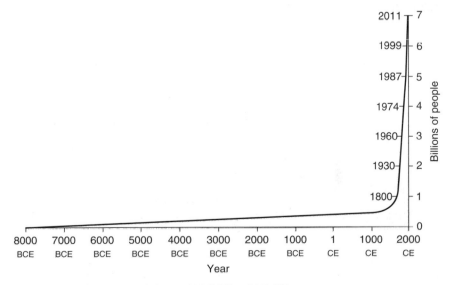

Figure 1.1   Population growth from 8000 BCE to 2011 CE

Source: Based on data from Population Reference Bureau, *2010 World Population Data Sheet*.

is growing at a slower rate than before: women throughout the world now have on average fewer than three children per woman whereas in the 1950s they had five. But an average of slightly less than three children per woman still means the population is growing dramatically.

Figure 1.2 shows that the largest growth in the future will be in the less wealthy countries, with India, China, and some nations in Africa leading the way. In 1950 about one-third of the world's people lived in economically wealthy countries. At the end of the twentieth century that total reduced to about 20 percent living in countries with relatively rich economies. During the present century, nearly all of the growth in population will occur outside of these historically wealthy countries. An ever larger percentage of the world's population will be relatively poor. The United Nations projects that by 2050 about 86 percent of the Earth's population will be residing in the poorer nations.[2]

Because no one knows for sure what the size of Earth's population will be in the future, the United Nations gives three projections: a high, medium, and low one, based on the possible number of children the average woman will have. Projections are educated guesses. The United Nations believes the middle projection is the most likely, and most authors writing on the subject use that number. The population in wealthy countries is expected to slowly grow to 1.3 billion in 2050,[3] with migration from poorer countries accounting for most population growth.[4] The vast majority of the global population will be in less wealthy countries, which are expected to increase from 6 billion people in 2015 to 8.2 billion in 2050.[5] From 2013 to 2100 about one-half of the annual growth is expected to occur in eight countries – India, Nigeria, Ethiopia, United States, Democratic Republic of the Congo, Tanzania,

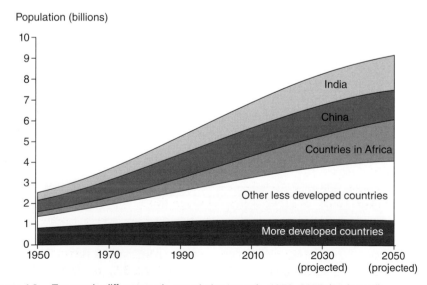

Figure 1.2   Economic differences in population growth, 1950–2050 (projected)

Source: UN Department of Economic and Social Affairs, Population Division, *World Population Prospects: The 2006 Revision, Medium Variant* (2007).

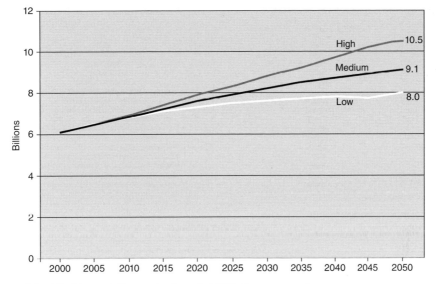

Figure 1.3   World population projections to 2050: three scenarios

Source: Based on data from UN Department of Economic and Social Affairs, Population Division, *World Population Prospects: The 2008 Revision* (2009).

Niger, and Uganda.[6] The largest growth is expected in India, which is likely to pass China as the largest country in the world by 2028 with 1.4 billion people.[7] At that time India and China will account for about one-third of the world's population. Figure 1.3 gives the three growth projections for the world population by the United Nations up to 2050.

High growth rates will take place in the less wealthy countries because a larger percentage of their population consists of children under the age of 15 who will be growing older and having children themselves. If we plot the number of people in a country according to their ages, we can see clearly the difference between rapidly growing populations, which less wealthy nations tend to have, and relatively stable or slowly growing populations, which tend to occur in wealthier nations. Figure 1.4 shows the difference between these two population structures. The age structure of countries with relatively stable populations is column shaped, while the age structure of growing countries is pyramid shaped.

Another major change occurring in the world's population is the movement of people from rural areas to urban areas. Although this is happening throughout the world, the trend is especially dramatic in poorer countries, where a significant portion of rural youth are fleeing to cities with hopes of a better life. But all too often jobs are not as available in the cities as hoped, pushing many rural migrants into poorer areas such as slums on the edges of big cities. In 2012, 32.7 percent of the urban population in developing regions lived in these informal settlements.[8] Table 1.2 lists the world's ten largest cities in 1990 and 2014 and the projected ten largest for the year 2030. Note the trend in the growth of cities in countries with economies that

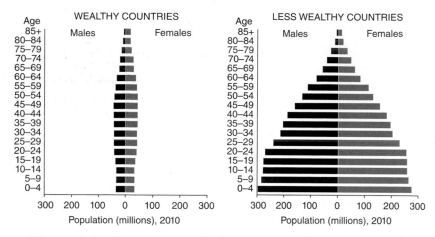

Figure 1.4 Population by age and sex in different groups of countries, 2010 (projected) *Source*: UN Department of Economic and Social Affairs, Population Division, *World Population Prospects: The 2008 Revision* (2009).

Plate 1.1 Rural migrants often settle in urban slums in developing nations

Source: United Nations.

have been rapidly growing. It is hard to imagine a city like Calcutta getting any bigger. In 1950, it had a population of about 4 million, with many thousands of people living permanently on the streets; in 1990 it had a population around 10 million and an estimated 400,000 lived on the streets.[9] If the present rate of growth continues, it will have a population of about 19 million by 2030.[10] Note also the increased size of the cities. Cities with over 5–10 million people are sometimes called "megacities."[11] In 1990, there were only six cities in developing countries with more than 10 million people. By 2014 there were 28 cities in the world with populations over 10 million

Table 1.2 Ten largest cities in the world, 1990, 2014, and 2030 (projection)

Population in 1990 (millions)		Population in 2014 (millions)		Population in 2030 (projected) (millions)	
Tokyo, Japan	32	Tokyo, Japan	37	Tokyo, Japan	37
Kinki M.M.A. (Osaka), Japan	18	Delhi, India	24	Delhi, India	36
New York-Newark, USA	16	Shanghai, China	22	Shanghai, China	30
Mexico City, Mexico	15	Mexico City, Mexico	20	Mumbai, India	27
São Paulo, Brazil	14	São Paulo, Brazil	20	Beijing, China	27
Mumbai, India	12	Mumbai, India	20	Dhaka, Bangladesh	27
Kolkata (Calcutta), India	10	Kinki M.M.A. (Osaka), Japan	20	Karachi, Pakistan	24
Los Angeles, USA	10	Beijing, China	19	Cairo, Egypt	24
Seoul, Republic of Korea	10	New York-Newark, USA	18	Lagos, Nigeria	24
Buenos Aires, Argentina	10	Cairo, Egypt	18	Mexico City, Mexico	23

Cites are formally called "urban agglomerations" in UN publications.
Source: Based on data from UN Department of Economic and Social Affairs, Population Division, *World Urbanization Prospects: The 2009 Revision*; *World Urbanization Prospects: The 2014 Revision, Highlights*.

people, the majority of these in emerging economies.[12] Many of these cities had vast areas of substandard housing and serious urban pollution, and many of their residents lived without sanitation facilities, safe drinking water, or adequate healthcare facilities.

Innovative sustainable cities

Shenzhen, China

In 2014, Shenzhen won the City Climate Leadership Award for Urban Transportation, sponsored by Siemens and the C40 Cities Climate Leadership Group. Known around the world as a leader in developing electric vehicles, the city aimed to add 24,000 electric vehicles to its transportation system by 2015. However, what sets Shenzhen apart from other cities is its push to start infusing public transportation sectors, such as buses and taxis, with hybrid and electric vehicles. The city's leadership collaborated with public and private actors to add over 3,000 new energy buses and 850 pure electric taxis to the city's general transportation circuit by late 2013. This project has already led to a reduction of 160,000 tons of carbon pollution between 2009 and 2013, and the city aims to reduce carbon emissions by another 0.82 million tonnes by 2015.

Buenos Aires, Argentina

Buenos Aires, another 2014 recipient of the City Climate Leadership Award, was honored for its Solid Urban Waste Reduction Project. By 2017, the city aims to treat 100 percent of waste sent to landfills and reduce the overall waste production by 83 percent. The city seeks to achieve these goals through a combination of public education and infrastructure development. Thirty-two public parks contain "Green Stations," at which residents may bring recyclable waste for sorting, and every city block has a waste disposal bin. This initiative has created 4,500 urban recoverer jobs and has reduced overall landfill waste by 44 percent in 2014.

Curitiba, Brazil

Curitiba has been called the most innovative city in the world. City officials from around the world visit Curitiba to learn how this city, with relatively limited funds, has been tackling urban problems. By using imaginative, low-cost solutions and low technology, Curitiba has created a pleasant urban life that many cities in the more developed nations have yet to achieve. Here is how the city achieved this.

Transportation The city has made public transportation attractive, affordable, and efficient. Instead of building a subway, which the city could not afford, it established a system of extended, high-speed buses, some carrying as many as 275 passengers on express routes, connecting the city center with outlying areas. Many people own cars in Curitiba but 85 percent of the commuters use public transportation. This has reduced traffic congestion and air pollution. There are 30 percent fewer cars on city streets than you would expect from the number of cars owned by its residents.

Trash collection The city's "garbage that is not garbage" initiative encourages residents to exchange their trash for goods such as food, bus tickets, and school supplies. This program has led to the recycling of 70 percent of Curitiba's trash.

Education Small libraries have been built throughout the city in the shape of a lighthouse. Called Lighthouses of Learning, they provide books (many schools in Brazil have no books), an attractive study room, and, in a tower, a strong light and guard to make the area safe.

Health Curitiba has more health clinics – that are open 24 hours a day – per person than any other city in Brazil.

Environmental education The Free University for the Environment was built out of recycled old utility poles next to a lake made from an old quarry. Short courses on how to make better use of the environment have been designed for contractors, merchants, and housewives. Taxi drivers are required to take a course there in order to get their licenses.

Governmental services Colorful, covered Citizenship Streets have been built throughout the city to bring government offices to where the people live and shop. Here people can pay their utility bills, file a police complaint, go to night court, and get a marriage license. Vocational courses are subsidized to help provide accessible classes to all residents.

The main credit for this innovative city has been given to its former mayor Jaime Lerner. Lerner, an architect and planner, headed an honest and very capable government. He served three terms as mayor of the city and later served two terms as governor of the state.

Sources: On Shenzhen: "City Climate Leadership Awards 2014: The Winners," at http://city climateleadershipawards.com/2014-ccla-winners/; UN Commission on Sustainable Development, *Electric Vehicles in the Context of Sustainable Development in China* (May 2–13, 2011), p. 26, at http://www.un.org/esa/dsd/resources/res_pdfs/csd-19/Background-Paper-9-China.pdf; C40 Cities, "Shenzhen: New Energy Vehicle Promotion," at http://www.c40.org/profiles/2014-shenzhen (all accessed July 2015). On Buenos Aires: C40 Cities, "Buenos Aires: Solid Urban Waste Reduction Project," at http://cityclimateleadershipawards.com/2014-project-buenos-aires-plan-integral/; Buenos Aires Ciudad, "Waste Management," at http://www.turismo.buenosaires.gob.ar/en/article/waste-management (both accessed July 2015). On Curitiba: Ali Soltani and Ehsan Sharifi, "A Case Study of Sustainable Urban Planning Principles in Curitiba (Brazil) and Their Applicability in Shiraz (Iran)," *International Journal of Development and Sustainability*, 1 (2012), p. 126; Robin Wright, "The Most Innovative City in the World," *Los Angeles Times*, June 3, 1996. Curitiba's accomplishments are also described in Jonas Rabinovitch and Josef Leitman, "Urban Planning in Curitiba," *Scientific American*, 274 (March 1996), pp. 46–53; Eugene Linden, "The Exploding Cities of the Developing World," *Foreign Affairs* (January/February 1996), p. 62; Arthur Lubow, "The Road to Curitiba," *New York Times Magazine*, May 20, 2007, pp. 76–83.

With respect to urbanization, although countries differ on their definitions of "urban" (the United States defines urban as places of 2,500 or more, Japan uses 50,000, and Iceland 200), by 2012, more than half of the global population lived in urban areas.[13] There has been a particular trend toward increased urbanization in poorer nations: in 1950 only about 20 percent of their population was urban, but that increased to 40 percent in 2000. In 2009, for the first time in human history, more people lived in urban areas in the world than in rural areas, and by 2012 less than 30 percent of the global urban population resided in wealthy countries.[14] Nevertheless, 60 percent of the population in Africa and 52 percent in Asia still live in rural areas.[15] The trend is toward more urbanization as megacities and other cities continue to grow. The United Nations expects nearly all the world's population growth in the future will be in the urban areas of less wealthy nations.[16]

Plate 1.2 Growing cities in less developed nations often have a mixture of modern and sub-standard housing

Source: United Nations.

Figure 1.5 Urban and rural population by development group, 1950–2050

Source: UN Department of Economic and Social Affairs, Population Division, *World Urbanization Prospects: The 2009 Revision, Highlights* (New York: United Nations, 2010), p. 3

Causes of the Population Explosion

Although it is easy to illustrate that the human population has grown exponentially, it is not so easy to explain why we are in a situation at present of rapidly expanding population. Exponential growth is only one of many factors that determine population size. Other factors influence how much time will pass before the doublings – found in exponential growth – take place. Still other factors influence how long the exponential growth will continue and how it might be stopped. We will consider these last two matters later in the chapter, but we will first look at some of the factors that drastically reduced the amount of time it took for the world's population to double in size.

The agricultural revolution, which began about 8000 BCE, was the first major event that gave population growth a boost. When humans learned how to domesticate plants and animals for food, they greatly increased their food supply. For the next 10,000 years until the industrial revolution, there was a gradually accelerating rate of population growth, but overall the rate of growth was still low because of high death rates, caused mainly by diseases and malnutrition. As the industrial revolution picked up momentum in the eighteenth and nineteenth centuries, population growth was given another boost: advances in industry, agriculture, and transportation improved the living conditions of the average person. Population was growing exponentially, but the periods between the doublings were still long because of continued high death rates. This situation changed drastically after 1945. Lester Brown explains why that happened:

> The burst of scientific innovation and economic activity that began during the forties substantially enhanced the Earth's food-producing capacity and led to dramatic improvements in disease control. The resulting marked reduction in death rates created an unprecedented imbalance between births and deaths and an explosive rate of population growth. Thus, while world population increased at 2 to 5 percent *per century* during the first fifteen centuries of the Christian era, the rate in some countries (in the late 1970s) is between 3 and 4 percent *per year*, very close to the biological maximum.[17]

It was primarily improvements in life expectancies around the world after World War II that gave the most recent boost to population growth. The spreading of public health measures, including the use of vaccines, to less developed countries enabled these countries to control diseases such as smallpox, tuberculosis, yellow fever, and cholera. Children and young adults are especially vulnerable to infectious diseases; thus, the conquering of these diseases allowed more children to live and bear children themselves.

While life expectancies around the world were increasing rapidly, birth rates generally remained higher than death rates. Birth rates have been high throughout human history. If this had not been true, you and I might not be here today since high birth rates were needed to replace the many people who died at birth or at an early age. (If you walk through a very old cemetery in the United States or especially in Europe, you can see evidence of this fact for yourself as you pass the family plots with markers for the many children who died in infancy and through adolescence.)

Birth rates remained high right up until the late 1960s, which was the beginning of a gradual lowering of birth rates around the world.

Sons preferred in India

Sons are preferred in many less developed countries. This has been particularly notable in India, where there are a number of places where a strong preference for sons has increased the ratio of men to women over the past century. A census in 2011 found an estimated 943 women for every 1,000 men nationally. Girls are more likely than boys to be neglected or mistreated, and India has a history of higher death rates and lower life expectancy for women than for men. Additionally, medical technology enables expectant parents to abort female fetuses, which has pushed the sex ratio at birth well above 105 boys to 100 girls, the normal ratio throughout the world. In the state of Haryana, just to the northwest of New Delhi, for example, a 2011 survey found that for children age 0–6, there were only 834 girls for every 1,000 boys.

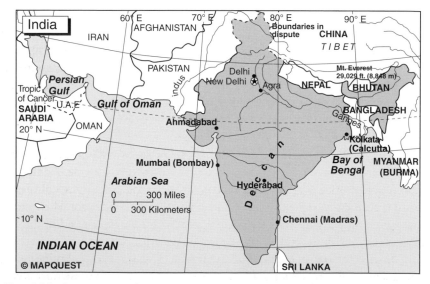

Map 1.1 India

Many families in India, as in China, Korea, and a number of other East and South Asian countries, value sons because sons usually live with their parents after marriage and contribute to family income. Sons provide vital financial support to elderly or ill parents, who often have no other source of income.

Traditionally daughters move away at marriage and transfer their allegiance to their husband's family. At least historically, parents would therefore expect less financial or emotional support from daughters after they leave home.

In many parts of India, daughters can mean an additional cost to parents – the obligation of paying her prospective husband's family a large dowry. Dowries often require parents to go into debt, and the amount families must pay has been increasing over the years.

The financial and social disadvantages of having a daughter prompt some women to abort their pregnancies if they are carrying a daughter. Pregnant women can determine the sex of their fetus through ultrasound and other examinations. As this technology becomes more widely available, more parents are using it to choose the number and sex of their children. Nearly all aborted fetuses in Indian hospitals are female. The national government has passed laws prohibiting sex-selective abortion, as have many Indian states, but abortion practices are difficult to regulate.

Sources: Nancy E. Riley, "Gender, Power, and Population Change," *Population Bulletin*, 52 (May 1997), pp. 14–15; Sanjay Kumar, "India: Where Are All the Girls?" The Diplomat, August 27, 2013, at http://thediplomat.com/2013/08/india-where-are-all-the-girls/ (accessed July 2015).

Birth rates have dropped close to or below replacement rates in wealthier nations but remain high in most other countries. There are a number of reasons for this. First, many people want to have many children. If many children die in infancy, as they still do in countries with relatively high infant mortality rates, more births are needed to replace the number of people surviving into adulthood. In many families, particularly in rural areas, children are tasked in helping with domestic and agricultural work, sometimes at the expense of their education. Before child labor laws severely restricted the use of children in factories in the United States and Europe, it was common for children to take paying jobs to help the family gain income. Additionally, the expectation is often that children (and specifically males in many cultures) are needed to ensure that the parents have someone to take care of them when they are old and can no longer work, which becomes a particularly acute need in the many countries where pensions or other assistance are unavailable.

Other reasons for continued high birth rates include tradition and religion. Cultural and religious norms are strong and one does not break with these norms easily. Tradition is very important in many societies, and traditionally families have been large in rural settings. Also, religion is a powerful force in rural societies and some religions either advocate for large families or against birth control. The unavailability or unacceptance of birth control options is a particularly significant factor for higher birth rates in some places. It has been estimated that about 143 million married women of reproductive age worldwide are not using contraceptives even though they do not want more children.[18] It is believed that these women have an unmet need, or demand, for family planning services.[19]

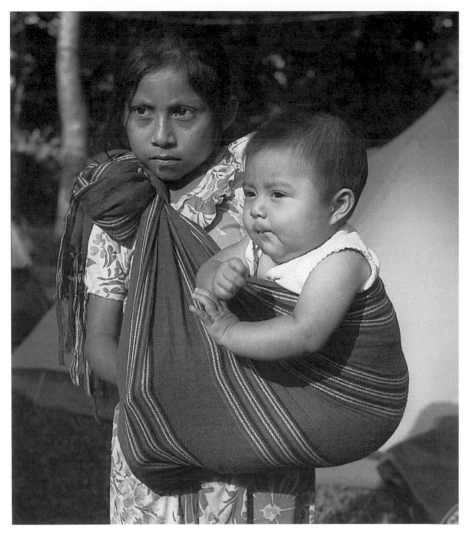

Plate 1.3 Children take care of children in many poorer countries, as this girl is doing in Mexico

Source: Mark Olencki.

How Population Growth Affects Development

How does population growth affect development? While there is no easy answer to the question of what is "too large" or "too small" a population for a country – a question we will return to in the final section of this chapter – we can identify some obvious negative features of a rapidly growing population, a situation which would apply to many less developed countries today.

Rapid growth

Let's look again at the age distribution of the population in less developed regions in Figure 1.4. It is striking that a large percentage of people is below the age of 15. This means that a large proportion of the population in these countries is mainly nonproductive. Food, education, and healthcare must be provided for children and youth until they become independent. Obviously, if a nation has a large portion of its population in the under-15 age group, its economy will be faced with a significant burden to provide for its younger members.

A rapidly growing population also puts a great strain on the resources of the country. If the population is too large or the growth too rapid, people's use of the country's resources for food and income can actually prevent the biological natural resources from renewing themselves. This can lead to the land becoming less fertile, and the forests being destroyed. An example of this is the making of patties out of cow droppings and straw by women in India and Pakistan. These patties are allowed to dry in the sun and are then used for fuel. In fact, dung patties are the only fuel many families have for cooking their food. But the use of animal droppings for fuel prevents essential nutrients from returning to the soil, thus reducing the soil's ability to support vegetation.

A large population of young people also means that there will be a terrific demand for jobs when these children grow old enough to join the labor force – jobs that are unlikely to exist. The ranks of the unemployed and underemployed will grow in many poorer nations, and this can easily lead to political and social unrest. As we saw earlier in this chapter, people from the rapidly growing rural areas of the global South are heading for the cities hoping to find work. What they find, though, is a scarcity of jobs, undoubtedly a contributing factor in the high rates of urban crime.

Rapid population growth can also impact the health of children and women. Malnutrition in infancy can lead to brain damage, and frequent childbearing can deplete certain minerals in a woman's body and bones.

A rapidly growing population also puts a tremendous strain on the ability of a nation to ensure adequate living conditions for everyone. The poor condition of much of the housing available to the poor is something that makes a lasting impression on foreign visitors to these countries – that is, if they venture beyond the Hilton hotels where they sometimes stay. A shortage of affordable housing can lead to overcrowding, which may be exacerbated by a rapidly growing population, impacting privacy and individual rights.

Urban crime: a personal experience by John L. Seitz

An experience in Liberia helped me to understand that urban areas are often less safe than rural areas. I lived at different times in Monrovia, the capital city of that country, and in a small village in a rural area. Once while I was in Monrovia, a thief entered my bedroom and stole my wallet and watch from under my pillow, which was under my sleeping head at the time. Such an event was unheard of in the rural areas, but was not that uncommon in the city. After the theft happened, I was happy to return to my "primitive" village, where I felt much safer.

Slow growth

Because it impacts the labor force, a slow population growth rate has the potential to impede a country's productive capacity, and therefore also its economic growth. Partly because of low birth rates, a number of European countries welcomed immigrants during the 1950s and 1960s from Turkey, southern Italy, and other relatively poor areas of Europe and North Africa. For some in the business world, a growing population signifies more consumers of products. But a number of the industrial countries have shown in the post–World War II period that a high level of economic growth is possible even when population growth is low.

Japan is a good example to look at. The country has experienced impressive economic growth in recent decades, and its population is projected to decline, dipping below 100 million by 2065.[20] However, the decreasing population has enabled the country's modest economic growth of recent years to trigger increased per capita income.[21] The healthcare advances that have enabled the people of Japan to reach an average lifespan of 84 years have also allowed for a healthier population that spends less on medical care.[22] Additionally, long-term benefits of reduced population pressure include greater availability of food, housing, and land.

An aging population and low birth rates

We saw earlier the types of problems that are created when a country has a large share of its population aged 15 or under. But special problems are also created when the proportion of a population that is over 65 starts to expand. As can be seen in Table 1.3, this is happening in many areas of the world, especially in Europe and North America. For example, as the percentage of the US population that is over 65 expands because of advances in healthcare and healthier lifestyles by some, and the number of new workers is reduced because of low birth rates, the ratio of working-age people to retired people declines and puts a strain on the social security system that provides financial support to retired persons. (It is the payments from the current workers that provide money for the retirement benefits.)

There are also increased healthcare costs as a population ages. More government funds are needed to care for the medical and social needs of the aged since the expectation in many countries is that families should not bear the exclusive burden to pay

Table 1.3 Regional trends in aging: percentage of total population 65 years or older, 2000, 2015 (projection), 2030 (projection)

Region	Year	65 years or older
Asia	2000	6
	2015	8
	2030	12
Europe	2000	15
	2015	18
	2030	24
Latin America/Caribbean	2000	6
	2015	8
	2030	12
Middle East/North Africa	2000	4
	2015	6
	2030	8
North America	2000	12
	2015	15
	2030	20
Oceania	2000	10
	2015	12
	2030	16
Sub-Saharan Africa	2000	3
	2015	3
	2030	4

Source: US Census Bureau, International Data Base, 2004.

for these services. This is a common concern in Europe, where by the year 2050 it is expected that about 34 percent of its people will be 65 or older, as compared to 23 percent in 2013.[23] At the beginning of the twenty-first century only about 15 percent were of that age. Also of concern in Europe is the more than doubling of the number of people 80 or over, from 4.5 percent in 2013 to 9.5 percent in 2050.[24]

Caring for the aged is a concern in nearly all developed countries. It certainly is for Japan. In 2013, 32.3 percent of the population was 60 or older, and by 2050 it is expected that this group will increase to about 42.7 percent in a population that will probably be smaller than it was in 2000.[25] By contrast, because of immigration and a relatively higher birth rate, in 2013 19.7 percent of the population in the United States was 60 or older and that group will grow to about 27 percent by 2050.[26]

Some developing countries, such as China, will also face an aging problem in the twenty-first century. Mainly because of the dramatic reduction in its birth rate, the percentage of people aged 60 or over in China is expected to increase from 13.9 percent in 2013 to 32.8 percent by mid-century.[27]

When a country has a low birth rate, and the number of young people entering the labor market is reduced, a situation now common throughout Europe and

Japan, this can lead to conflict over immigration policies. Hostility to foreign workers by extreme nationalists in Germany in the early 1990s led to fatal attacks on some foreigners in the country. Japan, a country that traditionally has been wary of outsiders, is also concerned about having to rely on foreign workers. (The Japanese are as worried as the Americans and Europeans that a shrinking workforce will be unable to support the increasing healthcare costs and welfare costs of an aging population.)

A number of European nations and Japan had such low birth rates in the mid-1990s that their populations had started to decline or would soon do so. Declining populations became common in Russia and the former Eastern European satellites, no doubt because of the harsh economic conditions these countries were facing as they tried to replace their planned economies with market economies. Long-term decline in population for most of Europe appears inevitable. In the first half of this century, the population of Europe is expected to decline from about 730 million to 690 million.[28]

Projections have been made that about 50 countries, most of them wealthy, will experience population declines between now and 2050. Germany is expected to go from 82 million to 72 million, Japan from 126 million to 108 million, and the Russian Federation from 142 million to 120 million.[29] The United States would also face a declining population in the twenty-first century were it not for its high immigration levels. Declining populations raise fears about the loss of national power, economic growth, and even national identities by some people in these countries. But most population experts believe that if population decline is gradual, the negative social and economic consequences can be handled. Much more difficult to manage, they believe, are situations where the decline is rapid.[30] It is possible that some nations will find a smaller population easier to maintain in a sustainable manner, a concept which will be discussed in the final chapter.

Some governments have tried different measures to encourage families to have more children – such as direct financial payments for additional children, tax benefits, subsidized housing preferences, longer maternity and paternity leave, childcare, and efforts to promote gender equality in employment – but these policies have had only modest effects in authoritarian states and minimal effects in liberal democracies such as France and Sweden.[31]

International conferences on population

The first international conference on population was held in 1974 in Romania under the sponsorship of the United Nations. It was anticipated that this conference would dramatize the need for population control programs in the less developed countries, but instead a debate took place between rich and poor countries over what was causing poverty: population growth or underdevelopment. The United States and other wealthy nations argued for the need for birth control measures in the poorer countries, while a number of the poorer countries argued that what they needed was more economic development. Some developing countries called for a new international economic order to support their development. They advocated more foreign aid from the richer countries, and more equitable trade and investment practices. The conference ended with what seemed to be an implicit compromise: that what was needed was both economic development and policies to manage population growth, and that an emphasis on only one factor and a disregard of the other would not work to reduce poverty.

In 1984 the United Nations held its second world population conference in Mexico City. The question of the relationship between economic growth and population growth was raised again. The United States, represented by the Reagan administration, argued that economic growth produced by the private enterprise system was the best way to reduce population growth. The United States did not share the sense of urgency that others felt at the conference concerning the need to reduce the world's increasing population. It announced that it was cutting off its aid to organizations that promoted the use of abortion as a birth control technique. (Subsequently the United States stopped contributing funds to the United Nations Fund for Population Activities and the International Planned Parenthood Federation, two of the largest and most effective organizations concerned with population control.)[32] The United States stood nearly alone in its rejection of the idea that the world faced a global population crisis, as well as in its advocacy of economic growth as the main population control mechanism. The conference endorsed the conclusion reached at the first conference ten years earlier that *both* birth control measures *and* efforts to reduce poverty were needed to reduce the rapidly expanding global population.

In 1992 the United Nations Conference on the Environment and Development – the so called Earth Summit held at Rio de Janeiro, Brazil, which will be discussed in detail in Chapter 6 – did not directly address the need for population control measures. The Rio Declaration says only that "states should … promote appropriate demographic policies," and Agenda 21, the action plan to carry out the broad goals stated in the declaration, does not mention family planning. The weak treatment of the population issue by this conference was, in part, the result of North–South conflicts over whether the poor nations or the rich nations were mainly responsible for the destruction of the environment. (When the population issue was raised, attention was focused on the harm to the environment that large numbers of poor people in the South could inflict, whereas the South held that overconsumption by the North caused most of the pollution that was harming the environment.) The rejection of any explicit connection between rapid population growth and environmental damage was also a result of opposition by the Vatican to any declarations which could be used to support the use of contraceptives and abortion to control population growth, practices that the Catholic Church has opposed. Also, some countries with conservative social traditions were opposed to raising any issue that could bring up the status of women in their countries.

While there was no explicit reference to population issues in its formal statements, the Rio conference, and the multitude of meetings around the world held to prepare for it, did cause increased attention to be placed on population, especially bringing to the forefront the perspectives of women.

The United Nations held its third conference on population – formally called the International Conference on Population and Development – in Cairo, Egypt in 1994. Although the Vatican and conservative Islamic governments made abortion and sexual mores the topic of discussion in the early days of the conference, the conference broke new ground in agreeing that women must be given more control over their lives if population growth was to be controlled. The conference approved a 20-year plan of action whose aim was to stabilize the world's population at about 7.3 billion by 2015. The plan called for new emphasis to be placed on the education of girls, providing a large range of family planning methods, health services, and economic opportunities for women. The action plan called for both developing and industrial nations to increase the amount they spent on population-related activities to $17 billion by the year 2000, a significant increase over the $5 billion that was then being spent.

Five years after the Cairo conference, the United Nations found that a number of new approaches to managing population had been initiated around the world, but that scarce resources and many needs led to population programs not receiving top priority in all developing nations. It found also that pledges of aid from developed nations were seriously underfunded.[33]

In 2003 the United Nations General Assembly voted to end the automatic holding of international conferences. Because of their large expense of funds and human energy and the danger that they were becoming routine, the United Nations decided that the decision to hold an international conference should be made on a case-by-case basis when there was a special need for international cooperation.

How Development Affects Population Growth

How does development affect the growth rate of population? There is no easy answer to that question, but population experts strongly suspect that there *is* a relationship, since the West had a fairly rapid decline in its population growth rate after it industrialized. In the nineteenth century, Europe began to go through what is called the "demographic transition."

Demographic transition

The demographic transition, which is shown in Figure 1.6, has four basic stages. In the first stage, which is often characteristic of preindustrial societies, there are high birth rates and high death rates that lead to a stable or slowly growing population.

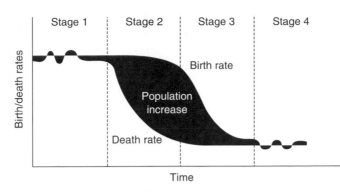

Figure 1.6 The classic stages of demographic transitions

Source: Joseph A. McFalls Jr, "Population: A Lively Introduction," *Population Bulletin*, 53 (3) (September 1998), Figure 12, p. 39.

Death rates are high because of harsh living conditions and poor health. In the second stage, there is a decline in the death rate as modern medicine and sanitation measures are adopted and living conditions improve. Birth rates continue to be high in this stage as social attitudes favoring large families take longer to change even as technology, health, and economic conditions evolve. This situation ignites what is known as the population explosion. In the third stage birth rates become more aligned with the lower death rate. Population growth remains high during the early part of the third stage but falls to near zero during the latter part. Most industrial nations passed through the second and third stages from about the mid-1800s to the mid-1900s. In the final and fourth stage, both the death and birth rates are low, and they fluctuate at a low level. As in the first stage, there is a stable or slowly growing population.

Most wealthy nations are already in the fourth stage of the demographic transition, but globally most countries are still in the second stage or the early parts of the third stage. There have been some significant differences between the developed and developing nations with regard to the second and third stages. For the developed nations, the reduction in the death rate was gradual as modern medicines were slowly developed and the knowledge of germs gradually spread. The birth rate dropped sharply, but only after a delay that caused the population to expand. For the developing countries, the drop in the death rate has been sharper than it was for the developed nations as antibiotics were quickly adopted, but because poverty lingered for many, the reduction in the birth rate has lagged more than it did for the developed nations. Both of these facts have caused a much larger increase in the population of the less wealthy nations than had occurred in the nations that shifted to industrialized economies in the nineteenth century. These two facts can be seen in Figure 1.7, which compares the demographic transitions of Sweden and Mexico.

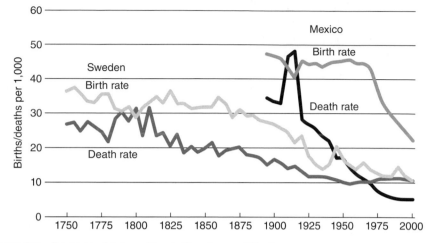

Figure 1.7   Demographic transition in Sweden and Mexico

Sources: B. R. Mitchell, *European Historical Statistics 1750–1970* (1976), Table B6; Council of Europe, *Recent Demographic Developments in Europe 2001* (2001), Tables T3.1 and T4.1; Centro Latinoamericano y Caribeño de Demografía, *Boletín demográfico*, 69 (2002), Tables 4 and 7; Francisco Alba-Hernández, *La población de México* (1976), p. 14; UN Department of Economic and Social Affairs, Population Division, *World Population Prospects: The 2002 Revision* (2003), p. 326. As presented in "Transitions in World Population," *Population Bulletin*, 59 (March 2004), p. 7.

The differences in the experiences of many nations have led many demographers to change the opinion they had in the 1950s that economic development would cause less wealthy nations to go through the same demographic transition as wealthy ones, and thus achieve lower population growth. There are obviously important differences between the experience of countries that industrialized early and that of the rest of the world. Probably as important as the fact that death rates dropped much faster last century than those prior is the fact that the industrialization that is taking place in emerging economies today is not providing many jobs and is not benefiting the vast majority of people in those regions. A relatively small, modern sector *is* benefiting from this economic development and the birth rate of this group is generally declining, but for the vast majority in the rural areas and in poor urban areas, high birth rates continue.

Factors lowering birth rates

If industrialization as it is occurring in the less developed world is not an automatic contributor to lower birth rates, what factors do cause birth rates to decline? As the West industrialized, it became more urban, and living space in urban societies is scarcer and more expensive than it was in rural societies. The availability of goods and services increased, which led to families increasing their consumption of these rather than spending their income on raising more children. Women now had job opportunities in the urban areas that hadn't existed in the rural areas and now could contribute to the family's wealth.

Certainly, better healthcare and better nutrition, both of which lower infant mortality and thus raise a family's expectations of how many children will survive, are important factors. (The irony here, of course, is that these advances, at least in the short run, tend to worsen the population problem since more children live to reproduce.)

Another factor tending to lower birth rates is the changing role of women. Better educated women are more likely to use some sort of contraception than are those women with little or no education.[34] Education for women tends to be associated with delayed marriage, increased knowledge about contraceptives, increased employment opportunities, and evolving views of their role in society.

As Western nations industrialized, child labor laws, compulsory education for children, and old age pension laws reduced some of the economic incentives for having many children. These laws made it more difficult for children to be viewed as producers on the farms and in the early factories; instead, they were considered consumers at some economic cost to their families. Traditional religious beliefs, which often support large families, also tended to decline.

There is little debate today that economic growth, especially if it benefits the many and not just the few, can lead to lower birth rates. There is also ample evidence that improving the social and economic status of women can lead to lower birth rates, even in areas which remain very poor – such as in the southern state of Kerala in India, where birth rates are significantly lower than in the rest of India. But there is also evidence that birth rates can decrease and are decreasing in poor countries – even in some where there has been little or no economic growth and where the education and social status of women remains very low, such as in Bangladesh – where an effective family planning program exists and modern contraceptives are available.[35] (Fertility rates dropped in Bangladesh from 6.7 births per woman in the early 1950s to 2.7 births per woman in about 2008.)[36]

The conclusion of some researchers who have reviewed the results of fertility studies conducted in various less developed countries is that "although development and social change create conditions that encourage smaller family size, contraceptives are the best contraceptive."[37] These researchers found that three factors are mainly responsible for the impressive decline in birth rates that has occurred in many less developed countries since the mid-1960s: more influential and more effective family planning programs; new contraceptive technology; and the use of the mass media to educate women and men about birth control.[38]

In the past several decades, fertility has declined significantly in the world, although as Figure 1.8 shows, the decline has been much greater in some regions than in others. Note that Europe is below replacement level, which is generally considered to be an average of 2.1 children per woman (the extra one-tenth compensates for the death of some girls and women before the end of their childbearing years). Also note that Africa still has high fertility.

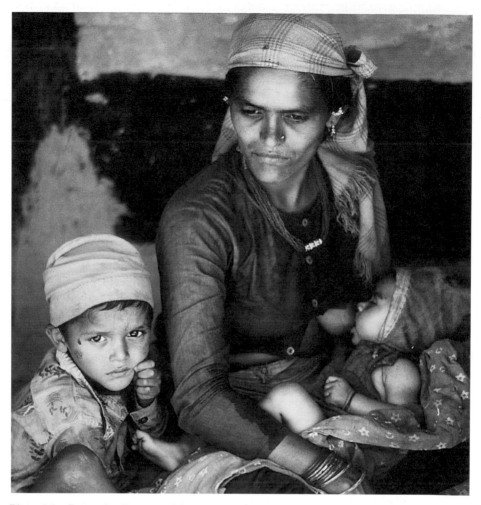

Plate 1.4　Breast-feeding can delay a woman's ability to conceive and provides the most healthful food for a baby

Source: United Nations.

Lowering fertility rates drastically in just 10–15 years – can it be done?

The answer is yes it can be done. We know it can because countries such as Iran, Tunisia, and Algeria have done it under a four-part strategy:

1　Promote child survival
2　Promote girls' education and gender equality

3　Promote availability of contraceptives and family planning, especially for the poor who cannot afford them

4　Raise productivity on the farm so mothers use scarce time in income-earning employment rather than childrearing

Source: Jeffrey D. Sachs, "Lower Fertility: A Wise Investment," *Scientific American*, 295 (September 2006), p. 42.

Governmental Population Policies

Controlling growth

Many governments today have some policies that try to control the growth of their populations, but this is a very recent trend. Traditionally, governments have sought to increase their populations, either through encouraging immigration (as the United States did in its early years) or through tax and other economic assistance to those families with many children. As late as the mid-1970s, many governments had no programs to help manage population levels. A survey of developing nations taken in conjunction with the 1974 United Nations population conference found that, out of 110 developing countries, about 30 had population control programs, another 30 had information and social welfare programs, and about 50 had no population limitation programs at all.[39] This United Nations conference ended with no explicit consensus

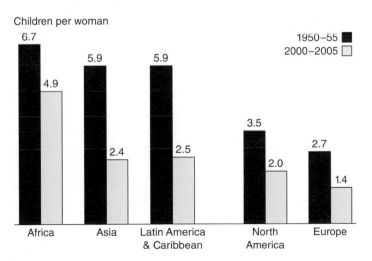

Figure 1.8　Fertility decline in world regions, 1950–1955, 2000–2005

Source: Based on data from UN Department of Economic and Social Affairs, Population Division, *World Population Prospects: The 2008 Revision* (2009).

Plate 1.5   Advertisement for contraceptives in Costa Rica

Source: George Shiflet.

among the participants that there was a world population problem at all. The delegates at the conference did pass a resolution stating that all families have the right to plan their families and that it is the responsibility of governments to make sure all families have the ability to do so.

The ability to control the number and timing of children a couple has is called family planning. Family planning services provide healthcare and information on contraceptives. The expansion of family planning services around the world in the past 40 years has been truly revolutionary. By 2011 about 63 percent of married couples worldwide were using contraceptives, a dramatic increase from the approximately 10 percent in the 1960s.[40] The average number of children per woman dropped from more than five in 1950 to less than three by 2012,[41] still more than needed for a population to stabilize. In the least developed countries, the average number of children per woman was still over four.[42] Most wealthy countries and a few rapidly industrializing countries maintain a birth rate at or below two children per couple, the replacement level.

Although more than half of married women worldwide used contraceptives in 2011, the rate among countries varied greatly. In sub-Saharan countries the contraceptive rate among married women was about 25 percent, while in Mexico and Thailand the use was closer to 70 percent and 80 percent respectively.[43] Wealthier countries had a contraceptive use rate of about 70 percent at this time.[44] As mentioned before in this chapter, at the beginning of the twenty-first century about 143 million women of reproductive age in the poor nations wanted no further children but were not using contraceptives. They are considered to be potential

Figure 1.9   Increases in modern contraceptive use in selected countries

Sources: Based on data from UN Department of Economic and Social Affairs, Population Division, *Levels and Trends in Contraceptive Use, 1998* (2000); C. Haub and B. Herstad, *Family Planning Worldwide* (2002); ORC Macro, Demographic and Health Survey data. As presented in "Transitions in World Population," *Population Bulletin*, 59 (March 2004), p. 8; UN Department of Economic and Social Affairs, Population Division, *World Contraceptive Use 2009*. Percentage of married women aged 15–49 using a modern contraceptive method. US figures are for women aged 15–44. Modern contraceptives include sterilization, oral contraceptives, IUDs, condoms, diaphragms, Depoprovera, Norplant, and other barrier and chemical methods.

family planning users if the services were made available to them. Figure 1.9 depicts increases in contraceptive use in selected countries.

Requests by countries for foreign aid to help them control their population growth now, for the first time, exceed the international assistance available for this activity. It was calculated in 2012 that providing family planning services to the estimated 222 million women whose potential demand remained unmet would cost an estimated $3 billion annually. While this seems like a huge amount, relative to other expenditures being made at present it is not. (The cost of one modern submarine in the United States is over $2 billion, and the US tobacco industry spends about that amount yearly on advertising.) Despite some controversial policies (see discussion earlier in this chapter about US policy in the 1980s), the US government has been the largest single donor of aid for population and family planning activities in the developing world. However, as we discuss in Chapter 2, its development assistance, which includes population assistance, is far below the recommended level.

Recognizing that many Member States were not on track to meeting their commitments pursuant to the 1994 International Conference on Population and Development (ICPD) and its Programme of Action, which had been set to expire in 2014, the UN General Assembly extended the Programme of Action by resolution in 2010.[45]

Plate 1.6   Family planning class

Source: United Nations.

Accordingly, the Commission on Population and Development adopted a resolution reaffirming the Programme of Action and its central implementation provisions in 2014, including the commitment of each Member State to provide 0.7 percent of its annual gross national product in assistance toward population and development programs.[46] However, the international assistance provided continued to fall below the cost of population assistance: in 2011 the total assistance provided for population programs amounted to $11 billion, while the ICPD estimated that global costs for that year were close to $67 billion.[47]

Mexico is a country that has had rather dramatic success with its family planning program. The government began this program only in 1972, when it had one of the highest rates of population growth in the world. In the early 1970s the annual population growth rate was estimated to be above 3 percent, while in 2010 it was estimated to be down to about 1.4 percent.[48] The average number of children per woman in Mexico dropped from about 7 in 1965 to about 2.5 in 2000.

In 1972 Mexico's President Luis Echeverria Alvarez announced a reversal of governmental policy on the population issue. His decision to support a strong effort to control the rapid growth of the Mexican population led the government to use Mexfam, the local affiliate of the International Planned Parenthood Federation, to set up family planning clinics throughout the country. (By the early 1990s Mexfam had set up 200 of these clinics.) Besides making contraceptives readily available, the government and Mexfam mounted a large propaganda campaign using television soap operas, popular songs, billboards, posters on buses and in subway stations, and spot announcements on radio and television. The leaders of the Catholic Church in Mexico did not oppose the government's efforts.

But if the present birth rate is not reduced further, Mexico's population will increase by 15 percent by 2050. To increase the use of contraceptives, the National Population Council began focusing its efforts on the rural population, adolescents, and men. Men are an especially important target since the rate of contraceptive use by men in Mexico is low and social and economic conditions have evolved such that men have become more receptive to the message that controlling family size makes sense.

A few countries have adopted more forceful measures than family planning to try to reduce their population growth. Japan drastically reduced its population growth by legalizing abortion after World War II, by some accounts in order to reduce the number of Japanese children fathered by American military men stationed in Japan.

India, which did not see significant changes with its voluntary family planning programs, enacted more forceful measures in the mid-1970s, such as the compulsory sterilization of some government workers with more than two children. Several states in India passed laws requiring sterilization and/or imprisonment for those couples who bore more than two or three children. A male vasectomy program was also vigorously pursued, with transistor radios and money being given as an incentive to those agreeing to have the sterilization operation. Public resentment against these policies mounted and helped lead to the defeat of Prime Minister Indira Gandhi's government in 1977. Birth control efforts slackened after that event. The government in India has now returned to voluntary measures to help manage the growth of its population. Fertility has declined substantially in India from about five children per woman in 1970 to about two children in 2015.[49] Even with this decline, population is now increasing by about 15 million a year,[50] an increase which leads the world. India now has about 18 percent of the world's population[51] on only 2.5 percent of the world's land, and is poised to soon become the most populous country on the planet.[52]

China, which has about 19 percent of the world's population[53] but only about 7 percent of its arable land, has implemented vigorous programs to limit its population growth and has drastically reduced its birth rate. For many years the communist government, under the leadership of Mao Zedong, encouraged the growth of the population, believing that there was strength in numbers. The policy was eventually reversed and the average number of children per woman dropped from about six in 1970 to about two in the year 2000. In 2015 China's population was about 1.4 billion, and the population is expected to decline to 1.2 billion by 2075.[54]

China employed a wide assortment of measures to limit the growth. These included broadly promoting contraceptives, encouraging sterilization, and making abortions readily available. The government, through extensive publicity efforts, promoted the one-child family as the ideal, encouraging late marriages and providing employment and housing incentives to one-child couples.

Partly because of a concern that there will not be enough adult children to care for their aging parents, the one-child policy is being moderated. It has been widely enforced in the urban areas, but in rural areas, where about 60 percent of the people still live, couples were usually allowed to have a second child if the first child was a female. The one-child policy was also not applied to ethnic groups in the country, partly because many of them live in strategic border areas and the government did not want to cause resentment among them. There is evidence that there was widespread disregard of the policy in some rural areas where it is not uncommon today to find families with three, four, five, or even more children.[55] A male child is still strongly desired in many areas to carry on the family name, to take care of his parents when they get old (an old age social security system still does not exist in the rural areas), and to help with agricultural work.[56]

China's birth control policies have been both admired and criticized in other countries. Admiration has been given for the spectacular accomplishment, for producing one of the fastest, if not the fastest, demographic transitions in history. The policy has been credited with having prevented the birth of an additional 400 million children,[57] which some experts believe could have caused a demographic disaster. The one-child policy was criticized because of the means used to enforce it, which included the use of abortions as a backup to contraceptives – sometimes on women who strongly preferred not to have one. The use of the coercive techniques of the past has mainly ended and emphasis is now placed on education and "family planning fees" for women who have unapproved children.[58] Concern has also been expressed at the unnaturally low numbers of female births being reported. Because of stringent family planning policies and a social preference for having a male child, there is speculation that many couples resorted to measures such as aborting pregnancies if the fetus was female – ultrasound equipment has become widespread to indicate the sex of the fetus.[59]

Population-related challenges in China's future include an aging population because of low fertility; fewer children to take care of aging parents; single children with no siblings, aunts or uncles; and a shortage of females for males to marry. Dissatisfaction is also spreading in parts of the country because of the increasing social and financial inequality that has come with China's increasing economic prosperity as it follows the market approach. Also, as the population continues to grow in tandem with consumption and industrialization expands, there will be increasing stress on the environment.

Promoting growth

Although most countries now recognize a need to limit population growth, a few have openly favored increasing their populations, among them the military governments that ruled in Argentina and Brazil in the 1960s and 1970s. Both countries have large areas that are still sparsely populated and both are rivals for the role of being the dominant power in Latin America. A few Brazilian military officers even advocated encouraging population growth so that Brazil could pass the United States in size and become the dominant nation in the Western hemisphere. It is doubtful that a larger population alone could ever put a country in this position without concurrent economic advances.

Aside from some pro-growth statements, the Brazilian military governments did not effectively promote population growth. They became basically neutral on the issue of population and gradually made it possible for the main nongovernmental family planning organization to operate in the country. After the military left power in Brazil in the mid-1980s, a new constitution acknowledged the right of women to family planning. This provision had the tacit approval of the Brazilian Catholic Church. By the mid-1990s about 75 percent of Brazilian women were using some form of contraception.[60] From 1960 to 2005 the average number of children born to a Brazilian woman dropped from about six to about two. Despite legal limitations, abortions have not been uncommon. One estimate is that there were about 1.4 million abortions performed annually in Brazil in the mid-2000s.[61]

Other countries, such as Mongolia and some in sub-Saharan Africa, have at times advocated larger populations both for strategic reasons and because of the belief that a large population is necessary for economic development. Even the US government, which generally recognizes the need for a check on population growth, has some policies that promote large families, such as income tax laws that allow deductions for children. Many developed nations have contradictory policies, some encouraging population growth while others discourage it. Some developing nations also have such contradictions, although the greater agreement now in these countries about the need to limit growth often causes the contradictions to be exposed and eliminated.

Romania: a disastrous pro-birth policy

Romania is an example of a country that tried to promote the growth of its population. After World War II, the birth rate there fell so sharply that within a few years the population of the country would actually have started declining. In the mid-1960s the communist government, headed by Nicolae Ceaușescu, decided to try to reverse this trend, not only to ward off a possible decline of population but to actually increase the number of people. Ceaușescu believed that a large population would improve Romania's economic position and preserve its culture, since Romania was surrounded by countries with different cultures. "A great nation needs a great population," said Ceaușescu. He called on all women of childbearing age to have five children. Monthly – and in some places, even weekly – gynecological exams were given to all working women 20 to 30 years old. If a woman was found to be pregnant, a "demographic command body" was called in to monitor her pregnancy to make sure she did not interrupt it. A special tax was placed on those who were childless.

The main techniques the government used to promote its pro-growth policy were to outlaw abortion, which was one of the main methods couples had used in the postwar period to limit the size of their families, and to ban the importation and sale of contraceptives. The birth rate immediately shot up, but within a few years it was nearly back to its previous low as couples found other means to limit their families. One of the means was secret abortions, and many women either died or ended up in hospital after abortions were performed or attempted by incompetent personnel. Another tragic result of Ceauşescu's pro-birth policy (as well as of his failed economic policies) was the abandoning of unwanted children. Tens of thousands of these children ended up in understaffed and ill-equipped orphanages (there are photo essays of Romania's orphanages in the sources below). Many babies were even sold for hard currency to infertile Western couples. The pro-growth policy ended in 1989 with the overthrow of the Ceauşescu regime and with his execution.

Sources: James Nachtwey, "Romania's Lost Children," *New York Times Magazine*, June 24, 1990, pp. 28–33; and Jane Perlez and Ettore Malanca, "Romania's Lost Boys," *New York Times Magazine*, May 10, 1998, pp. 26–9.

A generalization one can make about governmental policies that are aimed at influencing population growth is that, aside from drastic measures, governmental policies have not been very successful in either promoting or limiting birth rates very much if these policies are out of line with what the population desires. One can also generalize that matters pertaining to reproduction are still considered to be private decisions and not matters for public policy to control.

A growing number of industrialized countries are increasingly faced with a rapidly expanding retirement-age population and a shrinking labor force that will have to support its elderly citizens. Some of these countries, such as Sweden, Hungary, South Korea, and Japan, have tried various policies to encourage women to have more children. The policies have included paid maternity and paternity leave, free childcare, tax breaks for large families, family housing allowances, and even cash paid to parents raising a child. At the start of this century, a study of these efforts concluded:

> As we enter the next century, a growing number of countries will have near-zero growth or will decline in size. Experience in Europe, Japan, and other countries suggests that governments can encourage people to have more children, but at a high price and not enough to affect long-term trends.[62]

The Future

The growth of the world's population

In 2015 the world's population was estimated to be about 7 billion. The United Nations projects that the world's population will continue to grow to about 8 to 10 billion by 2050, depending on the success of efforts to control population growth.

The most likely total, according to the United Nations, is between 9 and 10 billion. The United Nations bases its projection on the assumption that the world's population growth rates, while still above their replacement rates, will continue the decline that started in the late 1960s.[63]

Unusually for a developed country, the population of the United States is expected to continue to grow significantly, increasing from about 300 million in 2010 to about 400 million around 2050. Rather atypical of Northern Europe, the United Kingdom's population is projected to grow from about 62 million in 2010 to about 77 million in 2050.[64]

The carrying capacity of the Earth

Will the Earth be able to support a population of 9 to 10 billion, 2–3 billion more than the present size, or will catastrophe strike before that figure is reached? (The world was 2 billion when one of your authors (Seitz) was born. Now it is more than three times that size, a remarkable change in just a single lifetime.) Understanding the concept of "carrying capacity" will help answer the question of potential catastrophe. Carrying capacity is the number of individuals of a certain species that can be sustained indefinitely in a particular area. Carrying capacity can change over time, making a larger or smaller population possible. Human ingenuity has greatly increased the carrying capacity of Earth to support human beings, for example, by increasing the production of food. (This was unforeseen by Thomas Malthus, who wrote about the dangers of overpopulation in the late 1700s.) But carrying capacity can also change so that fewer members of the species can live. A change in the climate might do this. Care must be exercised when using the concept of carrying capacity because, in the past, its definition implied a balance of nature. Many ecologists no longer use the concept of balance of nature because numerous studies have shown that nature is much more often in a state of change than in a balance.[65] Populations of different forms of life on Earth are usually in a state of flux as fires, wind storms, disease, changing climate, new or decreasing predators, and other forces make for changing conditions and thus changing carrying capacity.

There are four basic relationships that can exist between a growing population and the carrying capacity of the environment in which it exists. A simplified depiction of these is given in Figure 1.10. Graph (a) illustrates a continuously growing carrying capacity and population. Although human ingenuity as seen in the agricultural revolution (to be discussed in Chapter 3) and in the industrial/scientific revolution has greatly increased the capacity of the Earth to support a larger number of human beings, it is doubtful the human population can continue to expand indefinitely. A basic ecological law is that the size of a population is limited by the short supply of a resource needed for survival. The scarcity of only one of the essential resources for humans – which would include air, energy, food, space, nonrenewable resources, heat, and water – would be enough to put a limit on its population growth. It is unknown how much farther the carrying capacity can be expanded before one of the limits is reached, or whether the global population has already overshot its limit.

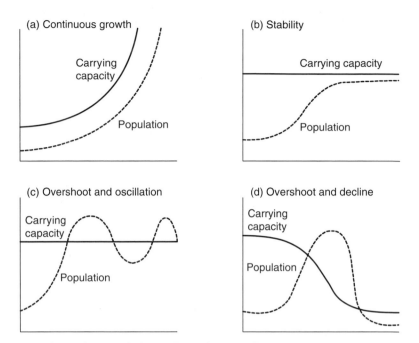

Figure 1.10   A growing population and carrying capacity

Graph (b) of Figure 1.10 illustrates a population that has stabilized somewhat below the carrying capacity. (In actuality the population may fluctuate slightly above and below the carrying capacity, but the carrying capacity remains basically unchanged.) Examples of this can be seen in relatively undisturbed tropical rainforests where many species are relatively stable in an environment where average temperature and rainfall vary little.[66] Graph (c) portrays a situation where the population has overshot the carrying capacity of the environment and then oscillates above and below it. An example of this situation may be the relationship between the great gray owls and their prey, lemmings and voles, in northern forests. Lemmings and voles are an important food source for the owls. Their populations rapidly increase over a period of four to six years and then, as predators increase their consumption of them, their numbers crash catastrophically, causing the owls to flee the area to escape mass starvation.[67] Graph (d) illustrates a situation in which the overshooting of the carrying capacity leads to a precipitous decline in the population, or even to its extinction, and also to a decline in the carrying capacity. Such a situation has occurred with deer on the north rim of the Grand Canyon in the United States,[68] and with elephants in Kenya's Tsavo National Park.[69] In both cases, the number of animals increased to a point where they destroyed the vegetation they fed upon.

It is our hope that the human species with its unique mental powers will create a situation that combines elements of graphs (a) and (b), using its abilities to increase the carrying capacity of Earth, where possible, and where it is not, making sure its numbers do not exceed that capacity. But there are many indications that the species has not yet recognized its danger and is not yet taking effective efforts to prevent either situation (c) – which would mean the death of millions – or situation (d), which could lead to the decline of the human race. There are places in the world where population expansion has already passed the carrying capacity of the land and the land itself is now being destroyed; in parts of Africa, for example, fertile land is turning into desert and in the Himalayan mountain area, land is being destroyed by human-made erosion and floods. There are many other examples of the reduction of the carrying capacity of the Earth that is taking place at unprecedented rates today around the world – the result of uncontrolled overgrazing, overfishing, overplanting, overcutting of forests, and the overproduction of waste which leads to pollution. (Some of this reduction of carrying capacity is being caused by population pressures and some by economic forces, for example the desire to increase short-term profits.) This deterioration has led many ecologists to believe that unless there is a rapid and dramatic change in many governmental policies, the human species may indeed be headed for the situations depicted in either the oscillation or decline graphs in Figure 1.10.

There is one other aspect of the carrying capacity concept that demonstrates some of the trade-offs in evaluating the global carrying capacity for humans: what quality of life should the population enjoy? Joel Cohen, a distinguished biologist, head of the Laboratory of Populations at Rockefeller University and Columbia University and author of the influential book *How Many People Can the Earth Support?*, persuasively argues that when asking the question "How many people can the Earth support?" an attempt must be made to answer questions such as the following:

- *How many at what average level of well-being?* What type of diet, transportation, and health system will be provided?
- *How many with what distribution of well-being?* If we are content to have a few rich and a large number poor, the Earth can probably support more than if the income distribution is fairly equal.
- *How many with what physical, chemical, and biological environments?* How much clean air, water, and wilderness do we want?
- *How many with what kinds of domestic and international political institutions?* How will conflicts be settled at home and internationally?
- *How many with what technology?* How food and goods and services are produced affects the Earth's carrying capacity.
- *How many with what values, tastes, and fashions?* Are we vegetarians or meat eaters? Do we commute to work by car, mass transport or bicycle?
- *How many for how long?* How long can that number of people be supported?[70]

The concept "sustainable development," which will be discussed in Chapter 9, is related to carrying capacity and is now being used more frequently than carrying capacity to convey some of the same concerns.

Optimum size of the Earth's population

What is the optimum size of the Earth's population? That question, like others we have asked in this chapter, is not going to be easy to answer, but it is worth asking. Paul Ehrlich, professor of population studies and of biology at Stanford University, defines the optimum size of the Earth's population as that "below which well-being per person is increased by further growth and above which well-being per person is decreased by further growth." What does "well-being" mean? Ehrlich explains what he believes it means:

> The physical necessities – food, water, clothing, shelter, a healthful environment – are indispensable ingredients of well-being. A population too large and too poor to be supplied adequately with them has exceeded the optimum, regardless of whatever other aspects of well-being might, in theory, be enhanced by further growth. Similarly, a population so large that it can be supplied with physical necessities only by the rapid consumption of nonrenewable resources or by activities that irreversibly degrade the environment has also exceeded the optimum, for it is reducing Earth's carrying capacity for future generations.[71]

Ehrlich believes that, given the present patterns of human behavior – behavior that includes the grossly unequal distribution of essential commodities such as food and the misuse of the environment – and the present level of technology, we have already passed the optimum size of population for this planet.

Julian Simon, author of *The Ultimate Resource*, believed that the ultimate resource on Earth is the human mind. The more human minds there are, said Simon, the more solutions there will be to human problems. Simon admitted that population growth in poor countries could lead to short-term problems since more children will have to be fed. But in the long run these children will become producers, so the Earth will benefit from their presence. Simon agreed that rapid population growth could harm development prospects in poor nations, but he was not disturbed by moderate growth in these countries. According to Simon, larger populations make economies of scale possible; cheaper products can be made if there are many potential consumers. Also, services can improve, as seen by the development of efficient mass transportation in Japan and Europe in areas of dense population.[72]

Simon's views won favor in the Reagan and Bush administrations (father and son) in the United States and were used to give academic support to a new US policy on population – popularly called the Mexico City policy. This policy basically saw the effect of population growth as a "neutral phenomenon … not necessarily good or ill," a position which Marxist ideology also held.[73] While many economists in the United States do not share Simon's view that "more is better," many do share his view that human ingenuity, especially new technology and resource management practices, can increase the carrying capacity of the Earth as it has in the past.[74]

Joel Cohen believes there is no way to estimate the optimum size of the human population on Earth because no scientifically based answers have been given to the questions he presented above. In simpler terms, no one has answered the fundamental question: "How many people can the Earth support with what quality of life?" Obviously the Earth can support a large number of people if they are all living at a subsistence level – with barely enough to eat – or if a relatively few are rich and the rest poor, or if they accept frequent risks of violent storms and droughts. But Cohen believes that even without an agreed-upon "optimum number," the many things that governments and individuals can do to improve conditions for the present generation and future generations are worth doing.[75]

Population-related problems in our future

Throughout this book we are going to be looking at many current problems related to population rates increasing in tandem with consumption. Here we mention a few of the most important ones. Hunger is an obvious problem in which overpopulation plays a key role, and the number of hungry people is huge. The news media are used to dramatizing this problem only when there are many children with bloated bellies to be photographed, but much more common than the starving child today, and probably in the future, will be the child or adult who is permanently debilitated or who dies because of malnutrition-related diseases. Pollution and the depletion of nonrenewable resources will increase as the world's population grows. Migration of people to lands that do not want them will probably increase in the future and this can cause international tension. At least 300,000 immigrants, and probably more, enter the United States through informal channels annually, many of whom come from Latin America looking for work.

In Assam, India, several thousand "unwanted" immigrants were massacred in 1983. Wars have taken place in the past in which overpopulation played an important role and they will probably occur in the future. In the 1960s a border war broke out between El Salvador and Honduras over "unwanted" Salvadorians in Honduras. In the 1990s numerous brutal civil wars occurred in Africa. While we cannot identify overpopulation as the main cause of these conflicts, it is likely that increasing population pressures made the ethnic conflicts more likely.

Growing populations in countries situated in regions with serious water shortages are a direct cause of competition and conflict over the scarce water. The most critical areas are the Middle East and North Africa where population more than tripled between 1960 and 2010, thus greatly reducing the amount of water available per person. About 1 billion people today, mostly in rural areas, do not have access to safe drinking water. According to the United Nations, 700 million people in 43 countries already face severe water shortages.[76] In some of these regions, droughts have been common throughout history. What is not common in these regions is the population density that is present and projected. While water scarcity can obviously promote conflict, it also has the potential of promoting cooperation as nations are forced to devise ways to conserve and share scarce water. It is projected that by 2025, 1.8 billion people will be living in areas with absolute water scarcity, while one-half of the global population will live in water-stressed areas.[77]

Plate 1.7   A more frequent picture in the future? A crowded train in Bangladesh
Source: World Bank.

Another potential problem is climate change, which will be discussed in Chapter 5. An increase in the average global temperature could intensify the water cycle. There could be more rain in some locations but also more droughts.

One bright development is that the industrialized countries are learning to conserve water and to use it more efficiently. Water use in the United States has actually declined about 20 percent since 1980. This decline came because of new water-saving technologies and practices such as less wasteful irrigation techniques and water-stingy toilets. (In the United States toilets used about 6 gallons of water per flush. After a law passed by Congress in 1992 set new standards, new toilets now use 1.5 gallons per flush, a big reduction.) Japan has made major reductions in water use in its industry. Some of these water-saving practices have spread to other nations, including less wealthy ones.[78]

Conclusions

While the population in many less wealthy countries is still growing, it is actually relatively stable or even decreasing in other countries. More economic growth raised the living standards in some countries to a level where having more children made it difficult for them to increase their living standards further. We see this happening in countries that have a high GNP or income per capita. At the same time, many other countries with lower GNPs continue to grow in population as they try to improve their living standards. Thus we find ourselves today with a relatively few countries considered "more developed" that have stopped growing in population, while the majority of countries are considered to be "developing" or "less developed" have higher growth rates that are contributing to a planet with unprecedented population growth.

We can use a more expansive concept of development to look at the progress or lack of progress many countries are making today in lowering their birth rates. First of all, we know that economic growth that benefits the majority in a country, and not just a few, is associated with lower population rates. As we have seen in this chapter, if the majority are receiving a higher standard of living, they tend to reduce the number of children a family has. And other parts of our definition of development help us evaluate why some countries are doing better than others in lowering the number of children women in those countries have. So we want to know how the increased wealth in the country that comes from the economic growth is affecting society. Is corruption increasing in the society, in the government? Is the wealth being used to provide more services to the majority of people, such as medical clinics for the rural poor who have the high birth rates, and family planning services that will help rural women receive contraceptives and help them plan their families, or is the wealth mainly benefiting the rich and urban class? All of these questions and others need to be answered when analyzing the type of development a country has. To put all nations with a certain range of GNP or national income per capita in the category of "developing" or "less developed" does not help us understand the differences that exist among countries regarding population growth. It is only when you look at a country's economic wealth *and* the social changes that are caused by or accompany that economic growth that you can begin to understand why some countries are doing much better than others in lowering their birth rates.

Looking over the statements by a number of population experts, they seem to share the conclusion that the Earth faces an overwhelming problem with its current population growth of about 1 million people every four days. This is a problem, along with climate change and the threat of nuclear weapons, which will be discussed later in this book, that has the potential for causing untold human misery. But many of these experts also emphasize that human thinking and governmental policies are starting to change and impressive reductions in birth rates are taking place in various countries around the world. We know how to reduce birth rates, and many countries have already transitioned to a stable or even shrinking population. But there are many places where population growth continues at exponential rates. Even if population growth were to halt immediately, the consumption habits of the world's population already demand more resources than the Earth can sustain. While population growth is slowing, the world is still expected to add billions more people in the coming decades, with societies that are increasingly adopting more resource-consumptive lifestyles. What is lacking at present is the political will to do what needs to be done to address the problem. We will do it if we take seriously the warning given in a joint statement by the US National Academy of Sciences and its British counterpart, the Royal Society of London:

> If current predictions of population growth prove accurate and patterns of human activity on the planet remain unchanged, science and technology may not be able to prevent either irreversible degradation of the environment or continued poverty for much of the world.[79]

Notes

1 UN Department of Economic and Social Affairs (DESA), Population Division, *World Population Prospects: The 2012 Revision*, at http://esa.un.org/unpd/wpp/unpp/panel_population.htm (accessed July 2015).
2 Ibid.
3 Ibid.
4 UN General Assembly Report A/68/190, para. 38 (July 25, 2013), at http://www.un.org/esa/population/migration/SG_Report_A_68_190.pdf (accessed July 2015).
5 UN DESA, Population Division, *World Population Prospects: The 2012 Revision*.
6 Ibid., p. xix.
7 Ibid., p. 3.
8 UN Habitat, *State of the World's Cities 2012/2013*, p. 127, at https://sustainabledevelopment.un.org/content/documents/745habitat.pdf (accessed July 2015).
9 Edward Gargan, "On Meanest of Streets, Salvaging Useful Lives," *New York Times*, January 8, 1992, p. A2.
10 UN DESA, Population Division, *World Urbanization Prospects: The 2014 Revision, Highlights*, p. 26, at http://esa.un.org/unpd/wup/Highlights/WUP2014-Highlights.pdf (accessed July 2015).
11 Ibid., p. 13.
12 Ibid., pp. 26–7.
13 UN Habitat, *State of the World's Cities 2012/2013*, p. 25.
14 Ibid.
15 UN DESA, Population Division, *World Urbanization Prospects: The 2014 Revision, Highlights*, p. 1.
16 UN DESA, Population Division, *World Urbanization Prospects: The 2009 Revision, Highlights*, at http://www.ctc-health.org.cn/file/2011061610.pdf (accessed July 2015).
17 Lester R. Brown, *The Twenty-Ninth Day: Accommodating Human Needs and Numbers to the Earth's Resources* (New York: Norton, 1978), p. 73.
18 UN DESA, Population Division, *World Contraceptive Patterns 2013*, wallchart, at http://www.un.org/en/development/desa/population/publications/pdf/family/worldContraceptivePatternsWallChart2013.pdf (accessed July 2015).
19 "Transitions in World Population," *Population Bulletin*, 59 (2004), p. 9.
20 UN DESA, Population Division, *World Population Prospects: The 2012 Revision*.
21 Fred Pearce, "Japan's Ageing Population Could Actually Be Good News," *New Scientist*, 221 (2951) (January 11, 2014), at http://www.newscientist.com/article/dn24822-japans-ageing-population-could-actually-be-good-news.html#.VQ9YmI54qtk (accessed July 2015).

22 Ibid.

23 UN DESA, Population Division, *World Population Prospects: The 2012 Revision*, vol. 1, p. 7.

24 Ibid.

25 UN DESA, Population Division, *World Urbanization Prospects: The 2014 Revision, Highlights*, p. 66.

26 Ibid., p. 68.

27 Ibid., p. 65.

28 UN DESA, Population Division, *World Population Prospects: The 2008 Revision* (New York: United Nations, 2008).

29 UN DESA, Population Division, *World Population Prospects: The 2012 Revision*.

30 Joseph A. McFalls Jr, "Population: A Lively Introduction," *Population Bulletin*, 46 (October 1991), p. 36. See also the third edition of this publication in *Population Bulletin*, 53 (September 1998), p. 42.

31 Kevin Kinsella, and David Phillips, "Global Aging: The Challenge of Success," *Population Bulletin*, 60 (March 2005), p. 15.

32 A discussion of the political forces that were instrumental in the Reagan and Bush administrations in developing this policy and in keeping it in force for ten years is contained in Michael S. Teitelbaum, "The Population Threat," *Foreign Affairs* (Winter 1992/1993), pp. 63–78. The policy was reversed in 1994 when the Clinton administration took office but reinstated when Bush's son became President.

33 "Transitions in World Population," *Population Bulletin*, 59 (2004), p. 25.

34 Bryan Robey, Shea Rutstein, and Leo Morris, "The Fertility Decline in Developing Countries," *Scientific American*, 269 (December 1993), p. 63.

35 Ibid., pp. 60–7. See also Susan Kalish, "Culturally Sensitive Family Planning: Bangladesh Story Suggests It Can Reduce Family Size," *Population Today*, 22 (February 1994), p. 5; Lina Parikh, "Spotlight: Bangladesh," *Population Today*, 26 (January 1998), p. 7; and Malcolm Potts, "The Unmet Need for Family Planning," *Scientific American*, 282 (January 2000), p. 91.

36 Population Reference Bureau, *2008 World Population Data Sheet* (2009).

37 Robey, Rutstein, and Morris, "The Fertility Decline in Developing Countries," p. 65.

38 Ibid., p. 60.

39 *New York Times*, August 18, 1974, p. 2.

40 UN DESA, Population Division, *World Contraceptive Patterns 2013*; John Cleland et al., "Family Planning: The Unfinished Agenda" (2006), p. 1, at http://www.who.int/reproductivehealth/publications/general/lancet_3.pdf (accessed July 2015).

41 UN DESA, Population Division, *Fertility Levels and Trends as Assessed in the 2012 Revision of World Population Prospects* (2012), p. vii, at http://www.un.org/en/development/desa/population/publications/pdf/fertility/Fertility-levels-and-trends_WPP2012.pdf (accessed July 2015).

42 Ibid., p. vii.

43 UN DESA, Population Division, "World Contraceptive Patterns 2013."

44 Ibid.

45 UN GA Res. 65/234 (December 22, 2010), p. 1, at http://www.un.org/ga/search/view_doc.asp?symbol=A/RES/65/234 (accessed July 2015).

46 UN Economic and Social Council, Commission on Population and Development, Report on the 47th Session, p. 12 (2014), at http://daccess-dds-ny.un.org/doc/UNDOC/

GEN/N14/312/08/PDF/N1431208.pdf?OpenElement; Programme of Action, para. 14.11 (September 1994), at http://www.unfpa.org/sites/default/files/pub-pdf/ICPD% 20PoA%20English.pdf (both accessed July 2015).

47   UN Population Fund, *Financing the ICPD Programme of Action: Data for 2011 Estimates for 2012/2013, Projections for 2014* (2013), p. 2, at http://www.unfpa. org/publications/financing-icpd-programme-action (accessed July 2015).

48   Population Reference Bureau, *2010 World Population Data Sheet* (2010).

49   UN DESA, Population Division, *World Population Prospects: The 2012 Revision*, vol. 1, p. 217.

50   UN DESA, Population Division, *World Population Prospects: The 2012 Revision*.

51   Ibid.

52   UN DESA, Population Division, *World Population Prospects: The 2012 Revision*, vol. 1, p. 3.

53   UN DESA, Population Division, *World Population Prospects: The 2012 Revision*.

54   Ibid.

55   Elisabeth Rosenthal, "Rural Flouting of One-Child Policy Undercuts China's Census," *New York Times*, April 14, 2000, p. A10.

56   Susan Scutti, "One-Child Policy Is One Big Problem for China," *Newsweek*, January 23, 2014, at http://www.newsweek.com/2014/01/24/one-child-policy-one-big-problem-china-245118.html (accessed July 2015).

57   Ibid.

58   Rosenthal, "Rural Flouting of One-Child Policy Undercuts China's Census."

59   Nancy E. Riley, "Gender, Power, and Population Change," *Population Bulletin*, 52 (May 1997), p. 39.

60   UN DESA, Population Division, *World Contraceptive Use 2009*, at http://www.un. org/esa/population/publications/contraceptive2009/contraceptive2009.htm (accessed July 2015).

61   Colin McMahon, "In Brazil, Abortion Illegal but Common," *Chicago Tribune*, November 1, 2006.

62   Mary Mederios Kent, "Shrinking Societies Favor Procreation," *Population Today*, 27 (December 1999), pp. 4–5.

63   UN DESA, Population Division, *World Population Prospects: The 2012 Revision*.

64   Population Reference Bureau, *2010 World Population Data Sheet*.

65   Daniel B. Botkin, "A New Balance of Nature," *Wilson Quarterly* (Spring 1991), pp. 61–72; and William K. Stevens, "New Eye on Nature: The Real Constant Is Eternal Turmoil," *New York Times*, July 31, 1990, pp. B5–6.

66   G. Tyler Miller Jr, *Living in the Environment: Principles, Connections, and Solutions*, 8th edn (Belmont, CA: Wadsworth, 1994), p. 153.

67   E. Vernon Laux, "In a Vast Hungry Wave, Owls Are Moving South," *New York Times*, March 8, 2005, p. D2; Peter Hudson and Ottar Bjornstad, "Vole Stranglers and Lemming Cycles," *Science*, 302 (October 31, 2003), p. 797.

68   Edward J. Kormondy, *Concepts of Ecology*, 2nd edn (Englewood Cliffs, NJ: Prentice-Hall, 1976), pp. 111–12.

69   Botkin, "A New Balance of Nature," pp. 61–3.

70   Joel E. Cohen, *How Many People Can the Earth Support?* (New York: W. W. Norton, 1995).

71   Paul R. Ehrlich, Anne H. Ehrlich, and John P. Holdren, *Ecoscience: Population, Resources, Environment* (New York: W. H. Freeman, 1977), p. 716.

72 Julian L. Simon, *The Ultimate Resource* (1981), later updated as *The Ultimate Resource 2* (Princeton: Princeton University Press, 1998). See also Julian L. Simon, *Population Matters: People, Resources, Environment, and Immigration* (Piscataway, NJ: Transaction, 1990).

73 Michael S. Teitelbaum, "The Population Threat," *Foreign Affairs* (Winter 1992/1993), pp. 71–2.

74 An interesting wager that Ehrlich and Simon made about whether the world's growing population was running out of natural resources (and which was won by Simon) is reported in John Tierney, "Betting the Planet," *New York Times Magazine*, December 2, 1990, pp. 52–81.

75 Joel E. Cohen, "Human Population Grows Up," *Scientific American*, 293 (September 2005), p. 55.

76 UN Water, "Water for Life Decade – Water Scarcity," at http://www.un.org/waterforlifedecade/scarcity.shtml (accessed July 2015).

77 UN Water, "Water Scarcity Fact Sheet," at ibid.; World Health Organization, "Water Fact Sheet No. 391" (June 2015), at http://www.who.int/mediacentre/factsheets/fs391/en/ (accessed July 2015).

78 Peter Gleick, "Safeguarding Our Water," *Scientific American*, 284 (February 2001), pp. 38–45.

79 "A Warning on Population," *Christian Science Monitor*, March 24, 1992, p. 20.

Further Reading

Cohen, Joel E., "Human Population Grows Up," *Scientific American*, 293 (September 2005), pp. 48–55. A relatively short summary of where we are at present and the challenges humanity faces as the Earth moves to a new stage of life.

De Souza, Roger-Mark, John Williams, and Frederick Meyerson, "Critical Links: Population, Health, and the Environment," *Population Bulletin*, 58 (September 2003). Three critical questions about population, health, and the environment are examined. First, the relationships among the three; second, how these relationships affect human well-being; and third, what communities and policymakers can do about these situations.

Kent, Mary M., and Sandra Yin, "Controlling Infectious Diseases," *Population Bulletin*, 61 (June 2006). We know how to control most serious infectious diseases but infectious microbes continue to evolve, requiring new methods and new drugs. This article includes special short sections on diarrheal diseases, malaria, tuberculosis, and the next pandemics.

Kinsella, Kevin, and David Phillips, "Global Aging: The Challenge of Success," *Population Bulletin*, 60 (March 2005). Kinsella and Phillips examine the causes of global aging and the changes it will bring to society. They also explore various public policies related to this development.

Livi-Bacci, Massimo, *A Concise History of World Population: An Introduction to Population Processes*, 5th edn (Oxford: Blackwell, 2012). A readable history of the growth of the human population from prehistoric times to the present. The author takes a position in between that of the optimists and those predicting a catastrophe; he presents an alternative way to understand and deal with population growth.

Longman, Phillip, "The Global Baby Bust," *Foreign Affairs*, 83 (May/June 2004), pp. 64–79. Longman does not believe that overpopulation is one of the worst dangers facing the world. Rather he argues that an aging population and falling birth rates, which we see now in many rich countries and some developing countries, should be our major concern.

O'Neill, Brian, and Deborah Balk, "World Population Futures," *Population Bulletin*, 56 (September 2001). This publication looks closely at population projections, how they are made, and their uncertainties. Based on these projections, the authors discuss what kind of world is likely in the future.

Potts, Malcolm, "The Unmet Need for Family Planning," *Scientific American*, 282 (January 2000), pp. 88–93. The author argues that falling birth rates have led some people to declare that overpopulation is no longer a threat, but it recently took just 12 years to add an additional billion people to the Earth. Many people still lack access to contraceptives. Unless they are given access to these, severe environmental and health problems will occur in large parts of the world in the twenty-first century.

Rogers, Peter, "Facing the Freshwater Crisis," *Scientific American*, 299 (August 2008), pp. 46–53. As world population increases, its need for fresh water as well as that of industry and agriculture soar. Yet with climate change, supplies of fresh water are becoming unpredictable. The article shows how existing technologies can be used to avert a water crisis if governments take action now.

Sanderson, Warren, and Sergei Scherbov, "Rethinking Age and Aging," *Population Bulletin*, 63 (December 2008). Demographers and policymakers have often not taken into account the fact that older people today are generally more active and healthier than in previous generations. New measures presented in this article take life expectancy differences into account.

Chapter 2

Wealth and Poverty

Wave of Hope: The Millennium Development Goals   55
A Pessimistic View: The Persistence of Poverty   57
Development Assistance and Foreign Aid   59
A Market Approach   63
The State as Economic Actor   67
A Blended Approach   70
Geography and Wealth, Geography and Poverty   72
Globalization   73
   Positive aspects   75
   Negative aspects   76
   An evaluation   77
Conclusions   78
Notes   80
Further Reading   83

The mere fact that opposing visions of economic development have grown to shape the international agenda is in one sense merely an indication that development concerns are receiving attention on a global scale for the first time in history.

Lynn Miller, *Global Order* (1985)

For most of history, human beings have lacked material wealth. A few individuals in many societies had a higher standard of living than their fellow humans, but the vast majority of people on Earth have shared a common condition focused on meeting their daily needs. The industrial revolution brought a fundamental change. Through

Global Issues: An Introduction, Fifth Edition. Kristen A. Hite and John L. Seitz
© 2016 John Wiley & Sons, Ltd. Published 2016 by John Wiley & Sons, Ltd.

a fundamentally faster rate of production and consumption, new wealth was created in the industrializing nations in Europe and eventually shared by larger numbers of people. And the differences between the rich and the poor in the world began to increase. A few nations began to achieve higher living standards, and they began to pull away from the rest of the world, which had not yet begun to industrialize. It is estimated that the difference between the per capita incomes of the richest and poorest countries was 3 to 1 in 1820, 11 to 1 in 1913, 35 to 1 in 1950, 44 to 1 in 1973, 72 to 1 in 1992 and 76 to 1 in 2009.[1] Another way to show this trend is to note that the real (i.e., controlling for inflation) per capita incomes for the richest one-third of countries increased nearly 2 percent annually from 1970 to 1995, while the middle third of countries increased only about 0.5 percent annually, and the poorest one-third had no increase in incomes.[2] After that period there was a more positive trend for the poorer countries. For low and middle income countries gross national incomes more than doubled from 1998 to 2008.[3] This was a significant increase from the previous decade.

One more way to demonstrate that the gap between the richest and poorest is increasing: in 1960 the richest 20 percent of the world's population had 30 times more income than the lowest 20 percent of the world's people. By 2009 the richest 20 percent had now more than 75 times the income of the poorest.[4]

Not only is the gap between the richer and poorer nations growing, but the gap between the rich and the poor *within* countries is also growing. According to a United Nations International Labor Organization report, from 2006 to 2010, the gap between the rich and poor increased markedly in Spain and the United States.[5] In 2012, the richest 1 percent of the US population earned 19.3 percent of the national income[6] and in Spain the richest 10 percent earned 25 percent of the national income.[7] While these figures are notable, this trend of concentrating wealth in the hands of the wealthy is not uncommon: in 2011–12 the richest 20 percent controlled about 43 percent of wealth in India and 47 percent in China.[8]

By the way, don't let all these numbers make your head ache. You don't have to remember them all to understand the subject. But read them carefully as they illustrate the points being made. For example, do the numbers show that the rich are getting richer and the poor poorer, a statement most people, no doubt, would say is true? Well it's not. Some people are getting poorer, but not the majority in the developing countries or the rich countries. The figures we have used don't support this false statement.

The growing gap between the rich and the poor is only one part of the picture of worldwide economic conditions. Another important part of that picture is the vast number of people still living in poverty.

Which are you – an optimist, or a pessimist? When one thinks about the living standards of the world's people there are figures that support both positions. On the positive side the total GDP (gross domestic product) of developing countries more than doubled from 1994 to 2009.[9] The growth rate of per capita income in developing countries was relatively high in the 1960s and 1970s but stagnated in the 1980s. In the early 1990s rapid growth began again, especially in East Asia (from Indonesia to South Korea), but a financial crisis in the late 1990s stopped that growth. Overall

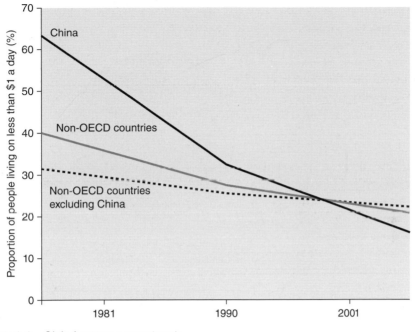

Figure 2.1 Global extreme poverty rate

Source: World Bank, *World Development Indicators*, 2005.

the decade of the 1990s was one of impressive economic growth for some countries, such as China and India, while other nations became poorer.[10] In the first half of the first decade in the twenty-first century, there was strong economic growth in much of the world that reduced the number of people living on less than $1.25 a day (the new international recognized standard for extreme poverty) from 1.8 billion in 1990 to 1.4 billion in 2005.[11] This improvement ended with the very serious economic crisis that occurred in the United States and spread to Europe and many other countries in 2008–9. The crisis led to abrupt declines in exports from developing nations and a lowering of the prices they received for their commodities (mainly minerals and agricultural products). Trade and foreign investments declined. The World Bank estimates the crisis left an additional 50 million people in extreme poverty in 2009.[12] Despite the global financial hardship, in 2010, the UN's Millennium Development Goal of reducing global poverty by one-half of the 1990 poverty level was achieved.[13] Figure 2.1 shows the overall reduction in extreme poverty in developing countries during the final decades of the twentieth century. A closer look at the impressive progress made in the decades of the 1980s and 1990s in reducing the number of people in poor countries living in extreme poverty, that is, living daily on $1 or less, can be seen in Figure 2.2.

Note that much of that progress took place in East Asia, where China is located, and in South Asia, where India resides. The impressive economic growth which both nations experienced in the late twentieth century, especially China, came after

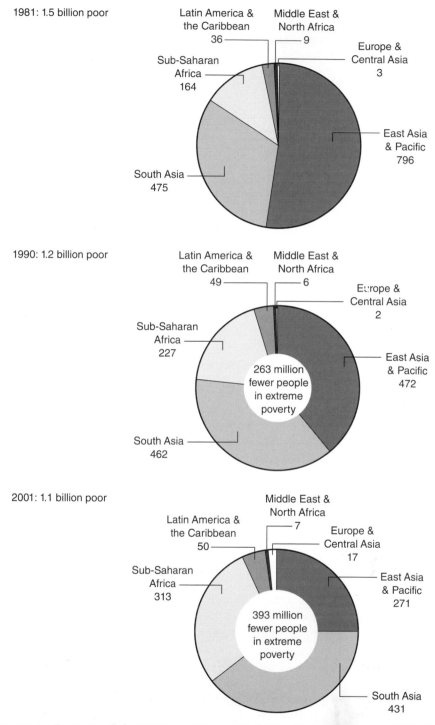

1981: 1.5 billion poor

Latin America &
the Caribbean
36

Middle East &
North Africa
9

Europe &
Central Asia
3

Sub-Saharan
Africa
164

East Asia
& Pacific
796

South Asia
475

1990: 1.2 billion poor

Latin America &
the Caribbean
49

Middle East &
North Africa
6

Europe &
Central Asia
2

Sub-Saharan
Africa
227

East Asia
& Pacific
472

263 million
fewer people
in extreme
poverty

South Asia
462

2001: 1.1 billion poor

Middle East &
North Africa
7

Latin America &
the Caribbean
50

Europe &
Central Asia
17

Sub-Saharan
Africa
313

East Asia
& Pacific
271

393 million
fewer people
in extreme
poverty

South Asia
431

Figure 2.2 Fewer people in extreme poverty: people living on less than $1 a day, 1981, 1990, 2001

Source: World Bank, *World Development Indicators*, 2005.

Figure 2.3 Reduction in extreme poverty in China and India, 1981–2001

Source: World Bank, *World Development Report 2005* (New York: Oxford University Press, 2004), p. 27.

they introduced free market measures which made foreign investments welcome. At the beginning of the 1980s China was one of the poorest countries in the world with about 60 percent of its people living in extreme poverty. Between 1981 and 2012, China reduced the number of people living on less than $1.25 per day by 660 million.[14] The unprecedented reduction of extreme poverty in China and India is shown in Figure 2.3. Poverty rates were estimated to fall from 51 percent in 1990 to about 24 percent in 2015.[15]

Overall, the global growth in wealth last century corresponded to marked increases in well-being, as illustrated in this excerpt from a report by the United Nations Development Programme (UNDP):

> Progress in human development during the twentieth century was dramatic and unprecedented. Between 1960 and 2000 life expectancy in developing countries increased from 46 to 63 years. Mortality rates for children under five were more than halved. Between 1975, when one of every two adults could not read, and 2000 the share of illiterate people was almost halved. Real per capita incomes more than doubled from $2,000 to $4,200.[16]

Wave of Hope: The Millennium Development Goals

Continuing to focus on positive developments, one can find many reasons to feel optimistic. In 2000, representatives of 189 nations met in a conference sponsored by the United Nations and adopted eight goals they would work to achieve in the new century. Each goal, which was stated in general terms, had specific targets to

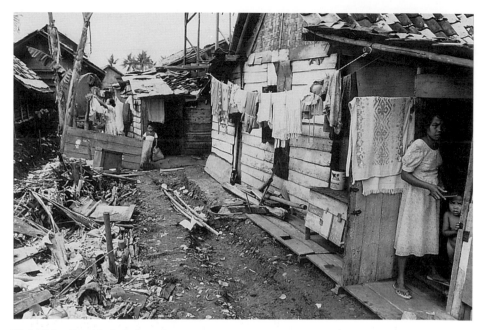

Plate 2.1   Poverty in Indonesia

Source: World Bank.

help measure progress in reaching the goal. The first goal was to eliminate extreme
poverty and hunger in the world.[17] The target under this goal was to reduce, during
the period 1990 to 2015, the number of people living on the equivalent of less than
$1 a day by one-half.

How did the world do in achieving the first goal – a goal, by the way, unprecedented in the world's history? As we have seen from the information presented
above, China and India are doing quite well, but the same cannot be said for many
other countries. Take the time to read the following paragraph from the *Millennium
Development Goals Report 2010* by the United Nations, as it presents a good summary of the world's progress up to that date in achieving this goal:

> Robust growth in the first half of the decade reduced the number of people in develop-
> ing regions living on less than $1.25 a day from 1.8 billion in 1990 to 1.4 billion in 2005,
> while the poverty rate dropped from 46 per cent to 27 per cent. The global economic
> and financial crisis, which began in the advanced economies of North America and
> Europe in 2008 …slow[ed] growth in developing countries. Nevertheless, the momen-
> tum of economic growth in developing countries is strong enough to sustain progress
> on the poverty reduction target. This translates into around 920 million people living
> under the international poverty line – half the number in 1990.[18]

By 2014, several targets of the Millennium Development Goals had been met,
including halving the extreme poverty rate: by 2010, 700 million fewer people lived
on $1.25 per day than in 1990.[19] Advances in malaria and tuberculosis treatment

saved an estimated 25.3 million lives by 2012, and 2.3 billion people gained access to drinking water from an improved source.[20]

A Pessimistic View: The Persistence of Poverty

Now, some information for the pessimist. The United Nations, in the same report as the above information, also mentions that about 1 in 8 people in the world, or 827 million people, endured chronic hunger between 2011 and 2013, and 1 in 4 children, or about 160 million, suffered from chronic undernutrition in 2012.[21] We review this in more detail in Chapter 3 (Food).

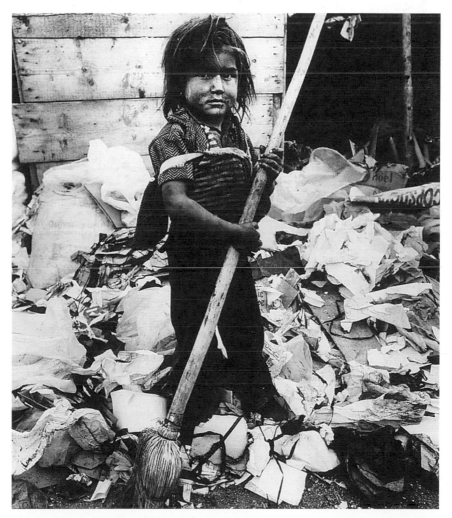

Plate 2.2 The weight of poverty falls heavily on children in less developed nations

Source: United Nations.

In 2010, about 9 percent of the population of China and about 33 percent of the population of India lived on less than $1.25 a day.[22] In the year 2014, more than 20 percent of the people in developing countries still lived in extreme poverty.[23] From 2012 to 2014, 11 percent of the global population, or about 770 million, still lacked clean drinking water, 1.2 billion had no electricity and about 2.5 billion lacked adequate sanitation.[24] In 2011, about 160 million people living in East Asia and the Pacific lived in extreme poverty, as did about 2 million in Europe and Central Asia, 27 million in Latin America and the Caribbean, 5 million in the Middle East and North Africa, 398 million in South Asia, and 415 million in sub-Saharan Africa.[25] A depressing number of countries (46) actually became poorer in the 1990s.[26] Many of these were in Africa and a few were in Latin America and in Europe and Central Asia. In Africa many of the countries growing poorer are in sub-Saharan Africa and are being hit by an HIV/AIDS epidemic, among other problems, while in Europe and Central Asia parts of the former Soviet Union found the transition to being an independent country difficult. For many the path from a planned, state-managed economy to a freer economy was filled with obstacles.

Who are the world's poor? According to the World Bank nearly half live in South Asia (e.g., India, Pakistan, Bangladesh), while a smaller but highly disproportionate number live in Africa, south of the Sahara desert. Within regions and countries the poor tend to be concentrated in rural areas with a high density of population, such as on the Ganges plain in India and on the island of Java in Indonesia. Although urban poverty is a growing problem due to demographic migration toward cities, 80 percent of extreme poverty occurs in the rural areas of the poorer countries. Part of this is due to how poverty is defined, part is due to differences between rural and urban livelihoods, and part is due to disparities in economic opportunities. Many poor also live in areas with scarce resources such as in the Andean highlands in Latin America and in the Sahel region in Africa.[27]

The weight of poverty in the less developed nations falls heaviest on women, children and minority ethnic groups. Figure 2.2 shows that the world's poor are concentrated in Africa, East Asia, and South Asia. Figure 2.4 shows an interesting contrast in the poverty situation. From 1980 to 2005 the proportion of those in two of the poorest regions in the world – sub-Saharan Africa and South Asia – who were living in extreme poverty actually decreased, while at the same time the number of people in both regions living in extreme poverty increased. Do you know why it was this way? As we saw in the first chapter on population, population is still increasing rapidly in both regions of the world so there are now more people living in these regions and thus more people at the bottom economic rung.

Fighting poverty – can an individual do it?

Is there any way an individual can aid the efforts to reduce poverty in our world? Yes there are ways. If you can't personally work with the poor, you can give some funds to an organization that is working to improve the lives of the poor. Here are a few of those we donate to annually: Doctors Without Borders, Grameen Foundation, International Rescue Committee, and Oxfam.

But you might ask, How can I be sure the organizations I give my money to will not waste my money? Several reputable organizations evaluate other organizations for this very characteristic. One of the best is the American Institute of Philanthropy, called by the *New York Times* "the pit bull of watchdogs."

Note: If you are one of those rare individuals who wants to personally aid those who are poverty-stricken, read the following article to learn how others are doing this: Nicholas D. Kristof, "The D.I.Y. [Do It Yourself] Foreign Aid Revolution," *New York Times Magazine*, October 24, 2010, pp. 49–53.

Development Assistance and Foreign Aid

Do the rich have a responsibility to help the poor? It's an age-old question, isn't it, and individuals and countries have throughout time given different answers to it. Most major religions answer it with a resounding "yes," as do many moral philosophies. In 2000, most of the nations of the world historically committed themselves to work toward helping the neediest when they endorsed the Millennium Declaration with its objective of eradicating poverty in the world. Before this, many nations had

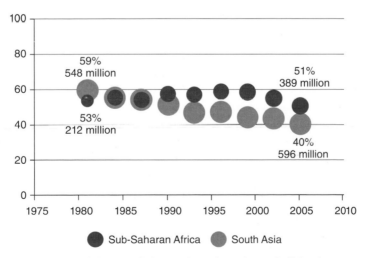

Figure 2.4 Percentage of the population and number of people living in extreme poverty (less than $1.25 a day) in South Asia and sub-Saharan Africa

Source: Data from World Bank, "2008 Poverty Data: A Supplement to the 2008 World Development Indicators."

given aid to foreign nations both for political and humanitarian reasons. Foreign aid is still used regularly to help the donor nation achieve its political objectives and can include military aid as well as economic assistance. Development assistance is usually given with the objective of helping a nation improve its economy. The eighth Millennium Development Goal focuses on the need for developed countries to increase their development assistance to developing nations. The United Nations has set an aid target for the rich countries of 0.7 percent of their wealth (as determined by their GNP. (Although it is still too early to evaluate a most unusual effort by two American billionaires – Bill Gates and Warren Buffett – to get other billionaires around the world to give half of their wealth to charities as they are doing, in 2010 at least 40 pledged to do this very act.)[28]

Plate 2.3   Street children in Nepal

Source: Ab Abercrombie.

In addition, the Millennium Development Goals presented the need for the rich countries to help the least developed by reducing tariffs and quotas on the poor country's exports, and granting debt relief. In return the nations receiving this aid are to show they are seriously working to reduce their poverty and improve their governmental administration, which, among other things, means reducing their corruption. Corruption, which is widespread in many poor countries, siphons off the aid for personal use by powerful governmental and private individuals. In 2014, a report by the ONE Campaign estimated that corruption deprived developing economies of 1 trillion dollars (that's $1,000,000,000,000).[29] To give perspective, this sum would be enough to provide about 165 million vaccines or educate 10 million children per year.[30]

A consequence of poverty: mothers who don't cry
by John L. Seitz

In trying to understand what it can mean to be very poor, consider this: some mothers don't seem to cry when their children die in certain parts of northeast Brazil. Why is this?

To consider this question, one needs to know that the death of a child is fairly common in the Brazilian northeast, the poorest region in Brazil, and one of the poorest in the world. One North American anthropologist offers this as an explanation:

Map 2.1 Brazil

The children of the Northeast, especially those born in shantytowns ... are at a very high risk of death ... marriages are brittle, single parenting is the norm, and women are frequently forced into the shadow economy of domestic work in the

homes of the rich or into … "scab" wage labor on the surrounding sugar plantations, where they clear land for planting and weed for a pittance, sometimes less
than a dollar a day … the women … cannot hire babysitters … In most cases,
babies are simply left at home alone, the door securely fastened. And so many
… die alone unattended.

This anthropologist found that for a number of mothers, no tears were shed
when an infant died and they never visited the graves after the burials. The
anthropologist concluded that the frequent deaths of children had become
such a commonplace tragedy that these mothers had learned to delay their
attachment to any child until that child had proven to be a survivor, hardier
than his or her weaker siblings. This reaction to the realities of their lives
allowed these particular women to continue living in a harsh situation and to
not let grief make their lives unbearable. Similar reactions have been observed
in parts of Africa, India, and Central America.

Source: Nancy Scheper-Hughes, "Death without Weeping," *Natural History* (October 1989),
pp. 8, 14.

How much are the richer nations doing at present to help the least developed
nations? Recently there have been some agreements to reduce the debt of developing
nations, but the need for reduction of trade barriers remains. Nontariff trade measures, such as quotas, subsidies, and restrictions on exports, are increasingly prevalent and may be enacted for policy reasons having nothing to do with trade. However,
they have a discriminatory effect on exports from developing economies that lack
the resources to comply with requirements of nontariff measures imposed by rich
countries.[31] For example, the huge subsidies that wealthy nations give to their farmers make it very difficult for farmers in the rest of the world to compete with them.
Another example would be domestic health or safety regulations, which, though not
specifically targeting imports, could impose significant costs on foreign manufacturers seeking to conform to the importer's market. Industries in developing markets
may have more difficulty absorbing these additional costs.[32]

The amount of foreign aid that wealthy nations have contributed in relation to the
donors' wealth fell rather dramatically in the second half of the twentieth century.
There was a slight upturn at the end of the century, but the aid is still far below the
United Nations target. While the United States gives the largest amount of aid, in
relation to its wealth as measured as a percentage of gross national income, it is near
the bottom of aid donors.[33] It shares this position with Japan and Italy, two other
higher income countries.

Let's end this section on a positive note. The Organisation for Economic Co-
operation and Development (OECD) reported that international development

assistance rose 6.1 percent in 2013, the highest level of development aid on record: $134.8 billion.[34]

Now that we have made a brief examination of poverty and international efforts to help alleviate it, let's focus on another question: Why are some countries rich and some poor? There is no agreement on the answer to that question, but various views have been presented over the years. Although vast differences among the nations of the world make generalizations hazardous, it can be useful to consider some of the most widely accepted approaches or views of economic development: The first is a relatively purely market-driven approach, in which the primary function of the state (if any) is to enable and govern the physical, infrastructural, social, and political conditions which allow free market transactions to occur. These conditions may range from transportation networks (though there are some who argue that even these should be privatized) to legal systems enabling enforcement by the state of private property contract rights that facilitate commercial transactions between relative strangers. The second approach envisions a more active role for the state, which has historically ranged from direct central control of production and labor by the state as described by Karl Marx and his intellectual descendants, to more indirect means of guiding or influencing market forces through direct government purchase and expenditure, regulation, subsidies, and/or incentives, as described in part by John Maynard Keynes and implemented recently in the US in the form of an economic stimulus package in response to the "Great Recession" in the first decade of the twenty-first century.[35] In both cases, it is important to consider inclusive governance in order to help address inequality and enable civil society to meaningfully participate in economic activities and benefit from development.[36] The third approach we describe is a blended approach.

A Market Approach

A decentralized, market-driven approach holds that nations can acquire wealth by following four basic rules: (1) the means of production – those things required to produce goods and services such as labor, natural resources, technology, and capital (buildings, machinery, and money that can be used to purchase these) – must be owned and controlled by private individuals or firms; (2) markets must exist in which the means of production and the goods and services produced are freely bought and sold; (3) trade at the local, national, and international levels must be unrestricted; and (4) a state-enforced system of law must exist to guarantee business contracts so as to ensure safe commercial relations between unrelated individuals.

Adam Smith, the eighteenth-century Scottish political economist sometimes credited as founder of the market approach, believed that the operations of labor are the key to increasing production. He argued that it is much more efficient for workers to specialize in their work, focusing on one product rather than making many different products. If workers do this, and if they are brought together in one location so their labor can be supervised, increased production will result. Smith

Plate 2.4   The market approach is followed on the streets in many countries
Source: Mark Olenski.

also presented the idea that, if the owners of the means of production are allowed to freely sell their services or goods at the most advantageous price they can obtain, the largest amount of products and services will be produced and everyone will benefit. It is the prices in the markets that suggest to the businessman or businesswoman new profitable investment opportunities and more efficient production processes. (For example, when oil prices rose dramatically in the 1970s, new investments occurred in alternative energy sources and some industries came up with ways to reduce the amount of oil they needed to buy. Some business people saw the alternative energy investments as a way for them to make money in the energy field, and some industries cut their costs, thus increasing their profits, by becoming more efficient in their use of energy.)

Smith did not focus on the role of the entrepreneur, but later market theorists did, making the entrepreneur – the one who brought the means of production together in a way to produce goods and services – a key component in this approach. Finally, Smith and other market theorists emphasized the importance of open trade. David Ricardo earned a place in economic history for positing that if a nation concentrates on producing those products in which it has a comparative advantage over other nations, advantages that climate, natural resources, cheap labor, or technology give it, and if it trades with other nations that are also concentrating on those products that *they* have the greatest advantage in producing, then all will benefit.

A market approach holds that government has a crucial but limited role in maintaining an environment in which economic transactions can flourish. Under this approach, government would confine its activities to providing for domestic tranquility that would ensure that private property is protected and contracts are secure; providing certain services, such as defense; enforcing private contracts; and helping to maintain a stable supply of money and credit. The reason some nations are poor, according to the market approach, is that they have not been successful in competing with other countries within the bounds of the basic rules listed above.

Advocates of the market approach point to the wealth of the United States and Western Europe as evidence of the correctness of their view. Even Karl Marx said that the hundred years of rule by capitalists were the most productive in the history of the world. And although an uneven distribution of income occurred in Western Europe during its early period of industrialization, the distribution of income later became much less uneven. This indicated that the new wealth was being shared by more and more people.

Nations such as Japan and West Germany, which came back from the devastation of World War II to create extremely strong economies by following the basic principles of the market approach, are also cited as evidence of the validity of the approach. Examples can also be found among developing nations that have achieved such impressive economic growth by following the principles of this approach that they have moved into a separate category of the less developed world: the newly industrializing countries. Many of these economies, such as China, South Korea, Taiwan, and Singapore, achieved their high economic growth at first mainly by exporting light manufactured products to the developed nations.

Finally, advocates of the market approach point to the decisions of many ex-communist countries and developing countries, during the 1980s, to adopt at least some market mechanisms in their efforts to reform their economies. Even China – the largest remaining communist government – has adopted many important aspects of the market approach; it is this adoption that is widely believed to be responsible for China's impressive economic growth.

Critics of the market approach point to the high rates of unemployment that have existed at times in Western Europe and the United States. At the present time, high unemployment exists throughout the developing world, even in a number of nations that follow the market approach and have had impressive increases in their GNP. Much of the industry that has come to the South has been capital intensive; that is, it uses large amounts of financial and physical capital but employs relatively few workers.

There is evidence from Brazil, which has basically followed the market approach for the past several decades, that the distribution of income within developing countries became more unequal during the period when the countries were experiencing high rates of growth. The same thing happened in China in the 1990s. The rich got a larger proportion of the total income produced in these countries than they had before the growth began. And even worse than this is the evidence that the poor in these countries, such as Brazil, probably became absolutely poorer during the period of high growth, in part because of the high inflation which often accompanied the growth.[37] (High inflation usually hurts the poor more than the rich because the poor are least able to increase their income to cope with the rising prices of goods.) The economic growth that came to some developing nations following the market approach failed to trickle down to the poor and, in fact, may have made their lives worse. High inflation was halted in Brazil in the 1990s, as was the trend for income inequality to worsen. At the end of the century the distribution of incomes in Brazil continued to be highly unequal. The poorest 20 percent of the population received about 3 percent of the income in the country, and the richest 20 percent received about 62 percent.

Critics of the market approach have also pointed out that prices for goods and services set by a free market often do not reflect the true costs of producing those goods and services. Damage to the environment or to people's health that occurs in the production and disposal of a product is often a hidden cost, which is not covered by the price of the product. The market treats the atmosphere, oceans, rivers, and lakes as "free goods," or as a global commons, and, unless prohibited from doing so by the state, it transfers the costs that arise because of their pollution to the broader community. In the language of economics this is called a "negative externality," a term rarely discussed in public. Some critics believe this flaw in the market system is what is really responsible for our changing of the climate on Earth, to be discussed in detail in the climate change chapter.

And finally, critics point to the cycles of positive and low or negative growth that are a normal part of the market approach. An extreme case of this was seen as recently as 2008/2009 when a near collapse of market economies started in the United States and spread to Europe and other parts of the world. A major recession occurred in the United States, which was only prevented from turning into a depression by major intervention by the state. Many economic analysts attributed this failure of the market system in the United States to a lack of regulation by the government or state.

The State as Economic Actor

Approaches to economic development that envision a role for the state beyond that described in the previous section vary widely. Advocates of Marxist-Leninist thought in early twentieth-century Russia built a communist state, the Soviet Union, which functioned as the *only* economic actor, overseeing a centrally planned economy and directing the production and distribution of all goods, services, and labor. In a socialist country most of the means of production – land, resources, and capital – are publicly controlled to ensure that the value obtained from the production of goods and services is used to benefit the nation as a whole. The prohibition on the private control or ownership of these so-called factors of production leads, according to this approach, to a relatively equal distribution of income, as everyone, not just a few individuals, benefits from the economic activity. Central planners set prices and invest capital in areas that are needed to benefit the society.

Some state-focused approaches to economic development envision a strong role for the state beyond direct central planning. With respect to the global distribution of wealth, one explanation popular among those who take a state-based approach to economic development attributes the causes of poverty in the world to international trade. According to the state approach, the root of the present international economic system, where a few nations are rich and the majority of nations remain poor, lies in the trade patterns developed in the sixteenth century by Western Europe. ("Dependency theory" is the name given to this part of the state approach, popularized by Immanuel Wallerstein.)[38] First Spain and Portugal and then Great Britain, Holland and France gained colonies – many of them in the southern hemisphere – to trade with. The imperialistic European nations in the northern hemisphere developed a trade pattern that one can still see clear signs of today. The mother countries in "the core" became the manufacturing and commercial centers, and their colonies in "the periphery" became the suppliers of food and minerals. Railroads were built in the colonies to connect the plantations and mines to the ports. This transportation system, along with the discouragement of local manufacturing competing with manufacturing in the mother countries, prevented the economic development of the colonies. The terms of trade – what one can obtain from one's export – favored the European nations, since the prices of the primary products from the colonies remained low while the prices of the manufactured products sent back to the colonies continually increased. It was the political power of the "core" that determined the global economic structure, rather than the economic "laws" of the market.

When most of the colonies gained their independence after World War II, this trade pattern continued. Many of the less developed countries still produce food and minerals for the world market and primarily trade with their former colonial masters. The world demand for the products from the poorer nations fluctuates greatly, and the prices of these products remain depressed. The political and social systems that developed in the former colonies also serve to keep the majority within these developing nations poor. A local elite, which grew up when these countries were under colonial domination, learned to benefit from the domination by the Western countries. In a sense, two societies were created in these countries: one, relatively modern and prosperous, revolved around the export sector, while the other consisted of the rest of the people, who remained in the traditional system and were poor. The local elite, which became the governing elite upon independence, acquired a taste for Western products, which the industrial nations were happy to sell them at a good price.

The present vehicle of this economic domination by the North of the South is the multinational corporation. Tens of thousands of these exist today. In 2009, 140 of the 500 richest corporations in the world had headquarters in the United States, while many others were headquartered in Europe and Japan.[39] These corporations squeeze out smaller local firms in the developing nations, evade local taxes through numerous devices, send large profits back to their headquarters, and create relatively fewer jobs than their local counterpart when the manufacturing firms they set up utilize the same capital-intensive technology that is common in the industrialized countries. Also, they advertise their products extensively, thus increasing demands for things such as Coca-Cola and color television sets while many people in the countries in which they operate still do not have enough to eat.[40]

Advocates for a state approach point to the adverse terms of trade that many developing nations face today. There is general agreement that there has been a long-term decline in the terms of trade for many of the agricultural and mineral products that the less developed nations export. There has also been great volatility in the prices of some of these products, with a change of 25 percent or more from one year to the next not uncommon for some products. Such fluctuations make economic planning by the developing nations very difficult. There is also clear evidence that the industrialized countries, while primarily trading among themselves, are highly dependent on other countries for many crucial raw materials, including chromium, manganese, cobalt, bauxite, tin, and, of course, oil.

Although international trade is still far from being the most important component of the US economy, it is a very important factor for many of the wealthiest corporations. In the early 1980s about one-half of the 500 wealthiest corporations listed in *Fortune* magazine obtained over 40 percent of their profits from their foreign operations.[41] Some multinational corporations have financial resources larger than those of many nations.

Finally, the defenders of a state approach argue that there is little chance for many poor nations to achieve as fair a distribution of income as that achieved by Europe after it industrialized. This situation has evolved because controlling elites have repressive tools at their disposal (such as sophisticated police surveillance devices and powerful weapons) that the European elites did not have. This allows

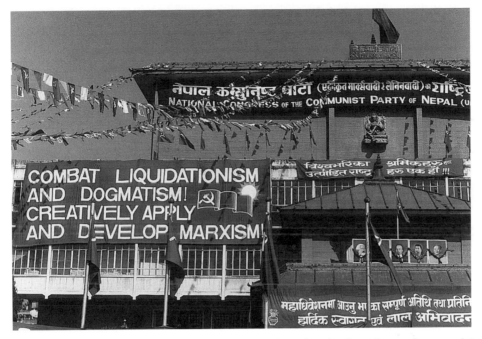

Plate 2.5 The state approach to development struggles to survive the collapse of communist regimes in Europe, as can be seen in the posters of a Communist Party conference in Nepal

Source: Ab Abercrombie.

them to deal with pressures from the "have-nots" in a way the Europeans never resorted to.

Critics of a state approach point to the breakup of the Soviet empire in Eastern Europe in the late 1980s and to the collapse of communism in the former Soviet Union and the breakup of that country in the early 1990s as support for their view that the state approach cannot efficiently produce wealth. In fact, it was the dissatisfaction of Eastern Europeans with their economic conditions that played a large role in their massive opposition to the existing communist governments and their eventual overthrow. Dissatisfaction with economic conditions also played a large role in the overthrow of the Soviet government, a startling rejection of the state approach by a people who had lived under it for 70 years.

Critics of the state approach also point to the suppression of individual liberties in the former Soviet Union, China, and other communist states as evidence that the socialist model for development has costs that many people are not willing to pay. In fact, most revolutions have huge costs, leading to much suffering and economic deterioration before any improvement in conditions is seen; even after improvements occur, oppressive political and social controls are used by leaders to maintain power.

Some critics say that central planning has proved to be an inefficient allocator of resources wherever it has been followed. Without prices from the free market to indicate the real costs of goods and services, the central planners cannot make good decisions. And if efficient central planning has proved to be impossible in a developed country such as the former Soviet Union, it has proved to be even worse in underdeveloped nations where governmental administrative capability is weak. A final criticism of central planning is that it always leads to a large, inefficient governmental bureaucracy.

Even less invasive forms of state involvement in the economy tend to provoke similar criticisms: that the state, lacking a profit motive or the threat of bankruptcy, is going to be less responsive to changes in economic conditions that may necessitate a change in policy; that excessive government involvement in the economy means the state is "picking winners and losers," a process that virtually invites corruption; and/or that the state cannot become involved in the economy without making value choices that are better left to individual consumers.

Additionally, some argue that the state approach generates less wealth than the free market approach. Multinational corporations have created jobs in the developing world that would not have existed otherwise; they have brought new technologies; and they have helped the balance of payments problems of those nations by bringing in scarce capital and by helping develop export industries that earn much-needed foreign exchange. These advantages help explain why multinational corporations are welcomed by many countries.

Finally, the critics of a state approach argue that political elites have used dependency theory, especially in Latin America where the theory is popular, to gain local political support among the bureaucracy, military, and the masses. To blame the industrial nations for their poverty frees them from taking responsibility for their own development and excuses their lack of progress. It also frees them from having to clean their own houses of governmental corruption and incompetence, and to stop following misguided economic development approaches. According to some critics, the newly industrializing countries have shown that when market principles are followed, economic progress can be made even by developing nations that have a dense population and few, if any, natural resources.

A Blended Approach

In practice, most countries blend state and market approaches to tailor them toward the political and economic priorities for a given country (or at least for those who hold much of the power). Friedrich List, a German political and economic theorist who began his career in 1817, posited (in contrast to those who push always for freer and more open trade) that in relatively underdeveloped economies, nascent industries may need state protection from foreign competitors in order to allow them to grow to the point where the country could truly exploit its competitive advantage in a given economic endeavor.[42] Some have even credited Friedrich List with first proposing the concept now known as "human capital,"[43] a concept often used by those who argue that states with less developed economies need to invest in their citizens, to ensure a healthy and educated workforce that can participate meaningfully in the economy.

Decentralized regulation: a catalyst for technological innovation?

In evaluating why the United States pioneered innovation in fracking technologies (see Chapter 8), Dan Merrill concluded that decentralized regulation was key to enabling innovation. In the article "Four Questions about Fracking," Merrill considers how governance structures impact innovation:

> Why does decentralized regulation promote innovation? The theory that explains this might go as follows. All regulators tend to be risk averse. If things go well, they get no credit. If things go badly, they get blamed. But the degree of risk aversion of regulators falls along a spectrum. Some are more risk averse than others. Where regulation is decentralized, a new technology like fracking can find at least one or two states where it is allowed to get going. This sets in motion a natural experiment. If the results are good, and the risks do not seem too great, then risk-averse regulators in other states will give it the green light to go ahead there, too. If the results are not so good, or the risks seem too large, then the regulators in other states will throw up roadblocks to the new technology, and the experiment will wither away. In a more centralized regulatory environment, which tends to be the norm in other parts of the world, the experiment is less likely to get off the ground in the first place. This is because the median regulator is risk averse. And being the only regulatory game in town, the risk aversion of the median regulator is likely to translate into hostility to technological innovation.

For more discussions on the role of technology in development, see Chapter 8

Source: *Case Western Reserve Law Review*, 63 (4) (2013) (internal citations omitted).

One relatively modern example of this blended approach is South Korea. From the 1960s through at least the 1980s, South Korean economic growth was predicated on massive government investment in its infrastructure and citizens, as well as heavy government intervention in the economy (through regulation, subsidies, and government-granted monopolies) that allowed certain family-controlled firms, such as Hyundai and Samsung, to become economic powerhouses that could drive the national economy.[44] While South Korea has now adopted a much more market-oriented approach, these nationally prioritized firms benefited directly from the state approach.

Geography and Wealth, Geography and Poverty

Adam Smith had a second theory of why some nations are rich and some poor. Modern economists usually ignore this part of Smith's writings. Not only did Smith believe that a free market economy would lead to wealth, but he also believed that nations bordering a sea would usually be richer than inland, landlocked countries. Recent research shows that geography does matter. As Table 2.1 shows, nations with access to the sea by coastal ports or by navigable rivers and those in the temperate climate zone are usually the wealthiest nations. Those nations landlocked and in the tropical zone or mainly desert or mountainous usually are the poorest.

Why does geography matter? The reasons are not hard to discover. First, shipping and receiving goods by sea is cheaper than shipping by land or air. For example, shipping a container to a major coastal city can cost only a fraction of the cost of shipping to a remote landlocked area (for example it might cost $3,000 to ship a container to the Ivory Coast and $10,000 more to send a similarly sized container to landlocked Central African Republic). Also people and new ideas often arrive in coastal areas first. Second, tropical climates are plagued by infectious diseases, such as malaria, which debilitate the workforce. An estimated hundreds of million of new cases of malaria occur each year, nearly all of them in the tropics. Winter is the great natural controller of many diseases. In tropical countries many diseases flourish all year long, making them difficult to control. And recognizing the economic wealth in many tropical countries is relatively limited, thereby limiting opportunities to profit commercially, pharmaceutical firms have tended to prioritize economically lucrative conditions such as erectile dysfunction over more critical health needs such as malaria.

Table 2.1 The wealth of tropical, desert, highland, and temperate regions

Climate zone	Percentage of world total	Near[a]	Far[a]
Tropical			
Population	40	22	18
GNP	17	10	7
Desert			
Population	18	4	14
GNP	10	3	7
Highland			
Population	7	1	6
GNP	5	1	4
Temperate			
Population	35	23	12
GNP	67	53	14

[a] "Near" means within 100 kilometers of sea coast or sea-navigable waterway; "Far" means otherwise.
Source: Jeffrey Sachs, Andrew Mellinger, and John Gallup, "The Geography of Poverty and Wealth," *Scientific American*, 284 (March 2001), p. 74.

Agricultural production is also usually higher in temperate and subtropical climates than in tropical climates. For example, a hectare of land in the temperate zone produces about 6 tons of corn or maize, while the same amount of land in the tropics produces about 2 tons. Developed countries spend much more on research to help their farmers in the temperate zone increase production than poorer developing countries spend on research that would benefit their tropical or semitropical farmers.

Geography alone does not explain why some countries are wealthier than others. While nearly all the wealthiest countries are in the temperate zone, such as North America, Western Europe, and Northeast Asia, the economic system they follow is also important. For example, the former Soviet Union and Eastern Europe are still struggling economically to overcome their socialist pasts. This fact is shown even more dramatically by looking at present and past countries with the same geographical characteristics but which have or had different economic systems and vastly different wealth: South Korea and North Korea, West and East Germany (before unification), Austria and the Czech Republic, and Finland and Estonia. In each case the first-mentioned state in the comparison followed a market system and greatly outperformed the second, originally socialist state.[45]

In addition to the difficulties caused by climate and lack of access to the sea, many landlocked countries face economic difficulties caused by borders with their neighbors that restrict the easy flow of goods, capital, and people.

According to Ricardo Hausmann, professor of the practice of economic development at the John F. Kennedy School of Government at Harvard University: "If current trends persist, countries that face high transportation costs and a high dependence on tropical agriculture will be left far behind, mired in poverty and income inequality. Will the rest of the world find this outcome morally acceptable?" Hausmann believes that the world has tried to help these countries, but its efforts have been insufficient, as shown by the widening gap between the rich and poor. He calls for more "globalized governance." By this he means more international agreements to make borders less of a barrier to people, goods, and capital. He also calls for international support for development projects that improve the transportation systems within and between countries, and lastly he calls for international aid in health and agricultural technology that benefits the tropical world.[46]

Globalization

After the killing in World War II ended in 1945 a number of world leaders asked, "What should be done to prevent a person like Adolf Hitler coming to power again?" One of the answers given was to prevent an international economic collapse, such as the Great Depression, which created the conditions that led to the rise of Hitler. With that idea in mind, it was agreed that trade among nations should be encouraged so that, it was hoped, prosperity would spread and economies would become more interdependent. In 1947, under the sponsorship of the United Nations, the General

Figure 2.5 World trade: merchandise exports, 1950–1998 (in 1990 dollars)

Source: Based on data from World Trade Organization.

Agreement on Tariffs and Trade (GATT) was signed by about 20 countries. These countries, later joined by about a hundred others, conducted a series of negotiations to promote free trade by reducing tariffs and other barriers to trade such as import quotas. The success of these efforts is clearly shown in Figures 2.2 and 2.4. Figure 2.2 shows that from 1950 to the end of the twentieth century world trade rose from about $500 billion to nearly $6 trillion. Figure 2.4 shows the expanding world exports from 2001 until 2008., after which time there was a sizable reduction caused by a world recession.

In 1995 GATT evolved into the World Trade Organization (WTO). The WTO was given the task of implementing the many agreements reached under the GATT negotiations and of setting up an arbitration mechanism to resolve trade disputes among its members.

The great expansion of international trade has created a highly interdependent world economy. That integration of the economies of many nations, combined with

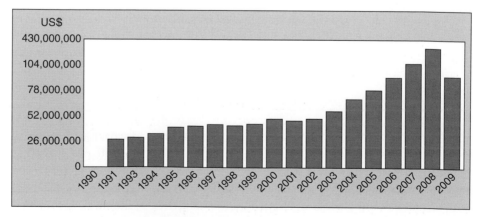

Figure 2.6 World trade: goods exports, 2001–2009

Source: World Bank, Global Economic Monitor database.

the proliferation of communication technologies that transcend national borders, and other factors, has been the main force in creating a new situation in the world called globalization. Globalization is mainly fueled by economic forces and sustained by new political, social, and technical integrative forces in the world today. Politically, international governmental organizations such as the United Nations, the International Monetary Fund, and the World Bank, along with regional organizations and agreements such as the European Union and the North American Free Trade Agreement, are playing an increasingly important role in global governance.

Social integration is proceeding at such a rapid pace that one can say that there is the beginning of a world culture. Much of this culture is coming from the United States, but it is also truly international as foods, music, dances, and fashions come from various countries. Technical integration comes from the information and transportation revolutions that are occurring in the world. Computers, the internet (and particularly social networks), television, and airplanes now link the world.

Globalization is a process that is leading to the growing interdependence of the world's people. Like many things, if not most things in life, it has positive and negative aspects and a critical reader should appreciate the implications of both.[47]

Positive aspects

The global economy has brought more wealth to both rich and poor nations. Although all nations have not benefited from it, "since 1950 there has been a close correlation between a country's domestic economic performance and its participation in the world's economy."[48] The United States, a country that has officially embraced globalization, had an unprecedentedly long period of economic growth and, as the information at the beginning of this chapter indicates, non-Western countries and areas such as China, the Republic of Korea, Taiwan, and Singapore that also embraced globalization have obtained high levels of wealth.

The formation of a global community has started. Nations around the world now face common problems, both economic and environmental, that they are working together to solve. More and more individuals are taking advantage of the new communication and transportation technologies to learn about and enjoy the whole planet.

For nations to become wealthier in this new world, it helps if they become freer, less corrupt, and more economically efficient. New ideas and more international contacts could even lead to an improvement of human rights in some countries, such as China, which has a poor record on human rights. It had this effect in other communist states.

Hunger and crime rates are lowered as poverty is reduced. Many types of crime dropped in the United States during its recent long period of economic growth, and during the decade of the 1990s "the number of hungry people [in the world] fell by nearly 20 million."[49]

New products are available and often at a lower price than if they had been produced locally. New jobs are created, not just in the developed countries but also in many less developed nations. Jobs lead to the reduction of poverty. The World Bank reports that "there are almost no examples of countries experiencing significant growth without reducing poverty."[50]

Although it is true that increased production can cause more pollution, many argue that once nations become richer and reduce their poverty, they tend to clean up their environments.

Negative aspects

A number of jobs are lost in rich countries when multinational corporations move some of their production or service facilities to less developed nations where labor costs are lower. It is true that many new jobs are being created in the United States, fewer in Europe and Japan, but the type of available jobs may be changing and it is not easy for certain (particularly older) workers who have been laid off to qualify for them.

Some have argued that corporations are moving facilities to developing nations to escape the necessity of complying with stricter environmental and labor laws in their home countries. Rapid economic growth in countries such as China and India has led to major pollution of air, water, and land.

Cultural imperialism by the United States, with its corresponding undermining of local cultures, is increasing. A world traveler can frequent many cities and dine on Big Macs, fries, and shakes in any of them. The largest single export industry in the United States is not aircraft or automobiles but entertainment, especially Hollywood films.

The gap between rich and poor nations is growing. Some poor nations are being left behind economically and technologically. The shift to knowledge-based industries is accelerating and creating an even greater gap. The United States has more computers than the whole of the rest of the world combined. From 2010 to 2014, about 87 percent of people in the United States had access to the internet, whereas only about 18 percent of Indians did, and even fewer in Pakistan and Bangladesh.[51]

Because nations' economies are so tied together today, an economic downturn in one can spread to others extremely quickly. We saw that happening in the late 1990s when a financial crisis hit Thailand, Indonesia, Malaysia, the Republic of Korea and other countries. Economic recessions and depressions also come with the dominance of the market. Capitalism has always had its cycles, and a "down" cycle can mean high unemployment and human suffering. Many of the fastest growing developing nations are tied to the US economy. If the United States goes into a period of slow or no growth it will affect many other countries whose wealth comes mainly from exports to the United States. We saw this very thing happening in the world recession of 2008–9, discussed above.

Nations are losing some of their national autonomy to institutions such as the International Monetary Fund, World Trade Organization, World Bank, and regional trade organizations.

The ease of transportation, of both people and goods, makes the transmission of diseases throughout the world easier than before. In the same way, rapid electronic communications and the huge number of people and goods moving through the world make criminal and terror activities more difficult to control.

An evaluation

Kofi Annan, as Secretary-General of the United Nations, had the following to say about globalization at the beginning of the twenty-first century:

> The central challenge we face today is to ensure that globalization becomes a positive force for all the world's people, instead of leaving billions of them behind in squalor. Inclusive globalization must be built on the great enabling force of the market, but market forces alone will not achieve it. It requires a broader effort to create a shared future, based upon our common humanity in all its diversity.[52]

In the box titled "The global village" he shows us what our world at the beginning of the twenty-first century looks like by asking us to imagine we are living in a small village with all the characteristics of our world.

The global village

"Let us imagine, for a moment, that the world really is a 'global village' – taking seriously the metaphor that is often invoked to depict global interdependence. Say this village has 1,000 individuals, with all the characteristics of today's human race distributed in exactly the same proportions. What would it look like?

Some 150 of the inhabitants live in an affluent area of the village, about 780 in poorer districts. Another 70 or so live in a neighborhood that is in transition. The average income per person is $6,000 a year, and there are more middle income families than in the past. But just 200 people dispose of 86 per cent of all the wealth, while nearly half of the villagers are eking out an existence on less than $2 per day.

Men outnumber women by a small margin, but women make up a majority of those who live in poverty. Adult literacy has been increasing. Still, some 220 villagers – two thirds of them women – are illiterate. Of the 390 inhabitants under 20 years of age, three fourths live in the poorer districts, and many are looking desperately for jobs that do not exist. Fewer than 60 people own a computer, and only 24 have access to the Internet. More than half have never made or received a telephone call.

Life expectancy in the affluent district is nearly 78 years, in the poorer areas 64 years – and in the very poorest neighborhood a mere 52 years. Each marks an improvement over previous generations, but why do the poorest lag so far behind? Because in their neighborhoods there is a far higher incidence of infectious diseases and malnutrition, combined with an acute lack of access to safe water, sanitation, health care, adequate housing, education and work.

There is no predictable way to keep the peace in this village. Some districts are relatively safe while others are wracked by organized violence. The village has suffered a growing number of weather-related natural disasters in recent years including unexpected and severe storms, as well as sudden swings from floods to droughts, while the average temperature is perceptibly warmer. … The village's water table is falling precipitously, and the livelihood of one sixth of the inhabitants is threatened by soil degradation in the surrounding coun-tryside."

Source: Kofi Annan, *We the Peoples: The Role of the United Nations in the 21st Century* (New York: United Nations, 2001), pp. 52–6.

Conclusions

The market approach to development places emphasis on the seemingly strong moti-vation individuals have to acquire more material goods and services. When people are freed from external restraints, the market allows them to use their initiative to better their lives. The release of creative energy that comes with the market approach is impressive. At the beginning of the twenty-first century most countries through-out the world were following it, at least to some degree, as the Western capitalist countries became the models to imitate. While the economic recession at the end of the first decade of 2000 has caused many countries to question a complete market approach, the model nevertheless is employed by many nations today.

With the collapse of communism and the breakup of the former Soviet Union, the state approach to development received a serious blow. The reliance on the state to create wealth was discredited. Yet in no country of the world is a state without some significant state functions relating to the economy. Within the capitalist world there is a debate among nations regarding how much involvement government should have in directing and guiding the economy. Traditionally Japanese and European capitalism relied on more government involvement than did capitalism in the United States.

This debate became of upmost importance in 2008 when the US market system nearly collapsed and a depression in the United States was prevented only by massive financial support by the national government of parts of the banking and insurance industries and automobile corporations. Alan Greenspan, the head of the Federal Reserve that monitored the economy and that had been given credit for the unprecedentedly long period of economic growth the United States had gone through, admitted to Congress that the model of the market economy he was following had an unknown flaw in it. This admission was rather shocking. If the chief "overseer" of the US economy didn't really understand how it worked, who did? Greenspan, who had favored loose government regulation of the economy, went from being a laissez-faire economist to one who now called for much tighter government regulation of the economy. As mentioned in this chapter, the unprecedentedly deep recession in the United States spread throughout the world and slowed the efforts to help millions of people escape from extreme poverty. Yet as the chapter's section on the UN's Millennium Development Goals shows, economic growth was still strong enough in the developing world to enable the United Nations to meet the goal of halving extreme poverty to 15 percent by the year 2015.

Even after the seemingly total victory of the market approach over the state approach in the 1990s, the state approach is not dead; what is dead is the total or near total reliance on it as the best way to create wealth. But the economic crisis of 2008–9 indicated that the world is still struggling to find the right balance between the market and state systems.

Today's globalization is still driven by market forces focusing on economic growth. That growth has done much to reduce world poverty. But large and vocal protests at international meetings dealing with aspects of globalization have drawn attention to some of the negative aspects of globalization. More emphasis on human governance appears to be needed. The United Nations Development Programme stated the need as follows: "When the market goes too far in dominating social and political outcomes, the opportunities and rewards of globalization spread unequally and inequitably – concentrating power and wealth in a select group of people, nations, and corporations, marginalizing the others." The UNDP believes that markets should continue to expand but that more governance is needed: "The challenge is to find the rules and institutions for stronger governance – local, national, regional and global – to preserve the advantages of global markets and competition, but also to provide enough space for human, community, and environmental resources to ensure that globalization works for people – not just for profits."[53]

There are dangerous signs that all is not well. Economic growth is reducing poverty and the market approach has produced that growth better than the state or blended approaches. The reduction of extreme poverty is universally praised, as it should be. No human being should have to live as the very poor live today. As the poor obtain new wealth, they tend to consume more goods and services. (The growing middle class in China is a good example of this with its desire for automobiles.) But rich nations historically have relied on fossil fuels to provide the energy needed to make their goods and provide their services. We now know how that kind of energy is placing a tremendous strain on our world; it is changing our planet in ways that will seriously hurt much of the life on the planet, both in rich and poor nations alike. This will be discussed more in our chapter on climate change.

The bottom line is that while achieving a certain level of economic wealth unquestionably affords critical opportunities to improve livelihoods, we cannot presume that economic wealth alone will lead to the development outcomes we desire. The classical use of the term "development" has defined progress by the increased growth of material goods by any means possible and this purely production-based notion of "development" is increasingly seen as not viable. It is for that reason that we focus in this book on sustainable development pathways that direct our attention toward human well-being, while considering both the costs and benefits of the growth of material goods and services.

Notes

1   United Nations Development Programme (UNDP), *Human Development Report 1999* (New York: Oxford University Press, 1999), p. 38. The 2010 number comparing the richest countries as a group with the poorest countries as a group is from the World Development Indicators database, World Bank, July 1, 2011, at http://siteresources. worldbank.org/DATASTATISTICS/Resources/GNIPC.pdf (accessed July 2015).
2   Bruce Scott, "The Great Divide in the Global Village," *Foreign Affairs* (January/February 2001), pp. 162–3.
3   Millennium Development Goals database, at http://databank.worldbank.org/ddp/home. do (accessed July 2015).
4   "World Bank Development Indicators 2009," gross national income per capita 2009.
5   International Labour Organization, *Global Wage Report 2014/2015: Wages and Income Inequality*, section 7.2, p. 23, at http://www.ilo.org/wcmsp5/groups/public/—dgreports/—dcomm/—publ/documents/publication/wcms_324678.pdf (accessed July 2015).
6   Josh Bivens and Elise Gould, "Top 1 Percent Receive Record High Share of Total U.S. Income," Economic Policy Institute blog, September 12, 2013, at http://www.epi.org/blog/top-1-percent-receive-record-high-share-2 (accessed July 2015).
7   World Development Indicators 2015, "Table 2.9: Distribution of Income or Consumption," at http://wdi.worldbank.org/table/2.9 (accessed July 2015).
8   Ibid.
9   World Development Indicators database, April 19, 2010 revision.
10 China increased its per capita GDP about tenfold from $440 in 1980 to $4,475 in 2002 (in international prices), while India's per capita GDP rose from $670 in 1980 to $2,570 in 2002. World Bank, *World Development Report 2005* (New York: World Bank and Oxford University Press, 2005), p. 27.
11 United Nations, *The Millennium Development Goals Report 2010* (New York: United Nations, 2010), p. 6.
12 Ibid., p. 7.
13 United Nations, *The Millennium Development Goals Report 2014*, p. 4, at http://www.un.org/millenniumgoals/2014%20MDG%20report/MDG%202014%20English%20web.pdf (accessed July 2025).

14 "Global Poverty: A Fall to Cheer", *The Economist*, March 3, 2012, at http://www.economist.com/node/21548963 (accessed July 2015).

15 United Nations, *The Millennium Development Goals Report 2010*, p. 7.

16 UNDP, *Human Development Report 2004* (New York: Oxford University Press, 2004), p. 129.

17 The other seven goals are Goal 2, Achieve universal primary education; Goal 3, Promote gender equality and empower women; Goal 4, Reduce child mortality; Goal 5, Improve maternal health; Goal 6, Combat HIV/AIDS, malaria and other diseases; Goal 7, Ensure environmental sustainability; Goal 8, Develop a global partnership for development.

18 United Nations, *The Millennium Development Goals Report 2010*, pp. 6–7.

19 United Nations, *The Millennium Development Goals Report 2014*, p. 4, at http://www.un.org/millenniumgoals/2014%20MDG%20report/MDG%202014%20English%20web.pdf (accessed July 2015).

20 Ibid.

21 Ibid., pp. 5, 12.

22 World Development Indicators, "Poverty and Equity Data" (2013 revision), at http://povertydata.worldbank.org/poverty/home/ (accessed July 2015).

23 World Bank, *World Development Report 2014: Risk and Opportunity* (Washington, DC: World Bank, 2014), p. 5.

24 United Nations, *The Millennium Development Goals Report 2014*, pp. 4–5; UN Department of Social and Economic Affairs, Population Division, *World Population Prospects: The 2012 Revision*, at http://esa.un.org/unpd/wpp/unpp/panel_population.htm; World Bank, "Energy," at http://www.worldbank.org/en/topic/energy (both accessed July 2015); World Bank, *World Development Report 2010* (Washington, DC: World Bank, 2010), p. xx.

25 World Development Indicators database, April 19, 2010 revision; World Bank, "Regional Aggregation Using 2005 PPP and $1.25/Day Poverty Line," at http://iresearch.worldbank.org/PovcalNet/index.htm?1 (accessed July 2015).

26 UNDP, *Human Development Report 2004*, p. 132.

27 World Bank, *World Development Report 1990: Poverty* (New York: Oxford University Press, 1990), p. 2.

28 Stephanie Strom, "Billionaires' Pledge to Give Away Half Gains Followers," *New York Times*, August 5, 2010, p. A15.

29 ONE Campaign, *The Trillion-Dollar Scandal* (2014), at https://s3.amazonaws.com/one.org/pdfs/Trillion_Dollar_Scandal_report_EN.pdf (accessed July 2015).

30 Ibid.

31 UN Conference on Trade and Development (UNCTAD), "Non-Tariff Measures to Trade: Economic and Policy Issues for Developing Countries" (2013), pp. vii–viii, at http://unctad.org/en/PublicationsLibrary/ditctab20121_en.pdf (accessed July 2015).

32 Ibid.

33 According to the OECD, US private foundations and other private US organizations provide about $6 billion a year in foreign assistance, much more than private groups give in most other counties. But even if this amount is added to US governmental aid, the total US aid given in relation to US GNP is still among the lowest ratios of all rich donor countries. Jeffrey Sachs, "Can Extreme Poverty Be Eliminated?" *Scientific American*, 293 (September 2005), p. 60.

34   OECD, "Aid to Developing Countries Rebounds in 2013 to Reach an All-Time High," April 8, 2014, at http://www.oecd.org/newsroom/aid-to-developing-countries-rebounds-in-2013-to-reach-an-all-time-high.htm (accessed July 2015).

35   See, e.g., the American Recovery and Reinvestment Act webpage at http://www.recovery.gov/arra/About/Pages/The_Act.aspx (accessed July 2015).

36   This framework derives from Alan Wolfe's classification of the three main views of development. He presented his ideas in a paper titled "Three Paths to Development: Market, State, and Civil Society," which was prepared for the International Meeting of Nongovernmental Organizations (NGOs) and United Nations System Agencies held in 1991 in Rio de Janeiro. Some of his views on this subject are contained in his book *Whose Keeper? Social Science and Moral Obligation* (Berkeley: University of California Press, 1989). In this book, we have adapted Wolfe's framework as Market, State, and a Blended Approach.

37   Censuses in Brazil have revealed that the percentage of national income going to the top 10 percent of the population was 40 percent in 1960, 47 percent in 1970, and 51 percent in 1980. During the same period the poorest 50 percent of the population received 17 percent of the national income in 1960, 15 percent in 1970, and 13 percent in 1980. Thomas E. Skidmore and Peter H. Smith, *Modern Latin America*, 2nd edn (New York: Oxford University Press, 1989), p. 180. In Latin America as a whole in the 1980s the poorest 10 percent suffered a 15 percent drop in their share of income. See UNDP, *Human Development Report 1999*, p. 39.

38   For a fuller discussion of dependency theory see Bruce Russett and Harvey Starr, *World Politics: The Menu for Choice*, 2nd edn (New York: W. H. Freeman, 1985), ch. 16; and John T. Rourke, *International Politics on the World Stage*, 7th edn (New York: Dushkin/McGraw-Hill, 1999), p. 400.

39   "Global 500," *Fortune Magazine*, July 20, 2009. Stacy VanDeveer, "Consuming Environments: Options and Choices for 21st Century Citizens," in *Beyond Rio+20: Governance for a Green Economy* (Boston: Boston University, 2011), pp. 43–51.

40   While it does not deal with the areas of the world now described as "developing nations," Victoria de Grazia's *Irresistible Empire: America's Advance through 20th Century Europe* (Cambridge, MA: Harvard University Press, 2005) explores how US political and commercial power combined to create and export new consumer habits in Europe, and is an enlightening look at how cultural, commercial, and economic power can interact.

41   Frederic S. Pearson and J. Martin Rochester, *International Relations: The Global Condition in the Twenty-First Century*, 4th edn (New York: Random House, 1998), p. 499.

42   See, e.g., H. Dunning, "Governments and the Macro-Organization of Economic Activity: An Historical and Spatial Perspective," *Review of International Political Economy*, 4 (1) (1997), p. 45.

43   See, e.g., David Levi-Faur, "Friedrich List and the Political Economy of the Nation-State," *Review of International Political Economy*, 4 (1) (1997).

44   Marcus Noland, "Six Markets to Watch: South Korea," *Foreign Affairs* (January/February 2014), at https://www.foreignaffairs.com/articles/south-korea/2013-12-06/six-markets-watch-south-korea (accessed July 2015).

45   Most of the analysis on the relationship between geography and wealth and poverty is taken from Jeffry Sachs, Andrew Mellinger, and John Gallup, "The Geography of Poverty and Wealth," *Scientific American*, 284 (March 2001), pp. 70–5; and Ricardo Hausmann, "Prisoners of Geography," *Foreign Affairs* (January/February 2001), pp. 45–53.

46 Hausmann, "Prisoners of Geography," p. 53.

47 For a good discussion of the potential for globalization doing good or harm see "Overview: Globalization with a Human Face," in UNDP, *Human Development Report 1999*, pp. 1–13.

48 Peter F. Drucker, "Trade Lessons from the World Economy," *Foreign Affairs*, 73 (January/February 1994), p. 104.

49 UNDP, *Human Development Report 2003* (New York: Oxford University Press, 2003), p. 6.

50 World Bank, *World Development Report 2005*, p. 31.

51 World Bank data, "Internet Users (per 100 people)," at http://data.worldbank.org/indicator/IT.NET.USER.P2 (accessed July 2015).

52 Kofi Annan, *We the Peoples: The Role of the United Nations in the 21st Century* (New York: United Nations, 2001).

53 UNDP, *Human Development Report 1999*, p. 2.

Further Reading

Bardhan, Pranab, "Does Globalization Help or Hurt the World's Poor?" *Scientific American*, 294 (April 2006), pp. 84–91. The answer according to this short article is that it does both. Bardhan discusses how to maximize the help and minimize the hurt.

Bhagwati, Jagdish, *In Defense of Globalization* (Oxford: Oxford University Press, 2004). The argument of this economics professor at Columbia University is that globalization has been overwhelmingly a good thing and its few downsides can be mitigated. His thesis that globalization leads to economic growth and economic growth leads to the reduction of poverty is the foundation for his belief that poor nations are not hurt by globalization but actually need more of it.

Chua, Amy, *World on Fire: How Exporting Free Market Democracy Breeds Ethnic Hatred and Global Instability* (New York: Anchor Books, 2003). A professor of law at Yale University, the author, who is a friend of globalization, argues that as the market and democracy have spread into the less developed nations, ethnic hatred and violence have increased, along with anti-Americanism. Chua explains why and identifies the urgent need for a greater sharing of the economic wealth that globalization has brought to various minorities.

Collier, Paul, *The Bottom Billion: Why the Poorest Countries Are Failing and What Can Be Done About It* (Oxford: Oxford University Press, 2007). Focusing mainly on Africa, where Collier states 70 percent of the world's poor live, he focuses on what he sees as the four main causes of poverty: civil war, the curse of rich resources, a landlocked location, and bad government.

Collins, Daryl, Jonathan Morduch, Stuart Rutherford, and Orlanda Ruthven, *Portfolios of the Poor: How the World's Poor Live on $2 a Day* (Princeton: Princeton University Press, 2009). The authors visited 100 households twice a month over a year in Bangladesh, India, and South Africa to record poor people's income, much of it from the informal economy. The authors also examine many microcredit operations.

Farmer, Paul, *Pathologies of Power: Health, Human Rights and the New War on the Poor* (Berkeley: University of California Press, 2003). Farmer presents case studies to support his three main points: the poor are not responsible for their situation, but have been hurt by their circumstances; the poor can be successfully treated and cured of disease, even those in the most dire conditions; good health is a human right, for without it all other human rights are meaningless.

McKibben, Bill, "Reversal of Fortune," *Mother Jones* (March/April 2007), pp. 33–43, 87–8. McKibben attacks the central concept of market economics: economic growth. Here, in his own words, is his justification for a position most people consider radical: "Growth no longer makes most people wealthier but instead generates inequality and insecurity. Growth is bumping up against physical limits so profound – like climate change and peak oil – that trying to expand the economy may be not just impossible but also dangerous."

Sachs, Jeffrey D., *The End of Poverty: Economic Possibilities for Our Time* (New York: Penguin Press, 2005). Sachs presents a plan to rid the world of extreme poverty by 2025. He does not dismiss the effectiveness of the market approach but believes that it is incomplete by itself. Poor countries that are weighed down by harmful geography, an inadequate healthcare system, and weak infrastructure (e.g., roads, ports, power, and communication facilities) cannot improve without significant, wisely given, foreign aid.

Singer, Peter, *One World: The Ethics of Globalization* (New Haven, CT: Yale University Press, 2002). Called one of the most provocative philosophers of our time, Singer writes, "How well we come through the era of globalization (perhaps whether we come through it at all) will depend on how we respond ethically to the idea that we live in one world."

United Nations Development Programme, United Nations Environment Programme, World Bank, and World Resources Institute, *World Resources 2005: The Wealth of the Poor: Managing Ecosystems to Fight Poverty* (Washington, DC: World Resources Institute, 2005). An attractive, easy-to-read reference source giving environmental, social, and economic trends of about 150 nations. In this volume the focus is on how the natural world can be utilized in a sustainable manner to benefit the rural poor.

Chapter 3

Food

World Food Production	86
How Many Are Hungry?	87
Causes of World Hunger	89
How Food Affects Development	91
How Development Affects Food	93
The production of food	93
The loss of food	97
Waste	97
Erosion	98
Urban sprawl	99
The type of food	100
The "Green" Revolution	105
Fertilizers	106
Pesticides	106
Irrigation	107
The future	107
Governmental Food Policies	108
Future Food Supplies	111
Climate	111
Arable land	112
Energy costs	114
Traditional/sustainable/organic agriculture	114
Biotechnology	115
Fishing and aquaculture	117
Future food production	119
Conclusions	120
Notes	121
Further Reading	127

Global Issues: An Introduction, Fifth Edition. Kristen A. Hite and John L. Seitz
© 2016 John Wiley & Sons, Ltd. Published 2016 by John Wiley & Sons, Ltd.

The day that hunger is eradicated from the earth, there will be the greatest spiritual explosion the world has ever known.

Federico García Lorca (1898–1936), Spanish poet and dramatist

One way a civilization can be judged is by its success in reducing suffering. Development can also be judged in this way. Is it reducing the misery that exists in the world? Throughout human history, hunger has caused untold suffering. Because food is a basic necessity, when it is absent or scarce humans need to spend most of their efforts trying to obtain it; if they are not successful in finding adequate food, they suffer, and can eventually die. In this chapter we will look at hunger and also at a problem the more developed countries face: how their own level of development affects the food they eat.

World Food Production

How much food is produced in the world at present? Is there enough for everyone? The answer, which may surprise you, is that yes, there is enough. Food production has kept up with population growth. At the beginning of the twenty-first century, food supplies were about 25 percent higher per person than they were in the early 1960s and the real price of food (taking inflation into account) was about 40 percent lower.[1] Impressive gains were made in the poorest nations during that timeframe, where the average daily food calories available per person rose from about 1,900 to 2,700. (What was available for consumption does not indicate what individuals actually consumed.) In wealthy countries the daily calorie supply increased from about 3,000 to 3,300 during the same period.[2] Enough food was available at the beginning of the twenty-first century to provide every person with more than 2,350 calories, the amount needed daily for a healthy and active life. But in the first decade of the new century, food prices rose sharply. After peaking in 2011, at just over 150 percent of 2000 prices, food prices declined gradually by February 2015 to a level that remains roughly double that of 2000.[3]

Over the past four decades, the world's output of major food crops increased significantly – the most dramatic increase happening in the production of cereals – as improved seeds, irrigation, fertilizers, and pesticides were used to increase production and new land was cultivated. Sometimes referred to as the "Green Revolution" (discussed later in this chapter), most of this growth in production came from an increase in yield per acre rather than from an increase in the amount of cropland. In 2014 the average grain yield was just over 3.5 tons (3,657 kilograms) per hectare, almost four times what it was in 1960.[4] This impressive performance was counterbalanced, however, by the rapid growth of population also taking place in the world at this time. But food production increased rapidly enough so that the output of food in the world has generally kept up with population growth, despite periodic food crises in certain regions. There was a decline in per capita food output in the former Soviet

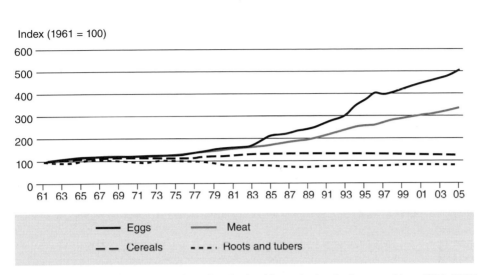

Figure 3.1 Per capita consumption of major food items in developing countries, 1961–2005

Source: FAO, *The State of Food and Agriculture, 2009*, p. 9.

Union after the collapse of that country in 1991 and in sub-Saharan Africa from the mid-1970s because of low production in agriculture (which was caused in part by droughts, civil wars, and nonsupportive government policies) and because of very rapid population growth.

In 2007–8 the global recession caused a massive food crisis. The recession dramatically reduced incomes and this along with persistently high food prices led to reduced access to food for many low income groups, especially those who spend a large portion of their incomes on food in both the urban and rural poor. In March of 2015, the United Nations Food and Agricultural Organization (FAO) reported that 37 countries were in need of external food assistance due to "crises related to lack of food availability, widespread lack of access to food, or severe but localized problems."[5] By 2010 the food crisis had lessened, but the FAO reported that "30 countries around the world are in need of external assistance because of crop failures, conflict or insecurity, natural disasters, and high domestic food prices."[6]

Figure 3.1 shows the per capita consumption of major foods in developing countries. Note the rapid increase in the consumption of livestock products (eggs and meat). We will discuss later in this chapter how nations' diets change as they become more wealthy.

How Many Are Hungry?

Unprecedented amounts of food in the world do not mean, unfortunately, that everyone is getting enough food. According to the FAO, over 800 million people were chronically undernourished in 2012–14, while undernourishment dropped from 19 to 11 percent globally.[7] In sub-Saharan Africa, 23.8 percent of the population is malnourished, as are about 15 percent of those in South Asia, 14 percent in Oceania, 10.8 percent in East Asia, 10.3 percent in Southeast Asia, 8.7 percent in West Asia, 7.4 percent in the Caucasus in Central Asia, about 5.1 percent in Latin America, and 20.1 percent in the Caribbean.[8] Nearly one-half of the children in large parts of South Asia (mainly India and Bangladesh) have stunted growth.[9] The World Health Organization (WHO) estimates that globally about 161.5 million children under five have stunted growth and 50.8 million have low weight for their height.[10] The percentage of hungry people is decreasing in most of the major regions in the developing world but the actual number of hungry people has stayed the same or even increased in some areas. In particular, the percentage of the population who were hungry increased in West Asia from 1990 to 2014, and sub-Saharan Africa has seen some progress in terms of percentage reductions but is the only area in the world where the prevalence of hunger is over 25 percent.[11]

The world economic crisis that occurred in 2007–9 hurt efforts to reduce global hunger. The FAO concluded that for the first time in decades, because of the crisis, there was "an increase … in both the absolute number and in the proportion of undernourished people."[12] In 2010 the FAO found that over 1 billion people went hungry in 2009, an increase from the previous decade which could be explained "not as a result of poor harvests but because of high food prices, lower incomes and increasing unemployment due to the economic crisis."[13]

Except for Africa, actual starvation is uncommon in the present world. A much larger number of people die today because of malnutrition, a malnutrition that weakens them and makes them susceptible to many diseases. Children die from diarrhea in poor countries – a situation nearly unheard of in rich countries – partly because of their weakened condition.

Who are the hungry and where do they live? The answer to the first question is that, according to World Bank estimates, 80 percent are women and children. A United Nations-sponsored Hunger Task Force estimated that about 50 percent of the hungry are small farmers; 20 percent are landless rural people; 10 percent are pastoralists, fishers and forest dwellers; and the remaining 20 percent are the urban poor.[14]

In the year 2014 the FAO estimated about 526 million hungry people lived in Asia, 227 million lived in Africa, 37 million lived in Latin America and the Caribbean, and 1.4 million lived in Oceania.[15] There are indications that the number of hunger-related deaths in the world has decreased during the past 30 years in spite of the world's growing population. In the mid-1980s, an estimated 15 million people were dying each year from hunger-related causes.[16] One estimate is that in the early 2000s about 200,000 people died yearly during famines, while about 11 million people died early from hunger-related causes.[17] Five million of these were reported to be children.[18] By 2011, an estimated 3.1 million children per year were dying of hunger – and almost half (45 percent) were under five years of age.[19]

Causes of World Hunger

If there is more than enough food being grown at present for the world's population but about 20 percent of the Earth's people are malnourished, what is causing hunger in the world? Food authorities generally agree that poverty is the main cause of world hunger. Millions of people do not have enough money to buy as much food as they need, or better kinds of food. This is the reason one food expert has written that "Malnutrition and starvation continue more or less unchanged through periods of world food glut and food shortage."[20] The world's poorest cannot afford to purchase the food they need, whatever its price. In tropical Africa and remote parts of Latin America and Asia, low agricultural productivity tends to be the main reason for hunger, with not enough food being produced.[21]

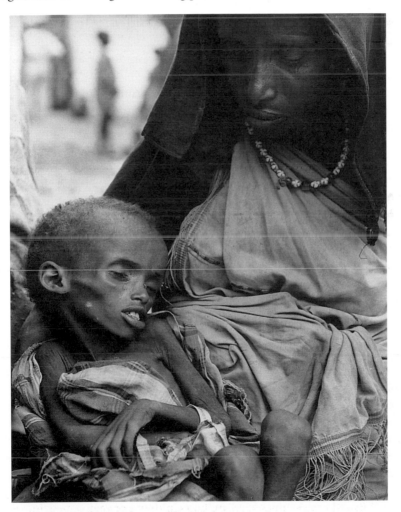

Plate 3.1 Starvation in Somalia

Source: CARE: Zed Nelson.

Other low-income people suffer during food shortages when the price of food increases dramatically, as it did during the early 1970s when world prices of rice, wheat, and corn doubled in just two years. A 2007 study of 13 countries found that food represented between 56 and 78 percent of consumption in poor households (with slight variation depending on whether the household was rural or urban), consistent with historic trends.[22] If world demand is high for certain foods, such as beef for the US fast food market, then the large landowners in developing countries grow food or raise cattle for export rather than for domestic consumption. This tends to cause domestic food prices to increase since the supply of local foods is reduced. A more recent example was the world recession of 2008–9, which combined with high food prices to disproportionately impact the world's poor.

The failure of families to understand that exclusively breast-feeding their babies for six months is to give them the best food for them, an unawareness that giving infants food mixed with unsafe water can cause diarrhea, and in some cases targeted advertising by formula milk manufacturers (at least in the past), leads to malnutrition in poorer countries. This malnutrition during the infant's first two years of life can lead to permanent damage to their mental capabilities in addition to stunted growth.[23] The World Health Organization believes optimal rates of breast-feeding could prevent globally about 15 percent of the deaths of children less than five years of age, while complementary feeding practices could save another 5 percent.[24]

With spreading economic development, famines are becoming rarer than they were in the past. But a number of major famines occurred in the twentieth century. In the Soviet Union in the early 1930s Stalin forcibly collectivized agriculture and deliberately caused a famine in the area where most of the grain was grown – the Ukraine and Northern Caucasus – in order to break the resistance of the peasants. An estimated 7 million people – 3 million of them children – died in that famine.[25] Another country with a communist government experienced the worst famine in the twentieth century. Although it was kept secret from the outside world while it was occurring, China had a famine in the late 1950s and early 1960s that led to an estimated 30 million deaths. The famine was caused mainly by misguided governmental policies during the period known as The Great Leap Forward.[26]

Much land was being used to grow export crops such as cotton and peanuts in the Sahel, a huge area in Africa just south of the Sahara desert, when a famine hit that area in the early 1970s. Six years of drought, rapid population growth, and misuse of the land led to widespread crop failures and livestock deaths. It is estimated that between 200,000 and 300,000 people starved to death in the Sahel and in Ethiopia before international aid reached them.[27]

Famine also hit Cambodia in the 1970s. Years of international and civil war, coupled with the genocidal policies of the communist government under the leadership of Pol Pot, led to an estimated 10,000 to 15,000 people dying every day during the worst of the famine in 1979. A highly successful international aid effort, first organized by private organizations and then joined by governmental agencies, saved the Cambodian people from being destroyed.

Famine hit again in Africa in the mid-1980s, and early and late 1990s. Television pictures of starving people in Ethiopia led to a large international effort by private organizations and by governments to provide food aid. The famines in Ethiopia, Somalia, and the Sudan, and in other sub-Saharan African countries, were not caused only by the return of a serious drought to the region. The causes of these famines were much the same as those that brought on the famine in Africa in the early 1970s: rapid population growth and poor land management. In addition the extensive poverty in the region, a worldwide recession which seriously hurt the export-oriented economies of the African countries, civil wars, and governmental development policies that placed a low priority on agriculture have been identified as likely causes.[28]

North Korea experienced a famine for about four years in the mid- and late 1990s. An estimated 2 to 3 million people died – about 10 percent of its population. The famine led to stunted growth in about two-thirds of the children under five. This made it, relatively, one of the worst famines in the twentieth century, comparable to the famines in the other two communist totalitarian regimes. Like the Soviet Union and China, North Korea was a closed society at the time of the famine and evidence of the famine was kept secret. Although a flood and drought were partly to blame, the main causes appear to be the inflexible political and economic systems and the downfall of the country's long-term patron – the Soviet Union. Serious food shortages continue to the present. Food donors have become increasingly reluctant to continue to help the country as the food shortage drags on, and North Korea has admitted making costly efforts to develop nuclear weapons at the same time that its people were starving.[29]

The Secretary-General of the United Nations appointed a Hunger Task Force in 2002 to recommend ways the Millennium Development Goal to reduce the number of hungry people in the world by one-half by 2015 could be reached. While the goal of halving hunger has not yet been met, global efforts to reduce the number of hungry people successfully reduced the proportion of undernourished people in developing regions from 24 percent in 1990–2 to 14 percent in 2011–13.[30]

Among various recommendations, the Task Force specified the need for about $10 billion in development assistance yearly from the developed world aimed at the reduction of hunger. From developing countries, the Task Force said hunger reduction policies at all levels of government were needed, as well as the reduction of corruption, the establishment of the rule of law, and respect for human rights. The Task Force's message to political leaders of both rich and poor nations was that "halving hunger is within our means; what has been lacking is action to implement and scale up known solutions."[31]

How Food Affects Development

The availability of food has a direct effect on a country's development. Possibly the most destructive and long-lasting development impact is the absence of food – or, more often, of the right kinds of food – for the children of the less developed nations.

(As mentioned in Chapter 1, the death of many children in poor nations at birth or in their first few years is one of the causes of high birth rates). From 2003 to 2008 about 30 percent of children under five in rural areas were undernourished, while about 20 percent of a comparable group in urban areas were hungry. About 60 percent of the 10 million annual deaths of children under five are directly or indirectly attributed to hunger.[32] Pneumonia and diarrhea appear to be the main immediate causes of children's deaths.

A deficiency of vitamin A leads to blindness in about 250,000 to 500,000 children a year in developing countries. About one-half of the children die during the first year after losing their sight.[33] More common than blindness are the harmful effects malnutrition has on the mental development of children. Eighty percent of the development of the human brain occurs before birth and during the first two years after birth. Malnutrition of the pregnant mother or of the child after birth can adversely affect the child's brain development and, along with limited mental stimulation, which is common in poor homes, can lead to a reduced capacity for learning.

Malnutrition also reduces a person's ability to ward off diseases since it reduces the body's natural resistance to infection. Measles and diarrhea, which are not generally serious illnesses in the developed nations, often lead to the death of children in the developing nations; in fact, diarrhea is the second greatest cause of death of children in the less developed world. When a child has been weakened by malnutrition, sickness is likely to come more frequently and to be more serious than that experienced by a well-nourished child.

Plate 3.2   The bloated belly is a sign of malnutrition, a major cause of stunting and death in children worldwide

Source: CARE: Joel Chiziane.

Malnutrition can play a role in productivity levels, particularly for people who are chronically obese or undernourished (and may also suffer from parasitism and disease). The World Health Organization believes that iron deficiencies among the hungry play a large role in their lack of productivity. According to the UN World Food Programme, iron deficiency is the most prevalent form of malnutrition worldwide, affecting productivity by impeding cognitive development and leading to lethargy.[34] A poor nation that must spend limited funds to buy imported food cannot use those funds to support its development plans. And, more importantly, a nation whose main and most important resource – its people – is weakened by malnutrition is unlikely to generate the kind of economic development that actually does lead to an improved life for the majority of its people. James Grant, former head of the United Nations Children's Fund (UNICEF), has described well the interrelatedness of all key elements of development:

> A cat's cradle of … synergisms links almost every aspect of development: female literacy catalyzes family planning programmes; less frequent pregnancies improves maternal and child health; improved health makes the most of pre-school or primary education; education can increase incomes and agricultural productivity; better incomes or better food reduces infant mortality; fewer child deaths tend to lead to fewer births; smaller families improve maternal health; healthy mothers have healthier babies; healthier babies demand more attention; stimulation helps mental growth; more alert children do better at school … and so it continues in an endless pattern of either mutually reinforcing or mutually retarding relations which can minimize or multiply the benefits of any given input.[35]

How Development Affects Food

The development that took place in Europe and the United States as they industrialized led to an increase in the average family's income, and this meant more money to buy goods, including food. As we saw in the preceding section, poverty is the main cause of malnutrition. As incomes rose in the West, hunger disappeared as a concern for the average person. Except for some subgroups in Western countries, malnutrition is no longer a common problem.

Development also affects food in other ways. As a nation develops, major changes start to take place in its agriculture. We will look first at how development affects the amount of food that is produced and how it is produced, and then at the way development affects the types of food people eat.

The production of food

Western agriculture produces an impressive amount of food. The US supermarket, better than any other institution, illustrates the abundance that modern agriculture can produce. The United States produces so much food that huge amounts of important crops such as corn, wheat, and soybeans are exported. Much of this US abundance has come since World War II. By 2000 American farmers were producing twice the output they had in 1930 with only one-third the number of farms.[36] Another way to show this accomplishment is to examine what happened to American farm production over the 60 years from 1948 to 2008. When we do this we find that US farm output increased nearly 160 percent during this period.[37]

What is the reason for this significant increase in production? There are many reasons, of course, but basically it is because American agriculture has become mechanized and scientific. By using new seeds, which can benefit from generous amounts of fertilizer, pesticides, heavy machinery, and irrigation, production has soared. But this accomplishment has had its costs, as we shall see below.

Western agriculture basically turns fossil fuel into food. This type of agriculture was developed when oil was inexpensive. Large amounts of energy are needed to build and operate the farm machinery, to build and operate the irrigation systems, to create the pesticides, and to mine and manufacture the fertilizers. Also, huge amounts of energy are needed to process the foods, to transport them to market, to package them, and to display them in retail stores. (Even in this period of increased energy prices, the open freezer in US supermarkets is still common.) It has been estimated that to raise the rest of the world's diet to the American level – especially one featuring its high consumption of beef – would consume nearly all the world's known reserves of oil in 15 years.[38] Even more important than energy to the success of Western agriculture is water, and agriculture consumes 70 percent of global fresh water use today. Anything that affects the availability of fresh water will seriously affect the production of food.

Although modern, mechanized agriculture is generally – but not always – much more productive than the traditional agricultural systems, traditional agricultural practices tend to occupy a higher share of a country's economy than they do in those countries where industrial agricultural practices are more widespread (see Figure 3.2 for the contribution of agriculture to countries' economies). Traditional agriculture is generally far more energy efficient than Western agriculture. In traditional agriculture the amount of energy used in the form of farm labor and materials is typically small compared with the yield in calories. Returns up to 50 to 1 are possible, although more common are 15 to 1 returns, whereas in modern industrial agriculture more energy is expended than produced.[39] To produce and deliver to a US consumer one can of corn which has 270 calories in it, a total of about 2,800 calories of energy must be used. To produce about 4 ounces of beefsteak, which also provides about 270 calories, an astounding 22,000 calories of energy must be expended.[40] A specialist on water use estimates it takes between 16,000 and 70,000 kilograms of water to produce one kilogram of beef.[41] Anthropologists Peter Farb and George Armelagos give us one perspective we need in order to judge the effects that development, as achieved in the West, is having on agriculture:

> In short, present-day agriculture is much less efficient than traditional irrigation methods that have been used by Asians, among others, in this century and by Mayans,

Mesopotamians, Egyptians, and Chinese in antiquity. The primary advantage of a mechanized agriculture is that it requires the participation of fewer farmers, but for that the price paid in machines, fossil fuels, and other expenditures of energy is enormous.[42]

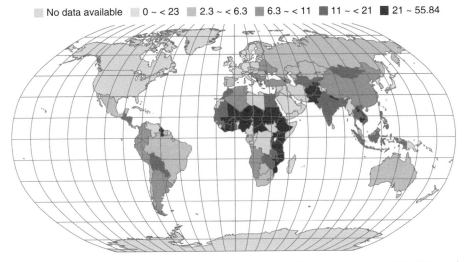

Figure 3.2 Contribution of agriculture as share of Gross Domestic Product, 2012 (percent)

Source: FAO, *Food and Nutrition in Numbers 2014*, p. 5, Figure 1.

The population of the United States comprises approximately 4 percent of the world population; yet in 2012, the average American consumed as many resources as 35 people living in India.[43] That statement, more than any other, presents the main argument of those who maintain that there is no way the rest of the world can adopt the agricultural methods followed by the United States at present.

Another feature of US agriculture is an increase in the size of farms and a reduction in their number. Table 3.1 shows how farm size and numbers have changed from 1940 to 2010. Increased demand for farm products, along with government price supports, enabled farmers to replace old sources of power (horses and mules) with new sources (first the steam engine and then the gasoline engine) and to begin using more machinery, improved seeds, fertilizers, and chemicals to control pests. Dramatic increases in farm productivity resulted so that by 1990 only about 2 percent of US citizens were farmers, down from about 30 percent in 1920. Since World War II there has been a 60 percent decrease in the number of farms in the United States as the mechanization of American agriculture proceeded, productivity increased, and the availability of nonfarm employment grew. A doubling of the average farm size occurred. With the increasing financial investment necessary to support the new type of agriculture, and the competition the large farms provide, there has been a noticeable decline in the small, family-owned farm in the United States. In 2002 the top 7 percent of the largest farms in the United States gained 75 percent of total farm

Table 3.1 Number and size of US farms, 1940–2010

Year	Number of farms	Average size of farms (acres)
1940	6,400,000	170
1950	5,600,000	210
1960	4,000,000	300
1970	2,900,000	370
1980	2,400,000	430
1990	2,100,000	460
2000	2,200,000	440
2010	2,200.000	418

Source: Data from *Statistical Abstract of the United States* (Washington, DC: US Bureau of the Census, 1970, 1992, 2006, 2012), p. 582 (1970), p. 644 (1992), p. 548 (2006).

sales and the smallest farms that were 80 percent of the farms in the country earned less than 10 percent of farm sales.[44]

Brazil, using Western agricultural methods, became a leading major exporter of foods. It claims more than a dozen commodities for which it is one of the world's top ten producer countries.[45] It has already surpassed the United States and Europe in productivity levels in some crops. In 2003 it passed the United States as the largest exporter of beef, although its market share has declined in more recent years. Using scientific research it has created varieties of crops that can grow in the tropical and savannah soils in its vast interior that were formerly considered poor for crops. According to the director of the Center for International Economic Policy at the University of Minnesota in the United States, "[the Brazilians] learned that with modest applications of lime and phosphorus, they can quadruple and quintuple their yields, not just with soybeans, but also with maize, cotton and other commodities."[46]

China, with 1.3 billion people but only about 7 percent of the world's arable land, has had an uneven record in producing grain (corn, rice, and wheat). In the late 1990s China produced a record amount of grain and was an exporter. But rapid urbanization and industrialization have led to the loss of large amounts of farmland. This, along with other factors, led to China's net import of cereal grains in 2013 reaching almost 20 million metric tons.[47] The size of the average farm in China is only about 2 acres, vastly different from the average of 400 acres in the United States and the large new farms in Brazil. China, reluctant to become dependent on the US and other countries for its food, is now struggling to find ways to produce enough food for its still growing population.[48]

The growth of what has become known as "agribusiness" – farms run like a big business – has meant an increased concentration of control over the production of food in the United States, although there are considerable subsidies as well as competition in agriculture so that food in the US remains relatively inexpensive. The large industrial farms can produce massive harvests of 100 million tomatoes, but sometimes with less efficiency than small operators can obtain. When committees, rather than farmers, make decisions, when attention is not given to detail, and when there is a lack of dedication – dedication that usually comes only when someone has a personal stake in the farm – one often finds waste and mismanagement. This happened on large state-owned farms in the Soviet Union, and it is happening on large industrial farms in the United States.

The loss of food

Waste   It is difficult to estimate food waste in the world. It is assumed that as national incomes increase, the amount of food wasted also increases. But some studies have found that food waste in various developing countries is widespread also. For example, a study in Egypt in the mid-1980s estimated 20 to 30 percent of all fresh fruits and vegetables were wasted in the post-harvest period. A 2006 study estimated this loss was as high as 40 percent in India.[49] A 2011 study commissioned by the FAO concluded that, at the global level, approximately one-third of food produced for human consumption is lost or wasted, amounting to roughly 1.3 billion tons per year.[50]

Mismanagement on an industrial farm: the case of the oversized carrots

When the author of a book on three different types of farms in the United States saw an entire crop of carrots being plowed under instead of being harvested on a corporation-owned farm in California, he was given the following explanation by a farm supervisor:

> There are enough carrots [in] the world right now without these … Price isn't so hot, and the warehouses were full when these got to the right size. We were held off harvesting. Someone let time go by and suddenly they were too big. More than eighty acres of them, which comes to sixty million carrots or so. They couldn't fit into plastic carrot sacks they sell carrots in unless they were cut, and that would have cost the processor a bundle. They offered us a hundred and twenty-five dollars an acre for the carrots – and it would have run us two hundred dollars just to have them contract-harvested. So this is the cheapest alternative.

Source: Mark Karma, *Three Farms: Making Milk, Meat and Money from the American Soil* (Boston: Little, Brown, 1980), p. 248.

In many developed countries consumers demand that the produce they buy look cosmetically perfect. This leads to the wasting of much of the food successfully harvested. One study in 2009 of fresh fruit and vegetables in the United

Kingdom found that about 25 to 40 percent of this food was "rejected" by the supermarkets.[51] Studies in the US and the UK have found that household food waste is also significant. The US Environmental Protection Agency in 2008 estimated about 15 percent of the solid waste collected in the country was food waste. And in the UK studies in 2008–9 estimated households wasted 25 percent of their food per year.[52] The agriculture ministry in Japan estimated 23 million tons of food was thrown away in 2007. About 30 percent of the food Japanese restaurants prepare is discarded.[53] In total, 2011 estimates of per capita food waste by consumers in Europe and North America were at 95–115 kilograms per year, while per capita food waste in sub-Saharan Africa and South/Southeast Asia was estimated at 6–11 kilograms per year.[54]

Erosion   Besides the waste of food, there is another waste occurring in the world, which could affect profoundly its ability to produce food in the future: the loss of its farmland by erosion. Although global soil erosion is not expected to seriously hurt world food production, it is a serious problem in a number of locations.[55] Cornell University biologist David Pimentel observed: "Our measuring stations pick up Chinese soil in the Hawaiian air when ploughing time comes. Every year in Florida we pick up African soils in the wind when they start to plough."[56] Nature makes soil very slowly – under normal agricultural conditions it takes from 200 to 1,000 years to form 2.5 centimeters of topsoil.

For years, close to 2 billion tons of topsoil a year were being lost in the United States alone, despite some more recent improvements.[57] A study by the US Department of Agriculture reported in 1999 that 30 percent of the nation's farmland was being eroded at an excessive rate. Globally, about 25 percent of the land has been either severely or very severely degraded by human activities. Of this amount, about one-third has been degraded by agriculture.[58]

Increasingly the world's food supply is relying on irrigation. Irrigation uses more water than any other human activity. Inadequate drainage of irrigated land can lead to waterlogging (an excessive amount of water remaining in the soil) or to salinization (toxic salts deposited on poorly drained land). It has been estimated that about 5 percent of all irrigated land at present seriously suffers from salinization and about 15 percent from waterlogging.[59]

Severe soil erosion is expected to seriously affect food production in southeast Nigeria, Haiti, the Himalayan foothills, some parts of southern China, Southeast Asia, and Central America. Salinization is expected to become a major threat in the irrigation systems of the Indus, Tigris, and Euphrates river basins. It is expected also to become a problem in India, Australia, northeastern Thailand, China, the Nile delta, northern Mexico, and the Andean highlands. Nutrient depletion is likely to become a serious problem in large areas of Africa and numerous other locations from Myanmar to the Caribbean Basin.[60] Desertification, the spreading of deserts, is found in the Sahel region of Africa, in Kazakhstan, and in Uzbekistan. In northern China the desert is growing and leading to massive dust storms that plague Beijing and other cities in China.[61]

Not all the news about erosion is negative. Some encouraging developments are taking place in the world. In the United States, Congress passed a law in 1985 that paid farmers to grow erosion-resistant grasses and trees on the land most susceptible to erosion. By the end of the 1980s about 30 million acres had been placed under this program. The US Department of Agriculture has reported that soil erosion in the US was reduced by 43 percent between 1982 and 2007.[62] No-till farming was one of the methods used to achieve this.[63] The World Resources Institute reported the following encouraging developments throughout the world:

> More soil-friendly farming practices that minimize tilling and reduce the erosive potential of the tilling that is done are coming into wider use, are spreading into countries such as Morocco, the Philippines, and Thailand, and are expanding region-ally in parts of sub-Saharan Africa and South America. These methods include contour farming, terracing, vegetative barriers, and improved land use practices at the farm and landscape levels. Better water management practices that control salinization and lower the amount of irrigation water needed per hectare are also spreading.[64]

Urban sprawl   Another situation in many countries that adversely affects their ability to produce enough food for their people is the loss of prime farmland to development. At the beginning of the twenty-first century the United States was losing about 2 acres of farmland every minute because of development; it was being covered over by houses, roads, shopping malls, factories, and by general urban sprawl. While the amount lost was small compared to the amount of actual and potential cropland in the US, the land lost was often prime farmland, including some of the best fruit orchards, and could be replaced only by marginal land, which was not as fertile, was more open to erosion, and was more costly to use. One-half of the lost farmland was carved into ten-acre lots, many probably for homes for the wealthy.[65]

The loss of farmland to development in the United States accelerated at the end of the twentieth century. While the population of the country grew about 15 percent from 1982 to 1997, the amount of land turned into urban areas grew nearly 50 percent. This resulted in the loss of 13 million acres of cropland, 14 million acres of pastureland, and 12 million acres of rangeland. The amount of forest land remained unchanged. Much of this loss in the United States came not only because of the sprawl of suburbs near large cities, but also because of the urban sprawl of small and medium-sized cities.[66] The same problem of urban sprawl devouring prime cropland is occurring also in other developed and developing nations. Although more people in wealthy nations live in urban areas than do in the rest of the world (about 75 percent compared to 40 percent), urbanization is increasing faster in the rest of the world than in the more wealthy countries.[67]

Plate 3.3   Street vendors sell food to many urban dwellers

Source: Ab Abercrombie.

The type of food

As a nation develops, its diet changes. The wealthier a nation becomes, the more calories and protein its citizens consume. The average citizen of a Western industrialized nation consumes many more calories and much more protein than he or she needs for good health. Much of the excess in protein comes from a large increase in meat consumption. Often the consuming of meat instead of grains in order to get protein, which is needed for human growth and development, is a very inefficient use of food.[68] For every 16 pounds of grain and soybeans fed to beef cattle in the United States, about 1 pound of meat for human consumption is obtained. About three-quarters of the food energy in the diet of people in Asia comes directly from grain (about 300–400 pounds a year), whereas someone in the United States consumes nearly 1 ton of grain per year, but 80 percent of it is first fed to animals.[69]

Plate 3.4 Tropical rainforests are being cut down to clear land to raise beef cattle for the US fast-food market – the so-called "hamburger connection"

Source: United Nations.

In 2005 about one-third of the total cereal harvest in the world, and an even higher portion of coarse grains, was fed directly to livestock.[70]

People in wealthy countries consume the highest amount of meat per person in the world – about 200 pounds annually (96 kilograms). Large amounts of meat are also consumed in some developing countries like Brazil, which consumes about 175 pounds (80 kilograms) annually per person. During the last 40 years of the twentieth century, per capita meat consumption in Europe went up about 100 percent, in Brazil about 150 percent, while in North America it increased about 30 percent.[71] It is generally agreed by experts on nutrition that excessive calories and excessive meat consumption can lead to serious health problems. Barbara Ward describes the harmful features of such a diet:

> The car and the television set and the growing volume of office work may well have produced the most literally sedentary population human society has ever known. But at the same time, diets stuffed with the proteins and calories needed for a lumberman or a professional boxer have become prevalent. Everywhere, high meat consumption demands grain-fed animals. Meanwhile, what little grain we do eat through bread

usually has little nutritional value and roughage, since these are removed when the flour is refined. Thus, the human bowel is deprived of the fiber it requires to function easily. The eating of fresh vegetables – which also give necessary fiber – has fallen off by between a third and a half in the last half century. Processed, defibered products have taken their place. The results are literally apparent. In all developed nations, obesity and diet-related illnesses are now a major medical problem. ...Many medical experts are now agreed that with fat, sugar, cholesterol, refined grains, food additives, and the general absence of roughage, modern citizens are literally – via heart attacks and cancer – eating and drinking themselves into the grave.[72]

A very disturbing development began at the end of the twentieth century, first in the United States, then in other Western developed countries, and finally in some developing countries. More fast foods with a high calorie content were consumed. Along with a sedentary lifestyle and lack of exercise, this led to an increasing number of people who were overweight and obese. The food industry contributed to this trend through its extensive advertising, vast expansion of outlets, and the increasing size of the portions of food and beverages served.[73] Table 3.2 gives the number of overweight and obese males and females in a select group of developed and developing countries. Medical personnel warned that this trend would lead to more diabetes, heart problems, high blood pressure, and possibly cancer.

Table 3.2 Percentage of adults overweight and obese (various countries)

Country	Male	Female
Greece (2003 self report)	67	48
Saudi Arabia (1995–2000)	69	76
Germany (2005–2007)	66	51
USA (2007/8)	72	64
Mexico (2006)	67	72
England (2008)	66	57
Spain (1990–2000)	58	48
Canada (2004)	65	53
Russia (2000)	41	49
Netherlands (1998–2002)	54	39
Italy (2005 self report)	53	35
Brazil (2003)	41	40
China[a] (2002)	19	19
Japan (2000)	27	21

"Overweight" and "obese" are labels for ranges of weight that are greater than what is considered healthy for a given height.

[a]China data are urban only.

Source: International Obesity Task Force (IOTF), "Global Prevalence of Adult Obesity," updated May 2010; see now data at http://www.worldobesity.org/ (accessed July 2015).

We end this section with a short explanation of how development has affected the first food North Americans receive after birth. If you are a North American and were born before 1940, the chances are good that the first food you received was human milk from your mother's breast, whereas if you were born after 1955,[74] your first food was more likely a human-made formula from a bottle, using cow's milk as the basic ingredient. In the second half of the twentieth century, a rapid decline in breast-feeding took place across the globe, although by the end the trend had reversed: from 1990 to 2000, there was a 15 percent increase in breast-feeding. By 2005, according to UNICEF, in the vast majority of countries, about 40 percent of infants were being exclusively breast-fed. Partly this was because of urbanization, the increasing number of women in the workforce, cultural attitudes, and the promotional efforts of formula-making companies (the latter more of a factor in the past than at present).

But is formula better for a child than breast milk? Except for mothers infected with life-threatening infectious diseases such as HIV, no, it's not.[75] Nutritionists agree that human milk is the best food for babies. According to UNICEF, breastfed children have a chance of survival in the early months that is at least six times greater than non-breastfed children.[76] Breast-feeding is also the safest, cheapest, and easiest way to feed babies. Breast-feeding probably improves bonding – a special feeling of closeness – between the mother and the baby, and it gives the baby antibodies which enable it to fight off infection; this is especially important since its own immune system is not fully developed during the first year. Studies have also shown that in India bottle-fed babies have diarrhea three times more often than breast-fed babies, and in Egypt infant deaths are five times higher among bottle-fed babies than among breast-fed ones.[77] Many of the harmful effects of bottle-feeding in the developing world occur because of the lack of refrigeration and the lack of knowledge about the importance of sterilization. Also, formula is expensive, so poor mothers often dilute it with water, making the formula too weak – and the water is often polluted.

There has been a return to breast-feeding in some European countries and partly in the United States. Norway, Denmark, and Sweden lead the way with close to 100 percent of all new mothers breast-feeding their infants at birth. After six months – the frequently recommended period for breast-feeding – 80 percent of new mothers in Norway are still nursing their infants. In Britain and the United States about 70 percent of new mothers breast-feed their infants at birth, but only about a third in the United States (2007) and 20 percent in Britain (2003) were breast-feeding six months after birth.[78] Working mothers in the United States find bottle-feeding more convenient, and the US culture is still unsettled by the sight of a woman breast-feeding in public. Due in part to shifting cultural attitudes where many of the previous generation did not acquire knowledge on breast-feeding to pass along to the next generation, a special organization – La Leche League – was formed by some women to help others learn about breast-feeding and to aid them with any difficulties they experience. What we find in this case is a modern society turning away from one of the most basic human functions and then having to relearn the advantages of this bodily function and how to practice it.

The general recognition of the harmful effects that were generated by the adoption of bottle-feeding by less developed nations led the World Health Organization in 1981 to adopt, by a vote of 118 to 1 (only the United States voted "no"), a nonbinding code restricting the promotion of infant formula.[79]

The Mediterranean diet

Would you like to lower your risk of high blood pressure, stroke, heart disease and cancer? Decrease your chance of getting Parkinson's or Alzheimer's diseases? Many in the medical profession now believe the closer a person follows the diet of people in countries bordering the Mediterranean Sea, the more likely they will achieve these benefits. Here are the main ingredients of the Mediterranean diet:

1 Eat a generous amount of fruits and vegetables, including whole grains and legumes (such as beans and peas)
2 Use olive oil or canola oil
3 Eat daily low to moderate amounts of cheese and yogurt
4 Use herbs and spices instead of salt to flavor foods
5 Drink red wine in moderation during meals
6 Eat fish or shellfish at least twice a week
7 Eat nuts in moderation
8 Consume very little red meat

Map 3.1   The Mediterranean

The "Green" Revolution

The widespread adoption of high agricultural technology has been called the "Green Revolution," which refers to enhanced food productivity as opposed to environmental benefits. This technological transition has two basic components: the use of new seeds, especially for wheat, rice, and corn; and the use of various "inputs," such as fertilizer, irrigation, and pesticides. The new seeds, developed over decades of cross-pollinating and engineering, are highly responsive to fertilizer. If they receive sufficient fertilizer and water, and if pests are kept under control, the seeds produce high yields. The introduction of this new agricultural technology in the mid-1960s brought greatly increased harvests of wheat and impressive increases in rice production in a number of Asian countries. Over a six-year period, India doubled its wheat production and Pakistan did nearly as well. Significant increases of rice production occurred in the Philippines, Sri Lanka, Indonesia, and Malaysia. Mexico's wheat and corn production tripled in only two decades. From 1960 to 2014, annual grain production around the world increased from approximately 823.5 million tons to 2.47 billion tons.[80]

Not only were the harvests much larger, but multiple harvests – in some places up to three – became possible in a year because of the faster maturing of the plants.

Increased food production led to lower food prices globally.[81] These lower prices enabled many people in less developed countries to increase their calorie intake, thus leading to better health and longer life expectancy.

There are now indications that grain production under the Green Revolution is slowing down. Between 1950 and 1990 grain production per acre increased about 2 percent per year, more than population growth, but then dropped to about 1 percent annually, less than population growth.[82] With its population continuing to grow, in the mid-2000s India had to import wheat for its grain stockpile in order to maintain desired stock buffers, something it had not had to do for many years.[83] Increased domestic production and enhanced stockpiles of wheat in India subsequently reversed this trend, and now economic conditions favor domestic production over imports.[84]

Part of the problem the Green Revolution is now facing is that funds for agricultural research in the developing world have plummeted, both within those countries and as a part of the shrinking foreign aid budgets of some developed countries. Also water tables, which feed the irrigation systems of the Green Revolution, are falling to unsustainable levels.

Ground water levels in a huge part of northern India, the most intensively irrigated region in the world, where 600 million people live, are now being depleted to unsustainable levels for the long term.[85] In China the water table under the North China Plain, where one-half of the country's wheat and one-third of its corn are grown, is falling fast.[86] Climate is also becoming unstable, in many places hotter and dryer, reducing core grain yields.

Some negative aspects of the new technology of the Green Revolution have become apparent. The new highly inbred seeds are often less resistant to diseases than are some of the traditional seeds. Also, the planting of only one variety of a plant – called monoculture – creates an ideal condition for the rapid spreading of disease and for the rapid multiplying of insects that feed on that plant. (The Irish potato blight in the mid-nineteenth century and the US corn blight of 1970 are examples of serious diseases that have attacked monocultures.) The new seeds can also be less tolerant of too little or too much water; thus droughts and floods have a more harmful impact on these plants than on the traditional varieties of the grains.

One other negative impact of the new technology is that some farmers and agricultural workers have been hurt by it. An evaluation of 40 years of the Green Revolution states: "Those who did not receive the productivity gains of the Green Revolution (largely because they were located in less favorable agroecological zones), but who nonetheless experienced price declines, have suffered actual losses of income."[87]

Probably the most serious potential negative aspect of the Green Revolution technology is the question about its sustainability. Critics have raised this question because of its tendency to increase chemical pollution, deplete aquifers, and lead to soil degradation.

Fertilizers

Synthetic fertilizers are usually needed with the new seeds associated with the Green Revolution. Fertilizer use has grown dramatically around the globe since 1970, especially in Asia and particularly in China. There is now evidence that the runoff of fertilizers from farmland is a significant source of pollution in rivers and lakes. Excessive nitrogen in the fertilizer and from other sources is overwhelming the natural nitrogen cycle with a variety of consequences such as a decrease in soil fertility and toxic algae blooms. Excessive nitrogen in lakes greatly stimulates the growth of algae and other aquatic plants, which, when they die and decay, rob the water of its dissolved oxygen, suffocating many aquatic organisms.

Seas such as the Baltic Sea, the Black Sea, and even the Mediterranean in Europe are especially vulnerable to this excessive fertilization – called eutrophication. Lake Victoria in Africa, Lake Erie in North America, and Lake Taihu in China are also threatened. A large "dead zone" – about the size of the state of New Jersey – of diminished productivity has developed at the mouth of the Mississippi River in the Gulf of Mexico because of the excessive amount of nitrogen from agricultural runoff.

There are now about 400 so-called "dead zones" around the world caused by fertilizer runoff and wastewater discharges.[88] Some of these dead zones are so large they can be seen from space. A number of measures can drastically reduce this runoff. These include better timing of fertilizer applications, more exact calculation of the amount of fertilizer the crops can absorb, and more accurate delivery of the fertilizer.

Pesticides

There was a large increase in the use of pesticides (insecticides, herbicides, and fungicides) around the world in the 1970s, 1980s, and 1990s, no doubt also connected with the spreading Green Revolution. It is difficult to know how many people are being harmed by pesticides, but it is believed that the number is significant. One estimate by the World Health Organization is that perhaps as many as 20,000 deaths occur annually around the world because of pesticide poisoning and 1 million people are made ill.[89] Many more may become sick from indirect contact through contaminated water or through food which has not been thoroughly washed. (We will look further at pesticides in Chapter 6.)

Irrigation

The Green Revolution also often requires irrigation. The use of fresh water, much of it for irrigation, has increased steadily since the 1960s. In many countries, for example in Africa and the Middle East – according to the World Resources Institute – "water withdrawals appear to be occurring at unsustainable rates."[90] At the height of the Green Revolution in the 1970s irrigated land on the planet increased about 2 percent annually. Since that time irrigation has been growing about 1 percent a year. The growth has slowed partly because of the high costs of installing irrigation, and the competition for fresh water. Besides the problems of waterlogging and salinization, which were mentioned earlier, increased use of irrigation can also lead to an increase in infectious diseases such as malaria and schistosomiasis. Between 2005 and 2007 the amount of irrigated land in the world actually decreased, dropping from about 2 percent in 2005 to about 1 percent in 2007.[91]

Improvements are being made in irrigation. New irrigation technology, such as highly efficient sprinklers and drip feeding, can lessen the amount of water used. By these methods, Israel reduced its water consumption for irrigation by about 35 percent between 1951 and 1990 with no loss of productivity.[92]

The future

Biotechnology will be discussed in a later section in this chapter. There is no doubt this technology, the transferring of desirable genes from one organism to another, is going to have a large effect on the Green Revolution. One possible serious problem is that the seeds produced by using this technology generally will not reproduce themselves, so farmers must purchase seeds from a commercial producer, such as the Monsanto Corporation, every year, whereas in the past plants reproduced seeds annually which the farmers could use to plant new crops the following year.

The Green Revolution technology has yet to be extensively applied to Africa. While Africa does have special problems that are difficult to overcome, such as limited water, poor soils, serious erosion, and much political conflict, there is evidence that if the government is supportive, the technology can be applied. Partly because former US President Jimmy Carter urged the new President of Ethiopia to view a demonstration site using Green Revolution technology, the new government of that country reversed the policy of the former military regime, which had focused on heavy industry, and began to focus on agriculture. The government began to lend money to farmers for improved seeds and fertilizer. Grain production in Ethiopia nearly doubled in just two years. Ten years after a major famine, the country began to export grain.[93]

About one-half of the world's people eat rice daily. China released version two of its high-yield hybrid rice in 2006, generating 9 tons of rice per hectare, and then started work on version three to yield 13.5 tons of rice per hectare.[94] China plants about 29 million hectares of the rice per year, with an average output capacity of about 6.5 tons of rice per hectare.[95] Among the total acreage of rice fields in China, hybrid rice accounts for about 57 percent and hybrid rice is about 20 percent more productive than traditional rice. According to the Chinese Ministry of Agriculture, China needs 500 million tons of grain annually to feed its present population of 1.3 billion people. It is hoping the new hybrid rice will help it achieve this total but admits difficulties such as in the summer of 2009 when the grain output was only about 123 million tons due to difficult climate conditions, including strong rainfalls in the south during the harvest season, droughts in northern grain areas, and persistent low temperatures in the south.[96]

Certainly, without the increased production that came with the Green Revolution many developing countries would have already lost the battle to have enough food available for their rapidly growing populations. The late Dr Norman Borlaug – a US scientist who received the Nobel Peace Prize for his work in developing high-yield wheat, and the person considered to be the "father" of the Green Revolution – has stated the Green Revolution was not meant to be the final solution for the world's food problem: it was designed to give nations a breathing space of 20 or 30 years during which time they could work to bring their population growth under control. Borlaug was as disappointed as many others are that this time has not been used by many nations to optimize their food supplies in proportion to their populations.

Governmental Food Policies

The availability of food is such a basic need that no government that we know of adopts a "hands off" policy regarding its production, price, and distribution. But many countries have given a relatively low priority to agricultural development and to relieving poverty in their rural areas, concentrating instead on industrial development. Most nations have scarce public funds, so decisions must be made judiciously about where to apply them. It should not be surprising to students of government that public funds usually go to benefit groups with political visibility and power. Political leaders want to stay in power, and it is often the traditional political and economic elites who will influence the leaders' length of stay rather than the scattered and weak – both physically and politically – small farmers and rural poor. In many developing nations the urban masses, who can riot, are much more of a threat to the leaders than the small farmers, and urban people demand plentiful and inexpensive food.

The desire to retain power, of course, is not the only reason why rural development has not been given a high priority in many less developed nations. The desire to achieve the high living standards of the West by following the route taken by the United States and other developed nations – both capitalist and communist in the past – with their emphasis on industrialization was hard to resist; it seemed like a relatively fast way to reduce poverty. US foreign aid in the 1950s and 1960s certainly encouraged developing nations along this route. Some of those in the foreign aid program then recognized that this development strategy was a gamble, that maybe benefits would not trickle down to the poor, but the other alternative of trying to work directly with the millions of rural poor did not seem viable. Barbara Ward shows how dominant this strategy of emphasizing industrialization over rural development became: "So far, on average, only 20 percent of the investment of most developing nations has gone to the 70 to 80 percent of the people who are in the rural areas."[97]

How does one respond to the argument that, given limited public funds, it is impossible to give any significant aid to the millions in the rural areas where most of the hunger exists? The response is that there have been a few Asian countries – namely Japan, South Korea, and Taiwan – that have brought significant prosperity to their rural areas by doing certain things. First, they enacted land reform measures – in Japan's case under the US occupation force's direction after World War II – which ended absentee landlordism and exploitative tenancy arrangements. The land was basically turned over to those who farmed it. Second, cooperatives were established to help small farmers purchase needed inputs such as seeds and fertilizers and market their harvests. The governments also provided information and aid to the farmers through an active agricultural extension service and by supporting agricultural research. Japanese small farmers now have some of the highest yields per acre in the world, and the mechanization they have used on their farms – mainly small machines – has tended to increase rural employment, not decrease it. Double and even triple harvests per year on the same piece of land became possible, and more laborers were required to handle these harvests.

China under Mao Zedong emphasized agriculture instead of industrialization after the disastrous "Great Leap Forward" (a crash program of economic development in the late 1950s). China, with only 7 percent of the world's arable land and about 1.3 billion people, has achieved impressive increases in its agricultural production, but because of its rapid population growth the increased food has mainly gone to feed the increased population. Hunger is certainly less of a problem in China today than it was before the communist takeover – except during the famine in the late 1950s and early 1960s – but the costs have been high. Political opponents have been dealt with harshly, and significant damage to the environment came from the efforts to increase the amount of agricultural land. Forests were cut down and marginal pasture land was converted to land for crops. Even though the communist government also made efforts to protect the environment, its actions directed toward increasing agricultural production led to an increased strain on the land. Significant losses of arable land are occurring because of the expansion of cities and industries, soil erosion, desertification, and deforestation. Experts are divided on whether China will be able to feed itself in the future without importing large amounts of food, which would affect the world food market.[98] In their first policy document of 2014, the

Central Committee of the Communist Party of China and the State Council focused on agricultural and land use issues.[99] The Central Committee identified 120 million hectares of arable land as the minimum required to ensure food security; as of 2012, China had approximately 133 million hectares of arable land, though the government conceded that the amount of land actually suitable for agriculture was only slightly above the target number after deducting land dedicated to forest or pasture restoration, and land deemed too polluted to be used for farming.[100] The same document also identified a target level of grain production for 2020 that fell below 2013 levels, shifting focus instead to the production of meat, vegetables, and fruit.[101]

Another historically significant set of centralized policies came from the Soviet Union, which pursued a radically different plan from China. Under Stalin's long rule, the country placed industrialization first, and agriculture was used to support that industrialization. Also, the desire to remove the political opponents of the ruling communists – the prosperous small farmers known as "kulaks" – and the desire to substitute state-owned and collective farms for privately owned farms, led to what is commonly recognized as the destruction of efficient agriculture in that country. The Soviet Union's inability to grow enough food to feed its people caused it to import large amounts of wheat from the United States and other capitalist countries.

There is space in this chapter to sketch food policies in the United States only briefly. The main point that should be made is that the US government is very active in this area. Up to the 1900s the government's policy was mainly to encourage farm production, but since the 1950s the policy has been directed mainly at coping with an excess of production. The basic policy has been to prop up low farm incomes by using price supports, by purchasing surpluses, and by paying the farmers to grow less food. During the 1950s and 1960s, the policy of the US (and Canadian) governments was to buy up farm surpluses, a process that led to huge public reserves. Food from this reserve often went to poor nations under the Public Law 480 program, whereby surplus food was given or sold to developing nations. World food prices were generally stable during this period since, during bad harvest years, food from the public reserve was released. Now it is no longer the policy of either the United States or Canada to encourage large public food reserves, which means that reserves can no longer act as a cushion during periods of poor harvests. More recently, the US government has encouraged and supported the export of US farm products to other nations. The United States has become the world's leading exporter of food. The government supports this because exports help correct the large trade imbalances that the country often experiences. Subsidy payments in the United States were designed also to protect the small family farm by boosting low agricultural prices, but the largest farms have benefited the most with the top 10 percent of agricultural producers receiving 60 percent of the subsidies.[102] As the United States faced serious security and environmental problems caused by its reliance on oil from the Middle East in the first decade of the new century, it diverted large amounts of corn and other grains to produce ethanol for its cars. In 2013, 40 percent of the US corn harvests were used to make ethanol, up from 25 percent in 2009. Diverting large volumes of corn for fuel has become one of the factors contributing to high food prices throughout the world.[103]

Developing nations have complained that large subsidy payments by the US government and the European Union to their farmers make it difficult for farmers in the poorer nations to compete with the Western farmers. Many less developed nations depend on agricultural exports to earn needed foreign exchange.

Future Food Supplies

How much food can be grown in the world? How many can be fed? Like most of the questions raised in this book, there are no simple answers. Also, it is not hard to find experts who give very different answers to these questions. In this final section we will look at seven topics which are directly related to these important questions: the effects of climate change, the amount of arable land, energy costs, alternative/sustainable agriculture, biotechnology, fishing and aquaculture, and, finally, expected future food production.

Climate

Experts are in general agreement that the Earth's climate is changing, and the global climate will continue getting warmer in the future. It is very difficult to predict how this will affect the world's agriculture. It could make conditions worse for the growing of food in some countries and better in others. This subject will be discussed more fully in Chapter 5 on climate change. Experts have also concluded that there will be more variability in the climate than there has been in the recent past. The climate over the past several decades in the United States and Canada has been unusually good for agriculture, but in the coming decades yields may suffer. Indeed, variability is the hallmark of the Earth's climate when it is examined over long periods; one sees long-term cycles of hundreds of years and shorter cycles of 15 to 20 years.

A greater variability of climate (higher and lower extremes of temperature and higher and lower amounts of rainfall) will probably lower agricultural production around the world because of the large amount of marginal land now being used for agriculture. On this land, such as parts of the American West, the Canadian West, and the Russian East, a slight reduction in rainfall or a slightly shorter growing season can spell the difference between a good harvest and little or no harvest.

A 2013 report from the world's leading scientists found that climate change has already reduced wheat and maize yields globally, and further that food prices spiked following extreme weather events in key producing regions.[104] Additionally, while climate impacts vary across regions, overall negative impacts are predicted to outweigh any positive changes such as those associated with a longer growing season.[105]

A warmer world is apt to have less organic material in its soils as vital nutrients decompose. The US National Academy of Sciences estimates that for every 1 degree Celsius (1.8 degrees Fahrenheit) rise in temperature above the norm, there will be a 10 percent decrease in rice, wheat, and corn yields.[106] Please refer to Chapter 5 for additional discussion on climate change.

Arable land

About 10 percent of the Earth's land free of ice, the arable land, can be cultivated and experts estimate that about one-half of the arable land is presently being used for agriculture. Large amounts of potential farmland exist in Latin America and Africa. The Brazilian *cerrado* and the grasslands of sub-Saharan Africa have the largest reserves of arable land. Yet most of the good farmland in the world is already being used. Much of the remaining potential arable land is far from population centers and a lot of it is marginal land, which is costly to bring into production and to maintain. Large amounts of energy would be needed to develop it – to build roads to it and to transport its products to market, to irrigate it, and to fertilize it.

Because of these challenges, plus the social and political obstacles that must be overcome to develop such areas, it is difficult to estimate the potential for increasing the amount of farmland. These estimates also must take into consideration the large amount of present farmland being lost to agriculture through urbanization, through erosion caused by the cutting down of forests and overcropping, through the spreading of desert-like conditions (desertification) because of overgrazing and farming on the edge of deserts, and through the loss of irrigated lands (salinization and waterlogging) because of poor drainage. The Earth's growing population and the

Plate 3.5   Much of the food in Africa is grown and prepared by women

Source: World Bank.

type of diet its people choose will also greatly affect the amount of land needed to feed them.

What's your footprint?

Your food choices have a big impact on the Earth. As illustrated in Figure 3.3, in 2008 the global population was already using approximately 1.5 times more of the Earth's resources than could be replenished, and if current trends continue the world will demand the resources of three Earths by 2050. Most people in wealthy nations use much more than their share, while the world's poor tend to tread very lightly. The world has a limited amount of arable land, and there is simply not enough land on the planet to support a global population following a diet high in processed foods, saturated fat, and large amounts of animal meat. Calculate your footprint at http://footprintnetwork.org/en/index.php/GFN/page/calculators/.

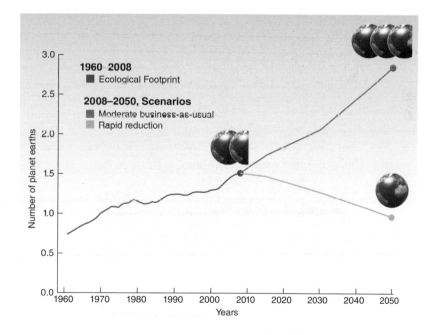

Figure 3.3   Number of Earths required to sustain global population, 1960–2008 and 2008–2050 (scenarios)

Source: Footprint Network, at http://www.footprintnetwork.org/en/index.php/GFN/page/world_footprint/.

A respected Canadian geographer, Vaclav Smil, has expressed concern that even if the total amount of arable land is sufficient to sustain the Earth's population for at least decades to come, many of the world's poorest may suffer. He sees the near future as follows:

> Undoubtedly, the total area of potential farmland is quite large, but its ... distribution is highly uneven and its initial quality will be generally inferior to the existing cropland. ... [T]he affluent countries should not experience any weakening of their food production capacity because of the declining availability of farmland [but] ... low income societies tell a different story. Combination of continuing population growth and uneven ... distribution of potentially available farmland will only increase substantial differences in per capita availability of arable land in those countries. ... [P]er capita land availability remains high in Latin America, and more than adequate in sub-Saharan Africa. The greatest concerns exist, and will intensify, in the Middle East and in South and East Asia.[107]

Energy costs

The dramatic increase in energy costs in the 1970s had a profound influence on agriculture, and expected rising energy costs in the future will strongly affect food production and the cost of food. As we have seen, modern, Western agriculture is energy intensive, and the spreading of that type of agriculture to the developing world via the Green Revolution also entailed a commitment to using large amounts of energy. In the past, a doubling of agricultural output required a tenfold increase in the amount of energy used.[108] There is hope that many countries and cultures can utilize agricultural methods that do not depend on the high use of energy and energy-related inputs common on large commercial farms in richer countries. This becomes increasingly possible when adopting a diet that is lower in processed foods and meat, which would suggest rejecting the Western diet as an ideal to strive for. Various experts have confirmed that a diet primarily based on plants is better for human health as well as the environment.

Traditional/sustainable/organic agriculture

One way to produce food with less contamination of the water and air and sometimes less impact on the natural fertility of the soil is through traditional, sustainable, or organic agriculture. This resource-conserving and lower impact agriculture utilizes a number of old, proven techniques and a sophisticated understanding of natural nutrient cycles and ecological relationships. According to the World Resources Institute, it includes "practices such as crop rotation, reduced tillage or no-till, mechanical/biological weed control, integration of livestock with crops, reduced use or no use of chemical fertilizers and pesticides, integrated pest management, and provision of nutrients from various organic sources (animal manures, legumes)."[109] A demand by consumers for foods free of possible contamination by chemicals led to a large increase in organic farming in the United States in the 1990s and 2000s. In 2002, for the first time, the US government developed organic certification standards.[110] Organic farming is supported with governmental subsidies in Europe, but the United States only partially supports the cost of certification.[111] In 2012, organic food sales reached $28.1 billion, over 4 percent of total food sales.[112] By 2013 total sales reached approximately $35.1 billion.

Whether organic farming will ever become widespread in the $500 billion food industry in the United States is unknown, but the trend is that organic food production and consumption are increasing. The main criticism of organic farming is that it is less productive than conventional farming, and thus the prices of its foods are relatively high. There is still some debate on this question. A Swiss study published in 2002, comparing organic and conventional farms – the most comprehensive study of its time – found that organic farming leaves the soils healthier and is more energy efficient, but average crop yields are about 20 percent lower.[113] A long-term US study found opposite results, with yields about equal in corn and soybean production using organic and conventional methods, and in drought years organic corn yields were significantly higher than conventional farm yields.[114]

Impressive evidence of the worth of alternative agriculture techniques came in China in the summer of 2000. At that time the results of one of the largest agricultural experiments ever undertaken were announced. Under the direction of an international team of scientists, tens of thousands of rice farmers in one province participated in a simple experiment that didn't cost them any money, didn't involve the use of any chemicals, and resulted in them gaining a nearly 20 percent increase in their yields of rice. What the farmers did was plant two varieties of rice in their fields rather than just one. The result of changing from a monoculture to using diversity was to nearly wipe out the most devastating disease that affects rice, one that destroys millions of tons each year, causing farmers losses of several billion dollars. Scientists involved in the study believe the startling results can apply beyond rice. An ecologist at the University of Washington stated that "what's really neat about this paper [which announced the results of the experiment] is that it shows how we've lost sight of the fact that there are some really simple things we can do in the field to manage crops."[115]

Biotechnology

Biotechnology has been called a technology that will transform modern agriculture. Genetic engineering, the transferring of desirable genes, or traits, from one organism to another, is the best-known part of this technology. New breeds of animals and plants are being created today with this technology. Plant and animal species have changed naturally throughout the evolution of life on this planet and human beings have, for thousands of years, influenced that evolution by encouraging the growth of those plants and animals which have traits that benefit humans. But now, as one scientist has stated, "we can do all at once what evolution has taken millions of years to do."[116]

Biotechnology is still controversial. While some raise concerns related to risks that engineered organisms may compromise conventional plants with irreversible genetic impacts, its defenders point out that food crops can be developed that are resistant to insects and viruses, thus reducing the need for pesticides. Plants can be developed that can tolerate herbicides, thus allowing herbicides, which would normally harm the plant, to be used to control the weeds threatening the plant. Fruits can be developed that are resistant to spoilage. A tomato has been developed in the United States that has a natural resistance to becoming overripe, which means the tomato does not have to be picked while it is still green and relatively tasteless. Plants that are more nutritious are being developed, such as a new variety of rice that will contain provitamin A, an essential nutrient that is missing in present rice. In Southeast Asia particularly high proportions of the children under the age of five are at risk from vitamin A deficiency, which leads to vision impairment and increased susceptibility to disease.[117] Plants that can grow under harsh conditions – for example, during droughts, or in salty soils, or in temperature extremes of heat and cold – are also being developed. With this technology, animals, such as pigs, can be developed to have more lean meat, and dairy cows can be developed to produce more milk. In the United States about 85 percent of corn, 85–90 percent of cotton, and 90 percent of soybeans are from seeds that have been genetically modified.[118] By 2002 genetically altered seeds were used widely in the United States, Argentina, and Canada.[119]

In 2002 a team of Chinese government scientists and scientists from a private Swiss biotech company jointly announced, and made public, a draft of the genetic code of two common varieties of rice, one that is commonly eaten in Japan and one widely eaten in China and India. Dr Ronald Cantrell, director of the International Rice Research Institute in the Philippines, said the decoding of the rice genome would "have a tremendous impact on the poor" by enabling researchers to improve the nutrient value and growing characteristics of rice.[120] Rice is the most important food for about 3 billion of the world's people, including many of its poorest. In 2005 the final, accurate version of the genetic makeup of rice was published by an international team from 11 nations, led by Japanese scientists. Rice has been called the Rosetta Stone of the cereals, since much of its genetic makeup is a part of the other main cereals such as corn, wheat, and barley, and can be used to study those plants.

The critics of this new technology, who tend to be more numerous in Europe than in the United States, claim that there is a possibility that genetic engineering will alter organisms in detrimental ways that will not be fully known for years. Herbicide-resistant crops might pollinate closely related plants that are now weeds, thus creating a new weed that is also resistant to herbicides. Much negative publicity for bioengineering was generated in the United States in 1999 when a study showed that the pollen from corn that had been genetically altered to produce a natural pesticide can kill caterpillars of the monarch butterfly. Since most of the research today in biotechnology is being performed by private corporations that see it as a way to increase their profits, it is not surprising that most of the present genetic engineering focuses on crops and animals that can be profitably sold in the rich nations, not in the poor nations. The critics point to several large corporations that produce herbicides and other farm chemicals as being leaders in efforts to develop herbicide-resistant crops. Instead of encouraging the development of less reliance on chemicals in the growing of foods, this research will increase such reliance.

The European Union requires labels on food identifying it as genetically altered if 1 percent or more of its ingredients have been genetically altered. A crack developed in European opposition in 2004 when the European Union ended its six-year moratorium on the approval of biotech foods. In 2010 the European Commission issued guidelines for the coexistence of natural and genetically altered corps appropriate to national circumstances. These guidelines are intended to prevent the unintended presence of biotech plants in conventional and organic crops.

A report by the US National Academy of Sciences in 2002 called for a more rigorous approval process by the government of biotech foods, although it had already given in 2000 cautious approval of the safety of genetically altered foods then on the market. With biotech companies developing plants with either a combination of genes or with an individual gene that enables the plant to produce pharmaceutical or industrial chemicals, stronger regulations are needed. The Academy warned that genetically altered crops have the potential to pose food safety risks and environmental harm. In a 2004 report the Academy stated that it will be difficult to contain all altered genes in plants and animals or prevent any of them from having unintended environmental and public health effects.[121]

Like many technologies, biotechnology appears to have positive and negative potential. It is impossible to predict at this point which potential will dominate. Being aware of the negative possibilities and taking steps to counter them may be the best we can do at this time. Government regulations need to be regularly updated to reflect the latest research and the plants and animals need to be monitored while being grown. (The negative side of technology will be discussed further in Chapter 8.) Biotechnology could lead to major advances in agriculture in the poorer nations. Some universities, such as the University of Ghent in Belgium, private foundations, such as the Rockefeller Foundation in the United States, and governmental agencies, such as the Swiss Federal Institute of Technology and the European Community Biotech Program, are supporting research in biotechnology that is directed toward that purpose.

Fishing and aquaculture

Not too long ago many people hoped that the world food problem would be solved by harvesting fish from the oceans, but it is now generally recognized that, as one marine biologist has put it, most of the ocean is a biological desert. Nearly all the fish in the world are harvested in coastal waters and in a relatively few places further from land where there is a strong up-welling of water that brings nutrients to the surface.

Over the past 50 years there has been increasing pressure on the world's fish. About two-thirds of the world's major varieties of fish are now fished at or above their capacity to renew themselves, and another 10 percent have been fished so heavily that it would take many years for their numbers to recover. Marine biologists estimate that in the past half-century about 90 percent of the large ocean predators such as sharks, tuna, marlin, swordfish, cod, halibut, skates, and flounder have been caught.[122]

According to the World Resources Institute ("WRI"), "substantial potential exists for increasing the ocean fish harvests with better management of fish stocks, although sound management is neither easy nor obvious."[123] WRI cites the examples of Cyprus and the Philippines where better management of fishing in their waters led to substantial increases in fish harvests in as little as 18 months. WRI also reported that Canada, the European Union, and the United States had recently adopted tougher controls over ocean fishing and reduced the size of their fishing fleets.

One type of fishing that does hold promise for an increase in catch is aquaculture, the farming of fish inland and in coastal waters. By 2005 about 30 percent of the fish eaten in the world came from fish farms.[124] Nearly nonexistent in the United States a generation ago, aquaculture had developed into a $900 million industry by the end of the twentieth century. Worldwide, aquaculture was a $45 billion industry. More than half of the salmon eaten in the United States, about one-third of the shrimp, most of the clams and oysters, and nearly all the trout and catfish come from fish farms.

Fish farming is popular in many countries, especially in Asia, which is the home for about 80 percent of the industry. China has about two-thirds of worldwide production.[125] Aquaculture was developed in China several thousand years ago. It is now becoming more popular in the developed nations because people there – partly for health reasons (because fish are low in fat, and fish oil is reported to have beneficial properties) – are consuming more fish and demanding that the fish they buy come from nonpolluted waters. Genetic engineering is also being used to create new species of fish. Here is the way one newspaper described the new techniques being used in aquaculture in the United States:

> Scientists are growing fish twice as fast as they grow naturally, cutting their feed requirement by nearly half, and raising them on a diet of ground chicken feathers and soybeans. Fish are now vaccinated against disease, sterilized so that their energy is spent growing not reproducing, and given hormones to turn females into males and males into females, changes that can be used to improve growth, taste and control of selective breeding.[126]

There are environmental concerns with this rapidly growing industry. Thailand has cleared a large part of its mangrove swamps to make way for shrimp ponds, thus losing a critical habitat for many aquatic species and opening its coasts to erosion and flooding. A 20-acre salmon operation can produce as much organic waste as a city of 10,000 people. There is also a fear that fish that escape from the farms can mate with their wild relatives and harm the natural gene pool. It has been estimated that in 2007 about 700,000 salmon escaped from fish farms in Norway, the largest salmon fish farm producer in the world.[127] On the east and west coasts of the United States from the mid-1980s to 2000, over 500,000 salmon were estimated to have escaped from their pens.[128]

Future food production

Will the world be able to produce enough food for its rapidly expanding population? This is a hard question to answer. Many experts failed to predict the progress that has been made in food production in the past few decades, so it would be easy to discount the warnings by some of them now. Yet some very disturbing signs exist.

Lester R. Brown, the founder of both the Worldwatch Institute and the Earth Policy Institute, the latter of which he heads at present, believes the availability of food in the future is threatened by four crucial factors: rapid population growth, loss of topsoil, spreading water shortages, and rising temperatures. Unless drastic action is taken to reduce these threats, he has warned that the food system could collapse in the future.

Here are some of the reasons Brown expressed concern. First, he cites the fact that during six of the years between 2000 and 2009, world grain production was less than consumption, necessitating the use of food reserves.[129] Second, Brown cites the study previously mentioned in this chapter by the National Academy of Sciences, the top science body in the United States, that as temperature increases there will be a significant decrease in rice, wheat, and corn production. Third, Brown notes the falling water tables in China, India, United States and other places that feed the irrigation systems of many major grain producing regions.

Brown also sees the changes to a more Western, meat-centered diet by many people in the world who have recently gained more wealth as being unsustainable. And adding on to that is the recent decision in the United States to use a large part of its corn production to make fuel for its automobiles. This last named action was one of the reasons for the large increase in food prices in world markets and food shortages in the latter part of the first decade of the twenty-first century, that led to food riots in several countries.

Many scientists agree with Brown regarding the dangers to agriculture caused by climate change. Here is what two of them said in a recent article published in the respected American journal *Science*:

In the past, heat waves, drought, and food shortages have hit particular regions. (But the future will be different.) Yields are going to be down everyplace. ... (Heat will be the main culprit). If you look at extreme high temperatures so far observed – basically since agriculture started – the worst summers on record have been mostly because of

heat (not drought). You have to go back at least several million years before you find
… temperatures (comparable to those being predicted).[130]

Conclusions

One of the most fundamental problems many nations face is how to end hunger in their lands. The rapid growth of their populations and the past neglect of agricultural development have resulted in increased suffering in rural areas. Although this may be changing, advances in technology have helped to keep the overall production of food in many poor countries ahead of their increased needs, although it is unclear how technological innovations have impacted traditional household incomes. Widespread poverty in the rural districts as well as in some urban areas has meant that many people cannot afford to purchase the food that is available in the market. An emphasis on agricultural development and on increasing employment in both rural and urban areas is needed in order to provide increased income to larger numbers of the poor.

Rich nations face major food problems also. Here the problems are quite different from those faced by poorer nations. The rich nations need to learn how to produce healthful food and to retain a prosperous agricultural sector, as well as to help make sure their poorest residents are able to obtain affordable and nutritionally adequate meals. Obesity is an increasing problem in some economies where foods high in calories are regularly available.

There are indications some people have increasing concerns about the types of food in the modern diet. Whether this desire for more healthful foods and the awareness of the connection between food and health will spread from a minority to the majority of people is not yet clear. Yet in economic systems where consumers can freely exercise their preferences, the potential exists for important changes to occur fairly rapidly. For example, in the United States the relatively recent awareness of the connection between fatty foods and heart attacks has led to the production of many types of lower fat foods.

The picture regarding the health of the farm economy in some developed countries does not look bright. The United States has not yet learned how to maintain a sustainable, prosperous agricultural sector. Its productive capabilities are impressive but, as this chapter has pointed out, its high dependency on uncertain, polluting, and potentially very costly energy supplies, and its tendency to undermine the land upon which it rests make its future uncertain.

The main factor that makes any conclusions about food so hard to make is the changing climate. A large amount of uncertainty still exists regarding this subject and agriculture, but we know climate and agriculture go together about as closely as any two subjects can. Temperature, rainfall, length and dates of growing seasons, and extreme weather events all directly affect harvests. We must study the scientific facts and predictions of climate change if we are to understand the possibilities for food in our future. We will have an opportunity to do this in the chapter on climate change.

Notes

1 United Nations Development Programme (UNDP), United Nations Environment Programme (UNEP), World Bank, and World Resources Institute (WRI), *A Guide to World Resources 2000–2001* (Washington, DC: WRI, 2000), p. 10.

2 UNDP, UNEP, World Bank, and WRI, *World Resources 2008* (Washington, DC: WRI, 2008), pp. 210–11.

3 UN Food and Agriculture Organization (FAO), "Food Price Index," at http://www.fao.org/worldfoodsituation/foodpricesindex/en (accessed July 2015).

4 World Bank, World Development Indicators, "Cereal Yield," at http://data.worldbank.org/indicator/AG.YLD.CREL.KG (accessed July 2015).

5 FAO, "Countries Requiring External Assistance for Food," at http://www.fao.org/giews/English/hotspots/index.htm (accessed July 2015).

6 FAO, *Crop Prospects and Food Situation*, No. 3 (September 2010), p. 1, at http://www.fao.org/docrep/012/ak354e/ak354e00.pdf (accessed July 2015).

7 FAO, *The State of Food Insecurity in the World 2014*, at http://www.fao.org/3/a-i4030e.pdf; see also FAO, *The State of Food and Agriculture, 2009*, Foreword, at http://www.fao.org/docrep/012/i0680e/i0680e.pdf (both accessed July 2015). In this chapter, "hunger" and "undernourishment" refer to the consumption of insufficient calories, whereas "malnutrition" refers to the lack of some necessary nutrients, usually protein. For the sake of simplicity, this chapter equates hunger with undernourishment and malnutrition.

8 UNDP, UNEP, World Bank, and WRI, *World Resources 2008*, pp. 210–11; see also "Use It and Lose It: The Outsize Effect of U.S. Consumption on the Environment," Earthtalk, *Scientific American* (September 14, 2012), at http://www.scientificamerican.com/article/american-consumption-habits/ (accessed July 2015).

9 According to the World Bank as reported in Celia Dugger, "Report Warns Malnutrition Begins in Cradle," *New York Times*, March 3, 2006, p. A6.

10 World Health Organization (WHO), "Infant and Young Child Feeding," Fact Sheet No. 342, updated July 2015, at http://www.who.int/mediacentre/factsheets/fs342/en/index.html (accessed July 2015).

11 FAO, *The State of Food Insecurity in the World, 2014*, p. 8.

12 FAO, *The State of Food and Agriculture, 2009*, p. 104.

13 FAO, "FAO and the Eight Millennium Development Goals: Goal 1: Eradicate Extreme Poverty and Hunger," Factsheet, 2010.

14 Pedro Sanchez and M. S. Swaminathan, "Cutting World Hunger in Half," *Science*, 307 (January 21, 2005), p. 357; see also World Bank, World Development Indicators, "Rural Poverty Headcount Ratio at National Poverty Lines (% of Rural Population)," at http://data.worldbank.org/indicator/SI.POV.RUHC (accessed July 2015).

15 FAO, "Hunger Map 2014," at www.fao.org/3/a-i4033e.pdf (accessed July 2015).

16 Roy L. Prosterman, "The Decline in Hunger-Related Deaths," *Hunger Project Papers*, No. 1 (San Francisco: Hunger Project, 1984), p. ii.

17 Marc Cohen, "Crop Circles," *Natural History*, 112 (October 2003), p. 64.

18 Brian Halweil, "Grain Harvest and Hunger Both Grow," in Worldwatch Institute, *Vital Signs 2005* (New York: Worldwatch Institute, 2005), p. 22.

19 World Food Program, "Hunger Statistics," at http://www.wfp.org/hunger/stats (accessed July 2015).

20   John R. Tarrant, *Food Policies* (New York: John Wiley, 1980), p. 12.

21   Sanchez and Swaminathan, "Cutting World Hunger in Half," p. 357.

22   Abhijit V. Banergee and Esther Duflo, "The Economic Lives of the Poor," *Journal of Economic Perspectives*, 21 (1) (2007), pp. 141, 167.

23   Celia Dugger, "Report Warns Malnutrition Begins in Cradle," p. A6; Caryn Finkle, "Nestle, Infant Formula, and Excuses: The Regulation of Commercial Advertising in Developing Nations," *Northwestern Journal of International Law and Interests*, 14 (3) (1994), p. 602.

24   WHO, "Infant and Young Child Feeding: Model Chapter for Textbooks for Medical Students and Allied Health Professionals," 2009, Section 1.3, at http://www.who.int/maternal_child_adolescent/documents/9789241597494/en/ (accessed July 2015).

25   Robert Conquest, *The Harvest of Sorrow: Soviet Collectivization and the Terror-Famine* (New York: Oxford University Press, 1986).

26   Jasper Becker, *Hungry Ghosts: Mao's Secret Famine* (New York: Free Press, 1997); and Penny Kane, *Famine in China, 1959–1961: Demographic and Social Implications* (New York: St Martin's Press, 1988).

27   *New York Times*, June 7, 1983, p. 1; John Mellor and Sarah Gavian, "Famine: Causes, Prevention, and Relief," *Science*, 235 (January 1987), p. 539.

28   For a fuller discussion of the causes of the African famines, see Carl K. Eicher, "Facing up to Africa's Food Crisis," *Foreign Affairs*, 61 (Fall 1982), pp. 151–74; a series of articles on Africa in the *Bulletin of the Atomic Scientists*, 41 (September 1985), pp. 21–52; and Michael H. Glantz, "Drought in Africa," *Scientific American*, 256 (June 1987), pp. 34–40.

29   Kavita Pillay, "The Politics of Famine in North Korea," in *Ninth Annual Report on the State of World Hunger 1999* (Silver Spring, MD: Bread for the World Institute, 1998), p. 24; James Brooke, "Food Emergency in North Korea Worsens as Donations Dwindle," *New York Times*, December 5, 2002, p. A16; "North Korea, Facing Food Shortages, Mobilizes Millions from the Cities to Help Rice Farmers," *New York Times*, June 1, 2005, p. A6; Jonathan Cheng, "United Nations' Food Aid Program for North Korea Lacks Donors," *Wall Street Journal*, August 26, 2014, at http://www.wsj.com/articles/united-nations-food-aid-program-for-north-korea-lacks-donors-1409047712 (accessed July 2015).

30   UNDP, *The Millennium Development Goals Report 2014*, at http://www.undp.org/content/dam/undp/library/MDG/english/UNDP_MDGReport_EN_2014Final1.pdf (accessed July 2015).

31   Sanchez and Swaminathan, "Cutting World Hunger in Half," p. 357.

32   WHO and UNICEF, *Global Strategy for Infant and Young Child Feeding* (2003), p. 5, at http://www.who.int/nutrition/publications/infantfeeding/9241562218/en/ (accessed July 2005).

33   WHO, "Micronutrient Deficiencies: Vitamin A Deficiency," at http://www.who.int/nutrition/topics/vad/en/ (accessed July 2015).

34   As reported by the UN World Food Programme in "Types of Malnutrition," at http://www.wfp.org/hunger/malnutrition/types (accessed July 2015).

35   As quoted in *A Shift in the Wind*, Hunger Project Papers, No. 15 (San Francisco), p. 4.

36   C. Peter Timmer, "Unbalanced Bounty from America's Farms," *Science*, 298 (November 15, 2002), p. 1339.

37 National Research Council, *Toward Sustainable Agricultural Systems in the 21st Century* (Washington, DC: National Academies Press, 2010), pp. 43–4.

38 Raymond Hopkins, Robert Paarlberg, and Mitchel Wallerstein, *Food in the Global Arena* (New York: Holt, Rinehart & Winston, 1982), p. 102.

39 William Ophuls, *Ecology and the Politics of Scarcity* (San Francisco: W. H. Freeman, 1977), pp. 42–3. The energy expended in modern agriculture is mainly nonhuman energy, of course, and most people consider that to be one of modern agriculture's most attractive features.

40 Peter Farb and George Armelagos, *Consuming Passions: The Anthropology of Eating* (Boston: Houghton Mifflin, 1980), p. 69.

41 Peter Gleick, "The Water to Grow Beef," blog post, May 5, 2009, at http://blog.sfgate.com/gleick/2009/05/05/the-water-to-grow-beef/ (accessed July 2015).

42 Farb and Armelagos, *Consuming Passions*, pp. 69–70.

43 Barbara Ward, *Progress for a Small Planet* (New York: W. W. Norton, 1979), p. 92.

44 National Research Council, *Toward Sustainable Agricultural Systems*, pp. 45–8.

45 FAOSTAT, "Food and Agricultural Commodities Production," at http://faostat.fao.org/site/339/default.aspx (accessed July 2015).

46 Larry Rohter, "South America Seeks to Fill the World's Table," *New York Times*, December 12, 2004, p. 1.

47 James Hansen and Fred Gale, "China in the Next Decade: Rising Meat Demand and Growing Imports of Feed," April 7, 2014, at http://www.ers.usda.gov/amber-waves/2014-april/china-in-the-next-decade-rising-meat-demand-and-growing-imports-of-feed.aspx#.VQIOidLF_HU (accessed July 2015)

48 Jim Yardley, "China Races to Reverse Its Falling Production of Grain," *New York Times*, May 2, 2004, p. 6.

49 Julian Parfitt, Mark Barthel, and Sarah Macnaughton, "Food Waste within Food Supply Chains: Quantification and Potential for Change to 2050," *Philosophical Transactions of the Royal Society: Biological Science*, 365 (September 2010), pp. 3065–81, Table 6

50 FAO, *Global Food Losses and Food Waste: Extent, Causes and Prevention* (Rome: FAO, 2011), Executive Summary.

51 Julian Parfitt et al., "Food Waste within Food Supply Chains," Table 6.

52 Ibid.

53 Philip Brasor, "Japan Loves Wasting Food," *Japan Times*, March 1, 2009.

54 FAO, *Global Food Losses and Food Waste*, Executive Summary.

55 Jocelyn Kaiser, "Wounding Earth's Fragile Skin," *Science*, 304 (June 11, 2004), p. 1616.

56 Bill McKibben, "A Special Moment in History," *Atlantic Monthly*, 281 (May 1998), p. 60.

57 William Stevens, "Sprawl Quickens Its Attack on Forests," *New York Times*, December 7, 1999. See also US Department of Agriculture (USDA), Natural Resources Conservation Service, "Soil Erosion on Cropland 2007," at http://www.nrcs.usda.gov/wps/portal/nrcs/detail/national/technical/nra/nri/?cid=stelprdb1041887 (accessed July 2015).

58 FAO, Terrastat database, "World Human-Induced Land Degradation Due to Agricultural Activities."

59 Ibid.

60 WRI, UNEP, UNDP, and World Bank, *World Resources 1998–99: A Guide to the Global Environment* (New York: Oxford University Press, 1998), p. 158.

61 Kaiser, "Wounding Earth's Fragile Skin," pp. 1616–17.

62 USDA, "Soil Erosion on Cropland 2007."

63 Kaiser, "Wounding Earth's Fragile Skin," p. 1618.

64 WRI, UNEP, UNDP, and World Bank, *World Resources 1998–99*, p. 158.

65 Elizabeth Becker, "Two Acres of Farm Lost to Sprawl Each Minute, New Study Says," *New York Times*, October 4, 2002, p. A19.

66 Stevens, "Sprawl Quickens Its Attack on Forests."

67 FAO, *The State of Food and Agriculture, 2009*, p. 11.

68 The consumption of meat (and, also, milk from cows and goats) can make nutritional sense. Cows and sheep, for example, can consume grasses, which people are unable to digest, in places where the climate or the condition of the land makes the growing of crops impossible.

69 Paul Ehrlich, Anne Ehrlich, and John Holdren, *Ecoscience: Population, Resources, Environment* (San Francisco: W. H. Freeman, 1977), p. 315.

70 FAO, *The State of Food and Agriculture, 2009*, p. 29.

71 Bill Marsh, "The Evolving World Diet," *New York Times*, August 20, 2002, p. D4.

72 Ward, *Progress for a Small Planet*, pp. 93–4.

73 Erica Goode, "The Gorge-Yourself Environment," *New York Times*, July 22, 2003, pp. D1, D7; and Anahad O'Connor, "Study Details 30-Year Increase in Calorie Consumption," *New York Times*, February 6, 2004, p. A19.

74 Bottle-feeding became more common in the United States than breast-feeding sometime between 1940 and 1955. A lack of good data makes it difficult to pin this down any further.

75 Because the HIV virus that causes AIDS can be transmitted from the mother to the baby through breast milk, it is recommended that mothers infected with the virus bottle-feed their babies. For a discussion of the advantages of breast-feeding for the baby and the mother see Meredith F. Small, "Our Babies, Ourselves," *Natural History*, 106 (October 1997), pp. 42–51.

76 UNICEF, "Breastfeeding," at http://www.unicef.org/nutrition/index_24824.html (accessed July 2015), citing *The Lancet*, 2008.

77 *New York Times*, December 17, 1982, p. 8.

78 Lizette Alvarez, "Norway Leads Industrial Nations Back to Breast-Feeding," *New York Times*, October 21, 2003, at http://www.nytimes.com/2003/10/21/world/norway-leads-industrial-nations-back-to-breast-feeding.html (accessed July 2015); M. A. McDowell, C.-Y. Wang, and J. Kennedy-Stephenson, "Breastfeeding in the United States: Findings from the National Health and Nutrition Examination Surveys 1999–2006," NCHS Data Briefs, No. 5 (Hyattsville, MD: National Center for Health Statistics, 2008).

79 Dugger, "Report Warns Malnutrition Begins in Cradle," p. A6; Finkle, "Nestle, Infant Formula, and Excuses," p. 602.

80 Calculated using data from the USDA Foreign Agricultural Service: Production, Supply, and Distribution online database, at http://apps.fas.usda.gov/psdonline/psdQuery.aspx (accessed July 2015).

81 R. E. Evenson and D. Gollin, "Assessing the Impact of the Green Revolution, 1960 to 2000," *Science*, 300 (May 2, 2003), p. 761.

82 Lester Brown, "Could Food Shortages Bring Down Civilization?" *Scientific American*, 300 (May 2009), p. 55. See also Keith Bradsher and Andrew Martin, "Crop Research Is

Neglected, and Third World Pays Price," *New York Times*, May 18, 2008, p. 12; Mark Welch, "World Grain Production: Keeping up with Demand," *Abilene Reporter-News*, January 18, 2015, at http://www.reporternews.com/business/agriculture/world-grain-production-keeping-up-with-demand_60766794 (accessed July 2015).

83 Somini Sengupta, "India's Growth Outstrips Crops," *New York Times*, June 22, 2008, p. 10.

84 USDA Foreign Agricultural Service, Global Agricultural Information Network (GAIN) Report: *India: Grain and Feed Annual, 2014*, at http://gain.fas.usda.gov/Recent% 20GAIN%20Publications/Grain%20and%20Feed%20Annual_New%20Delhi_India_2-14-2014.pdf (accessed July 2015).

85 Richard Kerr, "Northern India's Ground Water Is Going, Going, Going …" *Science*, 325 (August 14, 2009), p. 798.

86 Brown, "Could Food Shortages Bring Down Civilization?" p. 54.

87 Evenson and Gollin, "Assessing the Impact of the Green Revolution, 1960 to 2000," p. 762.

88 David Vaccari, "Phosphorus: A Looming Crisis," *Scientific American*, 300 (June 2009), p. 57. See also Robert Diaz and Rutger Rosenberg, "Spreading Dead Zones and Consequences for Marine Ecosystems," *Science*, 321 (August 15, 2008), pp. 926–9.

89 WHO, *Public Health Impact of Pesticides Used in Agriculture* (Geneva: WHO, 1990), p. 86.

90 WRI, *World Resources 1992–1993* (New York: Oxford University Press, 1992), p. 97.

91 World Development Indicators, "Agricultural Irrigated Land (Percent of Total Agricultural Land)," at http://data.worldbank.org/indicator/AG.LND.IRIG.AG.ZS/countries (accessed July 2015).

92 William Bender and Margaret Smith, "Population, Food, and Nutrition," *Population Bulletin*, 51 (February 1997), p. 33.

93 "Reseeding the Green Revolution," *Science*, 277 (August 22, 1997), p. 1041.

94 Jimin Li, Yeyun Xin, and Longping Yuan, "Hybrid Rice Technology Development: Ensuring China's Food Security", IFPRI Discussion Paper 00918, International Food Policy Research Institute, November 2009, at http://www.ifpri.org/sites/default/files/publications/ifpridp00918.pdf (accessed July 2015).

95 International Rice Research Institute, "China," at http://irri.org/our-work/locations/china (accessed July 2015).

96 Xinhua, "China to Finish Work on New Hybrid Rice in 2012," *China Daily*, October 26, 2010.

97 Ward, *Progress for a Small Planet*, p. 178.

98 Nancy E. Riley, "China's Population: New Trends and Challenges," *Population Bulletin*, 59 (June 2004), pp. 25–6; and Yardley, "China Races to Reverse Its Falling Production of Grain."

99 Dexter Roberts, "China Aims for Food Security as Pollution Destroys Crop Land," Bloomberg Business, January 21, 2014, at: http://www.bloomberg.com/bw/articles/2014-01-21/china-aims-for-food-security-as-pollution-destroys-crop-land; Ministry of Agriculture of the People's Republic of China, "No. 1 Central Document Targets Rural Reform", January 20, 2014, at http://english.agri.gov.cn/news/dqnf/201401/t20140120_21064.htm (both accessed July 2015).

100 Ministry of Agriculture of the People's Republic of China, "No. 1 Central Document targets Rural Reform."

101 Lucy Hornby, "China Scythes Self Sufficiency Policy," *Financial Times*, February 11, 2015.

102 Elizabeth Becker, "Far from Dead, Subsidies Fuel Big Farms," *New York Times*, May 14, 2001, p. A12; see also Alexei Barrionuevo, "Mountains of Corn and a Sea of Farm Subsidies," *New York Times*, November 9, 2005, p. A1.

103 Brown, "Could Food Shortages Bring Down Civilization?" p. 53.

104 Intergovernmental Panel on Climate Change, *Fifth Assessment Report: Adaptation, a Summary for Policy-Makers* (Geneva: IPCC, 2014), p. 5.

105 Ibid., p. 4.

106 Brown, "Could Food Shortages Bring Down Civilization?"

107 Vaclav Smil, *Feeding the World: A Challenge for the Twenty-First Century* (Cambridge, MA: MIT Press, 2000), pp. 36–9.

108 William Ophuls, *Ecology and the Politics of Scarcity* (San Francisco: W. H. Freeman, 1977), p. 54.

109 WRI, *World Resources 1992–1993*, p. 100. See also John P. Reganold, Robert I. Papendick, and James F. Parr, "Sustainable Agriculture," *Scientific American*, 262 (June 1990), p. 112. A fuller description of alternative agriculture is contained in National Resource Council, *Alternative Agriculture* (Washington, DC: National Academy Press, 1989).

110 USDA, National Organic Program website, at http://www.ams.usda.gov/AMSv1.0/nop (accessed July 2015).

111 USDA, National Organic Program: Organic Certification Cost Share Programs, at http://www.ams.usda.gov/AMSv1.0/NOPCostSharing (accessed July 2015).

112 Catherine Greene, "Growth Patterns in the US Organic Industry," *Amber Waves* (October 24, 2013), at http://www.ers.usda.gov/amber-waves/2013-october/growth-patterns-in-the-us-organic-industry.aspx#.VQIsW9LF_HU// (accessed July 2015).

113 Erik Stokstad, "Organic Farms Reap Many Benefits," *Science*, 296 (May 31, 2002), p. 1589; see also James Conca, "It's Final – Corn Ethanol Is of No Use," Forbes, April 20, 2014, at http://www.forbes.com/sites/jamesconca/2014/04/20/its-final-corn-ethanol-is-of-no-use/ (accessed July 2015).

114 David Pimentel, "Changing Genes to Feed the World," *Science*, 306 (October 29, 2004), p. 815.

115 Carol Kaesuk Yoon, "Simple Method Found to Increase Crop Yields Vastly," *New York Times*, August 22, 2000, p. D1. See also Dennis Normile, "Variety Spices up Chinese Rice Yields," *Science*, 289 (August 18, 2000), pp. 1122–3.

116 *New York Times*, December 27, 1988, p. 17.

117 Mary Lou Guerinot, "The Green Revolution Strikes Gold," *Science*, 287 (January 14, 2000), pp. 241–3.

118 "Adoption of Genetically Engineered Crops in the U.S.," USDA data set, at http://www.ers.usda.gov/Data/BiotechCrops (accessed July 2015).

119 David Barboza, "Development of Biotech Crops Is Booming in Asia," *New York Times*, February 21, 2003, p. A3.

120 Nicholas Wade, "Experts Say They Have Key to Rice Genes," *New York Times*, April 5, 2002, p. A19. For more on the scientific significance of this event see Ronald Cantrell and Timothy Reeves, "The Cereal of the World's Poor Takes Center Stage," and Dennis Normile and Elizabeth Pennisi, "Rice: Boiled Down to Bare Essentials," both *Science*, 296 (April 5, 2002), pp. 53, 32–6.

121 See Carol K. Yoon and Melody Peterson, "Cautious Support on Biotech Foods by Science Panel," *New York Times*, April 6, 2000, p. A1; Andrew Revkin, "Panel Urges US to Tighten Approval of Gene-Altered Crops," *New York Times*, February 22, 2002, p. A18; and Andrew Pollack, "No Foolproof Way Is Seen to Contain Altered Genes," *New York Times*, January 21, 2004, p. A10.

122 Worldwatch Institute, *Vital Signs 2005*, p. 26.

123 WRI, UNEP, UNDP, and World Bank, *World Resources 1998–99*, p. 196.

124 FAO, *The State of Food and Agriculture, 2005* (Rome: FAO, 2005), p. 134.

125 Ibid.

126 William Greer, "Public Taste and US Aid Spur Fish Farming," *New York Times*, October 29, 1986, p. 1.

127 Wilfred Vuillaume, "Escapes from Norway's Fish Farms Threaten Wild Salmon," Agence France-Presse, January 19, 2007, at http://www.spacedaily.com/reports/Escapes_From_Norways_Fish_Farms_Threaten_Wild_Salmon_999.html (accessed July 2015).

128 Erik Stokstad, "Engineered Fish: Friend or Foe of the Environment?" *Science*, 297 (September 13, 2002), p. 1797.

129 Brown, "Could Food Shortages Bring Down Civilization?", p. 50.

130 Constance Holden, "Climate Change: Higher Temperatures Seen Reducing Global Harvests," *Science*, 323 (January 9, 2009), pp. 193–4.

Further Reading

Brown, Lester R., *Full Planet, Empty Plates: The New Geopolitics of Food Scarcity* (New York: W. W. Norton & Co., 2012). Brown believes that present policies and human demands are undermining the Earth's capacity to provide enough food for an expanding population. He recommends a number of steps that could be taken to change this situation.

Gardner, Bruce L., *American Agriculture in the Twentieth Century: How It Flourished and What It Cost* (Cambridge, MA: Harvard University Press, 2002). This book has been called a definitive history. There is a tension in the book between the story of the amazing growth of productivity in American farms and the story of how that growth came about and who benefits from it.

Jacobson, Michael E., and the Staff of the Center for Science in the Public Interest, *Six Arguments for a Greener Diet: How a More Plant-Based Diet Could Save Your Health and the Environment* (Washington, DC: Center for Science in the Public Interest, 2006). This book argues a diet with less meat would reduce chronic diseases, reduce foodborne illnesses, benefit the soil, water, and air, and reduce animal suffering.

Nestle, Marion, *Food Politics: How the Food Industry Influences Nutrition and Health*, re. edn (Berkeley: University of California Press, 2013). Nestle, a professor in the Department of Nutrition and Food Science at New York University, seeks to show how the food industry, in order to increase its profits, works to encourage people to eat more, thus contributing to the obesity epidemic.

Pollan, Michael, *The Omnivore's Dilemma: A Natural History of Four Meals* (New York: Penguin Press, 2006). Written like a novel, this is a very interesting book. But it's not written by a novelist. Rather the author is a professor of environmental and science journalism at the University of California, Berkeley, one of the top universities in the United States. Pollan traces three very different diets from Earth to the plate: the industrial (the diet of most Americans), the organic, and the hunter-gatherer.

Postel, Sandra, "Growing More Food with Less Water," *Scientific American,* 284 (February 2001), pp. 46–51. With the population expanding and the climate getting warmer we will need to grow more food with less water. Postel shows how it can be done.

Pringle, Peter, *Food, Inc.: Mendel to Monsanto – the Promises and Perils of the Biotech Harvest* (New York: Simon & Schuster, 2003). A balanced account of a controversial subject, Pringle criticizes the extreme claims of both the biotech companies and the environmental critics.

Roberts, Paul, *The End of Food* (New York: Houghton-Mifflin/Bloomsbury, 2008). Roberts, the author of the best-selling book *The End of Oil,* argues that the globalization of our food supply and the increasing popularity of the Western-style diet has driven our food system out of balance. Roberts believes system-wide collapse is possible and recommends ways it might be prevented.

Ronald, Pamela C., and Raoul W. Adamchak, *Tomorrow's Table: Organic Farming, Genetics, and the Future of Food* (New York: Oxford University Press, 2008). This unique book presents the positive aspects of both organic agriculture and genetic engineering. The authors show how the two approaches can be used together to help solve our present food crisis.

Runge, C. Ford, Benjamin Senauer, Philip Pardey, and Mark Rosegrant, *Ending Hunger in Our Lifetime: Food Security and Globalization* (Baltimore: Johns Hopkins Press, 2003). In the first part of the book the authors discuss the difficulties we will face in the effort to end hunger during our lives. In the second part the authors give their solutions.

Chapter 4

Energy

The Energy-Climate Crisis	130
Energy and security	132
Government Responses to the Energy-Climate Crisis	133
The United States	134
Western Europe	136
Japan	136
China	138
The Effect of the Energy-Climate Crisis on Countries' Development Plans	140
The Relationship between Energy Use and Development	141
A shift in types of energy	141
Increased use	142
The decoupling of energy consumption and economic growth	142
The Energy Transition	147
Nonrenewable energy sources	147
Renewable energy sources	148
Conservation/energy efficiency	155
Nuclear Power: A Case Study	157
The potential and the peril	158
The choice	161
Withdraw support for nuclear power	161
Continue to support nuclear power	163
Conclusions	164
Notes	165
Further Reading	169

Global Issues: An Introduction, Fifth Edition. Kristen A. Hite and John L. Seitz.
© 2016 John Wiley & Sons, Ltd. Published 2016 by John Wiley & Sons, Ltd.

*A human being, a skyscraper, an automobile, and a blade of grass all represent
energy that has been transformed from one state to another.*

Jeremy Rifkin, *Entropy* (1980)

The Energy-Climate Crisis

Are we running out of energy? Of course not. Everything is made out of energy,
and, as college students learn when they study the laws of thermodynamics in their
introductory physics courses, energy cannot be destroyed. These laws also state that
energy cannot be created: all we can do is to transform it from one state to another.
And when energy is transformed, or in other words, when it is used for some work,
the energy is changed from a more useful to a less useful form. All types of energy
eventually end up as low-grade heat. A "law" in the physical sciences means that
there are no exceptions to it, and there are none to the laws of thermodynamics.[1]

So if everything is energy and energy cannot be destroyed, why is there an energy
crisis? The crisis has come because of the other laws, the laws that tell us that energy
cannot be created, and that, once used, it is transformed into a less usable form. At
present, the industrialized world relies on a very versatile, although polluting, fuel –
carbon, especially in the form of oil for transport and coal for electricity.

Countries are facing an energy crisis because they can no longer depend on abundant supplies of cheap energy from traditional sources, which generate massive
emissions of carbon dioxide (CO_2) and other pollutants. Unprecedented economic
growth and material prosperity took place in the United States during the 1950s
and 1960s, and this was made possible, in part, by cheap energy. Largely by default,
this became the "model" for development, where individual lifestyles and modes of
industrial production were based on plentiful, inexpensive, polluting energy.

Oil is being consumed at prodigious rates – about 90 million barrels a day were
produced in 2013.[2] Yet its supply is controlled by a limited set of producers, and its
price has fluctuated greatly. Table 4.1 shows this fact as well as any set of figures can,
as it focuses on the changes in the price of gasoline in the United States from 1950
to 2009. The table also helps us understand another important feature of the energy
crisis, especially as it has affected the United States. The period of cheap gasoline was
a relatively long one, and people in the United States got used to having an economy
based upon inexpensive petroleum products.[3] When oil prices skyrocketed in the
1970s, the shock to the US economy and to the economies of many other countries
was profound.

The first oil shock took place in 1973 and 1974. The 1973 Arab–Israeli war led a
number of Arab oil-producing countries to stop shipping oil to the United States and
other countries allied with Israel. American motorists lined up at gas stations, vying
for limited supplies. The Organization of Petroleum Exporting Countries (OPEC),
of which most oil-exporting nations are members, seized the opportunity to raise oil
prices significantly, and prices quadrupled.

The second oil shock came in 1979 and 1980. The event that prompted this shock
was the Iranian Revolution and the ousting of the Shah as the head of the Iranian

Table 4.1 US gasoline prices, 1950–2009

Year	*Retail price per gallon of regular gas ($)*
1950	0.27
1960	0.31
1970	0.36
1980	1.21
1990	1.16
2000	1.69
2009	2.35

Sources: Data from "Dollars and : Sense, July–August 1980," in Kenneth Dolbeare, *American Public Policy* (New York: McGraw-Hill, 1982), p. 113; *The World Almanac and Book of Facts 2006* (New York: World Almanac Books, 2006), p. 138; US Energy Administration, *Monthly Energy Review* (October 2010), p. 122.

government. Iranian oil shipments to the United States stopped, but the real shock came when OPEC doubled its prices. Many North Americans had refused to believe there was a real energy crisis after the first oil shock and had returned to their normal high consumption of petroleum products after the Arab embargo was lifted; but the second oil shock convinced most people that there was indeed an energy crisis. While many had blamed either US oil companies or the US government for creating the first oil crisis, the second shock clearly demonstrated that something had fundamentally changed in the world. What became apparent to many now was that the United States, and most other developed nations, were dependent on one section of the world for a significant part of their energy, and that they could no longer control events in that part of the world.

The large increases in the price of oil made by OPEC in the 1970s led to a massive transfer of wealth from the developed nations to part of the developing world. In the words of one commentator, "It may represent the quickest massive transfer of wealth among societies since the Spanish Conquistadores seized the Incan gold stores some four centuries ago."[4] Higher oil prices led to low economic growth, higher inflation, big trade deficits, and increased unemployment in the United States and other developed nations. Although developing nations use much less oil than do the developed nations, the cost of their imported oil also went up and caused some of them to acquire huge debts to pay for the oil they needed. Daniel Yergin, the coeditor of an important report on energy from Harvard Business School, assessed the potential consequences of the oil shocks in the following terms:

> The unhappy set of economic circumstances set in motion by the oil shocks contains the potential for far-reaching crises. In the industrial nations, high inflation, low growth, and high unemployment can erode the national consensus and undermine the stability and legitimacy of the political system. In the developing world, zero growth leads to misery and upheavals. Protectionism and accumulation of debt threaten the international trade and payments system. And, of course, there is the tinder of international politics, particularly involving the Middle East, where political and social

upheavals can cause major oil disruptions and where fears about and threats to energy supplies can lead to war.[5]

Energy and security

The third oil shock came in 1990 and 1991. Iraq invaded Kuwait and threatened Saudi Arabia. In order to prevent Iraq from becoming the dominant power in the Middle East and having significant influence on the production and pricing of oil from that region, the United States led a coalition of forces in driving Iraq out of Kuwait. The war, which lasted just six weeks, involved half a million US soldiers and token troops from other nations. A huge, sustained air attack on Iraqi forces in Kuwait and Iraq and on military facilities in Iraq (including on plants for poisonous gas and nuclear weapons) preceded the ground attack. The allied forces had few casualties, but the retreating Iraqi forces, which suffered large casualties, sabotaged more than 700 oil wells in Kuwait, setting about 600 on fire.

The United States persuaded other developed nations, including Japan, to contribute about $50 billion to help pay for the war. The United States spent about $10 billion for short-term costs. The war and its subsequent damage to their lands and economies cost all the Arab states an estimated $600 billion.[6] The price of oil increased dramatically right after the Iraqi invasion of Kuwait, but by the end of the war the price had dropped back to the prewar level. That price did not reflect the real cost of oil, which should have included the cost of the war. (It has been estimated that by the mid-1980s the United States was spending seven times as much keeping the shipping lanes open to the Middle East oil fields as it was for the oil itself.)[7]

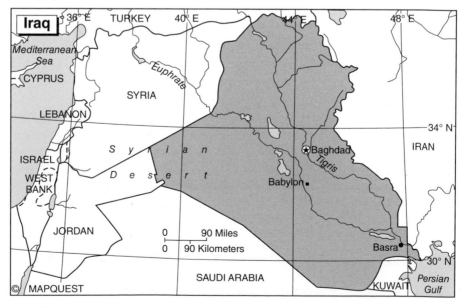

Map 4.1 Iraq

In 2003 the United States invaded Iraq and conquered the country after a relatively short war. Its main public reason for doing so was to destroy weapons of mass destruction, which the United States claimed Iraq possessed. No weapons of mass destruction were ever found and the United States later stated that faulty intelligence led it to believe Iraq had such weapons. A few allies of the United States supported the invasion – mainly the United Kingdom – with relatively small military forces, but the invasion was opposed by most nations of the world. It created intense hostility toward the United States in the Arab world. Many nations believed the main reason for the war was to help the United States secure its sources of oil, although some believed that President George W. Bush had personal reasons for wanting to depose the Iraqi president Saddam Hussein.

The Middle East, which supplies much of the oil imported into the United States and Western Europe, is a politically unstable area. It is torn by regional conflicts, religious conflicts, social and ideological conflicts, and, in the past, by East–West competition. A large amount of the oil involved in international trade is carried on ships that must pass through a single strait in the Persian Gulf – the Strait of Hormuz.

The United States has historically been the largest buyer of oil in the world. In the past, much of it came from a single country, Saudi Arabia. Over the past two decades, China became the fastest growing oil market in the world, buying more oil from Saudi Arabia than the United States. But that growth seems to have slowed in tandem with overall economic growth.[8] Many Western European countries are even more dependent on imported oil than the United States, as is Japan, the industrialized country most dependent on imported oil, producing virtually no oil itself and having few other domestic sources of energy.

This section has focused on the oil crisis, which has affected mainly the industrialized nations. But that is not the full story of the energy crisis that the world faces. Billions of people use very few fossil fuels at all, relying mainly on wood, charcoal, cow dung, and crop residues for cooking fuel and for heat. In Africa alone, 730 million people use traditional sources of energy.[9] The shortage of firewood in the south of the African continent is increasing as population growth has caused consumption of wood to exceed the growth of new supplies in many areas.

Now, due to climate change, experts are predicting that unless a breakthrough technology enables fossil fuels to be burned with dramatically lower carbon emissions, much of the existing oil reserves will need to remain untapped if the world is going to avoid catastrophic climate changes. So not only does the price of oil impact energy-intensive economies, but the availability and price of substitutes of cleaner energy sources present new challenges to conventional development pathways.

Government Responses to the Energy-Climate Crisis

Let us look at a few key countries and regions to see how their governments have responded to the energy crisis.

Plate 4.1 Shortage of wood is a part of the energy crisis, since many urban dwellers in developing nations rely on wood as their major source of fuel

Source: Ab Abercrombie.

The United States

The US energy sector remains overwhelmingly dependent on oil and coal, but that is starting to change as natural gas (particularly due to fracking, see Chapter 8) and renewable energy take up an increasing percentage of the market share, in part due to efforts to limit carbon dioxide emissions associated with climate change. In 2013, 36 percent of US energy came from oil, 27 percent from natural gas, 19 percent from coal (down 5 percent since 2008), 10 percent from renewable sources, and 8 percent from nuclear electric power.[10]

Historically, the United States has lacked a coherent energy policy, although a number of laws dealing with the crisis have been passed, and in 2015 the US Environmental Protection Agency announced a suite of new regulations for coal-fired power plants and other energy sources. In 1971 President Richard Nixon called for "Project Independence" to make the United States self-sufficient in energy by 1980, and in the late 1970s President Jimmy Carter stated that the energy crisis should be considered the "moral equivalent of war." By 2013, the United States was the world's biggest producer of oil (see Table 4.2), although about 40 percent of the oil consumed in the United States was still imported.[11] In 2010 the United States imported most of its oil from Canada, followed by Mexico, Saudi Arabia, Venezuela, and

Table 4.2 Top world oil producers, 2013

	Country	*Production(thousand barrels per day)*
1	United States	12,343
2	Saudi Arabia	11,702
3	Russia	10,764
4	China	4,459
5	Canada	4,074
6	United Arab Emirates	3,441
7	Iran	3,192
8	Iraq	3,058
9	Mexico	2,908
10	Kuwait	2,812
11	Brazil	2,694
12	Venezuela	2,689
13	Nigeria	2,372
14	Qatar	2,067
15	Angola	1,889

Source: United States Energy Information Agency (2015).

Nigeria – in that order. Meanwhile, government agencies at the federal and state levels began supporting policies to increase energy efficiency, reduce carbon emissions, and promote lower-carbon fuels. But despite these efforts, oil and coal have dominated US energy sources.

Why has it been so difficult for the United States to enact an effective policy to deal with the crisis? Part of the reason is that the inertia of an oil- and coal-intensive infrastructure is hard to overcome. The nation is used to abundance, in energy as well as in material goods, and the creation of a new outlook and new values is not easy. Also very large economic interests, such as those of the oil companies, benefit from the status quo and use their huge financial resources to influence government policy on energy. They spend large amounts in elections supporting favored candidates, benefiting from a 2010 US Supreme Court decision removing certain limits on campaign funding by corporations, unions, and others.

The cost of oil in the United States, in one sense, remains very low. Gasoline, for example, is about half the price in the United States as in Europe. What this means is that the "real," or true, cost of oil is not indicated by its price and thus consumers in the United States feel no urgency in demanding – or the government in producing – an energy policy that would break the dominance of oil in their society. As shown by some energy analysts, the real cost of oil would have to reflect not only the military costs necessary to secure it, but also the costs of the environmental degradation it causes – such as the effect it is having on the Earth's climate. Factoring in the full cost of oil would include not only military and climate costs but also the increased healthcare costs associated with the burning of petroleum, and the subsidies by the government to the oil industry.

The International Center for Technology Assessment once estimated that if the price of gasoline reflected all the environmental, military, and health costs of using it and subsidies to the oil industry, its price would be at least $14 a gallon.[12] Gasoline sales taxes can be used to cover some of these hidden costs – which otherwise are borne by the whole society in their general taxes and in healthcare costs – but the tax on gasoline in the United States has historically been much lower than that in other major industrialized nations.[13] In March of 2015 the typical price of a gallon of gasoline in the United States was under $3, approximately half of the price in many European countries.[14] But factoring out taxes, consumers in the United States paid more for gasoline ($2.47/gallon before taxes) than in Europe (closer to $2 per gallon pretax).

In 2007 Congress passed an energy law setting higher fuel efficiency standards for cars and supporting more US-produced biofuels for automobiles, mainly from corn, for the domestic market. Vehicles in the United States consume about 40 percent of its oil consumption. And beyond fuel standards, by 2015 national and federal initiatives were underway to limit carbon dioxide emissions from key sources such as power plants.[15]

Western Europe

Most Western European countries are more dependent on imported oil than is the United States, although oil/liquid fuel consumption is projected to decline slightly in the coming decades.[16] Traditionally, European governments have let the prices for imported fuel go up as determined by the world market and have tried to encourage energy conservation through the use of high taxes. France has emphasized nuclear power as its response to the energy crisis, and by 2012 it was producing about 83 percent of its electricity from that source – one of the highest rates in the world.[17] The discovery of oil and natural gas under the North Sea aided mainly Norway and Britain. This large deposit allowed Britain to be self-sufficient in oil for several decades, but production peaked in 1999 and has been declining since then. By 2004 Britain was importing more oil than it exported.[18] In 2012, 33 percent of Britain's energy came from natural gas, 37 percent from petroleum, 16 percent from coal, and 14 percent from nuclear and renewable and other sources, which tripled between 2000 and 2012.[19] Norway, which is a major oil producer at the global level, nevertheless generates nearly all of its electricity from lower-emitting hydropower.[20] In 2005 Finland began constructing one of the world's largest nuclear reactors, but that project has encountered many delays. The Finns were concerned with the growing threat of global warming, their increasing dependence on unreliable areas for oil and natural gas, and high and volatile energy prices.

Japan

Japan has no significant oil, natural gas, or coal deposits and, as stated above, in the mid-1970s it was the most vulnerable of all industrialized countries to OPEC's actions. A consensus quickly developed, after the first oil shock in 1973, that Japan's dependency on oil must be reduced. The government encouraged conservation and increased efficiency in using energy and the people responded. By the end of the first decade of the twenty-first century Japan had reduced its dependency on oil from about three-quarters of its energy consumed in the mid-1970s to less than one-half.[21]

It is interesting to note some of the differences between Japanese and US societies that have undoubtedly affected their different responses to the energy crisis. Because of their history and their limited land and resources, the Japanese have always assumed scarcity and insecurity of resources such as fuel, whereas the Americans have been accustomed to abundance and have assumed it will continue. Japanese industries have been traditionally more willing than their US counterparts to make long-term investments, the American companies often being more concerned with making short-term profits. The Japanese know that their goods must compete well in international trade if they are to maintain their high living standards. Japan is used to change and adaptation. The consensus that developed in Japan after 1973 emphasized a shift from consumption to restraint. It included a belief that the economy had to shift to "knowledge intensive" industries that use relatively little energy, and that energy efficiency was the key element in the adjustment the country needed to make to this new situation. It moved quickly into knowledge-based and electronic and computer-based industries.

Japan made significant progress in the period between the oil shocks in the 1970s and the third one in 1990 and 1991. By 1990 the energy efficiency of the Japanese economy had improved to such an extent that the production of goods and services took only one-half the energy it took in the late 1970s.[22] The increased efficiency in the automobile and steel industries came after the government set ambitious goals for them to reach.

Another action taken by the government after the early crises was to build large oil storage facilities. By the early twenty-first century, Japan had nearly six months' supply of oil in storage tanks, more than any other nation. The country also sought to diversify its sources of oil, and was successful for a while, but it has consistently relied on imported oil to supply much of its energy demands, with the vast majority (over 80 percent) supplied from the Middle East.[23] In 2013 the mix of Japan's energy sources was as follows: 44 percent oil, 27 percent coal, 22 percent natural gas, 1 percent nuclear, and 6 percent hydroelectric and other renewables.[24]

The Japanese government made nuclear power one of the key parts of its plans to reduce its dependency on imported oil. In 2007 Japan had 55 operating nuclear power plants. Japan also planned to build a number of fast-breeder reactors to reduce its dependency on imported uranium, and in the early 1990s it began importing plutonium from France (recycled from spent uranium fuel from Japanese power plants) for those reactors. By the early 2000s Japan had spent tens of billions on developing fast-breeder reactors that use plutonium as a fuel and, in theory, produce more nuclear fuel than they burn.

In 1999, because of human error, an uncontrolled chain reaction occurred in a Japanese nuclear fuel plant. Two people were killed and thousands were exposed to moderate levels of radiation. Safety concerns were again raised in 2002 when allegations were made that the largest privately owned electric utility in Japan was guilty of numerous serious safety violations in operating its nuclear power plants. Safety concerns, which include concerns with the aging of many of Japan's 55 nuclear plants, were beginning to erode the public's confidence in the safety of nuclear power.[25]

In 2011 a tsunami (tidal wave) caused the cooling systems of a group of nuclear reactors in northeast Japan to fail. This led to the release of large amounts of radiation into the air and sea and to the evacuation of nearby residents. As a result of the Fukushima disaster, Japan's energy mix has changed substantially. After the disaster, Japan's use of liquid fuels – such as petroleum – for energy generation increased by 22 percent in one year alone.[26] And by 2013, nuclear had declined to only 1 percent of Japan's total energy supply, 90 percent decrease below pre-tsunami levels.[27]

China

Although China's energy situation is not typical because of its vast reserves of coal, it does have a typical problem: how to provide a growing population with enough fuel in a manner that does not seriously harm the environment. China's population is so large, and its economy is transitioning at such a rapid pace, that its demand for energy is huge. In 2009 it overtook the United States as the largest total user of energy; China is also already the world's biggest importer of coal.[28] Beyond electricity use, the transportation sector accounts for much of China's projected growth in energy consumption. Other parts of Asia are expected to follow suit.[29]

In 2011, coal supplied 69 percent of China's energy demand. Despite a considerable commitment to increase renewable energy use, its current use of coal – the most polluting fossil fuel–is now having a significant effect on the world's environment. By 2010, China was burning 3 billion tons of coal yearly, amounting to half of global coal use.[30] In addition to massive increases in energy consumption, China is also a major energy producer, including commanding a full 45 percent of the world's coal supplies (the United States is the second biggest producer at about one quarter of China's yield), and its appetite for coal is so high that it also is the world's biggest importer of coal.[31] China plans to reduce its coal use to 65 percent by 2017 and this percentage of its overall supply is expected to continue to decline, although absolute consumption will continue to increase.[32]

China has now passed the United States as the largest emitter of carbon dioxide (CO_2), the main gas causing the changes in our climate, although its per capita emissions of this gas are still lower than those of the United States and some other developed nations. The country's air pollution levels are now among the world's highest. This extensive air pollution and serious water pollution were major contributing factors in the World Bank's rating of 20 Chinese cities among the 30 most polluted cities in the world.[33] Linfen, China, has been called the world's most polluted city.

Most of China's coal is situated in the northwestern part of the country, far from the eastern coastal provinces where much of the new economic growth is taking place. Tens of thousands of factories in the eastern provinces are experiencing serious energy shortages and must either shut down or limit their production at times. Energy shortages even led some cities – such as Shanghai – to try to modify the weather in an effort to reduce the demand for electricity.

China, now the largest user of energy in the world, is in a very energy-intensive period of its development as it focuses on manufacturing and exporting material goods. Two-thirds of China's electricity use is for industry.[34] As China continues to industrialize and living standards rise, there is concern about where the new energy will come from. Here are some of the steps China is taking to try to meet the growing demand for energy:

1 China built the world's largest program to create methane gas for use as fuel in rural areas. The gas is produced by fermenting animal and human wastes in simple generators; after the gas is produced, a rich organic fertilizer remains which can safely be used on crops.

2 China was self-sufficient in oil until the mid-1990s. Its use of oil is now growing rapidly. It is making large investments in foreign oil-producing nations from Sudan to Venezuela, and even tried, unsuccessfully, to buy an independent American oil company. In the 1990s, the Chinese economy grew at an amazing 10 percent a year, lifting millions of people out of poverty, while the new wealth created a demand for middle-class goods such as cars. The Chinese market for new cars is now the second largest in the world, only surpassed by the United States. The demand for cars is growing about 20 percent per year, putting new pressure on the government to increase its supply of oil.[35] China established higher fuel efficiency standards on its cars compared with the United States, but to save money China was importing so-called "sour" or "dirty" crude oil with much higher sulfur content than is allowed in Europe or the United States.[36]

3 China plans to increase its number of nuclear power plants, starting construction on as many as an additional ten each year. In 2010, it already planned to have in the next decade about three times the number of nuclear power plants as the rest of the world, located mainly in the industrial coastal areas. Since many of these plants will be located near large cities, safety concerns have been raised with this rapid expansion.[37] One nuclear energy expert at the Chinese Academy of Sciences said in 2005: "We don't have a very good plan of dealing with spent fuel, and we don't have very good emergency plans for dealing with catastrophe."[38] While plans may have improved, this underscores the manner in which rapidly scaled-up demand for electricity may be occurring without full considerations of the longer-term consequences and potential impacts.

4 China plans to significantly expand its renewable energy sources, such as solar and wind power, small hydroelectric dams, and biomass using plant and animal wastes. China's Twelfth Five-Year Plan set a course for the country to generate 15 percent of its energy from nonfossil fuel sources by 2020.[39] Its emphasis at present is on wind power, which it is significantly expanding in numerous windy areas from Inner Mongolia to the eastern coast.[40]

The Effect of the Energy-Climate Crisis on Countries' Development Plans

The early stages of industrialization are energy intensive. Modern transportation systems, upon which industrialization rests, utilize large amounts of energy, as does the construction industry. The huge increase in oil prices in the 1970s cast a cloud over the development plans of many developing nations. Most of these plans were based upon an assumption that reasonably cheap oil would be available, as it had been for the West, to support their industrialization. Most of the developing countries have little or no coal or oil themselves. The development plans called for these countries to export natural commodities, nonfuel resources, and light manufactured goods; it was assumed that the earnings from these exports would be sufficient to pay for the fuel they would need to import. The success of the development plans also depended upon the countries being able to generate enough capital locally so that funds for investment in businesses would be available.

When OPEC increased fuel prices, no exceptions were made for the poorer countries; they were required to pay the same high prices for their oil imports as the rich nations had to pay. Added to that burden was the one created by the global recession, which the higher oil prices had helped to create. As the recession deepened in the West, the industrialized countries cut back on their imports from the developing nations. Many of these countries borrowed heavily from commercial banks to pay for their higher oil bills and accumulated staggering debt. The foreign debt of the less developed countries in the mid-1990s rose to about $1.9 trillion. Brazil incurred the largest foreign debt of all the developing nations, over $150 billion, in the mid-1990s. One way Brazil subsequently reduced the amount of oil it needed was by using its huge sugar-cane wastes to produce alcohol (ethanol), which can be mixed with or substituted for gasoline, and produces less pollution than gasoline. At the end of the first decade of the twenty-first century, Brazil was exporting biofuels and petroleum products.[41]

The new situation created by high oil prices has led some experts to talk more about the energy needs of the world's poorest nations. Countries such as Bangladesh have few natural resources of their own and little ability to purchase the expensive oil supplies to enable large-scale industrialization. The least developed nations, sometimes called the "poor poor," have little prospect of developing along the path followed by the West, especially given the rising concerns of fossil fuel contributions to climate change. These nations are increasingly facing challenges in pursuing a development path radically different from the one followed by historically wealthy nations that developed their economies through cheap and abundant combustion of fossil fuels.

Many experts predict that the largest increase in demand for oil in the coming years will come from increasingly industrialized economies with large populations – such as China and India – and not from historically "developed" nations, which have mostly stabilized their energy use and are becoming more energy efficient.

Population pressures and the high cost of oil are increasing the demand for traditional fuels in the Global South. This problem has been mentioned above and it

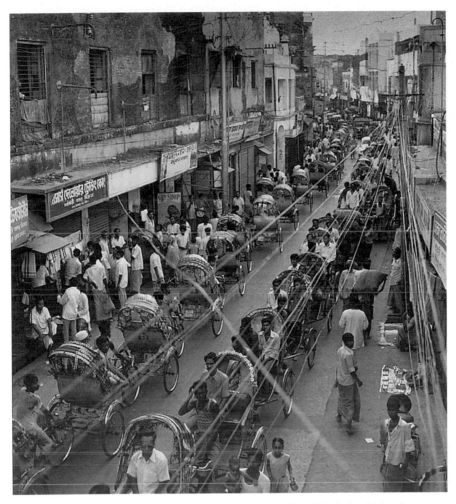

Plate 4.2 The replacing of human-powered vehicles with oil-fueled vehicles in poor and crowded countries, such as Bangladesh, will be difficult

Source: World Bank.

contributes to the pressures discussed further in the section on deforestation in Chapter 6. As firewood becomes expensive or unavailable in rural areas, people switch to burning dried cow dung and crop residues, thus preventing important nutrients and organic material from returning to the soil.

The Relationship between Energy Use and Development

A shift in types of energy

One way to study the progress of the human race is to focus on the way humans have used energy to help them produce goods and services. People have constantly sought ways to lighten the physical work they must do to produce the things they need – or feel they need – to live decently. The harnessing of fire was a crucial step in human evolution, as it provided early humans with heat, enabled them to cook their foods, and helped them to protect themselves against carnivorous animals. Next came the domestication of animals. Animal power was an important supplement to human muscles, enabling people to grow food on a larger scale than ever before. Wood was an important energy source for much of human history, as it still is for a large part of the world's population. The replacement of wood by coal to make steam in Britain in the eighteenth century enabled the Industrial Revolution to begin. In the late nineteenth century oil, and in the early twentieth century natural gas, began to replace coal since they were cleaner and more convenient to use. Oil had overtaken coal as the principal commercial energy source in the world by 1970. In the 1970s nuclear power was introduced and was producing about 5 percent of the world's energy by 2012, down from its peak since the 2011 Fukushima incident in Japan.

Increased use

The use of energy in the world has increased dramatically in the years since the end of World War II in 1945, a period of rapid development in the industrialized countries and one marking the beginning of industrialization in a number of developing countries. Figure 4.1 shows this well. Up through the end of the twentieth century, most of the increased energy use took place in the developed nations, but that trend changed by the twenty-first century. Figure 4.2 shows the world's supply of energy by type in more recent decades. In 2012 fossil fuels made up about 82 percent of the energy used, with oil about 31 percent, coal about 29 percent, and natural gas about 21 percent. Nonfossil fuels – mainly hydroelectric, nuclear, geothermal, biomass, wind, and solar – accounted for about 18 percent of energy production in 2012.

Table 4.3 shows per capita and total electricity consumption by region of the world. Consumption per capita and as a total tell different sides of the story. For example, per capita, the Chinese burn less coal (the most polluting fossil fuel) than North Americans do, but the total amount of coal used in China is twice that used in the United States.[42]

The decoupling of energy consumption and economic growth

Historically, there appeared to be a one-to-one relationship in the United States between economic growth and energy growth; for example, a 10 percent increase in the amount of goods and services produced in the country was accompanied by an approximately 10 percent increase in the amount of energy consumed. But the oil shock of 1973 seems to have broken this relationship. Between 1977 and 1985 the US economy grew about 30 percent but the amount of oil used dropped nearly 20 percent.[43] What happened was that the United States began to use energy much

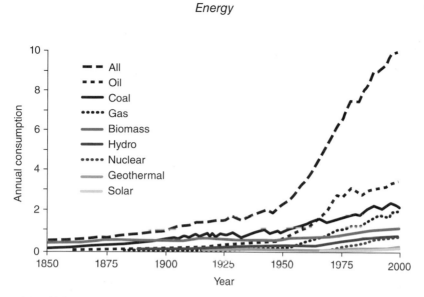

Figure 4.1 Global energy consumption, 1850–2000

Source: Robert Service, "Is It Time to Shoot for the Sun?" *Science*, 309 (July 22, 2005), p. 550.

more efficiently than it had before 1977, no doubt in response to higher oil prices. But then in the mid-1980s, the price of oil fell dramatically and remained relatively low for over a decade. Probably in large part because of that, the efforts to further conserve energy in the United States slowed down.

This partial decoupling of energy use and economic growth is not surprising once one realizes that there are a number of countries with high levels of economic prosperity that have traditionally used much less energy than does the United States. In 2012, the United Kingdom, Germany, and Japan – countries with high living standards – used about one-half of the energy per person that people living in Canada and the United States used. But the United States has been improving, and by the mid-2000s the United States was using nearly 50 percent less energy per dollar of economic output than it had 30 years before.[44] Part of this improvement in the United States came because there was a decrease in energy-intensive heavy industries and an increase in service industries, which use less energy.[45]

A number of studies of the US energy situation after the second oil shock concluded that a more efficient use of energy can actually lead to economic growth.[46] As early as the 1980s, official government recommendations determined the following:

Evidence is mounting that US economic growth, as measured by Gross National Product (GNP), need not be tied to a similar energy growth rate. The most important reason is that the US economy, including much of its building and transportation stock, its industrial processes and machinery, is inefficient in its use of energy, compared both with other economies and with the technological and cost-effective options that already exist. The opportunity is enormous for improving the energy efficiency of US capital stock – in effect creating "conservation energy" – to get the same desirable end result of warmth, comfort, jobs, and mobility that fossil fuel energy provides.[47]

Particularly in industrialized economies, energy conservation can promote economic growth because the cost of saving energy (through such measures as improving the fuel efficiency of cars, improving the efficiency of industrial processes, insulating houses, and so on) is lower than the cost of most energy today. Also, investments in improving the energy efficiency of US automobiles, homes, and factories create many new jobs and businesses throughout the country,

Figure 4.2   Global energy supply

Note: Mtoe is million tonnes of oil equivalent, the energy required to burn one tonne of oil; TPES is total primary energy supply; "Coal" includes peat and oil shale; "Other" includes geothermal, solar, wind, heat, etc.

Source: International Energy Agency, *Key World Energy Statistics 2014.*

Table 4.3 Per capita and total electricity consumption by region of the world, 2012

	Per capita electricity use (kWh/person)	Total electricity use (TWh)
World	2,972	20,915
OECD	8,089	10,145
United States	12,947	4,069
Canada	15,558	534
France	7,367	482
Australia	10,218	236
Japan	7,753	989
Middle East	3,704	790
Saudi Arabia	8,763	248
Qatar	15,904	33
Asia	893	2,071
China	3,475	4,694
India	760	940
Non-OECD Americas	2,094	979
Bolivia	646	7
Brazil	2,509	498
Africa	592	641
Kenya	157	7
South Africa	4,410	261

TWh refers to terawatt hours. A terawatt is equal to 1 trillion watts.
Source: International Energy Agency, *Key World Energy Statistics 2014*, pp. 48–57.

thus spurring the growth of the economy, in contrast to draining funds out of the economy by purchasing foreign oil.

Part of the reason many European countries use much less energy per person than does the United States is that they are smaller countries with populations not nearly as dispersed. One study has shown that the long distances people and goods move in the United States, in contrast with Europe and Japan, and the US preference for large, single-family homes account for about 40 percent of the difference between high US energy use and lower foreign use. The other 60 percent of the difference is accounted for by the fact that the fuel economy of US automobiles has historically been much poorer than that of many foreign cars, and the energy consumption per unit of output of many American manufacturing firms is higher than that of the foreign companies.[48] Also clearly contributing to the more efficient use of energy in Europe than in the United States are the high taxes placed on energy in Europe and therefore their higher cost. In much of America taxes are low and energy is relatively cheap, resulting in little incentive to use energy carefully and not waste it.

The United States cannot do anything about its size, but there are things that can be done to improve the energy efficiency of its transportation equipment. The federal government passed a law in 1975, over the strong opposition of the automobile industry, requiring the fuel efficiency of American automobiles to be gradually improved, doubling in efficiency by 1985.[49] During the 1990s no improvement was made in auto fuel efficiency in the United States. There was, in fact, some backsliding. US auto makers, exploiting a loophole in the fuel economy law that allowed them to classify minivans, sports utility vehicles (SUVs), and pickup trucks as "light trucks" (a category of vehicles that had a lower fuel economy requirement than did automobiles), produced many of these vehicles and heavily advertised them. They became very popular. Their fuel efficiency was low, an average of 21 miles per gallon, whereas automobiles averaged 28 miles per gallon. Some of the so-called "light trucks" (which were really passenger vehicles) averaged 15 miles per gallon or less, which was similar to the 14 miles per gallon that US autos averaged 25 years earlier, before the first oil shock. With relatively low gasoline prices, and fading memories of the energy crisis, US auto makers and consumers prioritized fashion and performance over fuel economy.[50]

From the early 1980s to the early 2000s, the US automobile industry used its improved technology to produce vehicles that had faster acceleration, were larger and heavier, and had slightly lower fuel economy. The average vehicle in 2002 had nearly 100 percent more horsepower, accelerated nearly 30 percent faster, and was also about 25 percent heavier.[51] Finally in 2007 the government instructed the auto industry to improve the fuel efficiency standards of its new cars to 35 miles per gallon by 2020, a significant improvement but still lower than many European, Japanese, and Chinese autos. And in 2012, the United States had plans to improve fuel efficiency standards to 55 miles per gallon by 2025.[52]

Most of the long-distance hauling of freight in the United States is by truck, and a truck uses much more energy to move a ton of freight than does a freight train. The US government, by its vast expenditure of funds on the interstate highway system (reported to be the largest public works project in history), its much lower tax on gasoline than in Europe and Japan, and its relatively small amount of expenditures that benefit the railroads, has done much to promote the use of trucks over trains in the country. This policy could be reversed.

In 1999, Japanese-made hybrid automobiles that used a gasoline engine and an electric motor appeared on the market. These hybrid vehicles were highly energy efficient and had low emissions. US companies followed suit in producing such cars in the early twenty-first century, but they were expensive compared with conventional cars.

Even a decade into the twenty-first century, governments continued supporting the burning of fossil fuels with huge government subsidies. Throughout the early 2000s, payments to the fossil fuel industries fluctuated annually according to the price of energy supplies, demand, domestic energy policies, and exchange rates. In 2008, when international energy prices were very high, subsidies were about $560 billion.[53] By 2009, subsidies totaled about $310 billion, including about $125 billion for oil products and $85 billion for natural gas.[54]

The information about governmental support of the use of fossil fuels through subsidies helped keep the price of fossil fuels low and is one of the crucial factors we need to know when we examine in Chapter 5 – climate change – perhaps the most important energy and environmental issue the world faces today.

The Energy Transition

The world is entering a period of transition from one main energy source – oil – to a new principal source or a variety of sources. This is the third energy transition the world has passed through: the first was from wood to coal, and the second from coal to oil. Many people, although not all by any means, now recognize that the industrialized world must shift from its reliance on nonrenewable and dangerously polluting fossil fuels to energy sources that are renewable and less polluting. Many in the industrialized countries, but fewer in the United States, understand that their dependence on imported oil must end since it is not a clean fuel, and neither is it cheap, abundant, or secure. But what will be the new principal energy source for the industries of the developed world and the new industries of the developing nations? As in many transitions, the end to be reached is not clear. The only clear thing now is that the present state of affairs is no longer viable. We are in the beginning years of the energy transition.

For the rest of this section, we will examine some of the potentialities of the most often discussed energy sources. Energy sources can be divided into those that are nonrenewable (i.e., it took millions of years to create them and they are being used up) and those that are renewable, in the sense that they can be readily replenished, such as energy from the sun, which is expected to continue to shine at its present brightness for at least one billion years more.

Nonrenewable energy sources

Oil, natural gas, coal, and uranium are the main sources of nonrenewable energy. According to many analysts the world is not about to run out of *oil*, but within a few decades shortages will become prevalent.[55] The world's demand for oil is now growing 1 or 2 percent each year.[56] Rapidly economically growing China and India are already competing with the West for oil. Fracking, a new technology, has enabled the United States to again become a major producer of oil and natural gas.

Canada has large deposits of tar sands from which oil can be extracted. In the mid-2000s about 1 million barrels of oil a day were being extracted from the oil sands. It is estimated that the tar sands hold as much as 175 billion barrels of oil, but it is relatively expensive and environmentally destructive to extract.

Proven reserves of *natural gas* are estimated to be larger than oil reserves. Large reserves exist in Russia, Iran, Qatar, and Saudi Arabia. Natural gas is the cleanest fossil fuel, emitting 40 percent of the carbon dioxide emitted by coal. Europe now uses natural gas for 20 percent of its energy, much of it coming from Russia. A quarter of the energy in the United States now comes from natural gas and there are plans to increase this. According to a well-known energy analyst, natural gas has become the "fuel of choice" for meeting the needs for more electricity in both the developed and developing countries.[57] Some energy analysts expect it to overtake coal and oil as the most important fossil fuel in the world by 2025.[58]

Coal is a much more abundant resource than oil or natural gas, and the United States has very large deposits of it, as do Russia, China, and Europe. It is estimated that the Earth has 1 trillion tons of recoverable coal, with one-quarter of it in the United States. China has about one-half as much as the United States but burns twice as much as the United States does at present. At the end of the first decade in the twenty-first century, China was burning more coal than the United States, Europe, and Japan combined.[59] It is coal that is fueling China's present economic boom.

Coal, partly because it is relatively cheap and abundant, made a resurgence in the United States under the George W. Bush administration. But its low price is deceptive and does not factor in many environmental costs, such as mercury pollution and particulate matter (see Chapter 6). Among the many serious pollutants emitted when it is burned, those contributing to climate change are some of the most significant. About 40 percent of carbon dioxide emissions around the world come from the burning of coal. According to the International Energy Agency (IEA), the pollution from coal will probably increase:

> The energy equivalent of some 1,350 thousand-megawatt coal-fired power plants will be built by 2030. Forty percent of them will be in China … India will add another 10 percent or so and most of the remaining half will be added in the West. In the United States the IEA predicts, about a third of the new electric-generating capacity built by 2025 will be coal-fired.[60]

Nuclear energy is the last nonrenewable source of energy we will examine. Please see the final section of this chapter for this examination. We have decided to give it its own section because of its controversy, importance, and complexity.

Renewable energy sources

Renewable energy can be obtained in a variety of ways: from wood, falling water, wind, wastes, hydrogen, and, of course, from direct sunlight. We will briefly examine each of these. In 2014 about 10 percent of the energy used in the United States came from renewable sources.

First, *wood, agricultural/forestry residues, and animal dung* are still the principal fuels in many developing countries. Rural peoples in sub-Saharan Africa, as in the South Asian countries of India, Pakistan, and Bangladesh, use these traditional fuels to cook their food and to provide heat and light. In fact, except for their own muscle power and the aid of a few domestic animals, the majority of the villagers in many developing nations have no other source of energy. Rapidly expanding populations in poorer countries are placing high demands on the use of wood; at the same time, modern agricultural requirements and development in general are leading to the clearing of vast acres of forests. Acute shortages of firewood already exist in wide areas of Africa, Asia, and Latin America.

Second, *hydroelectric power*, which is generated from falling water, is a potentially clean source of energy, causing little pollution. A large potential for developing this type of energy still exists in Africa, Latin America, and Asia, although many of the rivers that could be used are located far from centers of population. Large dams, which often need to store the water for the electric generators, usually seriously disturb the local environment, sometimes require the displacement of large numbers of people, and cause silting behind the dam, which limits its life. While most of the best sites for large dams in the industrialized countries have already been developed, a potential exists for constructing some small dams and for installing electric generators at existing dams that do not have them.

China has built the world's largest dam, the Three Gorges Dam, which is designed to produce annually an amount of electricity equal to that produced by 50 million tons of coal. The dam has its critics who, among many other complaints, point to the millions of people who had to be relocated to make room for its huge reservoir, and the possible large amounts of methane that will rise from the reservoir as the submerged vegetation rots. (Methane is many times more powerful as a greenhouse gas than is CO_2.)[61]

Third, *wind* is an energy source that was commonly used in the past for power as well as for the cooling of houses. It is still used for these purposes in some less developed countries and has recently gained respect around the world. In the United States, the state of California constructed 16,000 wind turbines in just three mountain passes, areas that have fairly steady wind. Actually, the Midwestern states in the United States – from North Dakota to Texas – have better wind conditions than California and have a great potential for generating more of their power from this source. The early dominance of California in producing wind power probably had more to do with the tax incentives that the state gave in order to promote this form of energy than with wind conditions. The California wind farms began going up in 1981 after the federal government passed a law that encouraged small energy producers, and after both the federal government and the State of California gave tax credits to wind producers. Texas has now surpassed California as the top producer of wind power in the US.[62] In 2010, Iowa, a state in the Midwest of the United States, was getting a US record of 14 percent of its electricity from wind.[63] During the same year, the United States was getting about 2 percent of its electricity from wind. While this was still a small amount, it was up from about nothing a few years earlier.

Attracted by the success of wind farms in California, a number of European countries such as Germany, Denmark, Spain, Italy, Britain, and the Netherlands have greatly increased their wind power. About 20 percent of Denmark's electricity now comes from wind power. In 2008 Spain got about 8 percent of its electricity from wind and Germany got about 7 percent. The European Union has set a goal of getting about 20 percent of its electricity from wind and other renewable sources by 2020. In 2010 Europe was getting about 5 percent of its electricity from wind.

China has begun installing wind turbines from Inner Mongolia to offshore of its eastern coasts as part of its goal to secure more of its energy from renewable sources. China has surpassed the United States as the world's largest market for wind turbines.

Plate 4.3   Wind turbines in Altamont Pass, California

Source: US Department of Energy.

In 2009 China was building six huge wind farms, each with the capacity of 16 large coal-fired power plants.

The main problem with wind, of course, is that it is usually not steady, and thus the energy it creates must be stored in some way so it can be used when the wind dies down. There is not yet any easy and inexpensive way to do this. Another problem with wind is that the choices of windy places in the world are relatively few and unevenly distributed. They are also often in remote locations, far from population centers, and in areas of great natural beauty, which some feel the windmills spoil. In an effort to defuse public opposition to the windmills' location and to benefit from strong and steady winds in coastal areas, many offshore wind farms are now in the planning stage in the United States and have been built in Europe and China. Past problems such as the noise the wind turbines make as the blades whirl (some blades are as large as the wingspan of a 747 aircraft) and the killing of birds have been partly solved by improvements in turbine design and more care given to their location. A study of wind power in the United States by the US Energy Department in 2010 concluded that wind power could replace coal and natural gas for 20 to 30 percent of the electricity used by the eastern two-thirds of the country by 2024, but the cost of changing the power grid would be large and it would have only a modest effect on cutting emissions linked to climate change.[64] According to the American Wind Energy Association, the total wind power operating in the United States in 2010 will avoid an estimated 60 million tons of CO_2 annually.[65]

Fourth, *biomass conversion* is the name given to the production of liquid and gaseous fuel from crop, animal, and human wastes; from garbage from cities; and from crops especially grown for energy production. Millions of generators that create methane gas from animal and human wastes are producing fuel for villages in India and China. Brazil is using its large sugar-cane production to produce low-pollution alcohol for fuel for automobiles. In 2007 Brazil obtained about one-third of its transportation fuel from alcohol (called ethanol in the United States). An important part of Brazil's success came when the automobile industry in Brazil developed new technology that permitted it to produce an engine that can use either gasoline, alcohol, or a combination of both. This allows drivers to select the cheapest fuel, which at present is alcohol.

In order to reduce its dependence on oil from the Middle East and other insecure areas, the United States granted large subsidies to farmers to encourage them to grow corn for processing into ethanol. By 2009 about 30 percent of the US corn crop was being grown to produce ethanol for automobiles. A debate has occurred over how much this move contributed to higher food prices around the world.

St. Louis and some other US cities are burning their garbage mixed with coal and/or natural gas to produce electricity. It is difficult to estimate how widespread this form of energy generation will become in the future. Some see good potential while others mention its negative aspects, such as the emission of harmful gases and of foul odors from burning garbage. Research into nonfood crops that can be used to make biofuels, such as wood waste, weed-like energy crops, agricultural residues, and cornstalks, is being conducted. A recent report has concluded: "Cellulosic biofuels – liquid fuels – made from inedible parts of plants – offer the most environmentally attractive and technologically feasible near-term alternative to oil."[66]

Fifth, the use of pollution-free *direct sunlight* probably has the greatest potential of all the forms of solar energy for becoming a major source of energy in the future, but it is not yet used in a major way. Each year the Earth receives from the sun about ten times the energy that is stored in all of its fossil fuel and uranium reserves. Direct sunlight can be used to heat space and water, and to produce electricity, indirectly in solar thermal systems, or directly by using photovoltaic or solar cells. Solar thermal systems collect sunlight through mirrors or lenses and use it to heat a fluid to extremely high temperatures. The fluid heats water to produce steam, which is then used to drive turbines to generate electricity.

China in 2009 produced the most solar cells in the world, Japan was second, Taiwan third, Germany fourth and the United States fifth. (The United States was once the world's leader in solar energy but the ending of governmental incentives after the 1980s and low natural gas prices ended its leadership.) In 2005 solar power was mainly used in the United States to heat swimming pools.[67] But this situation is rapidly changing. According to the Earth Policy Institute: "Total PV [solar photovoltaic cells] connected to the grid are doubling every two years ... [F]ederal tax credits along with various state and local programs, including renewable portfolio standards that require utilities to get a certain percentage of the electricity they sell from renewables, have been the main drivers of US PV growth."[68] Some regions,

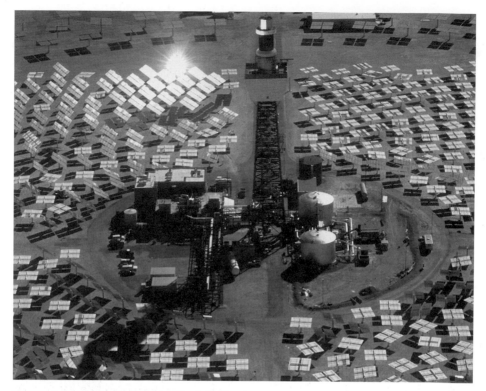

Plate 4.4   Solar thermal power plant, California

Source: US Department of Energy.

such as parts of the Middle East and North Africa, are particularly well suited for large-scale solar thermal plants, and these plants are becoming cost competitive.

Although dropping in cost, solar cells are still relatively expensive. Solar power, overall, in 2009 was far more expensive than energy produced from oil, natural gas, coal, and even wind. The high cost of solar cells is probably the most serious hindrance to their wider use. A major reduction in their cost will probably come about as their production scales up, but without a large demand for solar cells, which their high cost impedes, mass production facilities will not be built by private enterprise. A way out of this vicious cycle could come as the costs of oil and natural gas continue to rise, or if the world finally unites in an effort to combat climate change. Solar energy could be used well in moderately or intensely sunny places. Much of the developing world fits this criterion. The developing world is, in fact, often mentioned as a vast potential market for solar energy because many of its rural areas still lack electricity, and solar energy is collected more or less as efficiently by small, decentralized collectors as it is by larger, centralized units. Surprisingly, in spite of its frequently cloudy skies, Germany has become the world's leader in using solar power; this is largely due to government financial support. But solar is still a small part of the country's energy system, producing just 1 percent of Germany's energy.[69] Although still a small

Plate 4.5 Solar energy provides power for a water pump in Morocco

Source: USAID Photo Agency for International Development.

part, Germany uses solar as part of its renewable energy, which reached 14 percent of its electricity supply in 2008, putting it ahead of the European Union's target for 2010.[70]

The cost of solar energy from solar thermal plants has been dropping rather rapidly. If one includes the hidden costs of fossil fuels – that is, the costs society bears now and will bear in the future because of the pollution produced and the costs of military forces to ensure access to them – solar energy is probably less expensive than fossil fuels right now.

Sixth, *geothermal energy*, heat that is produced within the Earth's interior, is not a form of solar energy but is a renewable form of energy. Geothermal energy is stored

Plate 4.6   Geothermal power plant, California

Source: US Department of Energy.

often in pools of water or in rock, or as steam under the Earth's cool crust. Iceland
uses this form of energy to heat many of its homes, and Russia and Hungary heat
extensive greenhouses with it. Some US cities, including one in Oregon and one in
Idaho, use geothermal energy, and a geothermal power plant that produces electricity
has been built in northern California. In 2009 geothermal energy provided Iceland
and El Salvador with about 25 percent of their electricity, and the Philippines, Kenya,
and Costa Rica with about 15 percent of their electricity. For a few favorable locations
in the world, geothermal energy can be cost effective, but it is not expected to have
a wider potential.

Finally, *hydrogen-powered fuel cells* have the potential to become a major nonpolluting and efficient source of energy for vehicles. In fuel cells, hydrogen is combined at low temperatures with oxygen supplied from the air to produce electricity, which is used to run an electric motor. Vehicles powered by the electric motor
would be clean, quiet, highly efficient, and relatively easy to maintain. No battery is
required, and basically the only substance coming from the exhaust is water. Hydrogen can be obtained from water by a process that itself uses electricity. If the electricity used to make hydrogen comes from renewable and nonpolluting sources such as
solar power, wind power, or hydroelectric power, hydrogen fuel cells are a renewable

and clean source of energy. If a polluting fuel such as coal is used to make hydrogen, the fuel cell would be neither clean nor renewable.

By 2000 nearly all automobile companies were putting a major effort into developing cars using fuel cells, even though at the time hydrogen fuel cells cost about a hundred times as much per unit of power as the internal combustion engine powered by gasoline.[71] The US National Academy of Sciences in 2004 estimated that the transition to a hydrogen economy would take decades because of the serious challenges involved.[72] One major problem is the need to create thousands of hydrogen fueling stations, a challenge similar to cars that plug into an electrical source to recharge. One industrialist in the United States put it this way: "It's the classic chicken-and-egg dilemma. There's no demand for cars and trucks with limited fueling options, but no one wants to make the huge investment to create a fueling infrastructure unless there are fleets of vehicles on the road. So the question is: How do we create demand?"[73] Notwithstanding the infrastructure and cost challenges, in 2015 Toyota began piloting hydrogen cars for consumers.

Conservation/energy efficiency

Conservation is not commonly thought of as an energy source, but according to an influential study of the US energy situation by the Harvard University Business School in 1980, it should properly be regarded as a major untapped source of energy. "But is conservation really a 'source' of energy?" asked a bright student in author Seitz's class. "Good question," I responded. "Think of something that makes it unnecessary for you to use a product. Isn't it, in a sense, the same as the product?"

How much energy could the United States save by adopting conservation measures? The Harvard study found that the savings could be impressive:

> If the United States were to make a serious commitment to conservation, it might well consume 30 to 40 percent less energy than it now does, and still enjoy the same or an even higher standard of living. That saving would not hinge on a major technological breakthrough, and it would require only modest adjustments in the way people live.[74]

To many people, the term "conservation" means deprivation, or doing without something; but the Harvard study, and many others since, have shown that much energy conservation can take place without causing any real hardship. There are three ways to save energy: by performing some activity in a more energy-efficient manner (e.g., designing a more efficient motor); by not wasting energy (turning off lights in empty rooms); and by changing behavior (walking to work or to school).

Many businesses now recognize that making their operations more energy efficient is a good way to increase profits. (This subject was first discussed in an earlier section of this chapter on the decoupling of energy consumption and economic growth.) The investments the companies make to redesign their business operations so they reduce their energy usage are soon repaid by lower energy bills. Dow

Chemical discovered after the 1973 oil crisis that the company's standard practice up to then was to never turn off its de-icing equipment during the year, which meant that its sidewalks and service areas were being warmed even on the Fourth of July. More recently, DuPont was able to increase its production by about 30 percent but cut its energy use nearly 10 percent, saving more than $2 billion. Five other companies – IBM, British Telecom, Alcan, Norske Canada, and Bayer – collectively saved another $2 billion by reducing their CO_2 emissions by about 60 percent. British Petroleum (BP) met its 2010 goal in 2001 of reducing its CO_2 emissions 10 percent below its 1990 level, thus cutting its energy bill by about $650 million over ten years.[75]

One major conservation method US industry could adopt is called "cogeneration," which is the combined production of both electricity and heat in the same installation. Electricity is currently produced by private and public utilities, and the heat from the generation of the electricity is passed off into the air or into lakes and rivers as waste. In cogeneration plants, the heat from the production of electricity – often in the form of steam – is used for industrial processes or for heating homes and offices. The production of electricity and steam together uses about one-half the amount of fuel as does their production separately. Cogeneration is fairly common in Europe but not in the United States, where electric utilities often give cheaper rates to their big industrial customers, thus reducing the incentive to adopt the process.

If the United States ever does reach the goal of energy savings that the Harvard report believes is possible, it will be because of a combination of governmental policies encouraging conservation and action by millions of individuals. The United States is a country where people respond well to incentives to promote conservation practices, but such governmental incentives have so far been rather weak. In contrast to weak efforts by the federal government, some of the US states have done more to encourage conservation and the use of renewable energy. For example, the state of California allowed homeowners to deduct 55 percent of the cost of solar devices from their state taxes. (This law no doubt partly explains why California leads the nation in the number of solar devices installed in homes.) The city of Davis, California changed its building code so that all new homes in the city must meet certain energy performance standards.

American homes are not designed to use energy efficiently. If houses with large window surfaces were positioned to face the south, they could gain much heat from the low winter sun, and these windows could be shaded by deciduous trees or an overhang to keep out the high summer sun. The popular all-glass American skyscrapers built during the 1960s are huge energy wasters, since their large areas of glass absorb the hot summer rays. Since their windows cannot be opened, at times the buildings' air conditioners must work at high levels just to cool their interiors to the same temperature as the outside air. Simple measures like planting trees to obtain shade can have a significant cooling effect on a house, a city street, or a parking lot, reducing temperatures by as much as 10 to 20 degrees over unshaded areas. Townhouses, the modern name for the old row houses, are again becoming popular in many cities; they are much more energy efficient than the common, single-family house because of their shared walls.

Saving energy often takes an initial investment. Knowing this fact helps one understand why eliminating subsidies for oil and natural gas, which will lead to higher prices of those fuels, is probably not enough by itself to cause many people to use less energy. The better educated and more affluent might recognize that an investment in insulation or a more expensive water heater makes good sense and will save them money over the long run, but those with lower incomes do not have the extra money to make the initial investment. Some of the poor spend a higher portion of their income on energy than do those on higher incomes, and thus could benefit greatly from the better-insulated house or the more fuel-efficient car, but they usually end up with a poorly insulated house and a gas-guzzling car. Higher prices for fuel will probably help to reduce energy consumption, but stronger governmental incentives and regulations, such as substantially higher tax credits for installing insulation and substantially higher fuel efficiency standards for automobiles, could produce a significant movement toward conservation.

Some real progress is being made in conservation/energy efficiency efforts around the world, but much more can be done. Here is how Amory Lovins, an authority on the subject, sees the positive features:

> Many energy-efficient products, once costly and exotic, are now inexpensive and commonplace. Electronic speed controls, for example, are mass-produced so cheaply that some suppliers give them away as a free bonus with each motor. Compact fluorescent lamps cost more than $20 two decades ago but only $2 to $5 today; they use 75 to 80 percent less electricity than incandescent bulbs and last 10 to 13 times longer. Window coatings that transmit light but reflect heat cost one fourth of what they did five years ago.[76]

Lovins believes that Europe and Japan, although up to twice as energy efficient as the United States, can still make significant improvements in conserving energy. Even more opportunities to conserve energy exist in the developing countries, Lovins believes, where countries are on average three times less efficient than the United States. And finally Lovins is encouraged by what he sees in China, which has what he calls "ambitious but achievable goals" to shift from coal production to decentralized renewable energy and natural gas.[77] As we will mention in the next chapter on climate change, China is relying on conservation and energy efficiency improvements as its main way to achieve its stated goal of reducing the amount of carbon dioxide (its so-called "carbon intensity") it emits to produce economic growth. This has been difficult to do. Still, while China has become the world's chief producer of greenhouse gasses, it has also become a leader in producing renewable energy.

Nuclear Power: A Case Study

In this final section we will look closely at nuclear power, which historically has been surrounded by political controversy. An expansion of nuclear power is now taking place because of the increasing need for energy in rapidly growing economies, such as China, and as one of the ways to decrease the world's dependency on oil and coal, such as in the United States, which sees nuclear power as a way to deal with security and environmental concerns. There are strong arguments for and against this energy source, illustrating the complexity of many important issues today, with no easy right or wrong answers. Decision-makers should consider both the pros and cons of the issue. We have decided to present this subject to the reader as a case study instead of trying to give the "correct" decision, highlighting the need for decision-makers to set priorities.

The potential and the peril

Nuclear power was seen by many in its early years as the answer to the world's energy needs. Its promoters claimed it would be a nonpolluting and safe form of energy that could produce electricity "too cheap to meter." After the destructive power of the atom was demonstrated with the bombing of Hiroshima and Nagasaki, people welcomed the thought that atomic research could also be used for peaceful purposes. The first prototype of a commercial nuclear power plant began operation in the United States in 1957.

The first generation of nuclear power reactors takes the form of fission, light-water reactors. These reactors operate with the same process that was used to explode the early atomic bombs – the splitting of the core (the nucleus) of the atoms of heavy elements, which releases tremendous energy. Uranium 235 (U-235) is the fuel used in these reactors. The chain reaction that comes with the splitting of the uranium nucleus is controlled in the power reactors to produce sustained heat, which is then used, as it is in coal- and oil-fed power plants, to produce steam. The steam drives the turbines that generate electricity.

The uranium used in the common light-water reactors must be enriched so that it contains a higher percentage of U-235 than found in nature. This is done in very large, very expensive enrichment plants that utilize huge amounts of electricity themselves. Because of the difficulty of obtaining the required U-235, it was originally planned to reprocess the spent fuel rods from the power reactors to extract unused uranium, thus making uranium supplies last longer. Controversy has surrounded these reprocessing plants, partly because plutonium, one of the deadliest known substances and the fuel for the Nagasaki bomb (the bomb dropped on Hiroshima utilized uranium), is produced during the reprocessing. Three commercial reprocessing plants were built in the United States – one in Illinois, one in New York, and one in South Carolina – but none are operating at present. The shutdowns occurred because of technical difficulties, safety concerns, and the fear that such plants made plutonium too accessible.

Another way to handle the relative scarcity of fuel for the light-water reactors would be by building a second generation of power reactor. These reactors, known as the fast-breeder reactors, use plutonium as their fuel and will actually produce more fuel than they consume. The attractiveness of this feature was countered by the great complexity of the plants and the increased danger that would come from an accident, since plutonium was being used instead of the less radioactive uranium. Plutonium is extremely harmful if inhaled or digested and has a half-life (the amount of time for one-half of the substance to disintegrate or be transformed into something else) of over 24,000 years. Between the 1970s and the 1990s, the United Kingdom, Germany, the United States, France, Russia, and Japan built experimental fast-breeder reactors. By 2009 all, except the one in Japan, had been shut down because of technical difficulties, spiraling costs, and a concern for safeguarding the plutonium. But in that year China, India, and Russia were still planning or building a new generation of experimental fast-breeder reactors.

Fusion nuclear power, which is still in the experimental stage, might be called a third generation of nuclear energy. Fusion energy is created by the same process that creates the energy in the sun and is the process used in the hydrogen bomb, which is vastly more powerful than the fission atomic bombs. Instead of splitting atoms, as happens in fission, in fusion atoms are fused together. The process is highly complicated and demands temperatures (millions of degrees) and pressures with which scientists have little experience. The attractiveness of the fusion process is that it is an inherently safer process than fission and generates much less radioactive waste. Much of its fuel (deuterium) comes from seawater and is nonradioactive, while the other main component of its fuel (tritium), which is radioactive, can be obtained from a substance (lithium) that is fairly abundant.

In 1991, after nearly a half-century of research and many billions of dollars, a breakthrough in fusion research occurred as a European team for the first time produced a significant amount of energy from controlled nuclear fusion. Seven industrial and near-industrial powers (Europe, Japan, Russia, China, South Korea, India, and the United States) have agreed to cooperate in building a large experimental fusion reactor in France. The reactor is scheduled to be completed about 2018. Its cost is estimated to be 10 billion euros over the 30-year lifetime of its operation, which includes the cost of its construction and operation. The cost will be shared by the seven nations building it. One fact alone indicates the huge scientific challenge of this project. To be successful, the temperature within the reactor must reach 150 million degrees Celsius, or ten times the temperature at the core of our sun. The goal of the project is to deliver ten times the power it consumes.

In 2014, the United States began supporting new nuclear reactors for the first time since 1977 (and about 100 orders for plants were canceled during the 1970s).[78] The slowdown occurred because of the reduced demand for electricity (caused by the rapidly increasing cost of power, by conservation measures, and an economic recession), the skyrocketing cost of building the plants (plants that were originally estimated to cost from $200 to $300 million wound up costing from $1 to $2 billion), and increasing concern about the safety of the plants.

In 1979 the partial meltdown of the core of a nuclear reactor located at the power plant at Three Mile Island, Pennsylvania, United States, led to a release of some radioactive steam and gas from the plant and the consequent official recommendation that nearby pregnant women as well as young children be evacuated. Although no one was killed, and the release of the radioactive substances was later judged by a presidential investigation committee to have caused no danger to public health, the cleanup from the accident cost about $1 billion, and the accident increased public fears about nuclear power. It has been estimated that new safety requirements for nuclear power plants which were issued by the federal government after the Three Mile Island accident, as well as delays in the construction of new plants and more temporary shutdowns of existing plants caused by the concerns raised by that accident, added $130 billion to the cost of nuclear electricity in the United States between 1979 and 1992. Two lessons learned from the accident were that it was easier to destroy a reactor core than many experts had thought possible, but also it was harder to rupture the reactor vessel (the steel pot 5 inches thick that holds the core) than many had thought possible. On one hand, this confirmed concerns about the possibility of nuclear accidents and reactor meltdown; on the other, it demonstrated that not all accidents lead to catastrophic disaster.

In 1986 when the nuclear power plant at Chernobyl in the Soviet Union exploded, about 50 tons of radioactive particles – ten times the fallout at Hiroshima – fell across parts of the Soviet Union. The accident also spread radiation around the world, with significant amounts falling on some European countries. More than 100,000 people were evacuated from an area of about 300 square miles (78,000 hectares) around the plant. About 30 people died from the catastrophe during the following few months. It is believed that both flaws in the design of the reactor and mistakes by the operators of the plant were responsible for the disaster.

While the Soviet Union was much more candid about the accident than it had been about previous nuclear disasters (such as the explosion, which was kept secret, in 1957 of a tank that contained high-level nuclear waste and that contaminated thousands of square miles in the area of the Ural Mountains), it is now known that secret government decrees were issued one and two years after the accident, designed to cover up the full extent of the damage. Four years after the accident, the Soviet Union acknowledged that 4 million people were still living on ground contaminated by the explosion and the government voted to spend $26 billion on further Chernobyl-related expenses, including the resettlement of 200,000 people living in the most contaminated areas. A United Nations report released in 2005 estimated that 4,000 people were expected to die from cancer from the explosion's fallout. Some experts disagree with the United Nations estimate and believe the final cancer toll from the fallout could be in the tens of thousands.

After a three-decade withdrawal of interest in nuclear power in many countries, except a few such as France and Japan, more than 40 countries (including the United States), showed a new interest in nuclear power in late 2010. This interest came because of a serious shortage of electricity in countries such as China and India that were having major economic growth, rising prices of oil, insecure sources of imported energy, and global warming concerns. By mid-2010 there were about 440 nuclear power reactors operating in the world. Nearly 60 reactors were under construction at that time. (Figure 4.3 shows global nuclear production from 1971 to 2012.)

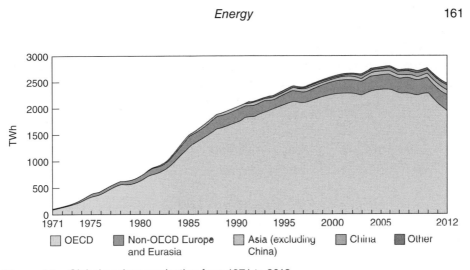

Figure 4.3 Global nuclear production from 1971 to 2012

Source: International Energy Agency, *Key World Energy Statistics 2014*, p. 16.

As mentioned before, in March 2011 a massive Earthquake near the northeastern coast of Japan was followed by a tsunami (tidal wave) that inflicted huge damage to the coastal region where the Fukushima nuclear facility was located. The reactors were seriously damaged. They released a large amount of radiation into the air and sea, and led to an evacuation of nearby residents. This became the biggest nuclear accident since Chernobyl. Since that time, nuclear power has significantly decreased.

The choice

Two basic political alternatives exist regarding nuclear power: the government can withdraw its support for the nuclear power industry, or it can continue to promote nuclear power and encourage its development. We will examine the main arguments being presented on both sides in this debate.

Withdraw support for nuclear power   As the accidents at Chernobyl and Fukushima show, nuclear power plants run the risk of having catastrophic accidents. Society should not have to accept such a risk. The Three Mile Island accident proved that the interaction of human error and failure of equipment can lead to events that no one had ever guessed could happen. One hundred alarms went off in the first few minutes at Three Mile Island, making it impossible for the operators to control the situation. And at Chernobyl a series of errors by the operators of a reactor which was inherently difficult to run generated forces and effects that up to then had never been experienced. Nuclear technology assumes better human performance and understanding than history shows can be achieved.

Nuclear power also increases the danger of the proliferation, or the spread, of nuclear weapons to additional nations. The knowledge and installations that a nation acquires when it develops nuclear power can be utilized to develop nuclear bombs. While it is true that most nuclear power plants do not use fuel that can readily be used to build bombs, the reprocessing of the spent fuel from the plants can produce fuel for weapons. Reprocessing technology is spreading around the world. For example, in 1975 West Germany sold Brazil reprocessing technology even though Brazil had never signed the Non-Proliferation Treaty, which would commit it not to use it to develop nuclear weapons. As more nations gain expertise in nuclear energy and acquire nuclear weapons, the chances that the weapons will be used will greatly increase.

The danger of terrorists stealing plutonium to make a bomb or to use as a poison to be spread in the atmosphere over a city or in its drinking water is real. The knowledge of how to make nuclear weapons is widespread, and only about 20 pounds of fissionable material is required to make a crude bomb. If, or probably more realistically when, terrorists do acquire a nuclear capability, threatened nations will probably respond by giving their police and governments increased power. The United States could become more authoritarian because of such a threat, with consequent restrictions on personal freedom and privacy.

Another disturbing consequence of nuclear energy is that large amounts of radioactive wastes from nuclear power plants are accumulating in the United States because no permanent way to store this material has yet been created. After spending $9 billion over 22 years to build a nuclear waste storage facility in Yucca Mountain, Nevada, concern over its ability to keep the wastes isolated led the United States to eventually abandon the effort. Some of the nuclear waste must be stored for a minimum of 100,000 to 200,000 years in such a way that it does not come into contact with humans or with any part of the environment. We show an overwhelming arrogance and unconcern for future generations when we say we can do this; this is made apparent when we remember that the United States is only 200 years old and human civilization about 5,000 years old. Several hundred thousand gallons of nuclear wastes have already leaked out of steel tanks at sites in Hanford, Washington and near Aiken, South Carolina, where military wastes are stored.

The high cost of nuclear power makes it economically unjustifiable. If one includes the cost of its development and the costs of the attempts to find a safe way to store wastes – both of which have been financed by public funds – nuclear power would not be competitive with other forms of energy. And the cost of decommissioning and possibly hauling away for storage worn out and highly radioactive nuclear power plants, which have a life expectancy of 30 to 40 years, will further add to the costs of nuclear power.

Nuclear power plants create thermal pollution, raising the temperature of the atmosphere and of the water in lakes, bays, and rivers often used to cool the reactors. The warmer water can be deadly to many kinds of fish and other forms of life in the lakes and rivers. The present light-water reactors convert only about 30 percent of their fuel into electricity; the rest is turned into waste heat.

Nuclear power cannot replace imported oil. Only about 10 percent of the world's oil is used to generate electricity; most of it is used to run vehicles, provide heat for homes and industry, and make chemicals. Nuclear power, for the foreseeable future, can be used only to make electricity, and, besides being of relatively limited use, electricity is a very expensive form of energy. The huge public investments which continue to go into nuclear energy (mainly through government subsidies) prevent public funds from being used to develop alternative sources of energy which would be more useful, safer, and cleaner.

Continue to support nuclear power   We accept chemical plants despite accidents associated with them, such as that at Bhopal in India in 1984 which killed more than 3,000 people, and we accept dams despite accidents associated with them, such as at the Vajont Dam in Italy in 1963, which killed about 2,000 people. So why should the accidents at Chernobyl, Fukushima, and Three Mile Island make us reject nuclear power? Nuclear power plants in the United States have become much safer because of new procedures and safety devices adopted since the Three Mile Island accident. And a number of highly respected scientists now believe that it is possible to build a nuclear power plant which is inherently safe, one which would be so designed that if anything unusual happened it would automatically cease functioning without any action needed by human beings or by machines.

A person gets more exposure to radiation in a year by taking a single round-trip coast-to-coast jet flight, by watching color television, or by working in a building made of granite than anyone would by living next to a nuclear power plant. Humans have evolved over millions of years living on a mildly radioactive planet and have prospered. Few things in life are risk-free, and the risks associated with nuclear power are relatively benign compared with the risks people take every day in their lives.

The accusation that nuclear power will contribute to the proliferation of nuclear weapons is exaggerated. A nation that wants to build a nuclear weapon can get sufficient plutonium from its nuclear research facilities. This is exactly how India got plutonium for the nuclear device it exploded in 1974. All of the major powers that have acquired nuclear weapons built these weapons before they acquired nuclear power.

It would be very difficult for a terrorist to steal plutonium in the United States. The US military has been shipping plutonium by convoy for many years and very effective means have been devised to protect the shipments from hijacking. Good security measures are also in effect in plants that produce plutonium. Although the knowledge of how to construct nuclear bombs is no longer secret, the actual construction of such a device is very difficult. If the construction of nuclear weapons were easy, more nations would have them than the handful that do at present.

A way to store nuclear wastes permanently has been devised and is actually being used in Europe. The wastes can be solidified, usually in glass, and then stored in geologically stable underground facilities. Sweden and Finland have chosen underground repositories in stable granite rock and France, Switzerland and Belgium are investigating potential repositories in clay. Most of the nuclear wastes in the United

States are being created in its military program, and these wastes will continue to build up even if every nuclear power plant was closed.

A great danger to the world is caused by the shortage of oil. Without secure sources of energy, such as nuclear power, it is likely that more wars will occur as nations fight to keep their sources of oil secure. The development of nuclear power can help to reduce this dangerous dependency on foreign sources of energy.

Nuclear power is much less polluting than the main alternative energy source – coal – that will be greatly expanded if nuclear power does not continue to be produced. Except for the construction of the reactor, nuclear power produces no carbon dioxide that causes climate change, no waste gases that produce acid rain, as coal burning does, and no smog or any of the other harmful effects commonly associated with coal. Nuclear power is generally much easier on the landscape than is coal; the average nuclear power reactor uses only about 30 tons of fuel a year while the average coal-burning electric plant uses about 3,000 tons of fuel per *day*. By slowing down the approval of new nuclear plants, the critics of nuclear power are causing nations to burn more coal. This causes many more people to die and more environmental damage from pollution than would have been the case if new nuclear plants had made the increased coal-burning unnecessary.

No energy option should be rejected during this period of transition. Nuclear power is one of the few alternatives we have to produce large amounts of energy during the rest of this century while the search for a sustainable fuel to take the place of oil and coal continues.

Conclusions

The energy transition the Earth is passing through is possibly the most important one human beings have encountered during their long evolution on the planet. The very suitability of the planet for high civilization is threatened by the fossil fuels they rely on to power the machinery that makes their products, runs their transportation systems, fuels their high-tech agricultural systems, and heats and cools their homes. The burning of these fossil fuels has led to wars as nations have fought over the control of oil, the main fossil fuel the people of the Earth depend on at present. As long as that dependency remains, more conflicts seem likely.

But more wars are not the main problem our use of energy might bring. The effect our reliance on fossil fuels is having on our climate at present and its possible effects in the future are why a transition to new energy sources is crucial. Time is limited. If too much time is taken for this energy transition to occur, the population of the Earth is large enough and its industrialization great enough – with both still growing – that the changing climate could bring widespread suffering and destruction to many, but especially to the poorest nations.

Other energy sources are available that don't cause conflicts among nations or threaten our climate, but it will take major efforts by governments and individuals to make them prominent. The careful reader of this book is learning about these renewable and nonpolluting sources of energy and of some of the difficulties standing in the way of their wider use.

Until only very recently, the efforts of the leading industrial nation, the country that produces more goods and services than any other and, in the past, has released more pollutants that affect the climate than any other – the United States – have been very disappointing. American scientists have been leaders in gathering the evidence that our climate is changing because of human actions, but so far the US Congress has been unresponsive, even as the executive branch has tried to scale up actions within the constraints of existing laws. Has this lack of legislative action in the US to address this threat been because of the political power of the fossil fuel and automotive industries which have opposed taking action, or is it because the American public lacks an understanding – or concern – that new energy initiatives are urgently needed for the long-term health of their country and of the planet itself? Or is it both?

Many European countries, along with Japan and others, are taking actions to address this issue. China is starting to address it, but because of its heavy reliance on coal and its rapid economic growth, it has now become the largest annual contributor to the problem of climate change. Will our descendants look back at this period and ask, "Why didn't they act sooner?" It's our challenge. Our societies are being tested. We, the writers of this book, and you, its readers, are trying to understand what is happening in our world. This is a vital first step, as no effective action can be taken without it. We have identified energy as a key component in our understanding of the way life is today. Next we will look at the climate challenges born out of historic fossil fuel-intensive development pathways such as those described in this chapter on energy. We are continuing to increase our knowledge of our world and our place in it. Congratulations, reader. If you are doing this seriously, you are becoming a possible part of the solution and not a possible part of the problem.

Notes

1   An interesting discussion of the laws of thermodynamics and what they tell us about energy is contained in Jeremy Rifkin, *Entropy: A New World View* (New York: Viking Press, 1980), pp. 33–43.

2   US Energy Information Administration (EIA), Energy in Brief: "Who Are the Major Players Supplying the World Oil Market?" September 30, 2014, at http://www.eia.gov/energy_in_brief/article/world_oil_market.cfm (accessed July 2015).

3   The era of relatively cheap energy in the United States extended into the twenty-first century. Prices in Table 4.1 are not adjusted for inflation. When inflation is considered, in the early twenty-first century gasoline was still relatively inexpensive in the United States.

4   Lester R. Brown, *The Twenty-Ninth Day: Accommodating Human Needs and Numbers to the Earth's Resources* (New York: W. W. Norton, 1978), pp. 205–6.

5   Daniel Yergin and Martin Hillenbrand (eds), *Global Insecurity: A Strategy for Energy and Economic Renewal* (Boston: Houghton Mifflin, 1982), p. 7.

6   *New York Times*, January 16, 1992, p. A7; and Youssef Ibrahim, "Gulf War's Cost to the Arabs Estimated at $620 Billion," *New York Times*, September 8, 1992, p. A4.

7   Joseph Romm, "Needed – a No-Regrets Energy Policy," *Bulletin of the Atomic Scientists*, 47 (July/August 1991), p. 31.

8   EIA, *International Energy Outlook 2014* (Washington, DC: US Department of Energy, 2014), p. 1.

9   International Energy Agency (IEA), *World Energy Outlook 2014* (Paris: IEA, 2014), Executive Summary, p. 6.

10 EIA, Energy In Brief: "What Are the Major Sources and Users of Energy in the United States?" May 30, 2014, at http://www.eia.gov/energy_in_brief/article/major_energy_sources_and_users.cfm (accessed July 2015).

11 EIA, Energy in Brief: "How Dependent Are We on Foreign Oil?" May 10, 2013, at http://www.eia.gov/energy_in_brief/article/foreign_oil_dependence.cfm (accessed July 2015).

12 "The Hidden Cost of Gas," *Sierra*, 87 (March/April 2002), p. 15. See also Harold M. Hubbard, "The Real Cost of Energy," *Scientific American*, 264 (April 1991), p. 36.

13 See, e.g., Sarah Lyall, "Britons Running out of Patience as Costly Gas Runs Out," *New York Times*, September 12, 2000.

14 There is a useful list of international gasoline prices at http://money.cnn.com/pf/features/lists/global_gasprices/ (accessed July 2015).

15 See, e.g., Environmental Protection Agency, "Overview of the Clean Power Plan," EPA Factsheet (2014), at http://www2.epa.gov/sites/production/files/2014-05/documents/20140602fs-overview.pdf (accessed July 2015).

16 EIA, *International Energy Outlook 2014*, p. 26.

17 EIA, International Energy Data and Analysis, at http://www.eia.gov/beta/international/ (accessed July 2015): France Country Data (2014).

18 EIA, International Energy Data and Analysis: United Kingdom Country Analysis (2014).

19 Ibid.

20 EIA, International Energy Data and Analysis: Norway Country Analysis (2014).

21 IEA, Energy Balances Statistics, at http://www.iea.org/statistics/topics/energybalances/ (accessed July 2015): Japan, 2008.

22 David Sanger, "Japan Joins in Embargo against Iraq," *New York Times*, August 6, 1990, p. C7.

23 EIA, International Energy Data and Analysis: Japan Country Analysis (2015); see also Ken Belson, "Why Japan Steps Gingerly in the Middle East," *New York Times*, September 17, 2002, p. W1.

24 EIA, International Energy Data and Analysis: Japan Country Analysis (2015).

25 Howard French, "Safety Problems at Japanese Reactors Begin to Erode Public's Faith in Nuclear Power," *New York Times*, September 16, 2002, p. A8.

26 EIA, *International Energy Outlook 2014*, p. 5.

27 Ibid.

28 IEA, "World Energy Outlook 2014 Factsheet," at http://www.worldenergyoutlook.org/media/weowebsite/2014/WEO2014FactSheets.pdf. See also EIA, *International Energy Outlook 2014*, p. 1; IEA, *Key World Energy Statistics 2014*, p. 15, at http://www.iea.org/publications/freepublications/publication/key-world-energy-statistics-2014.html (both accessed July 2015).

29 EIA, *International Energy Outlook 2014*, p. 29.

30 Keith Bradsher, "Green Power Takes Root in China," New York Times, July, 3, 2009, p. 5; Elisabeth Rosenthal, "Booming China Is Buying Up World's Coal," *New York Times* November 22, 2010, pp. A1, A10.

31 IEA, *Key World Energy Statistics 2014*, p. 15.

32 EIA, International Energy Data and Analysis: China Country Analysis (2014).

33 World Bank, "China Quick Facts," November 18, 2010.

34 EIA, International Energy Data and Analysis: China country Analysis (2014).

35 Keith Bradsher, "With First Car, a New Life in China," *New York Times*, April 24, 2008, pp. C1, C4.

36 Keith Bradsher, "China Pays a Price for Cheaper Oil," *New York Times*, June 26, 2004, p. B1.

37 Keith Bradsher, "China, Rushing into Reactors, Stirs Concerns," *New York Times*, December 16, 2009, pp. A1, A3.

38 Howard French, "As China Races to Build Nuclear Power Plants, Some Experts Still See Danger," *Spartanburg Herald-Journal*, January 16, 2005, p. A16.

39 EIA, International Energy Data and Analysis: China Country Analysis (2014).

40 Howard French, "In Search of a New Energy Source, China Rides the Wind," *New York Times*, July 26, 2005, p. A4.

41 IEA, Energy Balance Statistics: Brazil, 2008.

42 Jeff Goodell, "Cooking the Climate with Coal," *Natural History*, 115 (May 2006), pp. 40–1.

43 Amory Lovins, "More Profit with Less Carbon," *Scientific American*, 293 (September 2005), p. 81.

44 Ibid., p. 74.

45 Neela Banerjee, "Pushing Energy Conservation into the Back Seat of the SUV," *New York Times*, November 22, 2003, p. B2.

46 See, for example, Marc H. Ross and Daniel Steinmeyer, "Energy for Industry," *Scientific American*, 263 (September 1990), pp. 88–98; John H. Gibbons, Peter D. Blair, and Holly L. Gwin, "Strategies for Energy Use," *Scientific American*, 261 (September 1989), pp. 136–43; National Research Council, *Energy in Transition 1985–2010* (San Francisco: W. H. Freeman, 1980); Robert Stobaugh and Daniel Yergin (eds), *Energy Future: Report of the Energy Project at the Harvard Business School* (New York: Ballantine, 1980); Roger W. Sant, Steven C. Carhard et al., *Eight Great Energy Myths: The Least-Cost Energy Strategy, 1978–2000* (Arlington, VA: Energy Productivity Center of the Mellon Institute, 1981).

47 White House Council on Environmental Quality and the Department of State, *Global Future: Time to Act* (Washington, DC: Government Printing Office, 1981), p. 61.

48 Joel Darmstadter, *Economic Growth and Energy Conservation: Historical and International Lessons*, Reprint 154 (Washington, DC: Resources for the Future, 1978), p. 18.

49 In 1974 the average fuel efficiency of all American cars was 14 miles per gallon. The law required that this be increased to 27.5 miles per gallon by 1985.

50 For an explanation of how US auto companies were still able to build fuel-inefficient dinosaurs, and some of the tactics they used to keep from being fined for violating the fuel economy law, see James Bennet, "Trucks' Popularity Undermining Gains in US Fuel Savings," *New York Times*, September 5, 1995, pp. A1, C3; and Keith Bradsher, "Auto Makers Seek to Avoid Mileage Fines," *New York Times*, April 3, 1998, p. A14.

51 Danny Hakim, "Fuel Economy Hit 22-Year Low in 2002," *New York Times*, May 3, 2003, p. B1. See also Matthew Wald, "Automakers Use New Technology to Beef up Muscle, Not Mileage," *New York Times*, March 30, 2006, p. C4.

52 US White House, Office of the Press Secretary, "Obama Administration Finalizes Historic 54.5 MPG Fuel Efficiency Standards," August 28, 2012, at https://www.whitehouse.gov/the-press-office/2012/08/28/obama-administration-finalizes-historic-545-mpg-fuel-efficiency-standard (accessed July 2015).

53 IEA, "World Energy Outlook 2010 Fact Sheet," p. 4.

54 IEA, Organisation for Economic Co-operation and Development, and World Bank, *The Scope of Fossil Fuel Subsidies and a Roadmap for Phasing out Fossil Fuel Subsidies* (2010), at http://www.worldenergyoutlook.org/media/weowebsite/energysubsidies/second_joint_report.pdf (accessed July 2015).

55 Richard Kerr, "Bumpy Road Ahead for World's Oil," *Science*, 310 (November 18, 2005), p. 1106.

56 Richard Kerr and Robert Service, "What Can Replace Cheap Oil – and When?" *Science*, 309 (July 1, 2005), p. 101.

57 Daniel Yergin and Michael Stoppard, "The Next Prize," *Foreign Affairs*, 82 (November/December 2003), p. 108.

58 Simon Romero, "Demand for Natural Gas Brings Big Import Plans, and Objections," *New York Times*, June 15, 2005, p. C8. See also Matthew L. Wald, "Study Says Natural Gas Use Likely to Double," *New York Times*, June 25, 2010, p. B3.

59 Joseph Kahn and Jim Yardley, "As China Roars, Pollution Reaches Deadly Extremes," *New York Times*, August 26, 2007, p. 6.

60 Goodell, "Cooking the Climate with Coal," p. 37.

61 Richard Stone, "Three Gorges Dam: Into the Unknown," *Science*, 321 (August 1, 2008), pp. 628–32.

62 Clifford Krauss, "Move Over, Oil, There's Money in Texas Wind," *New York Times*, February 23, 2008, p. A13.

63 American Wind Energy Association, "Market Update: Record 2009 Leads to Slow Start in 2010" (May 2010).

64 Matthew L. Wald, "Wind Power Is Feasible but Costly, Study Says," *New York Times*, January 21, 2010, p. B6.

65 American Wind Energy Association, "Market Update."

66 George W. Huber and Bruce E. Dale, "Grassoline at the Pump," *Scientific American*, 301 (July 2009), p. 5.

67 Worldwatch Institute, *Vital Signs 2005* (New York: Worldwatch Institute, 2005), p. 36.

68 J. Matthew Roney, "Solar Cell Production Climbs to Another Record in 2009," Earth Policy Institute, Eco-Economy Indicators: Solar Power, September 21, 2010, at http://www.earth-policy.org/index.php?/indicators/C47/solar_power_2010 (accessed July 2015).

69 Felicity Barringer, "With Push toward Renewable Energy, California Sets Pace for Solar Power," *New York Times*, July 16, 2009, p. A17.

70 Mark Landler, "Solar Valley Rises in an Overcast Land," *New York Times*, May 16, 2008, p. C7.

71 Matthew Wald, "Questions about a Hydrogen Economy," *Scientific American*, 290 (May 2004), p. 68.

72 Matthew Wald, "Report Questions Bush Plan for Hydrogen-Fueled Cars," *New York Times*, February 6, 2004, p. A19.

73 Steven Ashley, "On the Road to Fuel-Cell Cars," *Scientific American*, 292 (March 2005), p. 68.

74 Stobaugh and Yergin, *Energy Future*, p. 10.

75 Lovins, "More Profit with Less Carbon," p. 74.

76 Ibid. p. 76.

77 Ibid. p. 83.

78 Ned Resnikoff, "US to Help Build First New Nuclear Reactors in Decades," MSNBC, February 19, 2014, at http://www.msnbc.com/msnbc/us-invests-big-nuclear-power (accessed July 2015).

Further Reading

Goodell, Jeff, *Big Coal: The Dirty Secret behind America's Energy Future* (New York: Houghton Mifflin, 2006). The secret is that much (about one-half) of America's electricity is generated from burning coal and this is rarely acknowledged. Coal is used because it is cheap and abundant. Goodell writes: "Our shiny white iPod economy is propped up by dirty black rocks."

Jacobson, Mark Z., and Mark A. Delucchi, "A Path to Sustainable Energy by 2030," *Scientific American*, 301 (November 2009), pp. 58–65. The authors argue that wind, water, solar, tidal, and geothermal technologies can provide 100 percent of the world's energy.

Klare, Michael, *Blood and Oil: The Dangers and Consequences of America's Growing Petroleum Dependency* (New York: Metropolitan Books, 2004). Since America's own supply of oil is drying up, its demand for imported oil is increasing, and the sources of oil in the world today are often in conflict-ridden areas with strongly anti-American sentiments, Klare sees conflict as inevitable.

MacKay, David J. C., *Sustainable Energy without the Hot Air* (Cambridge: UIT Cambridge, 2009). MacKay is a former Chief Scientific Adviser to the Department of Energy and Climate Change in the UK and a professor at the University of Cambridge who tries to help us understand what a realistic effort would look like if the UK switched to sustainable energy by mid-century.

Smil, Vaclav, *Energy at the Crossroads: Global Perspectives and Uncertainties* (Cambridge, MA: MIT Press, 2003). Smil has spent four decades studying energy. Here he presents an introduction to the complexities and uncertainties of the subject. He shows the difficulties of changing from our dependence on carbon-emitting fuels, while at the same time explaining the need to do so.

Taebi, Behnam, and Sabine Roeser (eds), *The Ethics of Nuclear Energy: Risk, Justice, and Democracy in the Post-Fukushima Era* (Cambridge: Cambridge University Press, 2015).

Wald, Matthew L., "Getting Power to the People," *Bulletin of the Atomic Scientists*, 63 (September/October 2007), pp. 26–43. Wald, a long-time correspondent of the *New York Times* specializing in energy, examines the different energy alternatives to fossil fuels in a time of climate change.

Chapter 5

Climate Change

The Evidence and Impacts	172
Warmer temperatures	172
Food and water	174
Extreme weather	174
Sea level rise	175
Coral reefs	176
Air pollution	178
Infectious diseases	178
Agriculture	178
Disruption of natural ecosystems	179
Regional impacts	179
Africa	179
Asia	179
Europe	179
Latin America	180
North America	180
Polar Regions	180
Uncertainties	180
Abrupt climate change	180
Slower Atlantic currents	180
More intense storms	181
Clouds and soot	181
Other positive and negative feedbacks	181
What Is Being Done at Present?	181
What More Can Be Done?	182
Conclusion	185
Notes	185
Further Reading	187

Global Issues: An Introduction, Fifth Edition. Kristen A. Hite and John L. Seitz
© 2016 John Wiley & Sons, Ltd. Published 2016 by John Wiley & Sons, Ltd.

The overwhelming majority of scientists who specialize in the study of the Earth's climate, "climatologists" (not economists, political commentators, or meteorologists), have unequivocally affirmed the human race is now involved in an experiment of unprecedented importance to the future of life on this planet. A change in the global climate is now taking place, mainly because of the burning, by humans, of large amounts of fossil fuels – coal, oil, and natural gas. When these fuels are consumed, carbon, which accumulated in them over millions of years, is released into the atmosphere as a gas, carbon dioxide (CO_2) (see Figure 5.1). CO_2 in the Earth's atmosphere has increased significantly since the Industrial Revolution: by about 40 percent between the mid-1700s and the present. This increase is causing a warming of the Earth's surface – called "global warming" or the "greenhouse effect" – since CO_2 in the atmosphere allows sunlight to reach the Earth but traps some of the Earth's heat, preventing it from radiating back into space. While CO_2 is the largest contributor to global warming, other gases – such as methane, which comes from both natural and human causes; nitrous oxide, which comes from fertilizers and other sources; chlorofluorocarbons (CFCs), widely used in the past in air conditioning and refrigeration; and other halocarbons – can also cause global warming. Many of these gases are increasing significantly in the atmosphere.

There is strong evidence that in the past CO_2 and methane in the atmosphere were closely connected in some way with the Earth's temperature. European scientists in the Antarctic drilled a hole about two miles deep in the ice and withdrew a core of ice. Like the rings of a tree, the core indicated changing conditions in the past   in fact, back about 650,000 years. The scientists measured the amount of CO_2, methane, and nitrous oxide (all greenhouse gasses) in the air bubbles in the ice and

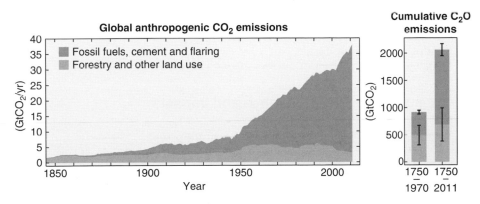

Figure 5.1   Global carbon dioxide emissions from human activity.

Note: Quantitative information is limited on emission time series of two other greenhouse gases, CH_4 (methane) and N_2O (nitrous oxide), from 1850 to 1970.

Source: IPCC, *Climate Change 2014: Synthesis Report*. Contribution of Working Groups I, II and III to the Fifth Assessment Report of the Intergovernmental Panel on Climate Change (Core writing team, R. K. Pachauri and L. A. Meyer (eds)). IPCC, Geneva, 2014. Summary for Policymakers, Figure SPM.1 (d), p. 3.

found two amazing facts. First, the amount of CO_2 and methane present in the Earth's atmosphere today is higher than in any previous time during those 650,000 years, and secondly, CO_2, methane, and the Earth's temperature went up and down closely together during that period.[1] The close relationship between the Earth's temperature and the carbon dioxide and methane levels is consistent with scientists' models for projecting climate impacts.

Under the sponsorship of the United Nations, in 1988 the Intergovernmental Panel on Climate Change (IPCC) was set up to study what was happening to the Earth's climate and the causes of the changes. Since its establishment, the IPCC has issued five of these "assessment reports" (the first in 1990 and the fifth in 2014) based on peer-reviewed, published scientific studies from thousands of scientists around the world. The IPCC is now recognized as the most authoritative organization on climate change. It won the Nobel Peace Prize in 2007 for its work. The IPCC's first report concluded that, probably because of the release of "greenhouse gases" by humans, an increase in the Earth's temperature would occur.[2] Since that first report, more evidence has increased scientists' confidence that something dramatic is happening to the Earth's climate, with humans largely responsible. In the IPCC's 2014 report, it reaffirmed that it is *"extremely likely"* that human influence has been the dominant cause of the observed warming since the mid-twentieth century.[3] It is one thing for politicians to call something "extremely likely," but for a Nobel laureate team of the world's leading climate scientists to do so based on scientific evidence signals that any debate on this matter is pretty much settled.

Notably, population and economic growth are the most important drivers of increased greenhouse gas emissions[4] – and as we have seen in earlier chapters, this growth continues to be significant at the global level. Numerous models of the Earth's climate have been made by climatologists and nearly all of these project that if current emission trends continue for even a few more decades, there is a significant likelihood of catastrophic impacts to the Earth's climate because of the increasing CO_2 and other greenhouse gases.

The Evidence and Impacts

Warmer temperatures

There is evidence, as can be seen in Figure 5.2, that since the Industrial Revolution began (1850) the temperature of the Earth has increased about 1.5 degrees Fahrenheit (about 0.85 degrees Celsius). Since the 1980s, every decade has been warmer than the previous one, which represents the warmest period since modern industrialization (1850) and likely the warmest in the last 1,400 years.[5]

The most common forecast of the computer models is that – if present trends continue – the amount of CO_2 in the atmosphere is expected to be double the preindustrial level before 2100, and according to the latest IPCC report, that will lead to an increase of 3.7 to 4.8 degrees Celsius (3 degrees Celsius equals about 5 degrees

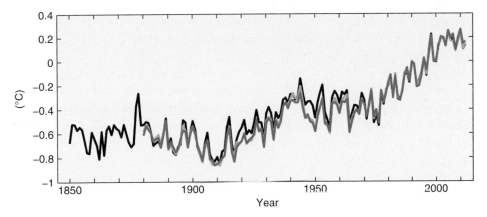

Figure 5.2 Globally averaged combined land and ocean surface temperature anomaly.

Source: IPCC, *Climate Change 2014: Synthesis Report*. Contribution of Working Groups I, II and III to the Fifth Assessment Report of the Intergovernmental Panel on Climate Change (Core writing team, R. K. Pachauri and L. A. Meyer (eds)). Geneva: IPCC, 2014. Summary for Policymakers, Figure SPM.1 (a), p. 3.

Fahrenheit) in average global temperature before the end of the present century; this increase can be moderated if the annual rate of greenhouse gas emissions can start declining at the global level.[6] (The amount of CO_2 in the atmosphere will not stop increasing after it has doubled, of course. Depending on how much carbon continues to be released on Earth, the CO_2 level in the atmosphere could keep rising.) Three degrees Celsius would be a more rapid change of temperature than has occurred in the past 10,000 years. While 3 degrees Celsius may not sound like very much, it would be a significant change. According to scientists of the US National Aeronautics and Space Administration (NASA), the temperature on Earth "would approach the warmth of the Mesozoic, the age of dinosaurs."[7] Scientists have concluded that, because of various "feedbacks," it is likely that the warming will be even more than they are predicting. They also warn that because of our incomplete knowledge about the processes involved in the Earth's climate, it is possible we will be confronted with "surprises" in the future.[8]

Heat waves are expected to become more common and more severe. Cities trap heat and their very young, elderly, and poor are especially vulnerable to heat stress. Mid-latitude urban areas such as Athens, Shanghai, and Washington, DC are more vulnerable than tropical and subtropical cities because their residents are less used to high temperatures. The death toll in cities during extreme temperatures can be surprisingly high, as was seen in Chicago where more than 700 people died during a four-day heat wave in the summer of 1995. In rural areas, hot, dry weather has been one of the main causes of many wildfires burning out of control in the western United States and other parts of the world.

Most global warming models predicted the Arctic region would be among the first regions to show significant effects caused by global warming. They have been proven to be correct. Average temperatures of the Arctic winters have risen about 10 degrees Fahrenheit over the past 30 years. The permafrost is thawing across the Arctic, leading to damage of buildings, pipelines, and roads in Alaska and Siberia as the land sinks. Temperatures have risen in the Arctic nearly twice as fast in recent decades as in the rest of the world.[9] Data from satellites since 1978 show on average annual Arctic sea ice has shrunk by about 4 percent per decade – and by even more during summer months.[10] In most computer models of the likely future, sea ice in both the Arctic and Antarctica is projected to continue to shrink. In several models the Arctic ice completely disappears by the latter part of the twenty-first century.

Food and water

Other evidence supporting the assertion that global warming has begun is the fact that most mountain glaciers in the world have been retreating since the late nineteenth century, affecting downstream water supplies.[11] Scientists have discovered the movements of some glaciers draining the great ice sheets in Antarctica and Greenland, the melting of which has recently accelerated.[12] Studies have shown that since the 1960s spring has come earlier and winter later for the higher latitude areas in the northern hemisphere. As shown in Figure 5.3, even as the growing season is extended, there have been overall reductions in crop yields, with climate change impacting wheat and corn yields across the globe, causing spikes in the price of food and cereals.[13]

Since the 1970s, droughts have become more intense, lasting longer and covering a wider area, especially in the tropics and subtropics. The IPCC in its 2007 report also cites evidence that over the past 50 years the number of cold days, cold nights, and frosts has decreased over most land areas and the number of hot days and hot nights has increased. In the northern hemisphere the average temperature during the second half of the twentieth century was higher than during any other 50-year period in the past 500 years, and likely 1,300 years.[14] Additionally, heat waves have become more frequent, breaking records and killing many thousands of people, especially those most vulnerable.

Extreme weather

The intensity of what is called "extreme weather events" (hurricanes/cyclones, violent thunderstorms, "winter storms," and windstorms) is expected to increase with higher peak wind speeds, and more heavy precipitation caused by warmer seas. Evidence is mounting that in North America, and potentially other regions, climate change is responsible for an increase in the intensity of extreme weather events like hurricanes.[15] The decade between 2005 and 2015 witnessed some of the most devastating storms in modern times, including major hurricanes causing billions of dollars of damage in the US cities of New Orleans and New York (and their surrounding

Figure 5.3   Climate impacts to agricultural production, by region and crop.

Note: Summary of estimated impacts of observed climate changes on yields over 1960–2013 for four major crops in temperate and tropical regions, with the number of data points analyzed given within parentheses for each category.

Source: IPCC, *Climate Change 2014: Impacts, Adaptation, and Vulnerability. Part A: Global and Sectoral Aspects. Contribution of Working Group II to the Fifth Assessment Report of the Intergovernmental Panel on Climate Change.* Cambridge: Cambridge University Press, 2014. Summary for Policymakers, Figure SPM.2 (c), p. 7.

regions), and typhoons wiping out entire villages or even islands in the Philippines and other Pacific countries.

Sea level rise

Warmer temperatures should cause the levels of the oceans to rise because melting glaciers and ice caps will add water to the oceans, and water expands when its temperature increases (thermal expansion of the oceans contributes about 25 percent of sea level rise).[16] Sea levels have risen on average by 3.2 millimeters per year from 1993 to 2010.[17] The rate has been higher in recent years. From 1993 to 2003 it was about 3.1 millimeters per year.[18]

A probable effect of a warming of the Earth's climate is that the level of the oceans will rise between 0.17 to 0.82 meters (about 0.5 to 2.5 feet) by the end of the twenty-first century.[19] Such a gradual rising of waters could lead to the evacuation of some coastal cities around the world. Sixteen of the largest cities with populations of over 10 million are located in the coastal regions. The rich countries will probably be able to build dikes to protect their cities, but poor countries such as Bangladesh probably cannot afford to do so. Also much coastal lowland around the world will be threatened. These lands are heavily populated at present, especially in the developing nations. Regions such as the Ganges–Brahmaputra Delta in Bangladesh, the Nile Delta in Egypt, and the Niger Delta in Nigeria are especially vulnerable. Island nations such as the Maldives in the Indian Ocean and the Marshall Islands in the Pacific Ocean could be inundated, and some islands are already seeing some residents leave: in 2014, a New Zealand court granted citizenship to a family evacuating Tuvalu in the South Pacific, prompting the *Guardian* newspaper to ask whether this marked a new era of climate refugees.[20] Higher sea levels cause much of their damage during storms when high sea surges hitting the coasts cause very destructive floods.

Coral reefs

Coral reefs are in serious decline around the world because of warmer seas, pollution, disease, and overfishing. An estimated 30 percent have already been severely damaged.[21] Here is what the United Nations Environmental Programme has to say about the situation in a recent report:

> Around 25 percent of the world's CO_2 emissions are being absorbed into the seas and oceans where it converts to carbonic acid. This is lowering the pH of the oceans and affecting its chemistry. For example, the concentration of carbonate ions is decreasing and is linked to the ability of many marine organisms to build reefs and shells.[22]

The chemistry of the oceans is being altered at a speed not seen for 65 million years – since the extinction of the dinosaurs. The ocean has absorbed almost one-third of all carbon dioxide emitted into the atmosphere, causing ocean acidification and other impacts.[23] The mean pH of the marine world has decreased by 0.1, corresponding to a 26 percent increase in hydrogen ions since the Industrial Revolution.[24]

Human interference with the climate system: assessment by the Intergovernmental Panel on Climate Change

Human influence on the climate system is clear. Yet determining whether such influence constitutes "dangerous anthropogenic interference" in the words of Article 2 of the UNFCCC [UN Framework Convention on Climate Change] involves both risk assessment and value judgments. This report assesses risks across contexts and through time, providing a basis for judgments about the level of climate change at which risks become dangerous.

Five integrative reasons for concern (RFCs) provide a framework for summarizing key risks across sectors and regions. First identified in the IPCC Third Assessment Report, the RFCs illustrate the implications of warming and of adaptation limits for people, economies, and ecosystems. They provide one starting point for evaluating dangerous anthropogenic interference with the climate system. Risks for each RFC, updated based on assessment of the literature and expert judgments, are presented [in this report]. All temperatures below are given as global average temperature change relative to 1986–2005 ("recent").

1 *Unique and threatened systems*: Some unique and threatened systems, including ecosystems and cultures, are already at risk from climate change (high confidence). The number of such systems at risk of severe consequences is higher with additional warming of around 1°C. Many species and systems with limited adaptive capacity are subject to very high risks with additional warming of 2°C, particularly Arctic-sea-ice and coral-reef systems.

2 *Extreme weather events*: Climate-change-related risks from extreme events, such as heat waves, extreme precipitation, and coastal flooding, are already moderate (high confidence) and high with 1°C additional warming (medium confidence). Risks associated with some types of extreme events (e.g., extreme heat) increase further at higher temperatures (high confidence).

3 *Distribution of impacts*: Risks are unevenly distributed and are generally greater for disadvantaged people and communities in countries at all levels of development. Risks are already moderate because of regionally differentiated climate-change impacts on crop production in particular (medium to high confidence). Based on projected decreases in regional crop yields and water availability, risks of unevenly distributed impacts are high for additional warming above 2°C (medium confidence).

4 *Global aggregate impacts*: Risks of global aggregate impacts are moderate for additional warming between 1–2°C, reflecting impacts to both Earth's biodiversity and the overall global economy (medium confidence). Extensive biodiversity loss with associated loss of ecosystem goods and services results in high risks around 3°C additional warming (high confidence). Aggregate economic damages accelerate with increasing temperature (limited evidence, high agreement), but few quantitative estimates have been completed for additional warming around 3°C or above.

5 *Large-scale singular events*: With increasing warming, some physical systems or ecosystems may be at risk of abrupt and irreversible changes. Risks associated with such tipping points become moderate between 0–1°C additional warming, due to early warning signs that both warm-water coral reef

and Arctic ecosystems are already experiencing irreversible regime shifts (medium confidence). Risks increase disproportionately as temperature increases between 1–2°C additional warming and become high above 3°C, due to the potential for a large and irreversible sea level rise from ice sheet loss. For sustained warming greater than some threshold, near-complete loss of the Greenland ice sheet would occur over a millennium or more, contributing up to 7 m of global mean sea level rise.

Source: IPCC, Fifth Assessment Report, *Climate Change 2014: Impacts, Adaptation, and Vulnerability*, Summary for Policymakers, p. 12 (footnotes omitted).

Air pollution

Higher temperatures tend to bolster the formation of pollutants such as ground-level ozone (O_3), which is one of the main components of smog. An increase in winds could disperse pollution whereas a decrease could help pollution levels to rise. An increase in rainfall can wash out pollutants, while a decrease can have the opposite effect.

Infectious diseases

A change in temperature and rainfall can affect the range of many infectious diseases. One obvious example is that the range of mosquitoes that spread malaria, yellow fever, and dengue fever could expand with increased temperatures and rainfall. The range of the black fly that carries river blindness is likely to expand, as also is that of the snail that carries schistosomiasis. People living on the edges of where these diseases are prevalent now are especially vulnerable because many have little resistance built up.

Agriculture

It is very hard to predict how climate change will affect agriculture in a specific area, but it is clear that overall agriculture can be severely disrupted by climate change. In a warmer world there would be major changes in the amount of rainfall and its location, with some areas getting more rainfall than at present and some less. Higher CO_2 levels can help some plants grow faster, but those higher CO_2 levels could also reduce nutritional values. Higher temperatures can extend the growing season in some regions and more rainfall can benefit crops in some areas, although more violent and extreme weather could significantly reduce yields. More droughts and extreme temperatures can devastate agriculture in other areas. The effect of climate change on plant pests and diseases is similar to that of infectious diseases. As mentioned in the chapter on food, a recent study by the US National Academy of Sciences concluded that overall a 1 degree Celsius increase in temperature over the norm would lead to a 10 percent decrease in corn, wheat, and rice yields.

An effort by the US government in 2000 to predict changes in food production in the country found that it was likely that crops would increase in the northern plains, where much of the country's wheat and corn is grown, but decrease in the southern states because of droughts and floods caused by heavy rains. The authors of the study admitted that many unknowns exist – for instance, they were unable to calculate the possible effects of flourishing weeds or migrating insect pests.[25]

Disruption of natural ecosystems

Natural ecosystems such as forests, rangeland, and aquatic environments provide a host of services to human and nonhuman life. Many of these services are still relatively unknown. Any disruption of these ecosystems because of climate change could have serious effects. Rough estimates now are that a doubling of CO_2 levels could cause from one-third to one-half of all plant communities and the animals that depend on them to shift their locations.[26] Some animals would not be able to do so because roads and urban sprawl would block their way. The shrinking sea ice in the Arctic is likely to make it much more difficult for polar bears to hunt for seals, one of their chief foods, thus leading to the bears' possible extinction.

Regional impacts

The IPCC previously reported regional changes in rainfall over the twentieth century, including increased precipitation along the eastern parts of the Americas, northern Europe, certain areas in Asia.[27] At the same time, already dry regions such as the Sahel have become even drier, as has the Mediterranean, southern Africa, and some areas in southern Asia.[28]

Here are a few examples taken from recent reports:[29]

Africa   By 2020, between 75 and 250 million of people are projected to be exposed to increased water stress due to climate change. … By 2020, in some countries, yields from rain-fed agriculture could be reduced by up to 50 percent.

Asia   By the 2050s, freshwater availability in Central, South, East and South-East Asia, particularly in large river basins, is projected to decrease. … Coastal areas, especially heavily populated megadelta regions in South, East, and South-East Asia will be at greatest risk due to increased flooding from the sea and, in some megadeltas, flooding from the rivers.

Europe   In southern Europe, climate change is projected to worsen conditions (high temperatures and drought) in a region already vulnerable to climate variability, and to reduce water availability, which impacts hydropower, tourism, and crop production generally. It is also projected to increase health risks due to heat waves, and the frequency of wildfires.

Latin America　By mid-century, increases in temperature and associated decreases in soil water are projected to lead to gradual replacement of tropical forest by savannah in eastern Amazonia. Semi-arid vegetation will tend to be replaced by arid-land vegetation ... Productivity of some important crops is projected to decrease and livestock productivity to decline, with adverse consequences for food security. In temperate zones, soybean yields are projected to increase.

North America　Warming in western mountains is projected to cause decreased snowpack, more winter flooding and reduced summer flows, exacerbating competition for over-allocated water resources. ... In the early decades of the century, moderate climate change is projected to increase aggregate yields of rain-fed agriculture by 5 to 20 percent, but with important variability among regions. Major challenges are projected for crops that are near the warm end of their suitable range or which depend on highly utilized water resources.

Polar Regions　The main projected biophysical effects are reductions in thickness and extent of glaciers and ice sheets, and changes in natural ecosystems with detrimental effects on many organisms including migratory birds, mammals, and higher predators.

Uncertainties

Abrupt climate change　Scientists examining the ice cores mentioned above have found evidence that at times in the past the climate of Earth changed abruptly to a new level which persisted for hundreds or thousands of years.[30] A threshold was crossed to cause each change, but scientists do not understand what these thresholds were. One scientist described our situation today as similar to when people in a canoe start to rock the boat. Nothing happens for a while until a threshold is crossed and the canoe suddenly tips over and the canoeists find themselves in the water. As strange as it may seem, the next section shows that one of these abrupt changes could be from warm weather to a rapid cooling for parts of our planet.

Slower Atlantic currents　Scientists have discovered some evidence that the currents that bring warm water from the tropics to North America and Northern Europe may be slowing.[31] The melting of the sea and land ice in the Arctic – especially in Greenland – may be diluting the ocean's salty water which is essential to keep the so-called "Atlantic heat conveyor" moving. While the evidence supporting this theory is still too incomplete to convince many scientists that this is happening,[32] there is wide agreement that if this did happen not only would North America and Northern

Europe face colder climates, but the monsoons that billions of people in Asia and Africa depend on to support their agriculture could be disrupted.

More intense storms   There is evidence that in at least some regions, storms have increased in intensity.[33] For example, in 2014, the US National Climate Assessment reported large increases in heavy precipitation in some parts of the country, leading to significant flooding and erosion.[34] This makes sense, as warmer air is able to hold more moisture.

Clouds and soot   Scientists admit unfamiliarity with the effects global warming will have on clouds. Some types of clouds could cool the Earth, while other types could heat it up more. Also largely unknown are the effect aerosols (soot) will have on weather. It is likely that large amounts of black carbon particles in the air over parts of India and China – from the burning of coal and biofuels by millions of villagers – are affecting the climate in various ways.[35] It is likely volcanic ash and human-produced soot are currently lowering some of the warming that would be occurring without it.[36]

Other positive and negative feedbacks   There are uncertainties over possible "positive feedbacks," those things that might occur as the warming takes place that will make it worse, such as a melting of the permafrost releasing more methane, and "negative feedbacks," those things that could make it cooler, such as an exploding algae population in a warmer ocean absorbing more carbon dioxide.

What Is Being Done at Present?

The 1992 Framework Convention on Climate Change, first presented at the Rio Earth Summit, has been ratified by 193 nations. The Convention called on nations to voluntarily reduce their emissions of greenhouse gases to 1990 levels. European nations, Japan, and about 40 small island and coastal states favored putting country-specific targets and timetables for reaching the targets in the treaty, but some countries, including the United States, opposed this and the timetables were not included. The industrial nations pledged to meet the goal of reducing greenhouse gases to 1990 levels by 2000. For the most part the industrialized nations did not meet this goal.

In 1997 many nations met at Kyoto, Japan, and agreed to a proposed treaty that did place legally binding limits on developed nations. No limits were placed on developing nations because they had historically produced few greenhouse gases and were making efforts to reduce their widespread poverty. The country-specific targets set in the 1997 treaty (called the Kyoto Protocol) meant that developed nations would reduce their greenhouse gas emissions by about 5 percent from their 1990 levels by 2008–12. As of 2014 the United States – the second largest annual producer of greenhouse gases (China is now the largest) – had still not ratified this treaty and there was no effort being made in the country to do so. The European Union did ratify it, and by 2002 the United Kingdom and Germany had reduced their emissions below their Kyoto targets. By 2005 enough nations had ratified the Kyoto Protocol to bring it into force. But by 2012 some high emitting countries such as Canada and Japan decided to withdraw from the treaty.

Since the ratification of the first treaty, countries have met at least annually to discuss the climate problem. In 2010 the nearly 200 countries at the annual UN climate conference rejected new treaty-based obligations in favor of a more decentralized approach to addressing climate change. They adopted a more formalized international system to report on and verify reductions made at the national level. They also set up a Green Climate Fund to help developing countries combat deforestation, shift to clean energy, and adapt to the impacts climate change will bring. However, whether enough funds will be available to pay for all of these needs remains uncertain.

As of mid-2015, countries had still not agreed on how they would reduce their collective climate emissions to avoid dangerous human-induced interference with the Earth's climate. Voluntary pledges to reduce greenhouse gases have been made by many nations, including the United States and China, but overall emissions reductions have not been in line with the level science predicts is necessary to stabilize the Earth's climate.

While the problem seems overwhelming at the global level, countries, cities, and many global citizens are all taking significant action to reduce their greenhouse gas contributions. Even some of the most historically intransigent – and highest emitting – countries such as the United States and China have been undertaking nationally significant actions to reduce their emissions. Whether this will lead to a transformative global effort remains uncertain, but one thing that is clear is that the problem of climate change is only getting worse, and will continue doing so until a critical mass of those causing the emissions make fundamental changes that shift the global development trajectory to a climate-safe pathway.

What More Can Be Done?

In the past, total CO_2 emissions and CO_2 emissions per capita have always been much higher in the more developed countries than in the less developed countries. Between 1970 and 2004 global emissions, mainly from the developed countries, of CO_2 and other greenhouse gases increased by 70 percent.[37] From 1990 to 2008 US greenhouse gas emissions rose by about 14 percent.[38] But as development spreads to some of the large emerging economies – such as China and India – and as their populations grow, they are producing a relatively larger percentage of the gases, especially as China relies mainly on coal, the fossil fuel that emits the most CO_2. At the same time, the world is beginning to decouple greenhouse gas emissions from economic growth: in 2015, for the first time in many decades, greenhouse gas emissions from the energy sector stabilized even though the global economy grew.[39]

The International Energy Agency (IEA) predicts that growing global energy demand and retired power plants will collectively result in an additional 7,200 gigawatts of energy production capacity by 2040.[40] How these new energy sources are built – whether through fossil fuels or renewable energy – will have a very large influence on global greenhouse gas emissions. If the IEA's prediction of a massive growth in the renewable energy sector proves correct, renewables will supply half of this new capacity–an unprecedented increase in the coming decades.[41] In fact, renewable energy capacity is expected to grow twice as much in poor countries as in wealthy ones.[42]

Given the urgency of the energy-climate crisis, many (particularly politicians in the United States) have called on higher-emitting countries in emerging economies, especially China and India, to take on nationally ambitious targets and actions to reduce their emissions. At the same time, while these countries command a substantial percentage of the global population and their total CO_2 emissions are relatively high, their per capita emissions still remain relatively low.

Eventually all nations, including the United States, will have to agree to reductions in greenhouse gas emissions well beyond those indicated in the Kyoto treaty if there is any possibility of stabilizing atmospheric CO_2 concentrations at even two or three times their preindustrial level. When, and whether, these actions will take place is unknown.

The prospects for the United States signing a new, binding multilateral treaty on climate change are not promising, but in recent years the United States has accepted its historical responsibility for climate emissions and has pledged to take action at the global level. Although the US Congress has not been able to pass significant climate legislation by both chambers despite concerted efforts to bring a bill forward in 2009, agency actions at the federal and state levels have generated key opportunities for the United States to reduce its greenhouse gas emissions. In 2015 President Barack Obama was the first US president to make a serious effort to address climate change. Since Congress would not act, he issued a number of executive orders designed to reduce US emissions. Meanwhile some individual states, cities, and companies are shifting to renewable energy sources such as solar and wind, but these efforts are far less than the national effort needed.

China is also pursuing many nonfossil fuel renewable energy sources. China hoped that improving the energy efficiency of its industry would be enough to cut emissions, but so far this has not produced the results hoped for. Its continuing reliance on coal as its main energy source makes it unlikely that China will, any time soon, reverse its growing production of CO_2 and other climate-destructive gases. But China has committed to taking nationally significant actions in the coming decades, as has the United States, which is a key global development given both countries' historical intransigence.

There are various policies that the United States and other nations could pursue that would help alleviate the threat of climate change. One would be to stop supporting and subsidizing programs to promote the increased use of coal and synthetic fuels made from coal and oil – such as tar sands – and to encourage the more efficient use of energy and its conservation. The development of renewable energy sources, such as solar and wind energy can be promoted.

Some experts have argued that a carbon tax – a tax on fuel according to the amount of CO_2 (and CO_2 equivalent) released – would give a big boost to the development of renewable energy and encourage technologies that make the use of energy more efficient. Because the prices of fossil fuels today are unrealistically low, not reflecting the health and environmental costs society will have to pay because that fuel is being used, there is little incentive to reduce their use. By the end of the twentieth century, five countries – Denmark, Finland, Norway, Sweden, and the Netherlands – had taken the lead in adopting carbon taxes.

In the short term, the United States and other high-energy users could switch from oil to natural gas as natural gas releases less CO_2 per equivalent amount of energy than petroleum or coal. If there is no methane leakage from production (which is far from certain), natural gas emits roughly 30 percent less CO_2 than oil and 40 percent less than coal.

Another policy would be to combat deforestation, since trees, along with other vegetation, absorb large amounts of CO_2.[43] Conversely, experts say deforestation is responsible for more than 10 percent of global emissions. The increasing destruction of the great tropical rainforests in Latin America, Indonesia, and the Congo Basin in Africa is cited by some experts as representing a real threat to the global climate.

The path for countries to develop and improve livelihoods without increasing CO_2 emissions is still being forged, but it is clearly in the interests of the global community – including wealthy historic emitters – to help countries develop sustainably.

Reducing our carbon footprints

I (Seitz) felt proud. As I sat on a bench on our campus I told a colleague I had recently calculated the amount of carbon dioxide I had avoided releasing into the atmosphere over the past 32 years by walking to work. Instead of driving a car to work I calculated I had reduced my personal carbon footprint by 13 tons (12 metric tons) of CO_2. Another colleague heard my statement and said, "I hate to say it, but Jack's actions were actually insignificant given the huge amount of CO_2 our society and the world produces every year." Was he right? From one way of looking at the huge climate change problem, of course he was. But from another perspective, my choices still made a difference.

I am responsible for my actions during my life and because my actions were better for the Earth and its living creatures (including myself), I was right to feel proud. Not everyone can or will walk to work, but many other ways exist to reduce the use of fossil fuels, and to cut our carbon footprints. What's your favorite way, reader? Have you stopped wasting energy, do you recycle, have you made your living and working areas more energy efficient, or have you even shifted away from using fossil fuels? If you have done any of these or others, you are taking steps to become part of the solution.

Conclusion

Addressing climate change demands institutional, technological, and behavioral changes orchestrated between global, national, local and even household scales at an unprecedented level. Greenhouse gas emissions have to peak and decline, led by historically wealthy countries whose economies grew in large part through the cheap combustion of fossil fuels. But even though wealthy historic emitters have to lead, the ultimate fate of the climate may be determined by faster growing economies in other countries – not just in India and China, but also in many other parts of the world. As billions of the world's poorest begin to shift from traditional fuels to electricity, billions more increase their consumption as demand for cars and modern conveniences grows in tandem with national economies. And while the energy sector is likely to be the biggest source of emissions, it also holds the biggest potential for reductions; land use choices regarding agriculture and deforestation will also play an important role in determining how much carbon the Earth both emits and absorbs. As the world works intently to decouple greenhouse gas emissions and economic growth, it seems that the daunting challenge of addressing climate change is shifting the very notion of "development" at a global level. Whether the world will rise to the challenge of following a more sustainable pathway remains to be seen. If it cannot, it is clear that severe, irreversible, and unprecedented changes will impact food security and economic production in other ways, meaning that in one way or another, climate change is "redeveloping" the world.

Notes

1 Edward Brook, "Tiny Bubbles Tell All," *Science*, 310 (November 25, 2005), pp. 1285–7.
2 J. T. Houghton, G. J. Jenkins, and J. J. Ephraums (eds), *Climate Change: The IPCC Scientific Assessment* (Cambridge: Cambridge University Press, 1990).
3 The Fifth Assessment Report of the Intergovernmental Panel on Climate Change (hereinafter IPCC AR5) consists of reports from three working groups and a synthesis report, see http://www.ipcc.ch/report/ar5/ (accessed July 2015). For the observation about human influence, see e.g. *Climate Change 2014: Synthesis Report*, Summary for Policymakers, p. 5.
4 IPCC AR5, *Climate Change 2014: Mitigation of Climate Change*, Summary for Policymakers, p. 8.

5   IPCC AR5, *Climate Change 2013: The Physical Science Basis*, Summary for Policy-makers, p. 5.

6   IPCC AR5, *Mitigation of Climate Change*, Summary for Policymakers, p. 9.

7   James Hansen *et al.*, "Climate Impact of Increasing Atmospheric Carbon Dioxide," *Science*, 213 (August 28, 1981), p. 966.

8   Houghton et al., *Climate Change*, pp. xi, xxvii.

9   Rodger Doyle, "Melting at the Top," *Scientific American*, 292 (February 2005), p. 31.

10 IPCC AR5, *Climate Change 2014: Impacts, Adaptation, and Vulnerability*, Summary for Policymakers, p. 7.

11 Houghton et al., *Climate Change*, p. xxix.

12 Richard Kerr, "A Worrying Trend of Less Ice, Higher Seas," and Ian Joughin, "Greenland Rumbles Louder as Glaciers Accelerate," both in *Science*, 311 (March 24, 2006), pp. 1698–721.

13 IPCC AR5, *Impacts, Adaptation, and Vulnerability*, Summary for Policymakers, pp. 5–6.

14 IPCC AR5, *Synthesis Report*, Summary for Policymakers, p. 2, and *Impacts, Adaptation, and Vulnerability*, Summary for Policymakers, p. 8.

15 IPCC AR5, *The Physical Science Basis*, Summary for Policymakers, p. 7.

16 Gabriele Hegeri and Nathaniel Bindoff, "Warming the World's Oceans," *Science*, 309 (July 8, 2005), p. 254.

17 IPCC AR5, *The Physical Science Basis*, Summary for Policymakers, p. 11.

18 Ibid., p. 2.

19 Ibid., p. 23.

20 Greg Harman, "Has the Great Climate Change Migration Already Begun?" *The Guardian*, September 15, 2014.

21 T. P. Hughes et al., "Climate Change, Human Impacts, and the Resilience of Coral Reefs," *Science*, 301 (August 15, 2003), p. 929.

22 United Nations Environment Programme (UNEP), "Acidification May Push Already Over-Stressed Oceans into the Red," press release, December 10, 2010, at http://www.unep.org/Documents.Multilingual/Default.asp?DocumentID=653&ArticleID=6849 (accessed July 2015), citing UNEP, *Environmental Consequences of Ocean Acidification: A Threat to Food Security* (2010).

23 IPCC AR5, *The Physical Science Basis*, Summary for Policymakers, p. 11.

24 UNEP, *Environmental Consequences of Ocean Acidification: A Threat to Food Security* (2010), at http://www.unep.org/dewa/Portals/67/pdf/Ocean_Acidification.pdf (accessed July 2015).

25 Andrew Revkin, "Report Forecasts Warming Effects," *New York Times*, June 12, 2000, pp. A1, A25.

26 World Resources Institute, UNEP, United Nations Development Programme, and World Bank, *World Resources 1998–99: A Guide to the Global Environment* (New York: Oxford University Press, 1998), p. 72.

27 IPCC, *Climate Change 2007: The Physical Science Basis* (Cambridge: Cambridge University Press, 2007), p. 7.

28 Ibid., p. 7.

29 IPCC, *Climate Change 2007: Impacts, Adaptation and Vulnerability* (Cambridge: Cambridge University Press, 2007), Summary for Policymakers, pp. 13–15.

30 Richard Alley, "Abrupt Climate Change," *Scientific American*, 291 (November 2004), pp. 62–9.

31 Detlef Quadfasel, "The Atlantic Heat Conveyor Slows," *Nature*, 438 (December 1, 2005), pp. 565–6.

32 "Overturning Assumptions," *Science*, 317 (August 17, 2007), p. 868.

33 Richard Kerr, "Is Katrina a Harbinger of Still More Powerful Hurricanes?" *Science*, 309 (September 16, 2005), p. 1807; and Claudia Dreifus, "With Findings on Storms, Centrist Recasts Warming Debate," *New York Times*, January 10, 2006, p. D2.

34 Justin Gillis, "Looks Like Rain Again. And Again." *New York Times*, May 13, 2014.

35 William Chameides and Michael Bergin, "Soot Takes Center Stage," *Science*, 297 (September 27, 2002), pp. 2214–15.

36 IPCC AR5, *Impacts, Adaptation, and Vulnerability*, p. 10.

37 IPCC, *Climate Change 2007: Mitigation of Climate Change* (Cambridge: Cambridge University Press, 2007), Summary for Policymakers, p. 3.

38 US Environmental Protection Agency, *Inventory of US Greenhouse Gas Emissions and Sinks: 1990–2008* (Washington, DC: US EPA, 2010), Executive Summary, p. 3.

39 International Energy Agency (IEA), "Global Energy-Related Emissions of Carbon Dioxide Stalled in 2014," March 15, 2015, at http://www.iea.org/newsroomand events/news/2015/march/global-energy-related-emissions-of-carbon-dioxide-stalled-in-2014.html (accessed July 2015).

40 IEA, *World Energy Outlook 2014* (Paris: IEA, 2014), Executive Summary, p. 4.

41 Ibid.

42 Ibid.

43 Humus, the organic material in topsoil, also stores large amounts of carbon.

Further Reading

Flannery, Tim, *The Weather Makers: How Man Is Changing the Climate and What it Means for Life on Earth* (New York: Atlantic Monthly Press, 2006). Originally a skeptic, the author is now convinced climate change is real. The book, in an interesting manner, describes the author's slow awakening to the dangers of global warming. He then provides the reader with a look at the climate shifts that have occurred over the past 65 million years, and ends with two contrasting futures – one in which we fail to act and the second where effective international action averts the worst effects of climate change.

Friedman, Thomas, *Hot, Flat, and Crowded: Why We Need a Green Revolution – and How it Can Renew America* (New York: Farrar, Straus & Giroux, 2008). Many American politicians and some economists believe confronting climate change will be bad for the US economy and hurt its competitive edge against those nations that are doing nothing or very little. Friedman believes they are wrong. He argues that going clean and green is the best way for America to remain an economic powerhouse.

Hoggan, James, and Richard Littlemore, *Climate Cover-Up: The Crusade to Deny Global Warming* (Vancouver: Greystone Books, 2009). The book seeks to explain the different tactics that have been used to create doubt in the public's mind that climate change is real.

Oreskes, Naomi, and Eric M. Conway. *Merchants of Doubt: How a Handful of Scientists Obscured the Truth on Issues from Tobacco Smoke to Global Warming* (New York:

Bloomsbury, 2010). One of the authors of this book, Dr Naomi Oreskes, Professor of the History of Science at Harvard University, has become the main object for attacks by deniers of climate change in the United States.

Tanner, Thomas, and Leo Horn-Phathanothai, *Climate Change and Development* (New York: Routledge, 2014). Climate change is redefining development pathways. This book provides a foundational exploration of the linkages and implications of climate change for development.

Weart, Spencer, *The Discovery of Global Warming* (Cambridge, MA: Harvard University Press, 2003). The *New York Times* called this book the intellectual journey to belief in global warming.

World Bank, *World Development Report 2010: Development and Climate Change* (Washington, DC: World Bank, 2010). This well researched and readable reference book has a wealth of information on how climate change is now affecting, and probably will affect in the future, both rich and poor nations. It also describes many ways the negative effects of climate change can be lessened.

Chapter 6

The Environment: Part I

The Awakening	190
The Air	192
Smog	192
Airborne lead	196
Ozone depletion	198
Acid rain	200
Climate change (global warming)	202
The Water	203
Water quantity	203
Water quality	203
The Land	206
Minerals	206
Deforestation	207
The Extinction of Species	211
The Extinction of Cultures	215
The Yanomami	216
Notes	218

We travel together, passengers on a little spaceship, dependent on its vulnerable resources of air and soil; all committed for our safety to its security and peace; preserved from annihilation only by the care, the work, and I will say, the love we give our fragile craft.

Adlai E. Stevenson, speech as US Ambassador to the United Nations (1965)

Global Issues: An Introduction, Fifth Edition. Kristen A. Hite and John L. Seitz
© 2016 John Wiley & Sons, Ltd. Published 2016 by John Wiley & Sons, Ltd.

The Awakening

The relationship between the environment and development has not been a happy one. Development has often harmed the environment, and environmental harm has in turn adversely affected development. Industrialization brought with it many forms of pollution, pollution that is undermining the basic biological systems upon which life rests on this planet. It took millions of years for these systems to evolve. Industrialization also vastly increased the rate of the extraction of natural resources.

The first world conference on the environment was held in Stockholm, Sweden, in 1972 under the auspices of the United Nations. At that conference the developed nations, led by the United States, pushed for greater efforts to protect the environment, while many less developed nations feared that an effort to create strict antipollution laws in their countries would hurt their chances for economic growth. The developing nations maintained that poverty was the main cause of the deterioration of the environment in their countries. What they needed, they said, was more industry instead of less.

Ten years later, the nations of the world again met together to discuss the state of the global environment, this time in Nairobi, Kenya. The positions of the rich and poor nations had changed dramatically. The developing nations generally were now more receptive to further efforts to protect the environment, since in the ten years between the conferences they had seen that environmental deterioration, such as desertification, soil erosion, deforestation, and the silting of rivers and reservoirs, was harming their efforts to develop and to reduce poverty. On the other hand, many of the rich nations at Nairobi, led by the United States, called for a slowing down of environmental initiatives until they had recovered from their economic recessions.

Even though the positions of the developed and developing nations had become somewhat reversed during the ten years between the two environmental conferences, there is no doubt that an awareness of the threat to the environment caused by human activities had by 1982 become worldwide. Only 11 nations had any kind of governmental environmental agency at the time of the first conference, whereas over 100 nations, 70 of them in the developing world, had such agencies by the time of the second. These agencies did much to educate their own governments and people about environmental dangers.

In 1992 the third environmental conference sponsored by the United Nations was held in Rio de Janeiro, Brazil. Popularly called the Earth Summit, and formally the Conference on the Environment and Development, it was attended by the largest number of leaders of nations in history for a conference of this type. They were joined by about 10,000 private environmentalists from around the world plus 8,000 journalists. Although frequent clashes happened between the representatives of northern rich countries and relatively poor southern countries in the preparatory meetings, which took place during the two years preceding the conference, three major treaties were signed by about 150 nations at the conference. One concerned the possible warming of the Earth's climate, which was discussed in Chapter 5. The Framework Convention on Climate Change called on nations to curb the release of greenhouse gases that may be causing a change in the world's climate that will prevent nations from developing in a sustainable manner. Because of the insistence of the United States, no specific targets or timetables were placed in the treaty, but it did call for nations to eventually reduce the emissions of their greenhouse gases to 1990 levels.

The second treaty – the Convention on Biodiversity, providing for the protection of plant and animal species – was signed by most nations. The United States did not sign it and stood fairly alone in its opposition to it. The opposition by the first Bush administration in the United States to these environmental initiatives can be explained partly by timing: 1992 was a presidential election year and President Bush was vulnerable to attack because of slow economic growth and a huge governmental deficit. (He was in fact defeated that year in large part due to the poor economic conditions in the United States.)[1]

Although the third treaty, the Convention to Combat Desertification, did not receive as much attention as the prior two, the United Nations is now focusing on it, especially as it relates to helping countries adapt to climate change.

The Rio Earth Summit made the term "sustainable development" known throughout the world. The term means that economic growth in the present should not take place in such a manner that it reduces the ability of future generations to meet their own needs. Economic growth and efforts to improve the living standards of the few or the many should be sustainable; in other words, they should be able to be continued without undermining the conditions that permit life on Earth, thus making future development impossible or much more difficult. The term represents an effort to tie economic growth, the protection of the environment, and social development together, a recognition that future economic growth is possible only if the basic systems that make life possible on Earth are not harmed. It also implies a recognition that the economy, the environment, and social conditions are all important, that economic development and the reduction of poverty are essential to the protection of the environment. Sustainable development was endorsed by the conference and a new organization – the Commission on Sustainable Development – was set up under the United Nations to monitor the progress nations are making to achieve it.

In 2002 the fourth UN environmental conference was held in Johannesburg, South Africa, under the title World Summit on Sustainable Development. One of the main clashes between nations was unusual. The European Union proposed a target that nations would set as their goal for switching to renewable energy from fossil fuels. The goal was to have 15 percent of world energy come from renewable sources by 2010. European nations felt that in order to hold nations responsible for their actions, specific targets were necessary; without them it is difficult to measure progress or lack thereof. The United States strongly opposed this and with the help of oil-producing nations such as Saudi Arabia and Canada, along with Japan, got the provision dropped from the final conference agreement. The final agreement endorsed many of the Millennium Development Goals, discussed in Chapter 2. Some cited the creation in the conference of "public–private partnerships" as an attempt at decentralized and voluntary efforts for sustainable development as an accomplishment of the conference. (But these have generally turned out to be ineffective.) Many environmentalists were disappointed with the results of the conference, frequently blaming the lack of leadership from the United States, whose president, George W. Bush, was one of the few country leaders who didn't attend the conference. In the words of the UN Secretary-General Kofi Annan, "Obviously, this is not Rio."[2]

Ten years later, in 2012, countries met again in Rio for another international conference on sustainable development. Countries shared progress they had made and discussed challenges going forward, but largely diverted conversations about targets to sustainable development goals as a part of the Millennium Development Goals discussions, whose target period ended in 2015. Countries also diverted conversations about climate and energy to parallel negotiations under the UN Framework Convention on Climate Change. There are two ways to view this development: one is that countries have found environmental problems challenging and wish to avoid taking on new, high-profile commitments. The other is that the concept of "sustainable development" has become so mainstream that environmental considerations have become integrated into the broader development dialogue.

Regardless of how countries approach sustainable development, environmental problems continue to grow as consumption and population increase. Nations vary greatly on how well they are treating the environment. In 2014, a study by Yale and Columbia universities in the United States rated Switzerland, Luxemburg, and Australia as the best, while the United States was ranked 33 of 178 countries.[3] This portion of the book, two environment chapters, considers the intersections between environment and development in light of traditional economic development pathways and their impacts. In this chapter, we will look at the air, water, and land as shared resources that not only serve as the base of development activities but also receive many of the impacts associated with modern development. After looking briefly at the use of natural resources in the world, we will learn why the extinction of species is accelerating, as well as the role of development in threats to human cultures.

The Air

Smog

Industrialization has brought dirtier air to all parts of the Earth. From factories and transportation systems, with their telltale smokestacks and exhaust pipes, harmful and sometimes toxic fumes are constantly emitted into the air. A few spectacular instances in the twentieth century resulted in large numbers of people becoming ill or dying because of the toxic gases in the air they breathed: 6,000 became ill and 60 died in the Meuse Valley in Belgium in 1930; 6,000 became ill and 20 died in Donora, Pennsylvania in 1948; and in London tens of thousands became ill and 4,000 died in 1952. (It was this last-mentioned instance that led the United Kingdom to pass various laws to clean up the air, which have proved to be quite successful: within just a few decades, 80 percent more sunshine reached London than had in 1952.)[4] But even more deaths are caused by accumulated daily levels of pollution: in 2012, the World Health Organization (WHO) estimated that air pollution caused 3.7 million premature deaths across the globe. Of these, 88 percent occurred in lower- and middle-income countries.[5]

Rapid economic growth may have benefited China from a financial standpoint, but not without serious environmental consequences. The rapid increase in air pollution has caused illness and premature death among the population. Estimates of the healthcare and non-healthcare costs of China's air and water pollution combined have totaled about $100 billion per year, or about 5.8 percent of the country's GDP.[6] Air pollution was a contributing factor in about 1.2 million of the country's premature deaths in 2010 and caused an eight-year-old girl to develop lung cancer in 2013, making her China's youngest lung cancer patient.[7] Though the situation is severe, China is not alone: many other countries face similar problems, and Earth's environment transcends state boundary lines.

Over recent decades, a number of industrialized countries, including the United States, have made significant progress in reducing air pollution in their large urban areas. In 1970 the Clean Air Act was passed in the United States, and it was then strengthened in 1990. During the first 20 years after the law was passed, lead was reduced by 95 percent, sulfur dioxide by about 30 percent, and particulates (tiny particles in the air) by about 60 percent.[8] According to the US Environmental Protection Agency, about 200,000 premature deaths and 700,000 cases of chronic bronchitis were avoided.[9] And during the second 20 years of the Act, emissions of six principal pollutants fell by about 40 percent, while the economy (i.e., GDP) grew by about 60 percent. The US Environmental Protection Agency estimates the economic value of the air quality improvements brought about by this law by 2020 will reach almost $2 trillion, a value which greatly exceeds the costs of efforts to comply with the law.[10]

In spite of this progress, much remains to be done. Even in countries with significant laws and enforcement regarding pollution, many cities still experience a number of days each year when the air is considered unhealthy. At the beginning of this century, southern California had the dirtiest air in the United States, with some areas claiming over 400 days in a two-year period when the air was unhealthy to breathe.[11] Since then, significant progress has been made in cleaning the air in Los Angeles. According to an article in the *Los Angeles Times*: "In 1979, the South Coast Air Basin [of which Los Angeles is a part] experienced 228 days above the state one-hour ozone standard; in 2007 the number of days in violation was down to 96. ... It is also broadly true for the other pollutants that comprise smog."[12] But despite the progress cited above, the reduction of particulates turned out to be less impressive than first thought. Studies in the 1990s and early 2000s indicated that extremely small particulates spewed by vehicles, factories, and coal power plants, which were not illegal to release until 1997, were the greatest risk to health and estimated to be causing up to 60,000 premature deaths per year in the United States.[13] These particulates generally pass through the nose and throat and enter the lungs, where they can have serious health effects on the lungs and heart.

Asthma rates among children in the United States have been increasing rapidly and may be linked to air quality, and have a disproportionate impact on the poor, who live in neighborhoods with dirtier air than the wealthy. A 2012 study found that of the 320,500 annual cases of asthma in children living in Southern California, about 27,000 (8.4 percent) are at least partially due to air pollution from major roads.[14] Poor and minority children in the inner cities had the highest rates of asthma.[15]

Europe has improved its air, but more needs to be done there as well. In 2012, air pollution in Europe caused more deaths than car accidents.[16] At the beginning of this century, ozone (a key component of smog) cost European farmers about 6 billion euros annually.[17] And a more recent UK government report found that air pollution lowered life expectancies in the UK by an average of 7–8 months, and also could lead to 50,000 premature deaths every year.[18] Overall in the European Union, the average life expectancy is 8.6 months lower due to exposure to certain particulate matter pollution.[19]

Your "friendly" coal power plant

Much of the world's electricity comes from power plants fueled by coal. A typical 500-megawatt coal plant, which can power a city of about 140,000 people, burns about 40 train cars of coal each day and yearly releases into the air the following pollutants: 3.7 million tons of carbon dioxide, 10,200 tons of nitrogen oxide, 10,000 tons of sulfur dioxide, 720 tons of carbon monoxide, 500 tons of small particles, 220 tons of hydrocarbons, 225 pounds of arsenic, 170 pounds of mercury, 114 pounds of lead, 4 pounds of cadmium and other toxic heavy metals.

Source: "A Typical Coal Plant," *Nucleus* (Spring 2000), p. 5.

Emerging economies are facing air pollution problems even greater than those in some of the countries which first developed industrial economies. At present, cities such as Mexico City, Bangkok, Beijing, Delhi, and Jakarta have serious air pollution. In most of the megacities, air pollution is worsening because of increased industry, vehicles, and population. Pollution levels sometimes exceed the air quality standards of the World Health Organization by a factor of three or more.[20] The WHO estimates that about half of all people living in urban areas in 91 countries breathe air with pollution levels at least 2.5 times higher than the WHO guidelines.[21]

Mainly because of its heavy use of coal, China has some of the worst air pollution in the world. In 2014, only eight of China's 74 largest cities met the government's air quality standards.[22] Levels of particulates in the air in Beijing have

Map 6.1 China

exceeded WHO levels by 20 times in early 2015.[23] In 2007 it was reported that "only 1 percent of the country's 560 million city dwellers breathe air considered safe by the European Union."[24] China's environmental agency estimated that 31 percent of the total air pollution came from motor vehicle exhaust. To improve the air quality, more than 300,000 vehicles in Beijing and an additional 5 million in other areas are expected to be decommissioned.[25] However, Chinese consumers purchased 20 million motor vehicles in 2012, the world's largest automobile market that year.[26] In 2004 Chinese refineries were purchasing a cheaper quality of petroleum which had a very high sulfur content, an amount high enough to ruin the catalytic converters being installed in China's new cars to reduce air pollution.[27] A significant percentage of deaths in China have been caused by lung disease at least partly attributed to serious urban and household air pollution.[28] By 2015 China's concern with pollution was growing, but efforts to reverse the damage done to the environment and being done by a quarter-century of rapid economic growth were still inadequate to the task.

Indoor air pollution can also be severe in poorer nations, mostly in rural areas, but also sometimes in urban areas. About one-half of the world's people rely on traditional fuels for heating and cooking.[29] Wood, crop waste, dung, and coal are often used as fuels, and women and children especially are exposed to the smoke when these fuels are burned. In many of these dwellings the air pollution indoors is far worse than outdoor pollution. The World Bank has identified indoor pollution in developing nations as one of the four most urgent environmental problems. Various clean-burning stoves have now been developed and efforts are being made, both by for-profit and by nonprofit organizations, to get them to poor households.[30]

The world's largest pollution cloud

A two-mile thick cloud of brownish haze, about 4 million square miles large, has been discovered high over the Indian Ocean by scientists. The cloud, about the size of the United States, is composed of pollutants, mainly from the burning of fossil fuels as well as from forest fires and wood-burning stoves in the Indian subcontinent, China, and Southeast Asia. Winds during the winter monsoons bring the pollution out to sea as the prevailing winds are coming down from the Himalayan Mountains. In the late spring and summer the winds reverse and the haze is blown back over the land. The pollutants combine with the monsoon rains and come back to Earth as acid rain.

In addition to this cloud, there are other similar clouds around the Earth, but the worst are in Asia, according to a 2008 United Nations report.

Sources: William Stevens, "Enormous Haze Found over Indian Ocean," *New York Times*, June 10, 1999, p. A23; Worldwatch Institute, "Air Pollution Still a Problem," in *Vital Signs 2005* (New York: W. W. Norton, 2005), pp. 94–5; Andrew Jacobs, "U.N. Report Points to Peril From Noxious Brown Clouds," *New York Times*, November 14, 2008, p. A6.

Airborne lead

The history of airborne lead in the United States is a success story, a good illustration of effective actions by government to reduce this dangerous pollution. While most of the lead pollution in the past was in the air, lead also is found at present in some household water and paint so the pollutant still exists, but in much more limited amounts than it did before.

Scientists are able to estimate the amount of lead there was in the world's air in the past by taking core samples of ice in the Greenland ice cap. The air bubbles in the ice, ice that represents past rainfall, show that from 800 BCE to the beginning of the Industrial Revolution, around 1750, the amount of lead in the air was low. There was a major increase after 1750 and a huge increase after World War II when the use of leaded gasoline for cars rose sharply. In 1965 the lead concentration in the Greenland ice was 400 times higher than the level in 800 BCE. Other studies showed that, in 1980, the bones of Americans contained 500 times more lead than those of prehistoric humans.[31]

Children are the most susceptible to harm from breathing lead. They inhale two to three times as much lead in the air per unit of body weight as do adults because their metabolic rates are higher and they are more active than adults. There is no known safe level of lead in the human body. High levels of lead poisoning can lead to death, but even low levels can cause learning difficulties and behavioral problems. In the early 2000s nearly a million children in the United States were estimated to have

Plate 6.1   Vehicles, such as this truck/bus, provide a lot of air pollution in the cities of the developing countries.

Source: Ab Abercrombie.

unhealthy levels of lead (as defined by the Centers for Disease Control (CDC), the US government's top health organization) in their blood, and black children were more likely to have high levels of lead than were white children.[32] Many of these children were living in old houses or apartments with lead-based paint flaking off from walls (which young children, who tend to put everything in their mouths, wind up ingesting), and old lead water pipes. (Disturbing research shows that the lead paint industry in the United States actively promoted the use of leaded paint for 40 years, even after studies showed that lead could poison children and its use had been banned or restricted in a number of countries.)[33]

Research published in the *New England Journal of Medicine* (one of the most respected health journals in the United States) in 2003 found that levels of lead even lower than the CDC acceptable level affected children's brains and that there was no known way to restore intelligence lost because of lead damage. These studies indicate the possibility that 90 percent of children in the United States have been harmed by lead poisoning.[34]

There has been a significant improvement in reducing the amount of lead in the blood of Americans. Between 1976 and 1991 the amount dropped by nearly 80 percent.[35] Because of tighter federal government air pollution requirements, new cars were required to use unleaded gasoline, and many experts believe that the reduced use of leaded gasoline was the cause of the lower lead levels in blood. About 90 percent of the lead in the air comes from leaded gasoline. A total ban on leaded gasoline in the United States came into effect in 1995. The European Union effectively banned all leaded gas in 2000. Some lead experts believe that recent lower levels of violent crime in the United States are the result of lower lead blood levels in US children born after 1980 rather than better enforcement.[36]

Aggressiveness and delinquency linked to lead in bones

A study of 800 boys in the United States showed a direct link between the amount of lead in the boys' bones and their behavior. Those with a relatively high level of lead in their bones had more aggressiveness and delinquency than those boys with low levels of lead. Other studies have shown that childhood antisocial behavior is a strong predictor of criminal behavior as an adult. The director of the study cautioned that the study did not show that lead was the cause of childhood delinquency, but only that it was probably one cause. That is not surprising, he stated in an interview, because "lead is a brain poison that interferes with the ability to restrain impulses."

Source: Jane E. Brody, "Aggressiveness and Delinquency in Boys Is Linked to Lead in Bones," *New York Times*, February 7, 1996, p. B6.

Another indication that the efforts to reduce the lead used in gasoline were having a beneficial effect can be seen in the Greenland ice caps. The study of the lead concentrations in Greenland snow showed a drop in the lead concentrations to about the levels existing in the early 1900s, before the widespread use of leaded gasoline.[37]

About 90 percent of gasoline used in the world is now lead-free and by 2009, according to the United Nations Environmental Programme, only 12 countries were still using leaded gasoline. Although significant progress has been made in the United States, the problem of lead has not been completely solved. Despite banning lead in gasoline decades prior, one-quarter of the homes in the country with children under six still contained lead-based paint at the turn of this present century.[38] In spite of this fact, we consider the efforts by the US government to significantly reduce the danger of lead in the air to be a real success story. In the United States in 2010, according to the Environmental Protection Agency, lead levels in the air were 92 percent lower than in 1980.

Ozone depletion

The ozone layer in the atmosphere protects the Earth from harmful ultraviolet rays from the sun. Scientists believe that life on Earth did not evolve until the ozone layer was established. That layer has been reduced by substances produced by humans, mainly in the developed nations. Chlorofluorocarbons (CFCs) – used as a propellant in aerosol spray cans, as a coolant fluid in refrigerators and air conditioners, as an industrial solvent, and in the production of insulating foams – can destroy ozone. Ozone can also be destroyed by halons, which are chemicals used in fire extinguishers, and also produced when nuclear bombs are exploded.

Scientists are agreed that major depletion of the ozone layer causes serious harm to humans, other mammals, plants, birds, insects, and some sea life. Skin cancer increases, as do eye cataracts. Increased ultraviolet light also adversely affects the immune system of humans, which protects them from many possible illnesses. As is mentioned in Chapter 8 on technology, one of the most harmful effects of a nuclear war would be the damage it would do to the ozone layer, which would affect life far beyond the combat area.

By analyzing past data, British scientists in the mid-1980s discovered that, during two months of the year, a hole was occurring in the ozone layer over the South Pole. Almost every year since it was discovered, the hole has continued to get larger. The hole (which is actually a significant reduction in the ozone normally found above that region, not a 100 percent decrease) galvanized the world to act to reduce the danger.

Nations first met to discuss this problem in Vienna in 1985. Two years later about 60 nations met in Montreal, Canada and created the Montreal Protocol, an agreement to cut the production of CFCs by 50 percent by 1998. But further evidence that the depletion of the ozone layer was progressing faster than expected led the nations of the world to meet again – this time in London in 1990. The 90 nations attending that meeting agreed to speed up the phasing out of ozone-destroying chemicals. They agreed to halt the production of CFCs and halons by the year 2000. Less developed nations were given until 2010 to end their production and a fund was set up, mainly contributed to by the industrialized nations, to help the poorer nations obtain substitutes for ozone-depleting chemicals.

New disturbing evidence of the ozone depletion danger was made public in the early 1990s. The US Environmental Protection Agency announced in 1991 that data from satellites, which had been collected over the previous 11 years, revealed that the ozone layer over large parts of the globe, including the layer above the United States and Europe, had been depleted by about 5 percent. This loss was occurring twice as fast as scientists had predicted. Based on the new findings, the agency calculated that over the next 50 years about 12 million people in the US would develop skin cancer and more than 200,000 of them would die from it.[39]

Based on the new US evidence and on new data collected by an international team of scientists, which showed that the depletion was occurring in the dangerous summer months as well as in the winter, 90 nations met in Copenhagen, Denmark, in 1992 and agreed to further accelerate the ending of ozone-destroying chemicals. All production of CFCs was to end by 1996 and halon production was to end by 1994. (Developing nations were again given a ten-year grace period to phase out the production of these two chemicals.)

Chlorine compounds enter the atmosphere mainly as a component of CFCs and it is chlorine and some other compounds that scientists now believe are causing the destruction of the ozone layer. One atom of chlorine can destroy 100,000 molecules of ozone. CFCs will remain in the atmosphere for about 50 to 100 years.

The depletion of the ozone layer: how to protect yourself

People prone to sunburns should try to keep out of the sun from 11 a.m. to 3 p.m. – when ultraviolet (UV) rays are at their strongest – and they should use hats and sunscreen lotion, which protect against both UV-A and UV-B rays, when exposed to the sun. Sunglasses that block UV rays should also be worn. While it is important to use sunscreen lotions, dermatologists agree that people who are at especially high risk of getting melanoma, a dangerous kind of skin cancer, should not rely on sunscreens but should stay out of the sun. At high risk are those with fair skin who sunburn easily, those with many moles, and those with a family history of skin cancer. Clouds offer little protection, but shade does. Melanoma rates are now on the increase in many countries, including the United States.

Sources: Walter Willett *et al.*, "Strategies for Minimizing Cancer Risk," *Scientific American*, 275 (September 1996), pp. 94–5; Jane Brody, "How to Save Your Skin in the Season of Sun," *New York Times*, May 24, 2005, p. D7.

The Montreal Protocol has brought impressive results. The transition away from the widely used CFCs and other ozone-depleting chemicals has been faster than many thought possible. In the ten-year period after the Protocol was signed in 1987, consumption of these chemicals dropped over 70 percent, with most developed nations meeting the Protocol's goal, as amended, to cease CFC production by 1996.

In 2014, for the first time in modern history, scientists discovered that the ozone is recuperating. CFC concentrations in the atmosphere have now peaked and started a slow decline. Ozone loss is expected to gradually diminish until about 2065, when the ozone layer is expected to return to its 1980 condition.[40] The global recovery of the Earth's ozone demonstrates a concrete success for international efforts based on science working in tandem with nations, businesses, and citizens to solve a major global environmental problem.

Acid rain

When fossil fuels are burned, sulfur dioxide and oxides of nitrogen are released into the air. As these gases react with moisture and oxygen in the atmosphere in the presence of sunlight, the sulfur dioxide becomes sulfuric acid (the same substance as is used in car batteries) and the oxides of nitrogen become nitric acid. These acids then return to Earth in rain, snow, hail, or fog. When they do, they can kill fish in lakes and streams, dissolve limestone statues and gravestones, corrode metal, weaken trees, making them more susceptible to insects and drought, and reduce the growth of some crops. The effects of acid rain on human health are not yet known. Some scientists fear that acid rain could help dissolve toxic metals in water pipes and in the soil, releasing these metals into drinking water supplies.

In the United States, acid rain comes mainly from sulfur dioxide produced by coal-burning electric power plants in the Midwest and from the nitrogen oxides from auto and truck exhausts. Acid rain has caused lakes in the northeastern part of the country to become so acidic that fish and other organisms are unable to live in them. Other areas of the country, such as large parts of the South, Northwest, Rocky Mountains, and the northern Midwest, are especially sensitive to acid rain since the land and lakes in these areas contain a low amount of lime. Lime tends to neutralize the falling acid. An international dispute was created between Canada and the United States because a large amount of the acid rain falling on huge sections of Canada came from industrial emissions in the United States. Pollution also came from Canada to the United States especially from a large Canadian smelter near the border. There are now acid rain agreements between the two countries to reduce this pollution.

Europe is facing a similar problem. Many lakes in Norway and Sweden are now so acidic that fish cannot live in them, and about one-third of the forests in Germany are sick and dying. Much of the acid rain falling in Northern and Central Europe comes from industry in Britain, Germany, and France. The section of Europe with the greatest damage from acid rain lies in Eastern Europe. The efforts of the communist governments in that region to keep up with the West led to industrial growth fueled with lignite coal, which is cheap and abundant in the region but also extremely polluting. In one area where former East Germany, former Czechoslovakia, and Poland met, more than 300,000 acres of forests have disappeared and the ground is poisoned by the huge amount of acid rain that fell there from the coal-fed power plants and numerous steel and chemical plants. Local foresters dubbed the area the "Bermuda Triangle of pollution," as winds carried the sulfur dioxide and other pollutants to other areas of Europe.

Acid rain was first observed in industrial England in the late 1800s, but nothing was done about it. In the 1950s the response to the increasing air pollution in the United States and Europe was to build tall smokestacks on factories so that emissions of toxic gases would be dispersed by the air currents in the atmosphere. These tall smokestacks led to a noticeable improvement in the air around many factories, smelters, power plants, and refineries, but the dispersal of noxious gases in the atmosphere gave more time for these gases to form into acid rain. We now realize that the tall smokestacks violated a fundamental law of ecology, one that biologist Barry Commoner has labeled the "everything must go somewhere" law.[41] Matter is indestructible, and there are no "wastes" in nature. What is excreted by one organism as waste is absorbed by another as food. When the food is toxic, the organism dies.

Thus is explained the beautiful clear water in lakes that have become highly acidic, where many forms of plankton, insects, and plants have ceased to exist.

In 1990 the US Congress passed major amendments to the Clean Air Act, which calls for a large reduction of sulfur dioxide emissions from power plants. An innovative provision was put into the law that allows polluters to buy and sell their rights to pollute (the total amount of emissions indicated in the law must not be exceeded and the level will be lowered over time). The hope was that this provision would encourage polluters to find the cheapest way to cut their pollution. This hope has generally been realized according to the US Environmental Protection Agency. During the decade of the 1990s the cost of the scrubbers on coal plants that remove sulfur dioxide fell by about 40 percent, thus making it cheaper for plants to remove the pollutant. Because of this result, the sulfur dioxide "cap and trade" program has been cited as a successful example of market-based environmental solutions and has served as a model for other programs along the same line.[42] A cost-benefit analysis of the acid rain program (including the cap and trade provision) shows that the benefits of the program outweigh the costs 46 to 1.[43]

But neither the 1990 Clean Air Act amendments nor the "cap and trade" system has entirely solved the acid rain problem in the United States. Some scientists believe the Clean Air Act is still too weak. Even after ten years of reducing sulfur dioxide, the acidic level in many lakes in the northeastern United States had still not decreased. The Environmental Protection Agency reported that sulfur dioxide emissions decreased about 70 percent from 1990 to 2008, but nitrogen dioxide emissions went down only 35 percent in the same period. Some scientists believe the failure to reduce nitrogen emissions – coming mainly from power plants, car and truck emissions, and gases released from fertilizer – is now the main factor preventing more progress in reducing acid rain in the United States.[44]

Acid rain is now becoming a major problem in Asia with the increased use of fossil fuels as industrialization spreads. China's acid rain now falls on Seoul, South Korea and Tokyo. According to the *Journal of Geophysical Research*, many of the particulates in the air of Los Angeles come from China. And China's State Environmental Administration in 2006 reported that in 2005 China became the leading source of sulfur dioxide pollution in the world.[45] High levels of acid rain have been reported in northeast India, Thailand, and South Korea, which are near or downwind from major urban and industrial centers in parts of China and elsewhere. According to a high government official in China, by 2004 acid rain was falling on two-thirds of the country.[46]

Climate change (global warming)

The release of carbon dioxide into the atmosphere from the burning of fossil fuels and other gases is causing a change in the Earth's climate. This subject has been discussed in Chapter 5. Along with water, it is likely to be the most serious environmental problem of the twenty-first century.

The Water

Water as a resource has two critical elements for development: quantity and quality. A very basic premise of human survival is that regular access to safe water supplies is necessary to sustain life. The world faces serious water problems. At the beginning of the present century it was estimated that about 2.5 billion people lived in river basins where water was scarce and of these about 1.5 billion people lived in areas of high water scarcity.[47]

Water quantity

A surprising positive development regarding the use of water occurred in the United States at the end of the twentieth century. After the amount of water used by industry and agriculture consistently grew faster than population growth for the first eight decades in the century, an unexpected change occurred. Instead of water use continuing to rise, from 1980 to 1995 it actually declined by about 10 percent even though the size of the population had increased about 15 percent during the same period. The main cause of the decrease was that industry and agriculture had learned to use water more efficiently rather than look for more water. Most of the best dam sites were already being used, the cost of new dams had risen, and the negative environmental effects of dams became well known. Also federal antipollution laws made it cheaper for industry to find ways to use less water and to recycle it rather than clean it before discharging waste water into rivers and lakes.

Modern agriculture, which uses more water than any other human activity – about 70 percent of all water withdrawals – can significantly reduce the water needed for irrigation with new methods such as drip irrigation at the roots of plants rather than spraying the water into the air where much of it is lost through evaporation and by the wind. In the United States, water use by individuals has not decreased but it has leveled off. Water use also decreased in Europe and there has been a slowdown worldwide in the expansion of irrigation.

Because of increasing population and rapid industrialization in some developing nations, water use in the developing world is expected to continue to grow. According to the World Bank, industry in China uses 4 to 10 times more water per unit of production than the average in industrialized countries.[48] But developing nations might adopt some of the more efficient ways to use water that the West has discovered and thus reduce their need.

Water quality

Development, to date, has tended to turn clean water into dirty water as often as it has turned fresh air into dirty air. In 2010 about 15 percent of the world's population had no access to clean drinking water. Of these people, most lived in rural areas.[49]

In the United States the deterioration of the nation's rivers was dramatized in the late 1960s when the Cuyahoga River in Ohio caught fire because it was so polluted. That event helped lead to the first Earth Day in 1970 and helped prod the US Congress into passing the Clean Water Act of 1972, which set a ten-year goal to return the nation's waterways to a state where they would be "fishable, and swimmable." Ten years later, many United States rivers, streams, and lakes were cleaner than they had been when the Act was passed, but many still remained too polluted to allow safe fishing or swimming.

By 1990 the $75 billion that had been spent in the United States on upgrading sewage treatment facilities during the previous two decades had resulted in a significant improvement of the nation's waters. A survey about that time revealed that 80 percent of the nation's rivers and streams were now safe for fishing and 75 percent were safe for swimming. But that survey also indicated that about 130,000 miles of rivers were still unsafe for fishing and 150,000 miles were unsafe for swimming.[50]

Why was there still a significant problem after this large expenditure and 20 years of effort? A large part of the reason was that little progress had been made in reducing the pollution from urban and agricultural runoff. Especially during storms, huge amounts of polluted water from city streets and the lawns of houses drain directly into rivers and lakes, untreated by local sewage treatment plants, and huge amounts of water drain from farms and golf courses, water laden with pesticides, herbicides, and fertilizers. In 2010 the Environmental Protection Agency reported about 40,000 bodies of water in the United States remain impaired (i.e., not fishable and/or swimmable).[51]

The status of freshwater fish in the United States reveals the extent of the problem of water quality in the country. In 2011 the Environmental Protection Agency reported that about 9,000 miles of rivers and streams had fish consumption advisories to limit or avoid eating fish caught there.[52] A 2004 Environmental Protection Agency report identified mercury and PCBs (polychlorinated biphenyls, an especially persistent and toxic class of industrial chemicals) as the leading causes of fish contamination.[53] Usually the warnings did not advise that no fish should be eaten but rather that their consumption should be limited. For example, the state of New York recommended in 2005 that people eat no more than one meal of fish weekly from any fresh water in the state.[54]

The Great Lakes are less polluted by PCBs than they were in the past – the use and discharge of the chemical is now tightly controlled and its production is banned – but concentrations of the chemical in fish have continued to rise as it works its way up the food chain. While PCB contamination in other waters in the country is still a problem, contamination of fresh waters also comes from air pollution, such as mercury from coal-burning power plants, industrial sites, and incinerators, and from other chemicals. In 2004 the head of the Environmental Protection Agency said that mercury emissions from human causes in the United States had declined nearly 50 percent from 1990 to 1999 but admitted that virtually every river and lake in the country had fish contaminated with mercury.[55] The contamination of water by mercury is now recognized to be a global problem, with countries having recently adopted an international treaty to address the global impacts of mercury pollution.

Other wealthy countries are also experiencing serious water pollution problems. In the 1970s and 1980s the river Rhine was commonly called the sewer of Europe. By the mid-2000s a cooperative effort, some of it begun in the 1950s, by the five nations on the Rhine to clean up the river was having significant results. About 20 to 25 billion euros were spent, much of them on new sewage treatment plants, and salmon have been restocked in the river.[56] Its success has led some to cite this effort as a model for other international efforts to reduce pollution.

Why does there continue to be so much dangerous water pollution? Industry must take a large part of the blame since traditionally industrial wastes have been dumped into nearby water as often as they have into the air overhead. Many industries are no longer dumping wastes into nearby rivers, but some dumping still goes on. In the United States some legal dumping is allowed after a permit has been issued and often some treatment of the waste by the polluter is required.

A particularly challenging problem for water pollution today is chemicals. The chemical industry has had a huge growth in the industrial world since World War II. Chemicals are now finding their way into waterways, many of which are being used for drinking water. A nationwide study of streams and lakes in the United States at the beginning of the twenty-first century found low levels of many chemicals. About half the waterways had trace amounts of insecticides, antibiotics, fire retardants, disinfectants, insect repellents, some nonprescription drugs, and steroidal compounds. It is not known if these levels are harmful to plants, animals or humans. Water treatment plants are unable to remove these substances from the water. Studies in Europe a decade earlier found similar results in European waterways.[57]

In the less wealthy countries – most of the world – some 50 percent of the waste water was discharged directly into waterways without being treated. About 60 percent of the urban population, but only 40 percent of the rural population, had access to an improved sanitation system.[58] In China in 2014 about 280 million people did not have safe drinking water, roughly half the level from the previous decade.[59] But the situation is not so promising in other parts of the world. Bangladesh has possibly faced the worst water problem of all. In an effort to help the country get clean water, the government and international aid organizations in the 1970s and 1980s funded the digging of tube wells, about 10 million overall, but no one tested the groundwater for arsenic. It is now recognized that many of the tube wells are contaminated with arsenic, a deadly pollutant, and 20 to 35 million people are drinking this water. The WHO declared the situation the "largest mass poisoning of a population in history."[60] A study of this situation in 2010 stated: "One in five deaths in Bangladesh stems from arsenic in drinking water …Up to half of Bangladesh's population of around 140 million people, and further millions around the world, are chronically exposed to arsenic through drinking water …"[61] With expected warmer temperatures coming with global warming, increasing deforestation that makes water supplies more erratic, and increased pollution, the scarcity of safe water supplies is expected to be a major concern in the twenty-first century. More conflicts between countries over the availability of water, such as those that have taken place in the past between India and Pakistan, Israel and Syria, and Mexico and the United States, may occur. New efforts by nations to cooperate to deal with water scarcity might also occur. (This cooperation could follow the example of the long-term successful efforts by nations bordering the Mediterranean Sea – both Arab and non-Arab – to reduce the pollution in that body of water.) It is not clear whether conflict or cooperation will be the main result of coming water scarcity.

The Land

Whenever development has occurred, its effect on the land has been profound. The economic growth that comes with development increases the amount of goods and services available for human consumption. More natural resources from the land are required for the production of these goods, of course, and their extraction disturbs the land greatly. But even more widespread are the changes to the land that come with the disposal of the goods after they are no longer of use, and of the wastes that are created in the manufacture of the goods. Many of these wastes are artificial substances that never existed before in nature; thus nature has few, if any, ways of breaking them down into harmless substances. Development also affects the vegetation on the land, in some ways reducing it and in some ways helping to preserve it. In this section we will focus on two of the many changes to the land that come with development: the use of minerals, and deforestation. These two changes are affecting many human beings in such direct ways today that it is important that we look at them closely.

Minerals

Since the world's population is growing exponentially, as we learned in Chapter 1, it is probably not surprising that the consumption of nonfuel minerals is also growing exponentially. But, unlike petroleum, the supplies of minerals are not becoming exhausted. Another great difference between nonfuel minerals and energy supplies is that the actual cost of producing most minerals decreased over the twentieth century.[62] This reduced cost occurred, even as lower-grade ores were being mined, because of advances in technology – such as better exploration techniques, bigger mechanical shovels to dig with, bigger trucks to haul the ore away, and bigger ships to transport it to processing plants. Whether new technology will continue to keep the cost of minerals low in the future is a subject that is debated by scientists and economists. As ores containing a lower concentration of the desired minerals are mined and less accessible deposits are turned to, processing costs will probably rise. More ore must be processed, more energy and water used, and so more wastes are produced. Huge strip mines are often used, with a devastating effect on the land.

Some analysts have observed that mineral prices in the past did not reflect the true environmental costs of extracting and processing the minerals, but with new pollution laws in most industrial countries, the mining industry will have to assume more of these costs unless they extract the mineral from less developed countries where environmental regulations are often lax.

One trend is apparent: most industrialized nations are becoming more dependent on foreign countries for their minerals. The United States is a mineral-rich country; in the 1950s it was nearly self-sufficient in the most important industrial minerals. By the late 1970s it was self-sufficient in only 7 of the 36 minerals essential to an industrial society. Western Europe and Japan are even more dependent on imported minerals than is the United States. This increasing dependency on ores from foreign countries, many of which are essential for the advanced technologies common in the West, has strongly influenced the developed nations' foreign policies toward the developing world, where many of the minerals are found. The export of minerals (an extractive industry) has often had a surprisingly negative effect on the developing country if the government is weak. Despite the hope for prosperity for the mineral-rich country, the large sums of money generated (at times called the "resource curse") often lead to widespread corruption and violent conflict over control of the resources.

Deforestation

The UN Food and Agriculture Organization (FAO) reported in 2012 that the destruction of the world's tropical forests continues at a high rate.[63] Most of the deforestation is taking place in the developing world. On average, about 20,000 square miles of forest was cut down annually from 2000 to 2010, including in areas never previously logged.[64] This loss was partially offset by the Russian Federation, the United States, China, India, and many European nations, which increased their forest coverage from 2005 to 2010.[65] During this period, 80 countries either increased their forest area or reported no change in forest coverage.[66] But, overall, the rate of deforestation remains high.

The cutting of the trees in a tropical forest puts a severe strain on the soil since the trees protect the soil from the violent rains that are common in the tropics. And once the soil is washed away, it is not easily recreated. Some studies have estimated that from 100 to 1,000 years are needed for a mature tropical forest to return after human disturbances have taken place.[67]

Over the past 5,000 years almost 7 million square miles of the world's forests have been cut down; this pace has accelerated in recent history to make room for farms, pastures, and other uses.[68] During the last few centuries, 50 percent of global forests have been degraded, with 30 percent of these being completely cleared.[69] In 2010, 36 percent of global forest coverage was comprised of original forests.[70] These forests are known as "primary forests" or "old growth forests," and they are very different from the human-modified forests that are prevalent in the world today. These forests contain between 50 and 90 percent of the world's plant and animal species. From 2000 to 2010, about 154,000 square miles of primary forests were lost.[71] At least 76 countries have lost all of their old growth forests, and much of what remains is endangered by human activities.[72]

The greatest threat to tropical forests in the future is from logging (much of it illegal), from making pasture land for cattle, for agricultural crops including tree crops such as palm oil plantations in Indonesia, and in the Brazilian Amazon, cutting down the forest for the growing of soybeans. About 20 percent of the Amazon has been deforested in the last 20 years.[73] Brazil, Indonesia, and Australia had the fastest rates of deforestation in the world from 2000 to 2010.[74]

In contrast to the situation in tropical forest countries, temperate forests (mostly in richer nations) actually increased in cover during the twentieth century as marginal farmland was taken out of production and trees were allowed to return to the land. In the United States, forest coverage expanded by about 1,500 square miles per year over the first two decades of this century.[75] In Europe the forests have expanded recently, although at a relatively slow rate, some of which depends upon how "forests" are defined and accounted for.[76] From 2000 to 2010 China, the United States, and India had the largest annual gain in forest cover.[77] This expanding tree cover contains much less diversity of life than the old growth forests, of course, and may even include industrial tree plantations – which many people do not even consider "forests" at all.

One more factor lessens the impressiveness of numbers in forest cover growth: the FAO does not include logging in some of its deforestation estimates because, at least in theory, the forest can grow back after it has been logged. In reality logging often degrades the forest, leading to serious erosion and making it less suitable as a habitat for a wide variety of plants and animals. China and Malaysia have stopped much of their own deforestation, but are now importing logs from Indonesia and other areas. So many fires are set in Indonesia annually by illegal commercial activity, poor farmers, and plantation owners to clear forest land that the smoke from the fires covers a huge area, causing disruptions in air and sea travel and health problems, and has even been attributed to massive haze clouds in Southeast Asia.[78] In 2006 Indonesia agreed to export logs from much of its remaining tropical forests to China and replace the forests with vast palm oil plantations. The oil is sold to countries like China and India for use in products such as detergents, soaps, and lipsticks.[79] Demands for palm oil continue to increase, providing powerful economic incentives to convert forest land to palm oil plantations, destroying trees, threatening orangutans, and sometimes even displacing families dependent on the forest.

Deforestation is a serious problem because it can lead to erosion of the land, it can cause the soil to harden, and it can make the supply of fresh water erratic. Scientific studies support the hypothesis that deforestation can lead to significant changes in the climate. In addition to more greenhouse gas emissions, these changes usually mean less rainfall. Sometimes deforestation leads to too much water in the wrong places. Serious floods are occurring now in India in areas that had never experienced flooding; it is believed that the cutting down of forests in the Himalayan mountains, the watershed for many rivers in India, is causing the flooding. Rioting has even been reported among some of the tribal peoples of India who are protesting the cutting of their forests by commercial firms. In just one year – 1998 – government officials in two countries admitted that the cutting of trees had led to disastrous events in which many people died. In China it was recognized that the clear cutting of forests along the upper reaches of the Yangtze River contributed to the unusually severe flooding that year. In Italy mudslides from a deforested mountain covered five villages.

China has started a massive reforestation program hoping to stop the expansion of its deserts. Billions of trees have been planted. But the deserts continue to expand and sandstorms (that can be detected as far away as the western United States) increased from about five a year in the 1960s to about 25 in the 1990s; in recent years, at least some of these sandstorms were so large and powerful that they eventually reached California.[80] As reported by the United Nations in 2009, China at present is planting forests on about 4 million hectares annually (10 million acres).[81]

Provided they remain standing, forests absorb a significant amount of CO_2 yearly, thus helping to combat climate change. Scientists working in the Amazon have estimated that the Amazon rainforest alone could be absorbing over 1 billion tons of CO_2 each year. These scientists have found that in the sections of the forest they are studying, more trees are growing per hectare than in the past and the trees are growing faster and larger than before. They attribute this surprising finding to the increased amount of CO_2 in the atmosphere. They have also concluded that only large, undisturbed sections of the forest absorb large amounts of CO_2. Sections of the forests that have been logged, burned or fragmented actually lose CO_2 to the atmosphere.[82]

A study published in *Nature* estimates that the world's remaining tropical rainforests remove about 5 billion tons of CO_2 from the atmosphere annually. The lead author of that report, Dr Simon Lewis, a Royal Society research fellow at the University of Leeds, said, "We are receiving a free subsidy from nature. Tropical forest trees are absorbing about 18 percent of the CO_2 added to the atmosphere each year from burning fossil fuels, substantially buffering the rate of climate change."[83]

Forests in the temperate zones of the Earth absorb far less CO_2 than do the tropical rainforests, but they do absorb a significant amount. Studies in high-latitude forests have shown that the soils of the forests actually absorb much more CO_2 than the trees themselves. Scientists estimate that peat and other organic matter in the soils absorb two-thirds of the CO_2, while the trees absorb the remaining one-third.[84]

Deforestation not only destroys a valuable "sink" for CO_2, but it also releases the gas. Trees that are burned after they are cut, which is common when the forest land is cleared for settlements or for farming, release significant CO_2 into the atmosphere. The Intergovernmental Panel on Climate Change has estimated that around 180 gigatons of carbon have been released into the atmosphere by deforestation and other land use change since 1750, meaning that land use changes have been responsible for nearly one-third of all anthropogenic emissions in recent centuries.[85]

Although there are many causes of deforestation, the United Nations has cited poverty, lack of enforceable property rights, and the lack of incentives for a proper

Plate 6.2   Deforestation in Mexico.

Source: Jamie Dwyer.

forestry management system as contributing to the problem. Research in Brazil indicates that now less than 20 percent of the deforestation in Brazil is caused by small subsistence farmers.[86] Logging – much of it illegal – leads to roads being built into previously inaccessible forests and landless peasants follow these roads looking for land to farm.

An example of a government-supported resettlement effort that led to serious deforestation took place in northern Brazil. In the early 1970s the Brazilian government began a large colonization project in the Amazon basin, moving people in from the poverty-ridden northeastern section of the country. It was hoped that the resettlements would help reduce the poverty in the northeast and provide food for an expanding population. Unfortunately, both hopes faded as colony after colony failed. The main reason for the failure was that tropical forest land is actually not very fertile, in spite of the huge trees growing on it. Such trees get their needed nutrients directly from decaying leaves and wood on the forest floor, not from the topsoil, which in many places is thin and of poor quality. This explains why many of the settlers had experiences similar to that of the following Brazilian peasant who described what happened to his new farm in the Amazon: "The bananas were two feet long the first year. They were one foot long the second year. And six inches long the third year. The fourth year? No bananas."[87]

If only small plots of the forest are cleared, regeneration of the forest is possible. Some peoples have practiced what is known as shifting cultivation in the tropical forests. They clear a piece of land and farm it for a year or two before moving on to a new piece of land. As long as this remains small in scale, the damage to the forest is limited, but any large-scale use of this type of agriculture can lead to irreversible damage to the forest.

Some tropical soils contain a layer known as laterite, which is rich in iron. When these soils are kept moist under a forest they remain soft, but if allowed to dry out, which happens when the forest cover is removed, they become irreversibly hard – so hard that they are sometimes used for making bricks.

In Central America and in Brazil, large areas of forests are being cut down to make pastures for the raising of cattle. The cattle are intended mainly to supply the fast-food hamburger market in the United States. The raising of cattle on large ranches for export does not, of course, do anything to solve the food problems in the exporting countries, or to provide land to the landless.

Local people can earn income from the forests through sustainably harvested forest products (fruits, coffee, rubber, etc.) and through "ecotourism." This type of tourism focuses on the growing number of tourists (generally from wealthier countries) who wish to visit tropical forests and other spots that have been left more or less in a natural state. Additionally, in some countries payments are being made to forest-dependent communities for "ecosystem services" such as carbon sequestration or watershed conservation. If evidence exists that local people can earn more income by letting the forests remain than by cutting them down, a strong argument can then be made supporting their preservation. Also, local people can be enlisted in the efforts to prevent deforestation since they will have an economic stake in the preservation of the forests.

Logging is one of the leading causes of deforestation. To a lesser degree, the landless and the poor around the world today are assaulting the remaining forests for agricultural land and for fuel. As poverty is the root cause of the hunger problem, discussed in Chapter 3, and one of the root causes of the population explosion, discussed in Chapter 1, so also is it one of the causes of deforestation. Development can reduce poverty, and when it does this for the multitude, it can reduce one threat to the world's forests. Development can also lead to the destruction of the forests as they are cleared for cattle farms, for lumber, for commercial ventures, and for human settlements. As with the population problem, development in its early stages seems to worsen the situation, but development that benefits the many and not just the few can eventually help relieve it. And "low-carbon development" is an emerging pathway some countries are following, which includes efforts to stem forest loss as a way to reduce greenhouse gas emissions.

The Extinction of Species

No one knows for sure how many species of living things there are on the Earth. Biologists today generally make educated guesses that the number is between 10 million and 100 million.[88] (Scientists have given a name to about 2 million of them, and of those named, only about 10 percent have been studied in any detail.) Through-out the Earth's history, new species have evolved and others have become extinct, with the general trend being that more new species are created than die out. It is now believed that because of human actions this trend has been reversed, with extinctions outnumbering the creation of new species. And the trend appears to be increasing.

The marvels of life on Earth

Can any living being using its own power travel 7,000 miles (11,265 kilometers) nonstop – without eating or resting – and end up at its desired destination? Can any human being do this? No human being can, but a little bird named the bar-tailed godwit can. The bar-tailed godwit flies over the Pacific Ocean from Alaska to its wintering grounds in New Zealand and Australia over nine days. Modern science does not understand how the bird can do this. It is truly one of life's marvels.

Unfortunately, some of the habitats of migrating marvels like the godwit are now under serious threat.

Source: Carl Zimmer, "7,000 Miles Nonstop, and No Pretzels," *New York Times*, May 25, 2010, p. D1.

According to Edward O. Wilson of Harvard University, probably the most respected of all US biologists, the world has experienced five major periods, or "spasms," of extinction of large numbers of species, from which it took millions of years to recover. These extinctions were caused by natural forces, such as a change of climate. Wilson believes that because of the vast growth of the human pop-ulation and the related widespread deforestation and overuse of grasslands that are now occurring on our planet, the Earth is heading into the sixth and worst period of extinction of species. Wilson estimates the present rate of extinction as about 27,000 species per year, or three per hour. (The normal "background" rate is about 10 to 100 per year.) If the present rate continues, Wilson estimates that 20 percent of all the species in the world will be extinct in 30 years.[89] Robert May, zoologist at the University of Oxford, who is a past-president of the Royal Society and until 2000 was chief science advisor to the British government, has estimated the present extinction rate as 1,000 times as great as before the arrival of human beings.[90]

Whereas hunting used to be the main way humans caused extinction, it is now generally believed that the destruction of natural habitats is the principal cause of extinctions. As the human population grows, humans exploit new areas of the world for economic gain and often destroy life forms as they do so. Biologists believe that about one-half of all species live in tropical forests, which as we have seen are being cut down at an increasing rate. There is now a growing recognition that climate change, discussed in Chapter 5, could become as dangerous to biodiversity as the loss of habitats.[91]

Many of the species in the tropics have never been studied by scientists. But based on past experience, it is believed that many of these unknown species contain properties that could directly benefit humans. Many prescription drugs have a key natural component in as an active ingredient. The importance of some of these drugs can be illustrated by the example of just one plant from the tropical rainforests, the rosy periwinkle. Drugs are now produced from this plant that have enabled 80 percent remission rates in leukemia and Hodgkin's disease patients.

Exotic species are vital to the health of modern agriculture. The wild varieties and locally developed strains of a number of major grains grown today have characteristics that are of vital importance to modern seed producers. Seeds are needed with natural resistance to the diseases and pests that constantly threaten modern agriculture. Many farmers today utilize only relatively few, highly productive varieties of seeds in any one year. The monocultures that are planted are especially vulnerable to diseases and to pests that have developed resistance to the pesticides being used. An example of how this works was shown in 1970, when 15 percent of the corn crop in the United States was killed by a leaf disease, causing a $2 billion loss to farmers and indirectly to consumers because of higher prices. That year, 70 percent of the corn crop used seeds from only five lines of corn. The disease was finally brought under control with the aid of a new variety of corn that was resistant to the leaf disease. The new corn had genetic materials originating in Mexico.[92]

Insects from tropical forests can at times prove extremely valuable to American farmers. Citrus growers in the United States saved about $25–30 million a year with the one-time introduction from the tropics of three parasitic wasps that reproduced and preyed on the pests attacking the citrus fruit.[93] (The introduction of exotic species by humans for profit, or amusement, or by accident into areas to which they are not native is now recognized as having great potential for harm. Since the new species usually has no natural predators in the new area, it can multiply rapidly, destroying or displacing other desirable animals or plants, as was the case with the introduction of rabbits into Australia, and of European starlings and the kudzu plant into the United States.)

American ecologist Paul Ehrlich does not believe that developing nations can preserve tropical habitats on their own since their financial needs are so great. What is needed in the world, he feels, is a new awareness that the diversity of life forms on Earth is a priceless treasure that benefits all humanity and that all share a responsibility for helping to preserve it. He states: "Over 95 percent of the organisms capable of competing seriously with humanity for food or of doing us harm by transmitting diseases are now controlled gratis by other species in natural ecosystems."[94]

As discussed earlier, at the 1992 UN Conference on Environment and Development in Rio de Janeiro, a proposed treaty to try to slow down the loss of species was presented. The treaty, formally named the Convention on Biological Diversity, called for the study of each nation's biodiversity and a commitment to preserve the biodiversity that exists on Earth. By the beginning of the twenty-first century nearly every nation in the world had ratified the treaty except the United States.

A suggestion for a practical way to combat this daunting problem of the extinction of species is that conservation efforts could be focused on a relatively few, highly vulnerable "hot spots" where there is a large concentration of species found nowhere else in the world. Of the more than 30 hot spots that have been identified, 25 of them contain the last habitats for about 45 percent of the Earth's plant species and 35 percent of its land-based vertebrate (fish, amphibian, reptile, bird, and mammal) species. The top eight spots of these 25 are southern coastal India and Sri Lanka, the island of Madagascar, Indonesia, Brazil's Atlantic forest, the Caribbean Islands, Burma and other parts of Southeast Asia, the Philippines, and the eastern mountains and coastal forests of Kenya and Tanzania.[95]

Edward O. Wilson has joined those who now believe that while protecting "hot spots" is important, and should be expanded, it may no longer be enough. To really protect biodiversity, we must be concerned with protecting the whole biosphere. The variety of species on Earth and their habitats provide essential services to life that the market cannot put a price tag on, services such as "nutrient cycling, the formation and enrichment of soils, the detoxification of pollutants and other forms of wastes, the provision of freshwater, the regulation of the atmosphere and climate, and the stability of ecosystems." Wilson believes that to preserve species "we must push back the deserts, replant the forests, preserve water supplies, reduce pollution, restore topsoil, and stabilize the climate."[96]

Two metaphors have been used to help people understand what the loss of biodiversity means. One is that of the loss of rivets and the other is of the loss of threads. In the first metaphor the extinction of a species is seen as being like taking a rivet out of an airplane. One probably doesn't matter, nor two, but if you keep pulling out the rivets eventually the airplane will crash. This metaphor conveys the idea of a collapsed ecosystem. The other metaphor says that the loss of a species is like pulling a thread out of a beautiful tapestry. You won't even notice a few pulled out but the more you pull the less rich in color is the tapestry. If you pull too many out in one location the tapestry may even tear.

Some scientists say that while these two metaphors can be useful to understand what the loss of biodiversity can mean, neither fully explains the complexity of real life. They point out that while it is true that the greater the species loss, the simpler and duller nature becomes, it is also true that the complexity of life forms can actually keep an ecosystem from collapsing, especially during times of stress such as a drought. Also, all species are not of equal importance in keeping an ecosystem healthy. There may be key ones that provide vital services to the others. If they are lost, the others depending on them are in danger.[97]

The Extinction of Cultures

There are about 15,000 nations on our planet and about 200 nation-states. The nation-states are the political entities, what are commonly referred to as countries. They are often made up of several or many individual nations, or different cultures. The nation is a group of people that share a common history, a common ancestry, and usually a common language and a common religion. They often have common traditions, common ways of doing certain things and of interacting with each other and toward outsiders. Because of these similar features that make them different from other peoples, each nation's people see the world and their place in it differently than others, approach problems differently, and have arrived at different solutions to situations humans face. The unique language of the culture is used to pass the common history and traditions down to the young. The United Nations now estimates that of the approximately 7,000 languages in the world, by the end of this century about 90 percent of them will be endangered.[98] The term "endangered language" means that the group that speaks the endangered language – which is often unwritten – is becoming so small that there is a real possibility the group will die out or become absorbed by the larger dominant culture around it and will disappear forever.

Should we care? What will be lost if a culture dies out? The answer to that question is in some ways similar to the answer this book has given to the growing extinction of species. Species represent the amazing variety of life forms on this planet. Their interrelationships are still imperfectly known – to put it mildly – and that can affect the health, and even survival, of one of the species, our own. Cultures also represent the amazing variety of human life on Earth. But here it is not the form of life that is different, but the different ways members of one species – the human species – have created to live. The culture represents the accumulated knowledge of one group, knowledge that is available to others to pick and choose from, so they can improve their own lives. In addition, as with species, the multitude of cultures makes life on Earth extremely rich and varied. The discovery of that variety often leaves an observer with a sense of awe and with a realization that the death of any species or culture leaves life less wonderful.

"Development," in a consumption-oriented sense, especially since World War II, has often been equated with the culture of the United States. The United States is the largest producer of goods and services and its culture is closely associated with material wealth. Freedom from the burdens of excessive control by government and freedom from the restrictions common in more traditional societies are also characteristics of United States society. These characteristics have contributed to an emphasis on innovation and change that has led to many new products and services. So it is not surprising that "development" and United States culture have seemed to go together. Some other cultures have found that many of their youth are more attracted to the US culture than to their own. Even within the United States, youth in communities with strong cultural identities of their own have found that it is extremely difficult to keep from being absorbed by the dominant culture. These youth may want to become successful and accepted, and some may believe that this will come only if they are more like the dominant culture, not different from it.

Because of the worldwide popularity of US movies, music, fast food, and clothes, and of the English language, it is common to read that the American culture is replacing local cultures in many countries. But some recent studies indicate that only some rather superficial aspects of the American culture are being adopted, such as Coca-Cola and Big Macs, while more important values are not. For example, a study has shown that the cultures of Northern Europe, such as those of the Nordic countries, are actually better representatives of "modernity" than is the American culture with its more widespread traditional religious and social values.[99] European cultures place a higher value on leisure and government social services than does the American culture, which emphasizes earning higher income so people can acquire more material objects. Many Europeans seem to be happy to trade income for more leisure to enjoy life and, maybe not surprisingly, Europeans have a higher "satisfaction with their lives" than Americans do.[100]

Some people are giving a new respect to the previously marginalized cultures of indigenous and tribal peoples. There is a slowly growing recognition that these traditional cultures may have knowledge that developed countries need if they are going to survive – such as an ability to live in harmony with nature, a concern for future generations, and a knowledge of how to foster a sense of community.[101] Indigenous and tribal peoples in tropical forests have been finally recognized as possessors of important knowledge regarding natural drugs in plants and of skills that have enabled them to live in the forests without destroying them. There is also a growing recognition that if we want to preserve the tropical forests and the multitude of species they harbor, we must make it possible for those living in them to survive and thrive without cutting down the trees. If these peoples cannot survive, probably the forests cannot either. If these peoples do survive, they can help protect the forests that are their homes. Let us now focus for a moment on a culture under stress at present and in danger of extinction. The culture, that of the Yanomami, is found in Brazil and Venezuela.

The Yanomami

In the Amazon region of Latin America live the Yanomami. It is believed that these people have lived in this region for thousands of years. The approximately 9,000 Yanomami represent the largest group of indigenous people living in the Americas who still follow hunter-gatherer methods.[102] Although they had very limited contact with other cultures for many years, this changed in the late 1980s when gold was discovered in the Brazilian Amazon region. Thousands of miners flew into the area where the Yanomami lived. The miners brought with them diseases to which the Yanomami had no natural immunity. Amnesty International estimates that from 1988 to 1990 about 1,500 Yanomami died.[103] In addition to the malaria that killed many, some Yanomami died from mercury poisoning, which came from eating fish poisoned by the mercury the miners had used in the streams to sift for gold. Others were killed by armed attack. Amnesty International reported: "These attacks are often carried out by private agents, including gunmen hired by land claimants, timber merchants or mining interests. They have gone almost entirely unpunished – in fact, state-level authorities have even colluded with them."[104]

The Yanomamis' situation became known throughout Brazil and around the world. Responding to pressures within Brazil and from some foreign countries (the attention given to Brazil because of the upcoming UN environmental conference probably played a role), the Brazilian government in 1991 set aside for the Yanomami about 36,000 square miles of land. When added to that set aside by Venezuela, which was slightly smaller than the Brazilian grant, this was an amount of land equal to the size of Portugal and the amount anthropologists said the Yanomami needed in order to survive. In 1990 the agency in charge of Indian affairs in the Brazilian government announced that it was forcibly removing all miners from Yanomami lands.[105] In 1993 Brazil used its police and military force to forcibly remove 3,000 miners who were still in Yanomami lands.

What will be the fate of the Yanomami? No one knows, of course, but if history is a guide, one would have to say that their prospects of surviving are not bright. While the actions by the Brazilian and Venezuelan governments to reserve a large amount of land for the use of these people is a hopeful step, disturbing signs exist. The presence of gold in their lands increased tension. Despite some success removing miners in the early parts of this century, by 2011, the nonprofit organization Survival International reported that about 1,000 gold miners were illegally working on Yanomami land. In 2002 the Brazilian army began building more bases along its largely undefended northern border, which crosses Yanomami lands. Some of the soldiers got Yanomami women pregnant and brought venereal diseases.[106] In 2009 swine flu hit the Yanomami.

Another disturbing fact is that there is abundant research now showing that many indigenous cultures confronted with modern development pressures increasingly find it challenging to preserve their traditional knowledge – such as specialized farming techniques, natural cycles, and natural healing methods and medicines. This can present a threat to their traditional livelihoods and increases dependencies on modern goods, which may have significant cultural, social, and environmental impacts.[107] In some cases, alcoholism and suicide rates and have increased dramatically.

This concludes the first part of our environment discussion, where we looked at the resources available to support human life and livelihoods, and the ways that increasing competition for resources, combined with increasing pollution of existing resources, has created new challenges for development. We now turn to the Part II on our environment, considering complications stemming from increased consumption of resources as people become wealthier and the population increases, creating additional challenges related to the consumption of resources.

Notes

1   Bill Clinton, who defeated President Bush, signed the biodiversity treaty, but the US Congress never ratified it.

2   UN Secretary-General Kofi Annan, press conference at the conclusion of the 2002 World Summit on Sustainable Development, September 2, 2002, at http://www.un.org/events/wssd/pressconf/020904conf4.htm (accessed July 2015).

3   Yale Center for Environmental Law and Policy and Center for International Earth Science Information Network, Columbia University, 2014 Environmental Performance Index, at http://epi.yale.edu/epi/country-rankings (accessed July 2015).

4   Lester R. Brown, *The Twenty-Ninth Day: Accommodating Human Needs and Numbers to the Earth's Resources* (New York: W. W. Norton, 1978), p. 44. One of the ways Britain reduced its air pollution was to build tall smokestacks, which has probably led to worse air in Scandinavia.

5   World Health Organization (WHO), "Ambient (Outdoor) Air Quality and Health," Fact Sheet No. 313 (updated March 2014), at http://www.who.int/mediacentre/factsheets/fs313/en/ (accessed July 2015).

6   World Bank, *Cost of Pollution in China: Economic Estimates of Physical Damages* (2007), at http://documents.worldbank.org/curated/en/2007/02/7503894/cost-pollution-china-economic-estimates-physical-damages; see also Meena Thiruvengadam, "Chinese Smog: At What Cost?" The Financialist, March 4, 2013, at https://www.thefinancialist.com/chinese-smog-at-what-cost/ (both accessed July 2015).

7   Beina Xu, *China's Environmental Crisis*, Council on Foreign Relations backgrounder, updated April 25, 2014, at http://www.cfr.org/china/chinas-environmental-crisis/p12608 (accessed July 2015).

8   Stephen Klaidman, "Muddling Through," *Wilson Quarterly* (Spring 1991), p. 76.

9   US Environmental Protection Agency (EPA), "40th Anniversary of the Clean Air Act," at http://www.epa.gov/air/caa/40th.html (accessed July 2015).

10 EPA, "Benefits and Costs of the Clean Air Act Amendments of 1990," factsheet, at http://www.epa.gov/cleanairactbenefits/feb11/factsheet.pdf (accessed July 2015).

11 Reed McManus, "Out Front in the Air Wars," *Sierra*, 89 (January/February 2004), p. 12.

12 Eric A. Morris, "Los Angeles Transportation Facts and Fiction: Smog," *Los Angeles Times*, February 17, 2009.

13 Jocelyn Kaiser, "Mounting Evidence Indicts Fine-Particle Pollution," *Science*, 307 (March 25, 2005), p. 1858. For more information on the connection between particulates and cancer see President's Cancer Panel, *Reducing Environmental Cancer Risk: What We Can Do Now*, Annual Report, 2008–2009 (April 2010), at http://deainfo.nci.nih.gov/advisory/pcp/annualReports/pcp08-09rpt/PCP_Report_08-09_508.pdf (accessed July 2015).

14 Gary Gardner, "Air Pollution Still a Problem," in Worldwatch Institute, *Vital Signs 2005* (New York: Worldwatch Institute, 2005), p. 94; and Genevieve Wong, "Study: Asthma Rates Rise Dramatically," *Spartanburg Herald-Journal*, May 1, 2004, p. B5.

15 Merrill Singer, "Respiratory Health and Ecosyndemics in a Time of Global Warming," *Health Sociology Review*, 22 (1) (March 2013), pp. 98–111.

16 European Commission, "Mobility and Transport: Road Fatalities in the EU since 2001," at http://ec.europa.eu/transport/road_safety/specialist/statistics/index_en.htm; WHO,

Air Pollution Estimates, p. 4, at http://www.who.int/phe/health_topics/outdoorair/databases/en/ (both accessed July 2015).

17 Worldwatch Institute, *Vital Signs 2005*, p. 95.

18 House of Commons Environmental Audit Committee, *Air Quality: Fifth Report of Session 2009–10,* Vol. 1 (March 22, 2010), p. 3. A summary of this report is contained in "Air Pollution Death Toll Could Hit 50,000 a Year, Say MPs," *Ecologist*, March 22, 2010.

19 WHO, "Ambient (Outdoor) Air Quality and Health."

20 Jim Yardley, "Bad Air and Water, and a Bully Pulpit in China," *New York Times*, September 25, 2004, p. A4.

21 WHO, "Air Quality Deteriorating in Many of the World's Cities," news release, May 7, 2014, at http://www.who.int/mediacentre/news/releases/2014/air-quality/en/(accessed July 2015).

22 BBC News, "Most China Cities Fail to Meet Air Quality Standards," February 3, 2015, at http://www.bbc.com/news/world-asia-china-31110408 (accessed July 2015).

23 BBC News, "China Pollution: Beijing Smog Hits Hazardous Levels," January 15, 2015, at http://www.bbc.com/news/world-asia-china-30826128 (accessed July 2015).

24 Joseph Kahn and Jim Yardley, "As China Roars, Pollution Reaches Deadly Extremes," *New York Times*, August 26, 2007, p. 1.

25 BBC News, "China to Scrap Millions of Cars to Improve Air Quality," May 27, 2014, at http://www.bbc.com/news/business-27583404 (accessed July 2015).

26 Meena Thiruvengadam, "Chinese Smog: At What Cost?"

27 Keith Bradsher, "China Pays a Price for Cheaper Oil," *New York Times*, June 26, 2004, pp. B1 2.

28 Nancy Riley, "China's Population: New Trends and Challenges," *Population Bulletin*, 59 (June 2004), p. 25.

29 WHO, "Indoor Air Pollution and Health," Fact Sheet No. 292 (June 2005).

30 For example, see John M. Broder, "Developing Nations to Get Clean-Burning Cook-stoves," *New York Times*, September 20, 2010.

31 *New York Times*, May 13, 1980, p. C3.

32 "Peddling Lead," *Science*, 299 (February 7, 2003), p. 795.

33 Ibid.

34 Jane Brody, "Even Low Lead Levels Pose Perils for Children," *New York Times*, August 5, 2003, p. D7.

35 *New York Times*, July 27, 1994, p. C20.

36 Brody, "Even Low Lead Levels Pose Perils for Children."

37 "Lead Concentrations Down in Greenland Ice," *New York Times*, October 15, 1991, p. B8.

38 Brody, "Even Low Lead Levels Pose Perils for Children."

39 William Stevens, "Ozone Loss over US Is Found to Be Twice as Bad as Predicted," *New York Times*, April 5, 1991, p. A1.

40 Kenneth Chang, "Scientists Say Recovery of the Ozone Layer May Take Longer Than Expected," *New York Times*, December 7, 2005, p. A25.

41 Barry Commoner, *The Closing Circle* (New York: Knopf, 1971), p. 39.

42 W. Wayt Gibbs, "How Should We Set Priorities?" *Scientific American*, 293 (September 2005), p. 110.

43 EPA, "40th Anniversary of the Clean Air Act."

44 Michael Tennesen, "Acid Rain Returns – This Time It Is Caused by Nitrogen Emissions," *Scientific American* (June 21, 2010).

45 Kahn and Yardley, "As China Roars, Pollution Reaches Deadly Extremes," pp. 1, 6–7.

46 Yardley, "Bad Air and Water, and a Bully Pulpit in China," p. A4.

47 N. Johnson, C. Revenga, and J. Echeverria, "Managing Water for People and Nature," *Science*, 292 (2001), pp. 1071–2.

48 Kahn and Yardley, "As China Roars, Pollution Reaches Deadly Extremes."

49 United Nations, *The Millennium Development Goals Report 2010* (New York: United Nations, 2010), pp. 58–9.

50 World Resources Institute (WRI), *The 1993 Information Please Environmental Almanac* (Boston: Houghton Mifflin, 1993), pp. 38–40.

51 EPA, "National Summary of Impaired Waters and TMDL information," Watershed Assessment, Tracking and Environmental Results, January 3, 2011, at http://iaspub.epa.gov/tmdl_waters10/attains_nation_cy.control#prob_source (accessed July 2015).

52 EPA, "National Summary of State Information": "National Summary: Causes of Impairment in Assessed Rivers and Streams," table, January 3, 2011, at http://iaspub.epa.gov/tmdl_waters10/attains_nation_cy.control#prob_source (accessed July 2015).

53 EPA, *National Water Quality Inventory: Report to Congress, 2004 Reporting Cycle*, January 2009, p. ES-2, at http://water.epa.gov/lawsregs/guidance/cwa/305b/2004report_index.cfm (accessed July 2005).

54 Lisa Foderaro, "Caution Urged in Eating Fish from Adirondacks and Catskills," *New York Times*, April 16, 2005, p. A11.

55 Michael Janofsky, "Mercury Taints Fish across US," *New York Times*, August 25, 2004, p. A19.

56 Richard Bernstein, "No Longer Europe's Sewer, but Not the Rhine of Yore," *New York Times*, April 21, 2006, p. A4.

57 Andrew Revkin, "Stream Tests Show Traces of Array of Contaminants," *New York Times*, March 13, 2002, p. A14; and Andrew Revkin, "FDA Considers New Tests for Environmental Effects," *New York Times*, March 14, 2002, p. A20.

58 United Nations, *The Millennium Development Report 2010*, p. 5.

59 Duncan Hewitt, "China Announces Ambitious Plan to Clean up Its Water, Close Down Polluting Factories," *International Business Times*, April 17, 2015, at http://www.ibtimes.com/china-announces-ambitious-plan-clean-its-water-close-down-polluting-factories-1886320 (accessed July 2015).

60 David Rohde, "Bangladesh Wells Pumping Poison as Cleanup Lags," *New York Times*, July 17, 2005, p. 6. For more on this problem see A. Mushtaque Chowdhury, "Arsenic Crisis in Bangladesh," *Scientific American*, 291 (August 2004), pp. 86–91.

61 "1 in 5 Bangladeshi Deaths Due to Arsenic," United Press International, June 26, 2010; Maria Argos et al., "Arsenic Exposure from Drinking Water, and All-Cause and Chronic Disease Mortalities in Bangladesh: A Prospective Cohort Study," *Lancet*, 376 (9737) (July 24, 2010), pp. 252–8.

62 Hans Landsberg et al., "Nonfuel Minerals," in Paul Portney (ed.), *Current Issues in Natural Resource Policy* (Washington, DC: Resources for the Future, 1982), p. 83.

63 UN Food and Agriculture Organization (FAO), *State of the World's Forests 2012*, p. 16, at http://www.fao.org/docrep/016/i3010e/i3010e.pdf (accessed July 2015).

64 Ibid.

65 Ibid., p. 17.

66 Ibid.

67 Christopher Uhl, "You Can Keep a Good Forest Down," *Natural History*, 92 (April 1983), p. 78.

68 FAO, *State of the World's Forests 2012*, p. 9.

69 WRI, "Global Map of Forest Landscape Restoration Opportunities" (September 2011), at http://www.wri.org/resources/maps/global-map-forest-landscape-restoration-opportunities (accessed July 2015).

70 FAO, "World Deforestation Decreases, but Remains Alarming in Many Countries," March 25, 2010, at http://www.fao.org/news/story/en/item/40893/icode/ (accessed July 2015).

71 FAO, *Global Forest Resources Assessment 2010*, p. 56, at http://www.fao.org/docrep/013/i1757e/i1757e.pdf (accessed July 2015).

72 WRI, United Nations Environment Programme (UNEP), United Nations Development Programme, and World Bank, *World Resources 1998–99: Environmental Change and Human Health* (Washington, DC: WRI, 1999), p. 188.

73 Scott Wallace, "Last of the Amazon," *National Geographic*, at http://environment.nationalgeographic.com/environment/habitats/last-of-amazon/#page=1 (accessed July 2015).

74 FAO, *Global Forest Resources Assessment 2010*, p. 21.

75 Ibid.

76 Ibid., p. 19.

77 Ibid., p. 21.

78 David L. A. Gaveau et al., "Major Atmospheric Emissions from Peat Fires in Southeast Asia during Non-Drought Years: Evidence from the 2013 Sumatran Fires," *Scientific Reports*, 4 (August 19, 2014). ("We expect major haze events to be increasingly frequent because of ongoing deforestation of Indonesian peatlands.")

79 Stella Dawson, "Indonesia Defends Deforestation for Palm Oil on Economic Grounds," Reuters, March 25, 2015, at http://www.reuters.com/article/2015/03/25/us-indonesia-palmoil-forests-idUSKBN0ML20020150325 (accessed July 2015).

80 Howard French, "Billions of Trees Planted, and Nary a Dent in the Desert," *New York Times*, April 11, 2004, p. 3.

81 UNEP, *Vital Forest Graphics*, p. 11, at http://www.unep.org/vitalforest/ (accessed July 2015).

82 William Laurance, "Gaia's Lungs," *Natural History*, 108 (March 1999), p. 96.

83 University of Leeds, "One-Fifth of Fossil-Fuel Emissions Absorbed by Threatened Forests," *Science Daily*, February 19, 2009. Simon L. Lewis, "Making the Paper," *Nature*, 457 (February 19, 2009).

84 "Resurgent Forests Can Be Greenhouse Gas Sponges," *Science*, 277 (July 18, 1997), p. 315

85 Intergovernmental Panel on Climate Change, Fifth Assessment Report, *Climate Change 2013: The Physical Science Basis*, Summary for Policymakers, p. 12.

86 Larry Rohter, "Relentless Foe of the Amazon Jungle: Soybeans," *New York Times*, September 17, 2003, p. A3. Also a similar percentage is cited in an analysis by Forests Dialogue (hosted at Yale University) as a background paper for the Global Forest Leaders Forum, 2007, pp. 1–2.

87   Anne LaBastille, "Heaven, Not Hell," *Audubon*, 81 (November 1979), p. 91.

88   Convention on Biodiversity, "Forest Biodiversity: Earth's Living Treasure" (2010), p. 12, at https://www.cbd.int/idb/doc/2011/idb-2011-booklet-en.pdf (accessed July 2015).

89   Edward O. Wilson, *The Diversity of Life* (Cambridge, MA: Harvard University Press, 1992).

90   W. Wayt Gibbs, "On the Termination of Species," *Scientific American*, 285 (November 2001), p. 42.

91   Stuart Pimm and Clinton Jenkins, "Sustaining the Variety of Life," *Scientific American*, 293 (September 2005), p. 68.

92   Norman Myers, "The Exhausted Earth," *Foreign Policy*, 42 (Spring 1981), p. 143.

93   Norman Myers, 'Room in the Ark,' *Bulletin of the Atomic Scientists*, 38 (November 1982), p. 48.

94   Paul Ehrlich and Anne Ehrlich, *Extinction* (New York: Random House, 1981), p. 94.

95   William Stevens, "The 'Hot Spot' Approach to Saving Species," *New York Times*, March 14, 2000, p. D3; and Conservation International, Biodiversity Hotspots webpage, at http://www.conservation.org/How/Pages/Hotspots.aspx (accessed July 2015).

96   Norman Myers, "A Convincing Call for Conservation," *Science*, 295 (January 18, 2002), pp. 447–8.

97   A fuller discussion of the strengths and weaknesses of the two metaphors is contained in William Stevens, "Lost Rivets and Threads, and Ecosystems Pulled Apart," *New York Times*, July 4, 2000, p. D4.

98   UN Department of Economic and Social Affairs, Secretariat of the Permanent Forum on Indigenous Issues, *State of the World's Indigenous Peoples*, document ST/ESA/328 (2010), p. 1, at http://www.un.org/esa/socdev/unpfii/documents/SOWIP/en/ SOWIP_web.pdf (accessed July 2015).

99   Rodger Doyle, "Measuring Modernity," *Scientific American*, 289 (December 2003), p. 40. For a contrary view, that the American culture is dominant in Europe, see Alan Riding, "A Common Culture (from the USA) Binds Europeans Ever Closer," *New York Times*, April 26, 2004, p. B1.

100 Katrin Bennhold, "Love of Leisure, and Europe's Reasons," *New York Times*, July 29, 2004, p. A8.

101 As one author has written: "[indigenous peoples] may offer living examples of cultural patterns that can help revive ancient values for everyone: devotion to future generations, ethical regard for nature, and commitment to community among people." Alan Durning, "Supporting Indigenous Peoples," in Lester R. Brown et al., *State of the World 1993* (New York: W. W. Norton, 1993), p. 100.

102 Minority Rights Group International, *World Directory of Minorities and Indigenous Peoples – Brazil: Yanomami*, 2008, at http://www.unhcr.org/refworld/docid/49749d49c.html (accessed July 2015).

103 James Brooke, "Brazil Evicting Miners in Amazon to Reclaim Land for the Indians," *New York Times*, March 8, 1993, p. A4.

104 Ibid.

105 James Brooke, "In an Almost Untouched Jungle Gold Miners Threaten Indian Ways," *New York Times*, September 18, 1990, p. B6.

106 Larry Rohter, "A New Intrusion Threatens a Tribe in Amazon: Soldiers," *New York Times*, October 1, 2002, p. A1.

107 One encouraging sign is that when Western scientists seek information from the medicine men of indigenous peoples about natural drugs and health cures, the medicine men are given new respect. This new respect might help encourage some of their youth to study under them. But, all too often today, when the medicine men die, the knowledge they have acquired dies with them. See Daniel Goleman, "Shamans and Their Longtime Lore May Vanish with the Forests," *New York Times*, June 11, 1991, p. B5. As an example of a study showing the harmful effects Western contact can have on the culture of indigenous peoples, see Katharine Milton, "Civilization and Its Discontents," *Natural History* (March 1992), pp. 37–43.

Chapter 7

The Environment: Part II

The Workplace and the Home	224
Cancer	224
Chemicals	225
Pesticides	226
Managing Waste	228
Solid wastes	228
Toxic wastes	230
Governmental and industrial responses to the waste problem	232
Responsible Use	233
Resource efficiency	233
Recycling	234
Substitution	235
Reducing needs	236
Environmental Politics	236
Overdevelopment	238
Conclusions	238
Notes	239
Further Reading	242

The Workplace and the Home

Cancer

Cancer is often considered to be a disease of the industrial revolution. The US National Cancer Institute estimates that one out of two males and one out of three

Global Issues: An Introduction, Fifth Edition. Kristen A. Hite and John L. Seitz
© 2016 John Wiley & Sons, Ltd. Published 2016 by John Wiley & Sons, Ltd.

females in the United States alive at present will contract cancer and one out of four males and one out of five females will die from it.[1] In the United States, cancer kills more children than any other disease, although accidents are still the number one cause of death of children. It is commonly believed by the general public that exposure of workers to cancer-causing substances – carcinogens – in the workplace, and the exposure of the general population to pollution in the air and water and to carcinogens in some of the food they eat, are the main causes of this dreaded disease. There is no question that many workers – such as the millions of people who worked with asbestos – have been exposed to high levels of dangerous substances. But scientists do not now believe that contamination at the workplace is the main cause of cancer; nor do they believe that water pollution or food additives are causing most of the cancer cases. While these remain difficult to fully understand, leading cancer experts have agreed that smoking greatly increases the risk of contracting cancer. Also, a long-term, very large study published in 2003 convinced most experts that being overweight or obese significantly increases the likelihood of a person contracting cancer.[2] Another study identified very small particles in polluted air from motor vehicle traffic as increasing the risk of lung cancer.[3]

Some experts fear that while chemicals cannot be proven to cause most cancers today, there is a possibility that chemical-related cancers may increase greatly in the future because of the large increase in the production of carcinogenic chemicals since the 1960s. Cancer can occur 15 to 40 years after the initial exposure to a carcinogen, so chemicals may yet prove to be a major culprit.

Chemicals

You probably will prefer not to read the following statement, but if we are to present this subject truthfully, we must give it: "Only a few hundred of the more than 80,000 chemicals in use in the United States have been tested for safety."[4] How could this be true, you might well ask? Read carefully the following explanation by the US President's Cancer Panel and you will learn how:

> The prevailing regulatory approach in the United States is reactionary rather than precautionary. That is, instead of taking preventive action when uncertainty exists about the potential harm a chemical or other environmental contaminant may cause, a hazard must be incontrovertibly demonstrated before action to ameliorate it is initiated. Moreover instead of requiring industry or other proponents of specific chemicals, devices, or activities to prove their safety, the public bears the burden of proving that a given environmental exposure is harmful.[5]

Not everything causes cancer, of course, but development has brought forth so many new products in such a short time that we cannot be sure which ones do and which do not. Barry Commoner shows that new products often bring large profits to the first industry that introduces them, so there is a strong incentive for industries to be innovative. New products, especially in the United States since World War II, are often made of synthetic materials that pollute the environment, but the pollution usually does not become evident until years after the introduction. Commoner states that "by the time the effects are known, the damage is done and the inertia of the heavy investment in a new productive technology makes a retreat extraordinarily difficult."[6]

Europe is active on this issue also. In 2007 the European Union approved a new law that places more responsibility on chemical companies to manage the risks of their chemicals and to provide safety information on the substances. Dangerous chemicals are to be withdrawn when suitable substitutes are found. The law is being phased in gradually, potentially impacting trade relations with the United States unless new legislation is passed.

While chemicals offer potentially powerful technological solutions to environmentally polluting activities, many industrial production processes still cause significant health and environmental risks due to the fossil fuel and other chemical discharges.[7] The vital need for major reforms in the chemical industry can be illustrated by one class of modern "miracle" chemicals that have been used to make such popular products as Scotchgard stain protector, Teflon nonstick cookware, and Gore-Tex water-resistant clothing. These fluorochemicals have been found in the blood of sea and land animals, birds, and women in the Arctic. It is possible that these chemicals will never break down into harmless substances, and, according to the American Red Cross, are now found in the blood of nearly all Americans from whom it receives blood donations.[8] To its credit, the 3M corporation stopped producing the chemical used to make its popular Scotchgard product when some of this information become known.

Pesticides

The story of pesticide use illustrates well the dangers that new substances, which have become so important to modern agriculture, have brought to people at their workplaces as well as in their homes at mealtime. Rachel Carson is credited with making a whole nation – the United States – aware of the dangers of persistent pesticides such as DDT. Her book *Silent Spring*, which appeared in 1962, shows how toxic substances can become concentrated as they go up the food chain, as big animals eat little animals. Since many toxic substances are not excreted by the plants or animals absorbing them, they accumulate and are passed on to the next animal that eats them. Carson's warning led to a sharp reduction in the use of long-lived pesticides in many developed countries; but if she were alive today (she died of breast cancer in 1964), she would probably be disturbed to learn that short-lived but highly toxic pesticides are now increasing in use in the United States. The use of herbicides has especially increased dramatically as farmers, railroad companies, telephone companies, and others find it cheaper and easier to use these chemicals to get rid of unwanted vegetation than to use labor or machines. These new highly toxic pesticides pose a special risk to the workers who manufacture them and to the farmers who work with them in the fields. Although DDT was banned for use in the United States in 1972, residues of it could still be found in most people in the United States 20 years later.[9]

Pesticide use is increasing in the less wealthy nations – not just the use of short-lived pesticides but of persistent pesticides such as DDT as well. The World Health Organization has approved the use of DDT under certain conditions in developing countries to control a resurgence of malaria. US law explicitly permits the sale to foreign nations of substances that are banned, highly restricted, or unregistered in the United States. US companies, as well as many in Europe, have increasingly turned to the overseas market to sell their products as more restrictions on the use of pesticides occur in the developed nations. But the developed world still uses most of the pesticides; actually three-quarters of pesticides are used mainly in North America, Western Europe, and Japan.[10] In 2007, the US Environmental Protection Agency estimated world use of pesticides exceeded 5 million pounds, while US use alone exceeded 1 million pounds.[11]

In the early 1990s the US government announced that it was going to try to reduce the amount of pesticides used on US farms. A five-year study by the US National Academy of Sciences on the effect of agricultural chemicals on children was published in 1993. It criticized the method the government had been using to calculate the safe amount of pesticide residue on foods. It found that the risk calculations by the government had not taken into account the fact that people are also exposed to pesticides from sources other than on foods, such as in their drinking water, on their lawns, and on golf courses. It found that infants and children might be especially sensitive to pesticide residues on food. They consume 60 times the amount of fruit adults do, in relation to their weight, so are getting higher doses of the pesticides that are used on fruits. And this is taking place early in their lives. The head of the committee that prepared the report drew the following conclusion: "Pesticides applied in legal amounts on the farm, and present in legal amounts on food, can still lead to unsafe amounts."[12] In 1999 the Environmental Protection Agency responded to these concerns and banned most uses of a pesticide widely used on fruit and vegetables, and tightened restrictions on another, because of their possible harm to children. This was the first time the agency had issued regulations specifically designed to protect children.[13] In 2005 the Environmental Protection Agency issued new guidelines on the use of many chemicals which recognized that children might be more at risk from the use of these chemicals than adults.[14]

Pesticides have played a significant role in the Green Revolution; it is doubtful food production would have stayed ahead of population growth in the world without them. What seems to be called for now is a highly selective use of pesticides, not their banishment. A number of agricultural experts are now advocating a more balanced program for controlling pests. A selective use of pesticides would go along with the use of biological controls, such as natural predators, and other nonchemical means to control pests.

Managing Waste

Solid wastes

It seems to be a common occurrence in a number of developed countries that, as more goods and services become available, more are desired and less value is placed on those already in hand. After the end of World War II, an unprecedented period of economic growth in the industrialized world took place, leading to a huge increase in the consumption of material goods.

As consumption rose, so did wastes. "Throwaway" products that were used briefly and then discarded became common, as did items that wore out quickly. Such facts disturbed few people in the United States since they found enjoyment in buying new, "better" products. Many such products were relatively cheap in the 1950s, 1960s, and early 1970s since energy and other raw materials were inexpensive. Between 1960 and 2000 the amount of solid wastes generated in the United States per person annually grew by about 60 percent, until it reached about 1,600 pounds.[15] On average each American generated about 2.7 pounds of waste per day in 1960, whereas in 2012 this figure had grown to 4.4 pounds.[16]

One obvious way cities can help reduce and manage their citizens' waste is to support recycling programs, which many communities did to reduce the amount of trash going to their landfills. Another way to reduce trash is to make citizens pay variable costs for the disposal of their solid wastes, based on amount and type. Seattle is an example of a US city that has successfully followed that principle.

Seattle began charging its citizens according to the amount of trash they put out for disposal. Yard wastes, such as grass clippings, if separated by the citizens so the city could use them for composting, were charged at a much lower rate than regular trash, and paper, glass, and metal (which could be recycled) were hauled away free. Seattle, which was already more environmentally conscious than most other American cities, found that during the first year it started charging its citizens for the amount of waste they produced, the total tonnage the city needed to haul to the landfills fell by about 20 percent. By the mid-1990s, 90 percent of the residents of Seattle were recycling their waste.

Seattle has a zero waste goal as does San Francisco, Austin, in Texas, and Canberra, Australia. San Francisco is now diverting about 70 percent of city waste from its landfills, mainly by its composting and recycling programs. It has been a grand success.[17]

A huge solid waste problem has been created by the growing use of plastics around the world. This modern achievement of the chemical industry takes petroleum and turns it into containers which are very difficult to break and won't decay in any individual's lifetime. This last quality is what is causing the problem. Current estimates are that sunlight might break plastic down over about 500 years but there is no known living organism that can digest even a single molecule of plastic.[18]

Plate 7.1 Water pollution in the United States is partly caused by large amounts of pesticides, herbicides, and fertilizers, which run off from fields during storms.

Source: Lynn Betts, US Department of Agriculture.

Every year about 250 billion pounds of plastic pellets are produced in the world. A research sailing ship in the early twenty-first century found an area in the Pacific Ocean about the size of the state of Texas – about 800 miles across (1,300 kilometers) – filled with floating plastic debris.[19] A Japanese scientist and his colleagues at Tokyo University have discovered that floating plastic fragments in the sea contain and absorb toxic chemicals such as DDT, PCBs, and other oily pollutants. Here is how this problem has been described:

> The potential scope of the problem is staggering. …When those pellets or products degrade, break into fragments, and disperse, the pieces may also become concentrators and transporters of toxic chemicals in the marine environment. Thus an astronomical number of vectors for some of the most toxic pollutants known are being released into an ecosystem dominated by the most efficient natural vacuum cleaners nature ever invented: the jellies and salps living in the ocean. After those organisms ingest the toxins, they are eaten in turn by fish, and so the poisons pass into the food web that leads, in some cases, to human beings.[20]

In 2003 the research vessel that documented the huge floating body of plastic debris in the Pacific took underwater photographs of transparent filter feeding

organisms with colored plastic fragments in their bellies.[21] In 2014, researchers estimated that the patch actually weighed 100 times more than previously believed.[22]

Toxic wastes

The first warning of the danger of toxic wastes came from Japan. In the 1950s and
1960s hundreds of people were paralyzed, crippled, or killed from eating fish contaminated with mercury that had been discharged into Minamata Bay by a chemical
plant. It took many decades, but in 2014 the global community eventually adopted
the Minamata Treaty to address mercury pollution.[23]

The United States has been actively working to manage toxic wastes since the last
quarter of the twentieth century. Many people in a residential district of Niagara
Falls, New York, were exposed to a dangerous mixture of chemicals that were seep-
ing into their swimming pools and basements. Most of these people did not know
when they bought their homes that the Hooker Chemical Company had dumped
over 20,000 tons of chemical wastes in the 1940s and 1950s into a nearby aban-
doned canal, ironically known as Love Canal. News of the Love Canal disaster spread
through the country as the story of the contamination slowly came out in spite of the
denials of the chemical company and the apathy of the local government. Eventually
hundreds of people were evacuated from the area. The state and federal governments
bought over 600 of the contaminated homes. After putting a "wall" of clay and plastic around the buried toxic waste, the federal government later declared much of the
Love Canal neighborhood fit for resettlement. The name of the neighborhood was
changed from Love Canal to Black Creek Village.[24]

For decades, the US Environmental Protection Agency required some of the
producers of toxic wastes to report annually how much they were releasing into
the environment. Two industries that produce the largest amount of toxic wastes
– the mining and oil exploration industries – were exempt from the reporting
requirement.[25] Half of all wastes subject to reporting were produced by the chemical
industry, with other significant amounts produced by the metal, oil refining, paper,
and plastics industries.

This reporting law, formally called the Toxic Release Inventory, has been considered to be a very effective piece of legislation. Even the chemical industry, which
has worked to weaken it, has admitted that because of it, toxic emissions have been
reduced by about 50 percent. Very soon after the first report was released, several
large corporations announced that they would voluntarily reduce their emissions by
90 percent over the next three years. States and local residents have used the report
to put pressure on companies to reduce their pollution.[26]

In 1996 the reporting requirements were expanded to include, for the first time,
electric utilities, incinerator operators, recyclers, and many mining companies,
an increase of 6,400 new plants over the previous 23,000 that had to report toxic
emissions. By 2001, US manufacturers reported a nearly 15 percent decline from
the previous year in toxic releases into the air, water, and ground. And in 2013, US

manufacturers reported an additional 7 percent decline in toxic releases into the air, water, and ground over the previous decade.[27] This was progress, but the EPA reported total land disposal of 2.75 billion pounds and air disbursement of 592.43 million pounds of waste in 2013.[28]

Oil in the Amazon: a legacy of toxic sludge

During the early years of Ecuador's oil boom, the government and oil companies alike rushed to capitalize on some of the rich oil reserves in the Amazon region. While technology enabled new reserves to be tapped and processed, efforts to regulate the waste of byproducts did not keep pace with the rush of extra activity. As such, pits of oil sludge were often left behind as companies moved on to fresh sources. Communities – many of whom are indigenous – continue to live with the legacy of the wastes. Many community members in the northeastern part of Ecuador claimed they became sick due to the toxic waste. Frustrated with the failure to clean up the oil sludge, they sued Chevron, a company that inherited the messy legacy of the oil contamination from earlier production activities. Although an Ecuadorian court held Chevron responsible for much of the pollution-related damages, lengthy legal disputes at the international level have impaired resolution, payments, and cleanup. Billions of dollars are at stake, much of which is associated with legal fees and some of which may be paid to the communities for damages.

For a list of news articles associated with some of the most significant developments over more than a decade of litigation on this case, see generally Huffington Post's webpage on this lawsuit, at http://www.huffingtonpost.com/news/chevron-ecuador-lawsuit/. For the Ecuadorian plaintiffs' side of the story, see www.chevrontoxico.org and for the defendant company's version of the story, see http://www.chevron.com/ecuador/ (all accessed July 2015).

The persistence of some toxic chemicals is shown by the fact that byproducts of the chemical used to make stain protectors in carpets and food wrappers are showing up in seals and polar bears in the Arctic and in dolphins in the mid-Atlantic.[29] And a number of studies have shown that indigenous peoples in the Arctic are being exposed to significant amounts of pesticides, industrial chemicals, and heavy metals, with uncertain health effects.[30] Why are Arctic peoples being exposed to such poisons? One reason is that many rivers and ocean and air currents carry toxins originating in other parts of the world. Also many indigenous people have a diet rich in fish and marine mammals; thus they absorb the toxins the fish and mammals have been exposed to. Breast milk and samples of blood in umbilical cords in women living in the Arctic contain moderate to extremely high levels of toxins such as DDT, PCBs, dioxins, mercury, lead, and a flame retardant.[31]

Governmental and industrial responses to the waste problem

In 1980 the US government created a $1.6 billion fund to finance the cleaning up of the worst toxic waste sites. The law that set up this fund (popularly called Superfund) allowed the government to recover the cost of the cleanup from the companies that dumped wastes at the sites. In 1986 $9 billion more for the cleanup was approved by the US government, to come mainly from a tax on industry and on crude oil. The Congressional Office of Technology Assessment has estimated that it will require about 50 years and $100 billion to clean up toxic waste dumps in the country.

By 2005 work had been completed at about 1,000 or 60 percent of Superfund sites and work was underway at an additional 400 sites.[32] Over the time from 1990 to 2014 about $4.6 billion was deposited in special accounts for cleanups and enforcement and nearly $3 billion has already been spent or committed. The remaining amount will be used for ongoing and future Superfund cleanups.[33]

There are other ways government can help control the waste problem. Barbara Ward, the late British economist, mentions four ways a government can encourage the reduction of wastes and promote the reuse of wastes: (1) it can make manufacturers pay a tax that could cover the cost of handling the eventual disposal of their products; (2) it can stimulate the market for recycled products by purchasing recycled products for some of its own needs; (3) it can give grants and other incentives to cities and industries to help them install equipment that recycles wastes; and (4) it can prohibit the production of nonreturnable containers in some instances.[34]

Inefficient and wasteful technologies and processes to produce goods are still common in the United States and other developed nations, since many of these were adopted when energy was cheap, water plentiful, many raw materials inexpensive, and the disposal of wastes easy. Some industries now realize that they can increase their profits by making their procedures more efficient and producing less waste. One such company is 3M, which, according to one study, reduced its pollution as well as increased its profits, "not by installing pollution control plants but by reformulating products, redesigning equipment, modifying processes ... [and] recovering materials for reuse."[35]

Germany is one of the leaders in creating imaginative ways to deal with toxic wastes. Recognizing that the ideal solution to this problem is to concentrate on reducing the production of toxic waste rather than focusing on its disposal or the cleanup, the country is implementing what is called a "closed-cycle economy." For decades, Germany has required manufacturers and distributors to take back packaging and reuse or recycle the contents. When products are built they are designed with concern with how they will be disposed of when no longer wanted. Parts are marked so they can later be identified electronically to facilitate their recycling. According to the head of Germany's environmental protection agency, as manufacturers are held financially and legally responsible for the safe disposal of their products, it is expected they will support the revolutionary concept of the environmentally friendly closed-cycle economy.[36]

Responsible Use

There are four steps a country can take to help manage limited supplies of resources and minimize the impacts of their use: (1) use resources more efficiently; (2) recycle waste products containing the desired material; (3) substitute more abundant or renewable resources for the scarce material; (4) reduce its need for the material.

Resource efficiency

Two concepts have emerged in the developed world that are designed to reduce the use of natural resources by using the resources more efficiently. One is called "eco-efficiency" and the other is called "product stewardship." The use of either or both of these concepts by some industries led to a 2 percent improvement in resource efficiency per year in the developed world from 1970 to 1995.[37]

Eco-efficiency involves redesigning products and the processes that are followed to make them so that fewer natural resources are used and less waste is produced. In the United States a pioneer in the use of this concept is the 3M corporation. 3M established a program it called "Pollution Prevention Pays," the 3P program. The corporation claimed in 2010, 3P ideas and initiatives from employees prevented 3 billion pounds of pollutants and saved 3M nearly $1.4 billion.[38] 3M Corporation has about 15,000 suppliers and it expects its suppliers to follow 3M's environmental standards. It monitors the suppliers' performances. The Seventh Generation company uses bottles which are 90 percent postconsumer resin and nearly all packaging is 100 percent postconsumer recycled. The company's total materials use actually decreased from 2008 to 2009.[39]

By following eco-efficiency principles, SC Johnson Wax from 1990 to 1997 increased its production by 50 percent while at the same time it cut its manufacturing waste by half, reduced packaging waste by a quarter, and reduced the use of volatile organic compounds by about 15 percent. The company saved more than $20 million annually from these changes.[40]

Some companies are attempting to drastically reduce their use of natural resources and their toxic emissions by adopting a "closed cycle" process. In this manufacturing process, wastes are completely recycled or reused.

Product stewardship is being practiced mainly in Europe at present. This is the principle that a company should be held responsible for the environmental impacts of its products throughout their whole life cycles. The trend is for more laws and agreements between government and industry that are based on the Polluter Pays principle. This principle embodies the idea that the manufacturer of a product should be responsible for the harm to the environment that comes from its production, use, and disposal, such as Germany's requirement for manufacturers to accept back their packaging wastes.

All of these concepts are leading to a revolutionary change in thinking about the responsibilities of the manufacturer. Instead of having society as a whole pay for the consequences of the manufacturer's actions, the principle is slowly spreading that the manufacturer should accept this responsibility. If the manufacturer is held responsible, it will have an incentive for redesigning products and manufacturing processes to cut their costs. In some instances, as the examples above show, the practicing of this principle can lead to a win-win situation as the manufacturer and the environment both benefit from the new way of thinking.

Recycling

It is generally agreed that more recycling of waste material needs to be done in the United States. In the late 1980s recycling became relatively popular in the country because more citizens became aware of environmental problems and because many towns were faced with trash dumps that were becoming filled. (New dumps were becoming very expensive to open because of tighter federal government regulations.)

A demand for recycled material grew in the United States as more industries started using it. By the mid-1990s this was taking place as a growing economy emerged and new plants able to process recycled material began operating. One solution that has been suggested to promote recycling is that government should require the use of more recycled material, such as in newsprint. The US government did take this step in 1993 when President Clinton ordered all federal government agencies, including the military, to purchase paper with a minimum of 20 percent recycled fibers in it. But even with respect to newsprint, there is no simple solution since newspaper cannot be recycled indefinitely because the quality of the fibers degrades.

Even with the new interest in recycling in the United States, the country is still not doing as much of it as other industrial nations do. In the early 1990s the United States was recycling about 15 percent of its trash, while Japan was recycling about 50 percent. Some European countries also do much more than the United States. Since 2002 the European Union has required all its members' auto manufacturers to be responsible for the recovery and recycling of all of its new autos. As of 2004 the European Union requires all the electronic companies of its members to pay for the collection and recycling of its products. And by July 2006 no electronics sold in Europe can any longer contain some of the most toxic materials such as lead, cadmium, mercury, hexavalent chromium, and the flame retardants PBDE and PBB.[41]

In 2009 the United States recycled about a third of its waste. In that year Americans generated about 240 million tons of trash and recycled and composted about 80 million tons.[42] Although in 2008 the average European Union recycling rate for municipal waste was only about 20 percent, there was great variety among the European nations. Bulgaria did not recycle anything, Romania recycled just 1 percent, the Czech Republic just 2 percent, and Lithuania and Slovakia only 3 percent. However, Austria recycled and composted about 70 percent of its waste, while Belgium, Germany, Sweden, and the Netherlands recycled and composted from 40 to 50 percent. The UK recycled only about 15 percent of its waste in 2005.[43]

To increase recycling in Japan, many cities have increased the number of categories into which items to be recycled must be separated. Yokohama, a city of nearly 4 million people, had ten categories in 2005. Recycling costs more than dumping but about the same as incineration, which land-scarce Japan uses for much of its garbage.[44]

One unfortunate trend is the shipping of electronic waste, including computer monitors and circuit boards, to developing countries, such as China, India, and Pakistan, for recycling. These items contain lead and other toxic material. The people recycling the items, often children or adults with no protective clothing, are being exposed to dangerous substances. A report at the beginning of the twenty-first century by five American environmental groups estimated that from 50 to 80 percent of electronic waste collected in the United States for recycling was being placed on container ships for use or recycling by developing countries. The United States was the only developed country that had not signed the 1989 Basel Convention which was designed to limit the exporting of hazardous waste. The producers of hazardous wastes were encouraged to deal with their waste problems within their own borders whenever possible. The European Union at that time was considering requiring manufacturers of products containing hazardous material to take responsibility for them from "cradle to grave."[45]

While recycling is desirable, it is only a partial solution to resource shortages and to pollution by the minerals industry. Recycling also creates pollution and uses energy. The move by the US soft drink and beer industry to use aluminum cans that can be recycled is obviously not the final solution to the litter problem (recall that nearly half of aluminum cans are never collected for recycling,[46] and the manufacturing of aluminum uses a lot of energy. Probably a better solution was the move by some American states to require returnable soft drink and beer containers to be used in their states instead of throwaways.

The "throwaway" economy that developed in the United States after World War II still exists. The efforts to recycle are a step forward, but much remains to be done. Denmark has banned throwaways, but this action is unlikely to be taken in the United States any time soon.

Substitution

When a material becomes scarce, it is sometimes possible to substitute another material for it that is more abundant or to use a renewable resource in place of the scarce item. For example, the more abundant aluminum can be used in place of the scarcer copper for most electrical uses. Difficulties arise at times when the substituted material in turn becomes scarce. Plastic utensils and containers replaced glass products in most US kitchens because of certain advantages plastic has over glass, such as being less breakable and lighter in weight. But plastics are made from petrochemicals, which are a finite resource. Also, the plastics industry produces more dangerous pollutants than does the glass industry. Another limitation to substitution is that some materials have unique qualities that no other materials have. Tungsten's high melting point, for example, is unmatched by any other metal. And substitutions can produce disruptions in the society, causing some industries to close and new ones to open. The last-mentioned point can mean, of course, new opportunities for some people and fewer for others. New ways of doing things can also be substituted for old ways, sometimes resulting in a reduced use of resources. The trend in some businesses to use communications in place of transportation (videoconferencing instead of physically being present) might be such a development.

Reducing needs

The fourth way to counteract shortages of a material is to reduce the need for the material. Many consumer goods – such as automobiles and clothes – become obsolete in a few years as styles change. This planned obsolescence leads to a high use of resources. Many products also wear out quickly and must be replaced with new ones. In the United States more durable products could be designed by industry, but they would often be more expensive. This is probably why the United States industry generally does not make such products. Higher prices would mean fewer sales, a slower turnover of business inventories, and thus probably lower profits. They could also mean fewer jobs.

Perhaps the best way to end this section is to repeat the popular phrase of environmentalists: "reduce, reuse, recycle" as the best ways – in that order – to use resources and to handle the wastes caused by the use of them.

Environmental Politics

In this section we will try to understand what makes environmental politics so controversial. Politics is a passionate business, but why are environmental issues often emotional? Clearly, conflicting interests and values are involved. Politics involves the making of laws and decisions that everyone must obey in a society. These laws and decisions are directed at settling conflicts that arise among people living together in a community, and at achieving commonly desired goals. As we will see, environmental politics does deal with very strongly held opposing values and interests. It also represents an effort by a community to achieve some goals – such as clean air and clean water – which cannot be reached individually, only by the community as a whole.

The political scientists Harold and Margaret Sprout believe that most participants in environmental politics show a tendency toward having one of two very different philosophies or worldviews and that these are at the root of most environmental conflicts. One they call "exploitive," and the other "mutualistic." Here is how they define them:

A[n] …exploitive attitude would be one that envisages inert matter, nonhuman species, and even humans as objects to be possessed or manipulated to suit the purposes of the exploiter. In contrast, a … mutualistic posture would be one that emphasizes the inter-relatedness of things and manifests a preference for cooperation and accommodation rather than conflict and domination.[47]

While conflicting worldviews are a part of environmental politics, so also is a conflict of basic interests. Economist Lester Thurow believes that environmental politics often involves a conflict between different classes having very different interests. He sees the environmental movement as being supported mainly by upper middle-class people who have gained economic security and now want to improve the quality of their lives further by reducing environmental pollutants. On the opposite side, he sees both lower income groups and the rich – lower income people because they see environmental laws making it more difficult for them to find jobs and obtain a better income, and the rich because they can often buy their way out of environmental problems and see pollution laws as making it more difficult for them to increase their wealth even further.[48]

Other conflicting interests are also involved in environmental politics. Antipollution laws often make it more difficult and costly to increase energy supplies, extract minerals, and increase jobs by industrial growth. Barry Commoner's Fourth Law of Ecology – There Is No Such Thing as a Free Lunch – means that for every gain there is some cost.[49] There are tradeoffs involved in making the air and water cleaner as there are in making more cars and television sets. Also, the costs of pollution control often increase substantially as you try to make the environment cleaner and cleaner. The cost required to make a 50 percent reduction in a pollutant is often quite modest, whereas if you try to reduce the pollutant by 95 percent, the cost usually increases dramatically   balanced against the impacts of unabated pollution.[50]

Much environmental destruction is extremely difficult for the political system to deal with, since the damage often shows up many years after the polluting action takes place. It is now clear that prevention is much cheaper than trying to clean up the damage after it has occurred, but the nature of politics does not lend itself to long-range planning. Generally, politicians have a rather short-term outlook, as do many business people. Both are judged on their performance in handling immediate problems; this promotes a tendency to take actions showing some immediate result. Such actions further the politician's chances for reelection and the business person's profits or chances for promotion. Yet environmental problems often call for actions before the danger becomes clear. A further complication is the fact that, even after action is taken to reduce a pollutant, because of the inherent delays in the system the harmful effects of the pollutant do not decrease until a number of years later. Thus the inclination of the public official – and the business person – is to do nothing and hope that something turns up showing that the problem was not as bad as feared or that there is a cheaper way to deal with it.

An additional factor in environmental politics is unique to the United States. The American dream has been one of continuing abundance. For much of the country's history, there has seemed to be an unlimited abundance of many things needed for the good life, such as land, forests, minerals, energy, clean air, and natural beauty. It is a country that seemed to offer unlimited opportunities for many to make a better life for themselves, and "better" has been usually defined as including more material goods. The setting of limits on consumption and production that environmentalists often promote is certain to cause dismay to many.

If the above were not enough to make environmental politics very difficult, there is also the fact that the costs in environmental matters are often very difficult to measure. One can calculate the cost of a scrubber on a coal-burning power plant, but how do you measure the cost of a shortened life that occurs if the scrubber is not used? How do you place a dollar figure on the suffering a person with emphysema experiences, or a miner with brown lung disease, or an asbestos worker with cancer? How do you measure the costs the yet unborn will have to pay if nothing is done now about climate change? And how do you put a dollar figure on the loss of natural beauty? Because it is so difficult to weigh the costs in conventional terms of measurement, the costs often were not weighed in the past.[51]

There is, of course, also the matter of values – the value individuals place on more material goods, the convenience of throwaway products, open spaces, and clean air. The resolution of conflicts over values can often be handled only by politics, in a democracy by the community as a whole making decisions through its representatives and then requiring all members of the community to obey them. That such stuff causes controversy and stirs passions should not be surprising. It is hard work.

Overdevelopment

Perhaps a good way to end this chapter is to explain the concept of overdevelopment. According to the Australian biologist Charles Birch, "Overdevelopment of any country starts when the citizens of that country consume resources and pollute the environment at a rate which is greater than the world could stand indefinitely if all the peoples of the world consumed resources at that rate."[52] From this perspective, it can be seen that the United States could be considered the most overdeveloped country in the world, followed closely by many other industrial countries. People in the United States, who constitute about 4 percent of the world's population, consume about 25 percent of the world's annual use of natural resources, and do so, as this chapter has shown, with devastating effects on the environment. This devastation is being reduced as new environmental laws are enacted and gradually enforced in the developed world, but it has not been reduced to such an extent that the concept of overdevelopment is outdated. We saw in Chapter 3 that present global consumption already requires the resources of 1.5 Earths.

Conclusions

Development is more than economic growth: it also includes the social changes that are caused by or accompany economic growth. As this chapter has shown, the increase in the production of goods and services that came with industrialization had, and still has, frightening costs. Poverty was dramatically reduced in a number of countries by industrialization – obviously an impressive benefit of the new economic activity. But that activity harmed both people and the environment. Slowly and painfully, people in the developed countries have come to realize that economic growth is not enough. Attention has to be paid to its effect on the Earth and on people. And awareness has grown in the industrialized nations, and continues to grow, that the question of how economic growth is affecting the environment needs to be asked and answered. The rich countries are slowly learning that it is cheaper and causes much less suffering to try to reduce the harmful effects of an economic activity at the beginning, when it is planned, than after the damage appears. To do this is not easy and is always imperfect. But an awareness of the need for such effort indicates a greater understanding and moral concern than did the previous widespread attitude that focused only on creating new products and services.

Developing countries are slowly realizing that the effects of economic activity on the environment should not be ignored. But here the new awareness is less widespread than in the rich countries. This is understandable because, except for some of the rulers and elite groups, the reduction of poverty is the first concern people have. It explains why some developing countries have welcomed polluting industries, such as factories that manufacture asbestos, since jobs today are more important than a vague worry that workers may contract cancer in 20 to 30 years. But also in developing countries, a slowly growing number of people realize that if the economic activity that gives jobs to people harms the environment at the same time, the benefits from that economic activity will be short-lived.

Poverty harms the environment, as we saw for example in the case of deforestation, where poor people searching for land to farm and for fuel are one cause of the extensive destruction of the remaining tropical rainforests. Economic growth that benefits the majority of people is needed to protect the environment. And a control on the rapidly expanding populations of many of the poorest countries is also needed to protect the environment, since increasing numbers of poor people hurt the land on which they live as they struggle to survive.

For both rich and poor nations, the environment is important. Economic growth is also important, especially for the poorer countries. The challenge remains for both poor and rich to achieve the optimal level of economic activity while simultaneously maintaining healthy ecosystems and sustaining the land, air, and water upon which all life depends.

Notes

1   American Cancer Society, "Lifetime Risk of Developing or Dying from Cancer," January 10, 2014, citing US National Cancer Institute's Surveillance Epidemiology and End Results (SEER) database, at http://www.cancer.org/Cancer/CancerBasics/lifetime-probability-of-developing-or-dying-from-cancer (accessed July 2015).

2   "Study Hailed as Convincing in Tying Fat to Cancers," *New York Times*, April 24, 2003, p. A23; and Jane Brody, "Another Study Finds a Link between Excess Weight and Cancer," *New York Times*, May 6, 2003, p. D7.

3   Robin C. Puett et al., "Particulate Matter Air Pollution Exposure, Distance to Road, and Incident Lung Cancer in the Nurses' Health Study Cohort," *Environmental Health Perspectives*, 122 (9) (2014), pp. 926–31; Solana Pyne, "Small Particles Add up to Big Disease Risk," *Science*, 295 (March 15, 2002), p. 1994.

4   President's Cancer Panel, *Reducing Environmental Cancer Risk: What We Can Do Now*, Annual Report, 2008–2009 (April 2010), p. ii, at http://deainfo.nci.nih.gov/advisory/pcp/annualReports/pcp08-09rpt/PCP_Report_08-09_508.pdf (accessed July 2015).

5   Ibid.

6   Barry Commoner, *The Closing Circle* (New York: Knopf, 1971), p. 261.

7   An encouraging development in the United States in the mid-2000s was the decision by the US chemical giant DuPont to spend about 10 percent of its research budget on trying to find biological-based substances, such as in corn and in sugar, to replace fossil fuels as the building blocks of its chemicals. But for the near future, DuPont, like other chemical companies, is counting on chemicals based on fossil fuels to make most of its profit. See Claudia Deutsch, "DuPont Looking to Displace Fossil Fuels as Building Blocks of Chemicals," *New York Times*, February 28, 2006, p. C1.

8   Rebecca Renner, "Scotchgard Scotched," *Scientific American*, 284 (March 2001), p. 18; and Jennifer Lee, "EPA Orders Companies to Examine Effects of Chemicals," *New York Times*, April 15, 2003, p. D2.

9   "Study Links DDT and Cancer," *New York Times*, April 22, 1993, p. A10.

10 US Environmental Protection Agency (EPA), Office of Pesticides Programs, *The Value of Countries Working Together to Regulate Pesticides and Food Safety*, April 2009, p. 1, at http://www.epa.gov/pesticides/international/2009/workingtogether.pdf (accessed July 2015).

11 EPA, "Pesticide News Story: EPA Releases Report Containing Latest Estimates of Pesticide Use in the United States," press release, February 17, 2011, at http://epa.gov/oppfead1/cb/csb_page/updates/2011/sales-usage06-07.html (accessed July 2015).

12 Philip Hilts, "Results of Study on Pesticide Encourage Effort to Cut Use," *New York Times*, July 5, 1993, p. 8.

13 Matthew Wald, "Citing Children, Environmental Protection Agency Is Banning Common Pesticide," *New York Times*, August 3, 1999, p. A1.

14 Michael Janofsky, "Environmental Groups Are Praising the EPA for Updating Cancer-Risk Guidelines," *New York Times*, April 4, 2005, p. A18.

15 "US Waste and Recycling," *New York Times*, August 20, 2002, p. D4.

16 EPA, *Municipal Solid Waste Generation, Recycling, and Disposal in the United States: Facts and Figures for 2012* (2014), p. 1, at http://www.epa.gov/solidwaste/nonhaz/municipal/pubs/2012_msw_fs.pdf (accessed July 2015).

17 Matt Baume, "San Francisco Watches Its Waste Line," *Grist*, October 13, 2010, at http://www.grist.org/article/2010-10-12-san-francisco-watches-its-waste-line. See also zero waste updates from the Institute for Local Self Reliance, at http://www.ilsr.org/tag/zero-waste/, and the San Francisco Department of Environment, at http://www.sfenvironment.org/zero-waste (all accessed July 2015).

18 Charles Moore, "Trashed," *Natural History*, 112 (November 2003), p. 51.

19 Ibid.

20 Ibid., p. 50. For a report on the increase of plastic fibers in the beaches and seabed of the British Isles see Andrew Revkin, "Plastics Permeate Even the Seabed," *New York Times*, May 11, 2004, p. D2.

21 Moore, "Trashed," p. 50.

22 National Geographic, "Great Pacific Garbage Patch," at http://education.national geographic.com/education/encyclopedia/great-pacific-garbage-patch/?ar_a=1 (accessed July 2015).

23 For general information on international efforts to regulate mercury, see the Minamata Convention website at www.mercuryconvention.org; for the text of the treaty, see http://www.mercuryconvention.org/Portals/11/documents/conventionText/Minamata %20Convention%20on%20Mercury_e.pdf (both accessed July 2015).

24 See, generally, Charlie Specht, "Choosing Love Canal for a Neighbor," *Buffalo News*, February 10, 2013, at http://www.buffalonews.com/20130210/choosing_love_canal_for_a_neighbor.html (accessed July 2015).

25 EPA, "Superfund's 25th Anniversary: Capturing the Past, Charting the Future," October 1, 2010.

26 In the United States, Scorecard, a pollution information website enables individuals to enter a US-based zipcode to see local toxic chemical releases, see www.scorecard.org (accessed July 2015).

27 EPA, "2013 TRI National Analysis: Releases of Chemicals," at http://www2.epa.gov/ toxics-release-inventory-tri-program/2013-tri-national-analysis-releases-chemicals (accessed July 2015).

28 EPA, "2013 TRI National Analysis: Land Disposal – Trend in Land Disposal," at http://www2.epa.gov/toxics-release-inventory-tri-program/2013-tri-national-analysis-land-disposal-trend-land-disposal; EPA, "2013 TRI National Analysis: Air Disposal – Trend in Air Disposal," at http://www2.epa.gov/toxics-release-inventory-tri-program/ 2013-tri-national-analysis-air-releases-trend-air-releases (all accessed July 2015).

29 Rebecca Renner, "Tracking the Dirty Byproducts of a World Trying to Stay Clean," *Science*, 306 (December 10, 2004), p. 1887.

30 Paul Webster, "Study Finds Heavy Contamination across Vast Russian Arctic," *Science*, 306 (December 10, 2004), p. 1875.

31 Ibid.

32 EPA, "Superfund's 25th Anniversary: Capturing the Past, Charting the Future," at http://www.epa.gov/superfund/accomp/news/25anniversary.htm (accessed July 2015).

33 EPA, "Superfund Special Accounts," January 12, 2015, at http://www2.epa.gov/ enforcement/superfund-special-accounts (accessed July 2015).

34 Barbara Ward, *Progress for a Small Planet* (New York: W. W. Norton, 1979), pp. 65–6.

35 Michael Royston, "Making Pollution Prevention Pay," *Harvard Business Review* (November/December 1980), p. 12.

36 Heinrich von Lersner, "Commentary: Outline for an Ecological Economy," *Scientific American*, 273 (September 1995), p. 188.

37 World Resources Institute (WRI), United Nations Environment Programme, United Nations Development Programme, and World Bank, *World Resources 1998–99: Environmental Change and Human Health* (Washington, DC: WRI, 1999), p. 167.

38 The 3M website on its environmental goals and achievements is at http://solutions.3m.com/wps/portal/3M/en_US/3M-Sustainability/Global/Environment/GoalsProgress (accessed July 2015).

39 Seventh Generation, "Measuring Our Environmental Footprint: Packaging and Materials," at http://www.7genereport.com/measuring/packaging.php (accessed July 2015).

40 WRI et al., *World Resources 1998–99*, p. 167.

41 Samuel Loewenberg, "Old Europe's New Ideas," *Sierra*, 89 (January/February 2004), p. 43.

42 EPA, *Municipal Solid Waste Generation, Recycling, and Disposal, in the United States: Facts and Figures for 2009* (2010), p. 1, at http://www.epa.gov/epawaste/nonhaz/municipal/pubs/msw2009-fs.pdf (accessed July 2015).

43 Pavol Stracansky, "Eastern Europe Lagging on Waste and Recycling, NGOs Warn," April 1, 2010, at http://www.guardian.co.uk/environment/2010/apr/01/waste-recycling; and BBC News, "Recycling around the World," June 25, 2005 at http://news.bbc.co.uk/2/hi/europe/4620041.stm (both accessed July 2015).

44 Norimitsu Onishi, "How Do Japanese Dump Trash? Let Us Count the Myriad Ways," *New York Times*, May 12, 2005, p. A1.

45 John Markoff, "Technology's Toxic Trash Is Sent to Poor Nations," *New York Times*, February 25, 2002, p. C1.

46 EPA, *Municipal Solid Waste Generation … 2012*, p. 3.

47 Harold Sprout and Margaret Sprout, *The Context of Environmental Politics* (Lexington: University Press of Kentucky, 1978), pp. 47–8.

48 Lester Thurow, *The Zero-Sum Society* (New York: Basic Books, 1980), pp. 104–5.

49 Commoner, *The Closing Circle*, pp. 45–6.

50 William Ophuls, *Ecology and the Politics of Scarcity* (San Francisco: W. H. Freeman, 1977), p. 75.

51 For an attempt to measure the hidden costs of today's energy see Harold M. Hubbard, "The Real Cost of Energy," *Scientific American*, 264 (April 1991), pp. 36–42. For an explanation of how the accounting system presently used by economists allows policymakers to ignore the deterioration of the environment caused by economic activity see Robert Repetto, "Accounting for Environmental Assets," *Scientific American*, 266 (June 1992), pp. 94–100.

52 Charles Birch, *Confronting the Future* (New York: Penguin, 1976), p. 35.

Further Reading

Arthus-Bertrand, Yann, *Earth from Above*, revised and expanded edn (New York: Henry Abrams, 2002). From a helicopter flying over 60 countries, the author records the beauty of the Earth as well as its spoiled places. These stunning photographs give a rarely seen view of the Earth.

Brown, Phil, and Edwin J. Mikkelsen, *No Safe Place: Toxic Waste, Leukemia, and Community Action* (Berkeley: University of California Press, 1990). This book documents the efforts of a small group of citizens – led by a mother whose son had acute leukemia – to uncover the source of illness in their community. It describes their battle to overcome resistance by their neighbors and the indifference of local and state government officials.

Clayton, Susan, and Gene Myers, *Conservation Psychology; Understanding and Promoting Human Care of Nature* (Oxford: Wiley-Blackwell, 2009). The authors use psychological perspectives to try to answer such questions as "What is the relationship between individuals learning about environmental problems and their conservation attitudes, knowledge, beliefs, and behaviors?"

Daily, Gretchen, and Katherine Ellison, *The New Economy of Nature: The Quest to Make Conservation Profitable* (Washington, DC: Island Press, 2002). The authors show that the environment provides services that have an economic value. That recognition can lead to arrangements (like carbon trading) based on mutual self-interest and an understanding by all that conservation pays. Highly readable.

McKibben, Bill, "A Special Moment in History," *Atlantic Monthly* (May 1998), pp. 55–78. In simple but powerful prose, McKibben argues that we live in a very important time in the history of the planet. He believes the fate of the planet for many years to come will be determined by the lifestyle, population, and technological choices we make in the next few decades.

Pearce, Fred, *When the Rivers Run Dry: Water – the Defining Crisis of the Twenty-First Century* (Boston: Beacon Press, 2006). An experienced science journalist, Pearce visits over 30 countries during his research for this book. With a growing population and increased urban and agricultural needs, the world is withdrawing increasing amounts of water from its rivers and aquifers. Unless new water efficiencies are soon adopted, a water crisis is ahead.

Safina, Carl, *The View from Lazy Point: A Natural Year in an Unnatural World* (New York: Henry Holt, 2010). This naturalist's base is a cottage in the United States. During a year he travels about the world returning from time to time to his cottage to tell of the perilous times in which we live and of which we seem to be unaware. As a review in the *New York Times states*, "Safina's account ... can be harrowing, but its impassioned, informed urgency is also filled with hope, joy, and love."

Speth, James Gustave, *Red Sky at Morning: America and the Crisis of the Global Environment* (New Haven, CT: Yale University Press, 2004). Speth explores some of the fundamental reasons for the environmental deterioration occurring in the world. He seeks to explain why a number of economic indicators continue to show growth at the same time that serious environmental deterioration is occurring.

Steingraber, Sandra, *Having Faith: An Ecologist's Journey to Motherhood* (Cambridge, MA: Perseus, 2001). What's it like for a woman who knows a lot about chemicals and their effects on human beings to have a baby today? Streingraber explains but also analyzes how we got to where we accept that residues of many toxic chemicals in our world are all right.

Williams, Michael, *Deforesting the Earth: From Prehistory to Global Crisis* (Chicago: University of Chicago Press, 2003). A reviewer in *Science* has called this book "the most comprehensive account ever written of when, where, and how humans have wrought what is surely the most dramatic change in Earth's surface since the end of the Pleistocene 10,000 years ago ..."

Chapter 8

Technology

Benefits of Technology   245
Unanticipated Consequences of the Use of Technology   245
   DDT   247
   Factory farms   248
Inappropriate Uses of Technology   250
Limits to the "Technological Fix"   253
War   255
The Threat of Nuclear Weapons: A Case Study   257
   The threat   258
   New dangers   260
      Nuclear proliferation   260
      The cleanup   262
      The threat of nuclear terrorism   263
Conclusions   264
Notes   264
Further Reading   266

*Will mankind murder Mother Earth or will he redeem her? He could murder her
by misusing his increasing technological potency.*
> Arnold J. Toynbee, *Mankind and Mother Earth* (1976)

Technology is the application of science to solve problems. To many people, technology and development are synonymous. Technology is what makes economic growth and social change happen. The limited use of high technology by the less developed

Global Issues: An Introduction, Fifth Edition. Kristen A. Hite and John L. Seitz
© 2016 John Wiley & Sons, Ltd. Published 2016 by John Wiley & Sons, Ltd.

nations is sometimes given as one of the reasons why they are less developed and less prosperous than the industrialized nations.

But the relationship between technology and development is a complicated one. At times the negative features of technology seem to outweigh the positive features. Technology can cause a society to change in some very undesirable ways. In this chapter, after a short section on the benefits of technology, we will look closely at some of the negative relationships between technology and development.

Benefits of Technology

A book such as this one, whose readers will probably be mostly from the developed nations and the rapidly rising developing countries, does not need to dwell on the benefits of technology. Advertising and the mass media herald the expected joys that will come with a new product, technique, or discovery. In the United States people are socialized to like new things; they are also pragmatic, which means that technology is commonly used to make things work "better." They would have to be foolish not to recognize the benefits that technology has brought.

One of the main reasons much of the world envies the United States is that its technology has in many real ways made life more comfortable, stimulating, and free of drudgery. People in the United States know this and need to remember it. But they and others also need to learn several other lessons: (1) short-term benefits from using a technology can have long-term negative consequences; (2) there can be unanticipated consequences of using a technology; (3) the use of some types of technology in certain situations can be inappropriate; and (4) there are many problems that technology cannot solve. The inability to learn these lessons could lead to our destruction, as the case study in this chapter on the threat of nuclear weapons will show.

Benefits of technology

In personal terms, technology has allowed the authors of this book to visit dozens of countries; to see a photograph of the Earth taken from space; to write this book from different states and countries on personal computers that greatly facilitated its composition; to wear shirts that don't need ironing; and to keep the glaucoma of one of the authors under control to prevent him from going blind. What items would your list include?

Unanticipated Consequences of the Use of Technology

Ecology is the study of the relationships between organisms and their environments. Without a knowledge of ecology, we are tempted to use technology to solve a single

Plate 8.1 Without modern technology to help, necessary tasks can be difficult. A woman in Nepal breaks up clumps of soil to prepare the land for planting

Source: Ab Abercrombie

problem. But there are many examples to illustrate the truth that we cannot change one part of the human environment without in some way affecting other parts. Often these other effects are harmful, and often they are completely unanticipated, as the box about cats nicely illustrates.[1]

The case of the parachuting cats

A situation in Borneo nicely illustrates the fact that the use of a new technology can lead to unanticipated consequences. In this situation health officials wanted to destroy malaria-carrying mosquitoes so they began to spray DDT on the outside and inside of the homes of villagers. After the spraying, the roofs of many homes began to collapse because they were being eaten by caterpillars.

The spraying had killed not just the mosquitoes but also a predatory wasp that had kept the caterpillars under control. The DDT spraying also killed many houseflies, which were then consumed by the gecko, a little lizard that inhabits many village homes and eats houseflies. The geckos died and were then consumed by household cats. When the cats died, rats invaded the homes and began consuming the villagers' food and brought a danger of plague. This led to the need to parachute cats into villages in order to try to restore the balance that the widespread spraying of DDT had upset.

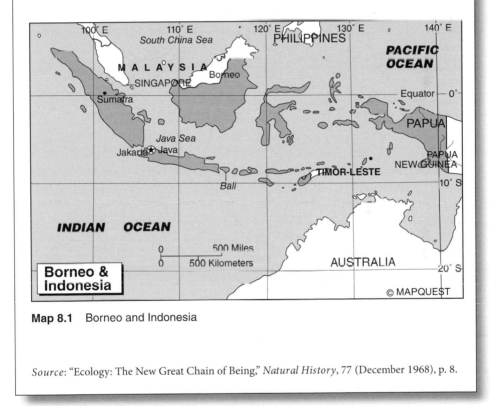

Map 8.1   Borneo and Indonesia

Source: "Ecology: The New Great Chain of Being," *Natural History*, 77 (December 1968), p. 8.

DDT

The use of DDT in the United States has also had major unanticipated effects since it is persistent (it does not easily break down into harmless substances) and is poisonous to many forms of life, as discussed in Chapter 7.[2] The reduced use of DDT in the developing nations, as the detrimental effects of DDT became known, led to a resurgence in malaria. The World Health Organization has now given conditional approval for the use of DDT for the control of malaria when "locally safe, effective, and affordable alternatives are not available."[3]

Natural gas fracking: when innovation advances faster than regulation

In the United States alone, natural gas production increased by roughly 50 percent in the decade between 2005 and 2015. This is due in large part to technological innovation, a combination of hydrological fracturing and directional drilling to extract oil and gas trapped in dense rock. This technique is commonly referred to as "fracking," and it is quickly changing national and even global energy supplies.

While many have touted natural gas as a "transition fuel" for climate change, as it is widely viewed as the most climate-friendly option among fossil fuels, gas production through fracking appears to be advancing at a faster pace than a full understanding of the risks, with regulation evolving at a slower pace than technological innovation. Some of the alleged risks include exploding wells, earthquakes, methane leaks that offset climate gains from reduced carbon emissions, and toxic pollution from fracking fluids that contaminate water and land.

Citing these risks, some groups of concerned citizens and landowners have called for more regulation of fracking activities. As a result, some governments are actively developing regulations governing fracking, but the fracking industry is not waiting for regulations to be put in place to scale up production. Proponents of fracking say that it reduces reliance on foreign energy supplies and lowers natural gas prices, which also helps reduce greenhouse gas emissions that cause climate change.

For the most part, fracking remains a weakly regulated activity with significant risks, even as its supplies are already impacting national and global energy supplies and prices.

Sources: Thomas W. Merrill, "Four Questions about Fracking," *Case Western Reserve Law Review*, 63 (2013); Scott Disavino, "Are the Good Times Over for Growth in US Shale Gas?" Reuters, March 17, 2015; Trevor M. Penning et al., "Environmental Health Research Recommendations from the Inter-Environmental Health Sciences Core Center Working Group on Unconventional Natural Gas Drilling Operations," *Environmental Health Perspectives*, 122 (11) (2014), p. 1155.

Factory farms

Let's look at factory farms and the unanticipated consequences that have come with the adoption of factory techniques to produce animals for human consumption. Such techniques have been adopted to raise poultry, pigs, veal calves, and cattle. The techniques allow large numbers of animals to be raised in a relatively small space. (Many of these animals never see the light of day until they are removed for slaughter.) The crowding of many animals in a small space and the confinement of individual animals in small stalls creates stress in the animals. Stress can lower the natural defenses of the animals to diseases, and the crowded conditions facilitate the rapid spreading of diseases among the animals. It is common in the United States for factory-raised animals to receive large doses of antibiotics in their feed to prevent the outbreak of diseases and to promote growth.

There is now evidence that the abundant use of antibiotics in animal food is creating bacteria that are resistant to treatment by modern drugs and that these bacteria can cause illness in humans.[4] In 2001 researchers in the United States reported in the *New England Journal of Medicine*, one of the country's main medical journals, that antibiotic-resistant bacteria were widespread in meats and poultry sold in the country and could be found in consumers' intestines. This means that many food-borne illnesses will not respond to the usual treatments and that some may be resistant to all current drugs.[5] Eighty percent of all antibiotics in the United States are used for animals.[6] In 2010 the US Food and Drug Administration asked farmers to stop giving unnecessary antibiotics to livestock, out of concerns that the antibiotics are contributing to drug resistant bacteria that endanger human lives.[7]

Following the recommendations of the World Health Organization, the European Union in 1998 banned the placing of antibiotics that are used to treat illnesses in human beings in animal food to promote growth of the animal and to prevent diseases. Denmark stopped their use in 1999 and found that by improving the sanitary conditions of its animals there were generally no negative consequences of the ban. The only exception was with pigs, where there were more intestinal infections and thus a small increase in production costs.[8]

McDonald's made an important decision in 2003 that could help reduce the use of antibiotics in foods. (Because McDonald's buys such a large amount of food for its fast-food outlets, its decisions influence the practices of the food industry.) It announced that it was going to require its poultry suppliers to eliminate the use of medically important antibiotics for growth promotion. It did not require this of its beef suppliers, but encouraged them to follow this policy also.

Controversy regarding factory farms in the United States is growing. In the late 1990s special attention was being given to large hog farms that were tending to dominate the industry. The number of hogs grown on an average swine farm rose from about 900 in the early 1990s to more than 8,000 in 2009.[9] Complaints came from small farmers who could not compete with large factory farms and also from nearby residents. The foul smell from the farms was at times very powerful and the large amount of animal waste presented a real danger to underground water supplies. Some of the large hog farms produce as much raw sewage as a middle-sized city, but without sewage treatment plants. Farm waste has always been treated more leniently in the United States than urban waste. The Environmental Protection Agency in 2008 issued a new rule requiring large factory farms to implement new manure management practices, including obtaining a permit for any discharges/runoff that the farm can't contain.[10]

The defenders of the large hog farms cite the demand by US consumers for low-cost, lean pork. Their farms can produce this because the pigs are artificially inseminated and genetically designed to produce an identical cut of meat. The defenders also cite the need for the jobs in rural areas and tax revenue that their farms provide.

The manure from large chicken factory farms is often spread as a fertilizer on crop farms. The manure has a high content of the nutrients nitrogen and phosphorus. Some of these nutrients wash into rivers and bays during heavy rains and are suspected of contributing to blooms of toxic algae in Chesapeake Bay and to the lack of dissolved oxygen in the Gulf of Mexico off Louisiana, one of the largest so-called "dead zones."

Experiences with foreign aid

The unanticipated consequences of the use of technology can be seen in a situation of which I (Seitz) have some personal knowledge. When I was in Iran in the late 1950s with the US foreign aid program, one of our projects was to modernize the police force of the monarch, the Shah of Iran. We gave the national police new communications equipment so that police messages could be sent throughout the country quickly and efficiently. The United States gave this kind of assistance to the Shah to bolster his regime and help him to maintain public order in Iran while development programs were being initiated. All fine and good, except for the fact that the Shah used his efficient police – and especially his secret police, which the US Central Intelligence Agency helped train – not just to catch criminals and those who were trying to violently overthrow his government, but to suppress all opponents of his regime. His secret police, SAVAK, soon earned a worldwide reputation for being very efficient – and ruthless. Such ruthlessness, which often involved torturing suspected opponents of the Shah, was one of the reasons why the Shah became very unpopular in Iran and was eventually overthrown in 1979 by the Ayatollah Khomeini, a person who had deep anti-American feelings.

For a fuller discussion of the unanticipated consequences of American aid to the Shah see John L. Seitz, "The Failure of US Technical Assistance in Public Administration: The Iranian Case," in Eric Otenyo and Nancy Lind (eds), *Comparative Public Administration: The Essential Readings* (Oxford: Elsevier, 2006), pp. 321–34.

Inappropriate Uses of Technology

In 1973, E. F. Schumacher published his book *Small Is Beautiful: Economics as if People Mattered*.[11] This book became the foundation for a movement that seeks to use technology in ways that are not harmful to people. Schumacher argued that the developing nations need intermediate (or "appropriate") technology, not the high (or "hard") technology of the Western industrialized nations. Intermediate technology lies in between the "low" technology common in the rural areas of the less developed countries – where many of the world's people live – and the technology of the industrialized world, which tends to use vast amounts of energy, pollutes the environment, requires imported resources, and often alienates the workers from their own work. The intermediate technology movement seeks to identify those areas of life in the South, and also in the industrialized West, where a relatively simple technology can make people's work easier while remaining meaningful, that is, giving them a feeling of satisfaction when they do it.

The high technology of the West is often very expensive, and thus large amounts of capital are needed to acquire it, capital that many in developing nations do not have. This technology is referred to as being capital intensive instead of labor intensive. This means that money – but not many people – is needed to obtain it and maintain it. In other words, high technology does not give many workers jobs. (This is the essence of the mass-production line: lots of products by a relatively small number of workers.) But the main problem in nations that are trying to develop – and, in fact, in the United States also when its economy is in a recession – is that there are not enough jobs for people in the first place. It is the absence of jobs in the rural areas that is causing large numbers of the rural poor in the South to migrate to cities both near and far looking for work, work that is often not there.

While it is fairly obvious, and widely recognized, that developing economies should select technologies that are appropriate to their needs, why don't they always do this? Why has this seemingly simple "lesson" not been learned? The authors of a study of World Bank experiences over nearly four decades explain why they believe inappropriate technology is frequently chosen:

> Why does this happen? Foreign consultants or advisers may advocate the technology with which they are most familiar. Local engineers, if educated abroad or the heirs of a colonial legacy, may have acquired a similar bias in favor of advanced technology, or they may simply presume, as do their superiors, that what is modern is best. Special interest groups may favor a particular technical approach. … Deep-seated customs and traditions may favor certain solutions and make others unacceptable. Economic policies that overprice labor (through minimum wage or other legislation) or underprice capital (through subsidized interest rates or overpriced currency) may send distorted signals to decision makers. A simple lack of knowledge or reluctance to experiment may limit the range of choice. … When aid is tied to the supply of equipment from the donor country … freedom to choose an appropriate technology may be compromised. With so many factors at work, it is not surprising that a "simple" lesson – such as selecting an appropriate technology – may prove far from simple to apply.[12]

I (Seitz) witnessed the inappropriate use of high technology in both Liberia and the United States. As part of US economic assistance to Liberia, we gave the Liberians road-building equipment. That equipment included power saws. As I proceeded to turn some of this equipment over to Liberians in a small town in a rural area, I realized that the power saws we were giving them were very inappropriate. To people who had little or no experience with power tools – which applied to nearly all the Liberians in that town – the power saw was a deadly instrument. Also, they would not be able to maintain or repair them when they broke down. Their noise would ruin the peacefulness of the area. A much more appropriate form of assistance would have been crates of axes and hand saws, tools that they could easily learn to use safely, that they would be able to maintain and repair themselves, and that would have provided work for many people.

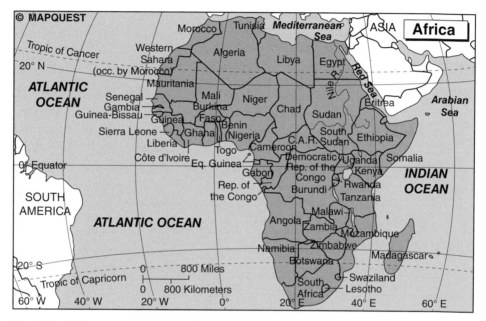

Map 8.2 Africa

In the United States both authors of this book became aware of the inappropriate use of high technology as their respective families began to prepare for the birth of their children. Most children in the world are born at home, but in the United States and in many other developed countries nearly all births take place in hospitals. An impressive number of studies now show that moving births into hospitals has resulted in unnecessary interventions in the birth process by doctors and hospital staff, which upset the natural stages of labor and can jeopardize the health of both the mother and the baby.[13] As many as 85 to 90 percent of women can give birth naturally, without the need for advanced mechanical technologies.[14] Prenatal care can usually identify the 10 to 15 percent that cannot deliver normally, and for them the use of high technology can help protect the lives of the mother and baby. But the major error that has been made is that procedures that are appropriate for these few are now routinely used for most births, often out of "convenience" as opposed to medical necessity. (Author Hite and author Seitz's wife were both grateful to use a low-technology midwife for the birth of their first children to minimize medical interventions).

A recent trend in the United States to use more appropriate technology is seen in the efforts to satisfy the growing demand for lower-intensity localized agriculture. (This subject was discussed in Chapter 3 on food under the section on alternative/sustainable/organic agriculture).

The intermediate technology movement is not against high technology as such (it recognizes areas where high technology is desirable – there is no other way to produce vaccines against deadly diseases, for example), but only against the use of such technology where simpler technology would be appropriate.

Limits to the "Technological Fix"

In US society, which makes wide use of technology, there is a common belief that technology can solve the most urgent problems. It is even believed that the problems that science and technology have created can be solved by more science and technology. What is lacking, according to this way of thinking, is an adequate use of science and technology to solve the problem at hand. In other words, we must find a "technological fix."

While the ability of technology to solve certain problems is impressive, there are a number of serious problems confronting humans – in fact, probably the most serious problems which humans have ever faced – which seem to have no technological solution. Technology itself has often played a major role in causing these problems. Let's look at a few of them.

The population explosion appears to have no acceptable technological solution. Birth control devices can certainly help in controlling population growth; without such devices a solution to the problem would be even more difficult than it is. But as we saw in Chapter 1, the reasons for the population explosion are much more complicated than the lack of birth control devices. Economic, social, and political factors play a significant role in this situation and must be taken into consideration in any effort to control the explosion. A technological advancement was one of the causes of the population explosion – the wiping out of major diseases, such as smallpox, which used to kill millions. Some people, such as Garrett Hardin, have argued that many of those people who are advocating technological solutions to the population problem, such as farming the seas, developing new strains of wheat, or creating space colonies, "are trying to find a way to avoid the evils of overpopulation without relinquishing any of the privileges they now enjoy."[15]

Huge municipal sanitation plants were once considered the solution to our polluted streams, rivers, and lakes, but the rising costs of these plants and the fact that they treat only part of the polluted water are bringing this solution into question.[16] As much water pollution is caused by agricultural and urban runoffs, both of which are not treated by the plants, as by sewage. To talk about a technological fix for this problem is to talk about spending astronomical sums of money to treat all polluted water, and even then the solution would still be in doubt.

A final example will be given to illustrate the limits to the technological fix. As we will see in the case study below, the nuclear arms race between the Soviet Union and the United States after World War II threatened the world with a holocaust beyond comprehension. Many believed that technology would solve this problem; all that was needed to gain security was better weapons and more weapons than the other side. But the history of the arms race, which lasted nearly half a century until the disintegration of the Soviet Union in the early 1990s, clearly shows that one side's advantage was soon matched or surpassed by new weapons on the other side. Momentary feelings of security by one nation were soon replaced by deepening insecurity felt by both nations as the weapons became more lethal. "Security dilemma" is the phrase that has been coined to describe a situation where one nation's efforts to gain security lead to its opponent's feeling of insecurity. This insecurity causes the nation that believes it is behind in the arms race to build up its arms, but it also causes the other nation to feel insecure. So the race goes on. The temptation to believe that a new weapon will solve the problem is immense. A brief history of the arms race shows how both superpowers were caught in a security dilemma.

The United States exploded its first atomic bomb in 1945 (see below) and felt fairly secure until the Soviets exploded one in 1949. In 1954 the United States tested the first operational thermonuclear weapon (a hydrogen or H-bomb), which uses the A-bomb as a trigger, and a year later the Soviets followed suit. In 1957 the Soviets successfully tested the first intercontinental ballistic missile (ICBM) and launched the Earth's first artificial satellite, Sputnik. The United States felt very insecure but within three years had more operational ICBMs than the Soviet Union. (This "missile gap," in which the Soviets trailed, could have been the reason they put missiles in Cuba in 1962, which led to the Cuban missile crisis, the world's first approach to the brink of nuclear war. The humiliation the Soviet Union suffered when it had to take its missiles out of Cuba may have led to its buildup of nuclear arms in the 1970s and 1980s, which caused great concern in the United States.)

The Soviet Union put up the first antiballistic missile system around a city – around Moscow – in the 1960s, and in 1968 the United States countered by developing multiple, independently targetable reentry vehicles (MIRVs), which could easily overwhelm the Soviet antiballistic missiles. The Soviets started deploying their first MIRVs in 1975, and these highly accurate missiles with as many as ten warheads on a single missile, each one able to hit a different target, led President Reagan in 1981 to declare that a "window of vulnerability" existed, since the land-based US ICBMs could now be attacked by the Soviet MIRVs. Reagan began a massive military buildup.

The technological race was poised to move into space when President Reagan in 1983 announced plans to develop a defensive system, some of which would probably be based in space, which could attack any Soviet missiles fired at the United States. This system (formally known as the Strategic Defense Initiative, and informally called "Star Wars") was criticized by many US scientists as not being feasible and by the early 1990s it had been greatly reduced in scope. The United States in the first decade of the twenty-first century was still planning to build a much-reduced missile shield to guard against accidents and possible attack by unfriendly developing countries that have recently acquired nuclear weapons. An unexpected end to the nuclear arms race between the Soviet Union and the United States came in the late 1980s with the collapse of the Soviet empire in Europe and with the breakup of the Soviet Union itself in the early 1990s. The huge financial strain on its economy caused by the arms race undoubtedly contributed to its collapse. But the nuclear arms race also placed serious strains on the US economy. The end of the Cold War brought the world a nearly miraculous release from the danger of a third world war, which likely would have been the world's last one.

In the first decade of the twenty-first century – over the objection of China and Russia – the United States started to build a limited defense against nuclear missiles, supposedly from so-called "rogue states," or from an accidental launch. Countries such as North Korea and Iran were unfriendly to the United States and to the West in general and had some ability already, or would have in the future, to build nuclear missiles. Meanwhile, some of the biggest emerging threats became not large-scale nuclear weapons but rather smaller ones with a more limited radius that could be made with materials whose supplies are more difficult to limit and control.

War

Why do human beings make war? Some of the people who have studied the causes of war believe that war is caused by the negative aspects of human nature, such as selfishness, possessiveness, irrationality, and aggressiveness. Other students of war have come to the conclusion that certain types of government – or, more formally, how political power is distributed within the state – make some countries more warlike than others. And other analysts have concluded that international anarchy, or the absence of a world government where disputes can be settled peacefully and authoritatively, is the main cause of war. Kenneth Waltz, a respected US student of war, concluded that human nature and/or the type of government are often the immediate causes of war, but that international anarchy explains why war has recurred throughout human history.[17]

War reflects the relatively primitive state of human political development. When Albert Einstein, the theoretical physicist who is considered to have been one of the most brilliant people of the twentieth century, was reportedly asked why it is that we are able to create nuclear weapons but not abolish war, he responded that the answer was easy: politics is more difficult than physics.

At the end of the first decade of the twenty-first century, the nations of the world spent about $1.5 trillion a year on military expenditures. The United States spent about $700 billion, China about $100 billion, France and the United Kingdom about $60 billion, and Russia, Japan, and Germany about $50 billion.[18] In 2009 the average cost for each US citizen for the country's military budget was about $2,000.[19]

Since World War II there have been more than 150 wars, with 90 percent of those occurring in the less developed nations. Wars have been frequent in the South since 1945 for a number of reasons. During the Cold War the United States and the Soviet Union supported with arms various political groups in the less developed nations that favored their side in the East/West conflict. Although the Cold War has now ended, the huge amounts of weapons supplied by the superpowers are now still circulating widely across the globe. Conflicts have been frequent in the developing world also because many of these nations received political independence relatively recently and territorial disputes, power struggles, ethnic and religious rivalries, and rebellions caused by unjust conditions are common.

With the exception of the Persian Gulf wars – which could be called "resource wars" – wars since the end of the Cold War have been mainly civil wars involving three categories of participants: first, ethnic groups fighting for more autonomy or for a state of their own, such as the Kurds in Turkey and the Chechens in Russia; second, groups trying to get control of a state, such as in Afghanistan; and third, so-called "failed states" where the central government has collapsed or is extremely weak and fighting is occurring over political and/or economic "spoils," such as in Liberia.

Wars over the control of natural resources will no doubt become more common as global consumption increases, exacerbating scarcities.

A characteristic of modern war is that often more civilians are killed than soldiers. In many wars in the past the military combatants were the main casualties but this has now changed so that civilians often bear the greatest burden. In the first half of the twentieth century about 50 percent of the war-related dead were civilians. In the 1960s the proportion of the war dead who were civilians rose to about 65 percent, and in the 1980s it reached about 75 percent. The United Nations estimates that civilians comprised 90 percent of war casualties in the 1990s.[20] If one adds to the number of civilians killed and wounded during the fighting the vast number of civilians who flee the fighting and become refugees – sometimes finding no place that will accept them – civilians indeed bear the largest burden of modern war. Also the destruction from the fighting is often immense so that when the fighting finally ends, those civilians able to return often find destroyed towns and an ecologically damaged land.

Another characteristic of modern wars is that technology has been used to greatly increase the destructive capacity of the weapons. The case study on nuclear weapons that follows will illustrate that point well, but even so-called conventional weapons are now much more destructive than they used to be. In addition to the increase in destructive capacity, technology has been used to increase the weapons' accuracy, penetration ability, rates of fire, range, automation, and armor. Now, unarmed airplanes are able to wage sophisticated and destructive warfare ranging from bombing to assassinations through remote-controlled technology.

At the beginning of the twenty-first century there seemed to be both positive and negative signs regarding war. For the first time the North Atlantic Treaty Organization (NATO) was used several times to end fighting and killing in the former

Yugoslavia. Other peacekeeping military forces under the United Nations were active in many locations throughout the world – 16 in June of 2015.[21] Under nuclear arms reduction agreements between the United States and Russia, by the mid-1990s nuclear arsenals had been reduced from about 18,000 megatons of explosive power to about 8,000 megatons.[22] In 2011 the United States and Russia signed a new nuclear arms control agreement, which provided for a 30 percent reduction in nuclear weapons over the following seven years and a verification process so each side can be sure the cuts are being made.

On the negative side, it is clear that although war among the great powers has increasingly become unlikely because of the threat it would become a nuclear war, war is still a political instrument in the world. In the Democratic Republic of the Congo nearly 4 million people have died since a conflict began there in 1998. Sudan's civil war, which lasted 22 years, led to about 2 million deaths and displaced about 4 million people.

The 2003 US-led invasion of Iraq left an estimated 134,000 Iraqi civilians dead.[23] Many military and civilian deaths continued as the US-led NATO force attempted to defeat the Taliban, the local radical Muslim group trying to restore its control of Afghanistan. The United Nations reported 17,774 civilian deaths between 2009 and 2014, with 3,699 of those occurring in 2014 alone, representing an increase in civilian deaths by 25 per cent from the previous year.[24] Elsewhere in the region, both political (Arab Spring) and more violent conflicts have surged in recent years in countries such as Syria, Mali, Egypt, and Libya.

According to the respected Stockholm International Peace Research Institute, while there was a decrease in the number of wars in the late twentieth century and early twenty-first century, dropping from a high of about 30 in 1991 to about 16 in 2008, those numbers, and particularly nonstate conflicts, are now increasing.[25]

The reduced stockpile of nuclear weapons still represents over 700 times the explosive power used in the twentieth century's three major wars, which killed about 44 million people. As we will see in the next section, nuclear weapons represent the darkest part of the "dark side" of our species.

The Threat of Nuclear Weapons: A Case Study

The threat of nuclear weapons is a subject that touches on many of the themes we have examined in this chapter. It is the "ultimate" development subject since it is the achievements of weapons technology by the developed nations that have brought the survival of human life into question. It is a problem that cries out for a political solution. Carl von Clausewitz, the famous Prussian author of books on military strategy, described war as a continuation of politics by other means. But, given the probable consequences of a nuclear war as presented below, one must ask whether war between nations with nuclear weapons can remain a way of settling their disputes. Let us look at the nature of the threat created by nuclear weapons and then at four contemporary problems related to these weapons.

The threat

It has taken 4.5 billion years for life to reach its present state of development on this planet. The year 1945 represents a milestone in that evolution, since it was then that the United States exploded its first atomic bombs on Hiroshima and Nagasaki, Japan, and demonstrated that humans had learned how to harness for war the essential forces of the universe. After 1945, when the United States had no more than two or three atomic bombs, the arms race continued until the two superpowers, the United States and the Soviet Union, had a total of about 50,000 nuclear weapons, the equivalent of 1 million Hiroshima bombs – or, to put it another way, about 3 tons of TNT for every man, woman, and child in the world. The Hiroshima bomb was a 15 kiloton device (a kiloton having the explosive force of 1,000 tons of TNT); some of the weapons today fall in the megaton range (a megaton being the equivalent of 1 million tons of TNT).

Plate 8.2   Underground nuclear weapons testing in the United States

Source: Los Alamos National Laboratory.

What would happen if these weapons were ever used? We cannot be sure of all the effects, of course, since, as the author Jonathan Schell has stated, we have only one Earth and cannot experiment with it.[26] But we do know from the Hiroshima and Nagasaki bombings, and from the numerous testings of nuclear weapons both above and below ground, that there are five immediate destructive effects from a nuclear explosion: (1) the initial radiation, mainly gamma rays; (2) an electromagnetic pulse, which in a high-altitude explosion can knock out electrical equipment over a very large area; (3) a thermal pulse, which consists of bright light (you would be blinded by glancing at the fireball even if you were many miles away) and intense heat (equal to that at the center of the sun); (4) a blast wave that can flatten buildings; and (5) radioactive fallout, mainly in dirt and debris that is sucked up into the mushroom cloud and then falls to Earth.

The longer-term effects from a nuclear explosion are at least three: (1) delayed or worldwide radioactive fallout, which gradually over months and even years falls to the ground, often in rain; (2) a change in the climate (possibly a lowering of the Earth's temperature over the whole northern hemisphere, which could ruin agricultural crops and cause widespread famine); and (3) a partial destruction of the ozone layer, which protects the Earth from the sun's harmful ultraviolet rays. If the ozone layer is depleted, unprotected people could stay outdoors for only about ten minutes before getting an incapacitating sunburn, and people would suffer a type of snow blindness from the rays which, if repeated, would lead to permanent blindness. Many animals would suffer the same fate.

Civil defense measures might save some people in a limited nuclear war but would not help much if there were a full-scale nuclear war. Underground shelters in cities hit by nuclear weapons would be turned into ovens since they would tend to concentrate the heat released from the blast and the firestorms. Nor does evacuation of the cities look like a hopeful remedy in a full-scale nuclear war, since people would not be protected from fallout, or from retargeted missiles, and could not survive well in an economy that had collapsed.

Since most of our hospitals and many doctors are in central-city areas and would be hit by the first missiles in an all-out nuclear war, medical care would not be available for the millions of people suffering from burns, puncture wounds, shock, and radiation sickness. Many corpses would remain unburied and would create a serious health hazard, which would contribute to the danger of epidemics spreading among a population whose resistance to disease had been lowered by radiation exposure, malnutrition, and shock.

What could be the final result of all of this? Here is how Jonathan Schell answers that question in probably the longest sentence you have ever read, but in one with no wasted words:

> Bearing in mind that the possible consequences of the detonations of thousands of megatons of nuclear explosives include the blinding of insects, birds, and beasts all over the world; the extinction of many ocean species, among them some at the base of the food chain; the temporary or permanent alteration of the climate of the globe, with the

outside chance of "dramatic" and "major" alterations in the structure of the atmosphere; the pollution of the whole ecosphere with oxides of nitrogen; the incapacitation in ten minutes of unprotected people who go out into the sunlight; the blinding of people who go out into the sunlight; a significant decrease in photosynthesis in plants around the world; the scalding and killing of many crops; the increase in rates of cancer and mutation around the world, but especially in the targeted zones, and the attendant risk of global epidemics; the possible poisoning of all vertebrates by sharply increased levels of vitamin D in their skin as a result of increased ultraviolet light; and the outright slaughter on all targeted continents of most human beings and other living things by the initial nuclear radiation, the fireballs, the thermal pulses, the blast waves, the mass fires, and the fallout from the explosions; and considering that these consequences will all interact with one another in unguessable ways and, furthermore, are in all likelihood an incomplete list, which will be added to as our knowledge of the Earth increases, one must conclude that a full-scale nuclear holocaust could lead to the extinction of mankind.[27]

New dangers

Despite the end of the Cold War and of the threat of a cataclysmic war between two superpowers, nuclear weapons still remain a danger for the world. Three problems exist with which the world will have to deal: (1) the proliferation of nuclear powers; (2) the cleanup of the huge amount of toxic wastes produced in both the United States and the former Soviet Union when they built their large numbers of nuclear weapons; and (3) the threat of nuclear terrorism.

Nuclear proliferation   The spread of nuclear weapons to new countries represents a growing danger because the larger the number of countries that have these weapons the greater the likelihood that they will be used. Figure 8.1 indicates those countries with nuclear weapons and related capacity to generate weapon-grade nuclear material. Many of these new nuclear powers – either actual or potential – are authoritarian regimes that have serious conflicts with their neighbors in the less developed world. For example, the Middle East is a region plagued by conflict. It is widely believed that Israel has already acquired nuclear weapons and has them ready for use or could have them ready in a very short time. After the defeat of Iraq in the Gulf War in 1991, UN inspectors discovered that Iraq had been making major efforts to build both atomic weapons and the much more powerful hydrogen weapons. This was in spite of the fact that Iraq had signed the Nuclear Nonproliferation Treaty, in which it had agreed not to acquire nuclear weapons, and in spite of the fact that officials from the International Atomic Energy Agency had inspected nuclear facilities in Iraq just prior to the war and had found no evidence that Iraq was building nuclear weapons.

Despite the suspicion that Iraq had again started developing nuclear weapons after the Gulf War – and one of the reasons the United States gave for invading Iraq in 2003 – no evidence after the war was found that Iraq had started up such a program. It is

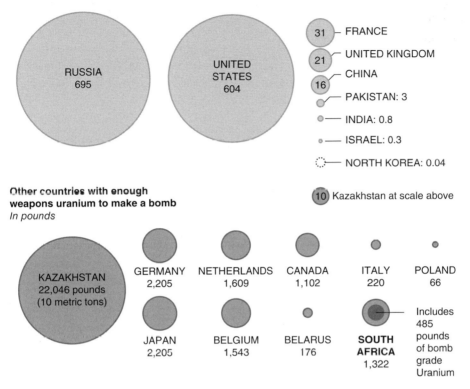

Countries with nuclear weapons
In metric tons

RUSSIA 695

UNITED STATES 604

31 — FRANCE

21 — UNITED KINGDOM

— CHINA

16 — PAKISTAN: 3

INDIA: 0.8

ISRAEL: 0.3

NORTH KOREA: 0.04

Other countries with enough weapons uranium to make a bomb
In pounds

10 Kazakhstan at scale above

KAZAKHSTAN 22,046 pounds (10 metric tons)

GERMANY 2,205

NETHERLANDS 1,609

CANADA 1,102

ITALY 220

POLAND 66

JAPAN 2,205

BELGIUM 1,543

BELARUS 176

SOUTH AFRICA 1,322

Includes 485 pounds of bomb grade Uranium

Figure 8.1 Countries with nuclear weapons capacity

Source: Douglas Birch and R. Jeffrey Smith, "U.S. Unease about Nuclear-Weapons Fuel Takes Aim at a South African Vault," *Washington Post*, March 14, 2015. Data from January 2013 report by the International Panel on Fissile Materials, James Martin Center for Nonproliferation Studies, former and current US officials, Center for Public Integrity.

now generally accepted Iraq had been forced to dismantle its nuclear program under the supervision of UN inspectors before the US invasion.

Another example of proliferation is in South Asia. In this region two countries – India and Pakistan – have already fought each other three times in the past 40 years and both tested nuclear weapons in 1998. A dispute over the territory of Kashmir, which was the central issue in two of their previous wars, flared up again in the late 1990s and the fear was raised that if the two countries fight again it could be with nuclear weapons.

North Korea has admitted it has an active nuclear weapons program and has tested nuclear weapons. It is believed that the state may have the capacity to launch a nuclear missile.[28]

Iran has claimed it has no nuclear weapons program but many in the West believe it does. The permanent five members of the UN Security Council – Britain, China,

France, Russia, and the United States – and Germany have spent many years negoti-
ating an international agreement to prevent Iran from developing a nuclear weapon.
The intent is to permit Iran to continue to enrich uranium for peaceful purposes
and under heavy international monitoring in exchange for reduction of economic
sanctions on the country.[29]

Regional conflicts in which these weapons could be used are not the only concern;
also disturbing is the possibility of accidental or unauthorized use of nuclear weapons
by these countries. In 2013 the list of actual and potential nuclear powers was as
follows:

- *Confirmed nuclear powers*: United States, Russia, United Kingdom, France,
  China, India, Pakistan, North Korea.
- *Suspected nuclear powers*: Israel.
- *Past suspected aspiring nuclear powers*: Algeria, Argentina, Brazil, Iraq, Libya,
  South Korea, Taiwan, South Africa.
- *Present suspected aspiring nuclear powers*: Iran.[30]

The cleanup   The production of vast quantities of nuclear weapons in both the
Soviet Union and the United States led to huge environmental contamination with
highly toxic chemical and nuclear wastes. In both countries wastes from the plants
producing components for the nuclear weapons were released into the air and
dumped onto the ground, and they have leaked from temporary storage facilities.
The extent of this contamination did not become public until the late 1980s in the
US case, when the US government released a number of reports outlining the huge
extent of the problem, and in the Soviet case in the late 1980s and the early 1990s, in
the last years of the Soviet communist state.

It is painful to read about the deliberate inflicting of harm by a government on its
own citizens. Although the Soviet contamination is probably greater than the American, both governments used "national security" to justify their actions and to keep
them secret. In the United States the plants were exempt from state and federal environmental laws, and actions were carried out that had long before been declared
illegal for private industry and individuals. An estimated 70,000 nuclear weapons
were made in the United States over a 45-year period, in 15 major plants covering an
area equal in size to the state of Connecticut. They cost about $300 billion (in 1991
dollars). Estimates in 2008 by various government agencies of the cost of cleaning
up the environmental damage at the plants, which will take decades to accomplish,
is about $250 billion.[31]

Even though cleanup is recognized as an important priority, it has not been easy to
decontaminate sites previously associated with nuclear weapons production. At the
beginning of the twenty-first century the National Academy of Sciences, the most
prestigious scientific group in the United States, declared that most of the sites related
to the production of nuclear weapons are so contaminated that they can never be
cleaned up. Of the 144 sites, the Academy has stated that only 35 can be cleaned
up enough so there is no potential harm to human beings, with 109 sites remaining

dangerous for tens and even hundreds of thousands of years. The Academy found that the government's plans for guarding permanently contaminated sites are inadequate and that the government does not have the money or technology to keep the contamination from "migrating" off the sites.[32] In 2013, an investigation published in the *Wall Street Journal* confirmed these cleanup efforts have proven challenging, particularly in residential areas, and that in some cases the government has not been able to adequately track the location of the contaminated sites.[33]

The threat of nuclear terrorism When Mohamed ElBaradei, the then head of the International Atomic Energy Agency (IAEA), accepted the Nobel Peace Prize in 2005 for his agency's work in preventing the spread of nuclear weapons, he warned that terrorists are actively trying to obtain nuclear weapons. The IAEA's Incident and Trafficking Database (ITDB) reported 2,477 incidents of unauthorized conduct involving nuclear material between 1993 and 2013, including 424 incidents of unauthorized possession and related criminal activities.[34] Of these, 146 incidents occurred in 2013 alone, including six incidents of unauthorized possession and related criminal activities.

Terrorism

Terrorism is a major problem today. The modern industrial state is relatively open to anyone who wants to harm the public. The challenge for the modern world is to decide how to defend itself against those who hold extremist beliefs, both religious and political, which call for the elimination of all those who do not believe as they do. There is a great need to strengthen defense against terrorists, which includes better intelligence and a greater ability to prevent attacks before they occur. At the same time, we believe, there is a need to resist the desire for revenge, which can easily create more hatred and more terrorists as innocent people are killed during the revenge action. To try to guard every vulnerable place and spy on every potential terrorist could lead to the creation of a police state, the use of uncivilized means the Western world has rejected, such as torture, and the loss of freedoms. A long-term effort is also needed to remove legitimate grievances of oppressed groups from which terrorists recruit their members.

One fear is that terrorists might make a so-called "dirty" nuclear bomb that would spread radioactive material over a large area, making that area uninhabitable for decades. Especially vulnerable to air attack are nuclear power plants, where in the United States nuclear waste that is still highly radioactive is stored above ground on the site. Globalization with its greatly increased trade and contacts among people has dramatically increased the possible targets and ways to deliver explosive devices.

Conclusions

This chapter has focused on the negative aspects of technology. It has done so because many of the readers of this book will probably be citizens of developed countries who already have a strong belief in the advantages of technology. It is not our intent to undermine that belief, because technology has benefited human beings in countless ways, and its use is largely responsible for the high living standards in the industrialized nations. Rather, our intent is to bring a healthy caution to the use of technology. An ignoring of the negative potential of technology has brought harm to people in the past and could cause unprecedented harm in the future. Much technology is neither good nor bad. It is the use that human beings make of this technology that determines whether it is mainly beneficial or harmful. Some technology has sufficiently harmful or excessively dangerous qualities that serious thought should be given as to whether it should be rejected. It is of course not always easy to place technologies in these categories, but an effort should be made.

Technology is absolutely necessary to help solve many of the planet's most awesome problems. But often intermediate technology should be used rather than the high technology favored by the industrialized nations. The temptation to imitate the West is strong, but ample evidence exists to show that this could be a serious mistake for developing nations. Economic, environmental, and social conditions and needs can vary tremendously depending on geography, and the best development plans will take from Western science only what is appropriate.

The industrial nations face another task. They must become more discriminating in their use of technology and lose some of their fascination with and childlike faith in it. The fate of the Earth could depend on technologically appropriate use of their hands. The wisdom or lack of wisdom these nations show in using military and industrial technology affects all – the present inhabitants of Earth, both human and nonhuman, and future generations, who depend on our good judgment for their chance to experience life on this planet.

Notes

1 A description of 50 case studies of development projects in the developing world that had harmful and unanticipated effects on the environment is contained in the following conference report: M. Taghi Farvar and John P. Milton (eds), *The Careless Technology: Ecology and International Development* (Garden City, NY: Natural History Press, 1972).

2 See also Rachel Carson, *Silent Spring* (New York: Houghton Mifflin, 1962; anniversary edn 2002).

3 World Health Organization, *Pesticides and Their Application*, 6th edn (2006), p. 2, at http://whglibdoc.who.int/hq/2006/WHO_CDS_NTD_WHOPES_GCDPP_2006.1_eng.pdf; see also the 2011 WHO Position Statement, "The Use of DDT In Malaria Vector Control," at http://apps.who.int/iris/bitstream/10665/69945/1/WHO_HTM_GMP_2011_eng.pdf (both accessed July 2015).

4   Dan Ferber, "Livestock Feed Ban Preserves Drugs' Power," *Science*, 295 (January 4, 2002), pp. 27–8.

5   Jane Brody, "Studies Suggest Meats Carry Resistant Bacteria," *New York Times*, October 18, 2001, p. A12.

6   Ralph Loglisci, "Animals Consume Lion's Share of Antibiotics," *Food Safety News*, December 27, 2010, at http://www.foodsafetynews.com/2010/12/animals-consume-lions-share-of-antibiotics (accessed July 2015).

7   Lindsay Layton, "FDA Seeks Less Use of Antibiotics in Animals to Keep Them Effective for Humans," *Washington Post*, June 10, 2010.

8   Denise Grady, "WHO Finds Use of Antibiotics in Animal Feed Can Be Reduced," *New York Times*, August 14, 2003, p. A5.

9   William D. McBride and Nigel Key, *U.S. Hog Production from 1992 to 2009: Technology, Restructuring, and Productivity Growth*, Report Summary, US Department of Agriculture, October 2013, p. 1, at http://www.ers.usda.gov/media/1207983/err158_summary.pdf (accessed July 2015).

10 US Environmental Protection Agency, "New Requirements for Controlling Manure, Wastewater from Large Animal Feeding Operations," press release, October 31, 2008.

11 E. F. Schumacher, *Small Is Beautiful: Economics as if People Mattered* (New York: Harper & Row, 1973).

12 Warren C. Baum and Stokes M. Tolbert, *Investing in Development: Lessons of World Bank Experience* (Oxford: Oxford University Press, 1985), p. 574.

13 See, for example, Suzanne Arms, *Immaculate Deception: A New Look at Women and Childbirth in America* (Westport, CT: Bergin & Garvey, 1984); Robert A. Bradley, *Husband-Coached Childbirth* (New York: Harper & Row, 1974); Robbie E. Davis-Floyd, *Birth as an American Rite of Passage* (Berkeley: University of California Press, 1992).

14 John S. Miller, "Foreword," in Lester D. Hazell, *Commonsense Child-Birth* (New York: Berkley Books, 1976), p. x.

15 Garrett Hardin, "The Tragedy of the Commons," *Science*, 162 (December 13, 1968), p. 1243.

16 Jon R. Luoma, "The $33 Billion Misunderstanding," *Audubon*, 83 (November 1981), pp. 111–27.

17 Kenneth A. Waltz, *Man, the State and War: A Theoretical Analysis* (New York: Columbia University Press, 1959).

18 Stockholm International Peace Research Institute, *2010 Yearbook*, see http://www.sipri.org/yearbook/2010 (accessed July 2015).

19 Ibid.

20 Robin Wright, "The New Way of War: Killing the Kids," *New Yorker*, July 3, 2014, at http://www.newyorker.com/news/news-desk/the-new-way-of-war-killing-the-kids; UNICEF, Impact of Armed Conflict on Children, "Patterns in Conflict: Civilians Are Now the Target," (1996), at http://www.unicef.org/graca/patterns.htm (both accessed July 2015).

21 United Nations, "Peacekeeping Fact Sheet," at http://www.un.org/en/peacekeeping/resources/statistics/factsheet.shtml (accessed July 2015).

22 Ruth Sivard, *World Military and Social Expenditures*, 16th edn (Washington, DC: World Priorities, 1996), p. 7.

23 Patrick J. Buchanan, "King Pyrrhus and the War on Iraq: Was Iraq Worth It?" *Washington Report on Middle East Affairs*, 32 (4) (May 2013), p. 40.

24   UN Assistance Mission in Afghanistan, *Afghanistan: Annual Report 2014: Protection of Civilians in Armed Conflict*, February 2015, p. 1, at http://unama. unmissions.org/Portals/UNAMA/human%20rights/2015/2014-Annual-Report-on-Protection-of-Civilians-Final.pdf (accessed July 2015).

25   Stockholm International Peace Research Institute, *2015 Yearbook: Armaments, Disarmament and International Security*, Summary, p. 7, at http://www.sipri.org/ yearbook/2015/downloadable-files/sipri-yearbook-2015-summary-pdf (accessed July 2015).

26   Jonathan Schell, *The Fate of the Earth* (New York: Avon Books, 1982).

27   Ibid.

28   Rob York, "Will North Korea Ever Use Its Nuclear Weapons?" *The Guardian*, October 31, 2014, at http://www.theguardian.com/world/2014/oct/31/sp-north-korea-nuclear-weapons (accessed July 2015).

29   M.S., "Everything You Want to Know about the Iranian Nuclear Deal," *The Economist*, April 5, 2015, at http://www.economist.com/blogs/economist-explains/2015/04/ economist-explains-3 (accessed July 2015).

30   CNN, "Nuclear Weapons: Who Has What?" at http://www.cnn.com/interactive/ 2013/03/world/nuclear-weapon-states/ (accessed July 2015).

31   National Governors Association, *Cleaning up America's Nuclear Weapons Complex* (2008), at http://www.nga.org/files/live/sites/NGA/files/pdf/0811NUCLEARCL EANUP.PDF (accessed July 2015).

32   "Nuclear Sites May Be Toxic in Perpetuity, Report Finds," *New York Times*, March 13, 2003, p. A1.

33   John R. Emshwiller and Jeremy Singer-Vine, "A Nuclear Cleanup Effort Leaves Questions Lingering at Scores of Old Sites," *Wall Street Journal*, October 30, 2013, at   http://www.wsj.com/articles/SB10001424127887323342404579079483154040874 (accessed July 2015).

34   International Atomic Energy Agency, "Incident and Trafficking Database (ITDB)," at http://www-ns.iaea.org/security/itdb.asp (accessed July 2015).

Further Reading

Allison, Graham, *Nuclear Terrorism: The Ultimate Preventable Catastrophe* (New York: Henry Holt, 2004). This Harvard scholar believes that without bold measures to prevent terrorists from getting a nuclear weapon, they will get one and will use it. He outlines the aggressive steps the world will need to take to prevent this disaster.

Ashford, Nicholas and Ralph Hall, *Technology, Globalization, and Sustainable Development: Transforming the Industrial State* (New Haven: Yale University Press, 2011). A high-level and technical exploration of the interplay between technology and industry as influencing development pathways and their associated implications for sustainability.

Chiles, James, *Inviting Disaster: Lessons from the Edge of Technology* (New York: Harper Business, 2001). Human beings are prone to error. Chiles takes us inside many famous technological disasters, showing us what led up to the events. With our increasing technological power comes the potential for greater disasters. We are unable to eliminate all risks – no system is perfect – so there are some technologies that we should not accept because they are very dangerous.

Cirincione, Joseph, *Bomb Scare: The History and Future of Nuclear Weapons* (New York: Columbia University Press), 2007. Cirincione describes how the world got to its present situation and suggests solutions to some of the most urgent problems with these weapons.

Glaser, Alexander, and Frank von Hippel, "Thwarting Nuclear Terrorism," *Scientific American*, 294 (February, 2006), pp. 56–63. For the authors, the best way to remove the danger of nuclear terrorism is to eliminate wherever possible the use of highly enriched uranium and remove accumulated stocks.

Hamburg, David, *No More Killing Fields: Preventing Deadly Conflict* (Lanham, MD: Rowman & Littlefield, 2002). As preventive medicine is better than treating an illness, so is preventing conflict better than fighting a war. By analyzing the rise of war makers such as Hitler and Milosevic, Hamburg believes the international community could have prevented their wars. He shows how an early warning and response system could be created today.

Klare, Michael, *Resource Wars: The New Landscape of Global Conflict* (New York: Henry Holt, 2001). Klare focuses on oil, water, timber, and minerals, such as diamonds. In this readable book the author shows that many wars that seem to be ethnic or sectarian are really over resources.

Lewis, H. W., *Technological Risk* (New York: W. W. Norton, 1990). Lewis examines the perceived risks associated with our technological society and argues that bad policy, misused resources, and lack of education rather than technology itself are the culprits. He argues that many things people fear the most actually pose no real risk to them, whereas some things that do pose a real risk to people are not perceived as being dangerous.

McKibben, Bill, *Enough: Staying Human in an Engineered Age* (New York: Henry Holt, 2003). McKibben is not against genetic engineering to repair defective genes but he warns against genetic engineering that tampers with fundamental behavioral traits. He also looks at the darker side of nanotechnology and robotics.

Tenner, Edward, *Why Things Bite Back: Technology and the Revenge of Unintended Consequences* (New York: Knopf, 1996). This book is based on a huge amount of research. Tenner says this of his book: "I am arguing not against change, but for a modest, tentative and skeptical acceptance of it." To deal with what Tenner calls "revenge effects," he calls for more use of our brains, not more "stuff." By examining a large number of cases, from low-tar cigarettes, black-lung disease, Chernobyl, and Windows 95, Tenner recommends we use technology cautiously.

Winner, Langdon, *The Whale and the Reactor: A Search for Limits in an Age of High Technology* (Chicago: University of Chicago Press, 1986). The sight of a whale surfacing near a nuclear reactor causes the author to contemplate the connections between nature and technology and to call for a more conscious effort by people to think about how technology can affect human life.

Chapter 9

Alternative Futures

Development Pathways: Evaluating Our Current Situation   269
Current Outlook: Business as Usual   270
Collapse and Sustainable Development   272
Choices   274
   Improve production   275
   Reduce demand   275
Governance: Deciding How to Act on the Choices We Make   276
   Governing the commons   276
   Inclusive governance and the role of civil society   278
Conclusion   282
Notes   284
Further Reading   287

> *In human affairs, the logical future, determined by past and present conditions, is less important than the willed future, which is largely brought about by deliberate choices – made by the human free will.*
>
> René Dubos, "A Celebration of Life" (1982)

Where is development leading us? What can we say about the future? If the dismal record of past predictions leads us to believe that the future is essentially unknowable, then we might ask, "Does it make any sense to think about the future at all?" Our answer is, "Yes, it does." While we cannot predict the future with certainty, we can prepare for what the future holds based on our best available information about the past and present. Even if the *precise* future is unknowable, we do know that

Global Issues: An Introduction, Fifth Edition. Kristen A. Hite and John L. Seitz.
© 2016 John Wiley & Sons, Ltd. Published 2016 by John Wiley & Sons, Ltd.

our present actions can make one outcome more likely than another. Human beings and societies have the power to make choices that have far-reaching impacts. Our options are not unlimited because of the times and places in which we live and our individual circumstances. But as rational human beings, we do have some freedom to make choices. It is this ability to influence the future that we consider in this final chapter.

If we can accurately describe our current situation and recognize some of the major trends in the past and present, we can make an educated guess about where we are heading. An old Chinese proverb states if you do not change the direction in which you are headed, you will end up where you are headed. So if we do not like the direction in which the world is heading, we can examine our individual behaviors and governmental policies to determine if they should be changed to improve our future outlook. This chapter considers our current outlook for development pathways under different scenarios and then explores the choices we can make to improve the opportunity for a better future.

Development Pathways: Evaluating Our Current Situation

Development models help evaluate how the choices that societies make impact their future economic and social well-being. In the twentieth century, development models focused primarily on achieving economic growth through increased production and less government regulation, reasoning that if nations could increase their GDP then their citizens would benefit from increased wealth, and more resources would be available to provide for education, healthcare, and other needs. Experts argued that technological innovations and supply-and-demand economics could solve problems of short-term supply shortages. The late Julian Simon, the author of several influential books, for example, insisted that natural resources were not finite in any real economic sense, arguing that scarcity of resources leads to increased prices, more efficient processing methods, and cheaper substitutes. The assumption at that time was that increasing production would lead to increased progress. Natural resource limits and pollution damage were generally not factored into the production considerations or were seen as "external" concerns (called "externalities" in economics).

Now, updated development models are working to better integrate natural resources and environmental costs. Even growth-focused experts have challenged the assumption that increased production alone will lead to broad development. For example, while the World Economic Forum recognizes that the price of natural resource commodities declined from 1950 to 2000 despite rapidly rising demand, they disagree with Julian Simon that such declines are likely to continue and instead say that resource scarcity will be a major factor in our future economic development.[1] This has led to more sophisticated development models that not only forecast what society will look like in the future if we continue to follow a development pathway focused on economic growth, but also consider alternative pathways.

Current Outlook: Business as Usual

The first step in considering the future is to understand where we are and where we are headed if we do nothing to change our actions. To this effect, we can identify certain key factors and trends that are likely to impact our future. The earlier chapters of this book identified many of these trends. We learned that the global population is increasing and that the population in high-income countries is aging while youth dominate the populations of many lower-income countries (Chapter 1). We saw in Chapter 2 that vast inequalities of wealth exist in the world and that production/gross domestic products (a conventional indicator of progress) continue to increase. We also saw that globally the consumption of food is increasing and agriculture now requires more water and land space (Chapter 3). Energy demands are significantly increasing in both high- and low-income countries, while energy supply comes primarily from fossil fuel resources (Chapter 4), which is contributing significantly to changes in the climate with long-term consequences across the globe. At the same time, modern societies are utilizing natural resources at ever increasing rates (Chapters 6 and 7). Combining these trends, we can create a picture of our current situation and make projections for where we are headed in the future if we continue our current trends – a scenario we call "business as usual."

What does the world look like under a business-as-usual scenario? In the first decade of the twenty-first century, the world population was increasing by more than 70 million people every year.[2] If this trend continues until 2050, we will have 9 billion people on the planet, the vast majority of whom will be living in developing countries.[3] (Remember we have about 7 billion people at present.) Recalling the discussion in this book's population chapter, we also know that people are generally living longer and moving away from rural areas and into cities.[4] By 2050, 25 percent of wealthy and about 14 percent of the population in lower income countries will be over 65 years of age, and 70 percent of the world's population is expected to live in cities.[5] This will require rural areas to produce more food for those living in cities.

Consider the implication of population trends on food, as discussed in Chapter 3. With more people on the planet, demand for food increases. According to the UN Food and Agriculture Organization, there will be a 50 percent increase in demand for food by 2030.[6] Correspondingly, according to the International Food Policy Research Institute, there will be a 30 percent increase in demand for water, and some estimates predict an increase of over 40 percent.[7]

Given business-as-usual projections of a need for at least 50 percent more food on the planet by 2030, predictions are that farmers may not be able to meet global demand due to supply-related challenges.[8] As the World Economic Forum has explained, key major grain-producing areas (including China, India, and the United States) already depend on unsustainable mining of groundwater, and climate change is affecting precipitation patterns in many areas (including North Africa and Australia) in a way that limits freshwater supplies.[9] For example, in China's primary grain-producing northeast region, drought losses from climate change are projected to increase over 50 percent by 2030.[10] The United Nations Environment Programme

(UNEP) forecasts "water stress will worsen, impacting population growth, agriculture and industrial production."[11] On land, "the increased use of chemical fertilizers is projected to increase yields in the agriculture sector in the short term at the expense of a longer-term decline of soil quality. This will require more land – converted from forest area to farmland – to feed the growing population."[12]

We can also consider the impacts of a growing population and more consumptive economies (see Chapter 2) on the energy and climate crisis. According to the International Energy Association, there will be at least a 40 percent increased demand for energy by 2030.[13] Continuing with a business-as-usual pathway focused on fossil fuels will result in exacerbated climate change and place more stress on already limited freshwater resources.[14] "Over 75% of the global increase in energy use from 2007–2030 is expected to be met through fossil fuels, especially coal, and an estimated 77% of the power stations required to meet demand are yet to be built," according to the World Economic Forum in 2011.[15]

As we saw in Chapter 5, the world's leading climate scientists have stated definitively that it is "*extremely likely*" that human influence has been the dominant cause of global warming since the middle of the twentieth century, driven by high rates of both population and economic growth.[16] The Intergovernmental Panel on Climate Change (IPCC) has warned that if we do not change our course, global greenhouse gas emissions will grow 25 to 90 percent between 2000 and 2030, and fossil fuels will constitute most of global energy supply even beyond 2030.[17] According to UNEP, increased fossil fuel use under business as usual "will further jeopardise energy security and tend to slow economic growth, through higher energy (especially oil) prices." Continuing to emit these gases at or above current rates "would cause further warming and induce many changes in the global climate system during the twenty-first century that would very likely be larger than those observed during the twentieth century."[18] According to UNEP, under a business-as-usual scenario, atmospheric carbon concentrations are projected to rise over 1,000 parts per million by 2100, more than double the threshold that scientists have determined is likely to lead to irreversible and catastrophic climate impacts.[19]

Not only will this business-as-usual trajectory for global population and consumption trends threaten global food supplies, the Earth's climate, and freshwater resources, but a number of analyses conclude that it will also reduce economic growth and increase poverty.[20] In 2010, the World Economic Forum analyzed how current consumption could influence future trends and concluded, "For such increased demand for water, food and energy to be realized, significant and perhaps radical changes in water use will be required as well as new sources for food and energy production exploited."[21] They also predict "extreme volatility" in commodity and energy prices as resource demands increase due to population growth and higher per-capita consumption.[22] Moreover, due to natural limits, "in the long-term, the world should expect at best, sustained increases in commodity prices, and at worst, shortages of key resources."[23] As resource prices rise and are transferred to consumers, the poorest will suffer the most, "increasing economic disparity and the interconnected risks that this implies."[24]

Looking at these different factors, it seems clear that business as usual sets us on a course of ever increasing future consumption, pollution, and population growth. If the Earth's resources were unlimited, this future trajectory could more easily sustain our society and its current values and trends. However, the Earth does have limits, and those limits require that we make important choices about our future.

Collapse and Sustainable Development

Can the world continue on its current development pathway that focuses on economic growth by the intensive use of natural resources? As we saw in Chapter 3, if current trends continue, absent a major technological breakthrough, we would need the resources of almost three Earths by 2050 in order to maintain existing levels of consumption.[25]

For many decades, popular books have warned of disaster due to industrial pollution, food scarcity, overpopulation, or depletion of nonrenewable resources. One of the best known is Rachel Carson's *Silent Spring*, which predicted premature death to humans and other animals because of the growing use of pesticides and other chemicals.[26] Another book, which received nearly as much publicity as Carson's book, was *The Population Bomb* by Paul Ehrlich, which looked at food supplies and other resource limits and starkly concluded: "The birth rate must be brought into balance with the death rate or mankind will breed itself into oblivion."[27]

Beyond these particular books, international predictions looking at natural resource limits in the context of population and society have grown increasingly grim. One of the first such predictions came in the 1970s from the Club of Rome, a group of experts that employed computer modeling from the Massachusetts Institute of Technology to determine limits to the Earth's arable land and nonrenewable resources, and its ability to absorb pollution. The study's main conclusion was as follows:

> If the present growth trends in world population, industrialization, pollution, food production, and resource depletion continue unchanged, the limits to growth on this planet will be reached sometime within the next 100 years. The most probable result will be a rather sudden and uncontrollable decline in both population and industrial capacity.[28]

These studies have become increasingly mainstream and have been undertaken by governments, academics, UN institutions, and even the private sector. In the late 1970s the US government predicted what the world would look like in year 2000 based on prevailing trends and concluded (consistent with the Club of Rome study):

> If present trends continue, the world in 2000 will be more crowded, more polluted, less stable ecologically, and more vulnerable to disruption than the world we live in now. Serious stresses involving populations, resources, and environment are clearly visible ahead. Despite greater material output, the world's people will be poorer in many

ways than they are today ... Barring revolutionary advances in technology, life for most people on Earth will be more precarious in 2000 than it is now – unless the nations of the world act decisively to alter current trends.[29]

Jared Diamond, an award-winning author, published in 2005 a popular book called *Collapse* that looked at what caused societies to fail in the past. He concluded that one of the main causes of their collapse was the inability of a society to live within its natural limits by holding destructive values and making choices to overconsume their resources.[30]

Studies and predictions of doomsday scenarios have persisted for decades, concluding that "business as usual" population trends combined with global consumption patterns cannot be sustained given the Earth's existing natural limits. Their predictions have generally been true that resources will be more stressed, though the time frames have sometimes overestimated the pace of destruction. While some of the near-term disasters forewarned by earlier predictions have not manifested as quickly as predicted, overall, experts agree that business-as-usual behavior will result in natural resource scarcity so severe that it cannot support the global population, leading to increased poverty, insufficient water for survival, and increased conflicts and political instability due to natural resource shortages.

Technological innovations can help remove an immediate limiting factor such as a resource shortage, but they generally do not solve the bigger problem. For example, the Green Revolution of the 1970s resulted in a large infusion of chemical fertilizers that significantly increased crop yields. But it also led to increased water pollution from all of the fertilizer runoff – so much that this has created new environmental problems. For example, there is now a large "dead zone" where fish cannot survive where the Mississippi River discharges all the fertilizer pollution into the sea off the coast of the United States. This is an example of technology removing one limiting factor (poor soil quality) while exacerbating another environmental problem (polluted water). It may buy more time to address the overall crisis of food production, but it has not changed the long-term predictions of resource scarcity.

The threat of collapse based on business-as-usual trajectories is what has driven experts to reexamine traditional development models and find ways to better incorporate ecological limits. New technologies to increase production have the power to either improve or worsen our long-term outlook, depending on how we choose to use them.[31] As the World Economic Forum explains, governments must consider integrated models for economic growth, low-carbon development, and water efficiency, as tradeoffs between uses of these resources by various resource users are key to decisions regarding their long-term management.[32]

Many growth-minded and environmental experts concur that given current population and consumption trends combined with natural resource limits, a future with a secure supply of natural resources for future generations must be one geared toward sustainable development, which enables current generations to "meet their needs without compromising the ability of future generations to meet their own needs."[33]

UNEP recently modeled what a future "business as usual" economy would look like and then compared that with the short-, medium- and long-term impacts of investing in sustainable development geared toward a green economy focused on resource efficiency, renewable energy, and job creation.[34] Based on UNEP's predictions, continuing with business as usual (even in the best case) could result in higher GDP and employment over the short term, but this increase would increasingly deplete natural resources, leading to the potential for collapse over the medium and long term. On the other hand, investing a small percentage of GDP in the green economy resulted in much more sustainable economic growth projections.[35] UNEP describes the future based on a green economy as a low-carbon development pathway that manages natural resources sustainably, such as by shifting away from fossil-fuel use, respecting the ecological limits in fishing, reducing deforestation, and using organic fertilizer.[36] This shift to a "green" economy serves to slow resource depletion and helps to restore the use of resources to sustainable levels, enabling "resilient economic growth in the medium and long term."[37]

Choices

Are we a society that is willing to continue on a business-as-usual trajectory and risk global collapse, or will we change course toward more sustainable development? If we understand our current trajectory and natural limits, we can develop a range of options that allow us to make choices toward a better future. As Joel Cohen explains:

> In human terms, almost nothing is inevitable about the twenty-first century. For example, urbanization offers exciting opportunities for educational and cultural enrichment. Urbanization also threatens frightening hazards from infectious diseases unless adequate sanitary engineering supplies clean water and removes wastes ... A healthy aging population offers unprecedented opportunity for longer use of acquired skills and experience, but threatens to bring unprecedented numbers of abandoned oldsters unless we anticipate the consequences of differently constructed families ... The future of many natural systems and their future effects on us depend in part on how well we come to understand our options, and what we decide to do.[38]

Based on predicted population growth, resource constraints, and our social structure, we have two principal options available to avoid collapse: (1) improve production within sustainable limits, or (2) reduce demand by slowing population growth and having less consumptive lifestyles. An alternative path may be possible if the issue is more related to the distribution of resources as opposed to scarcity challenges, and this focuses on more efficient management and equitable distribution of resources through improved governance of society, such as by undertaking legal, political, economic, and institutional reforms.[39] Deciding how to employ these strategies requires a better understanding of the tradeoffs between natural limits, social needs, and political realities.

Improve production

How can production improve within sustainable limits? Increases in resource efficiency can help mitigate hardships, as individual changes reduce demand and "government policies (such as removing hydrocarbon subsidies and stronger laws to conserve natural resources) provide incentives to change."[40] According to UNEP models, by 2050, changes in production practices could improve forest cover by 21 percent, fish stocks by 64 to 106 percent, and soil quality by 21 to 27 percent.[41] Additionally, through increased efficiency and new technologies, water use could improve 19–24 percent, fossil fuel consumption could be reduced 34–50 percent, and greenhouse gas emissions could be significantly lower than business as usual. Based on these projections, GDP could increase significantly in the medium to long term and employment could increase 3–5 percent by 2050.[42] The World Economic Forum echoes these overall projections, explaining: "In the long term, a model of truly sustainable consumption where private sector business models adopt resource limits as a driver of business innovation – as advocated by the Forum's Driving Sustainable Consumption Initiative – could shift [our] current set of risks to an opportunity for renewed growth and competitive advantage."[43]

As promising as it is to improve resource efficiency and sustainable production, this strategy alone may still not be enough to avert a trajectory headed toward collapse. "However, beware of false dichotomies," warns the World Economic Forum, as "trade offs exist primarily when policy-makers and resource-users act in a short-term, reactive and hurried fashion."[44] The Forum says that there are "soft" temporary limits based on production capacity but there are also "hard" or absolute limits of a natural resource's availability. They explain that the "hard" resource limits suggest that over the long term, technology and innovation may not be able to continually increase the supply of core resources at the rate required by population and economic growth, as certain resources like water do not have easy substitutes.[45] As such, we also need to consider two additional strategies: reducing demand and improving the management and governance of society and our natural resources.

Reduce demand

Reducing demand for resources can help us shift to a more sustainable future. The primary factors impacting resource demand are population and consumption. Stacy VanDeveer explains, "Frankly, the earth cannot sustain the material throughput of seven to nine billion people in the coming decades, if all consume as many resources as the wealthiest billion do now."[46] Similarly, Nobel laureate Murray Gell-Mann says that without a major demographic transition that can stabilize the human population, "talk of sustainability seems pointless."[47]

René Dubos, the late well-known bacteriologist, coined the phrase "Think globally, act locally." This is one way, according to Dubos, that an individual can see tangible results that contribute to a better future. Dubos no doubt realized that the great benefit of local action is that not only does it help solve problems, but the results of the action can provide satisfaction and motivation that we do have the power to change some key things that can impact our future. Wendell Berry, a US author and farmer who writes about sustainable living, gave the following tribute to "local action": "The real work of planet-saving will be small, humble, and humbling, and (insofar as it involves love), pleasing and rewarding. Its jobs will be too many to count, too many to report, too many to be publicly noticed or rewarded, too small to make anyone rich or famous."[48]

While we cannot predict the future, we can certainly influence the likelihood of future outcomes by our current choices. We know that given population and consumption trends, if we choose to do nothing, our business-as-usual trajectory will deplete some crucial natural resources in the coming decades. We can choose to invest in technology to improve the efficiency of production, but that alone may only slow our path toward collapse instead of avert it. We can encourage individual choices to reduce consumption and to voluntarily limit family size. That will contribute to a more sustainable rate of natural resource consumption. If we choose to make policy choices to invest in a green economy, protect the poor, and improve the way we govern our common resources, we can reduce the threat of wars over water and other natural resources and improve the likelihood of achieving a secure and sustainable future.

Governance: Deciding How to Act on the Choices We Make

One of the most challenging elements of global issues is that by definition they transcend political boundaries. Even if we understand our choices and want to pursue a responsible development pathway, our society has to be able to make collective decisions that allow us to manage our economy and resources sustainably. The process a society uses to achieve commonly desired goals and to settle conflicts among groups with different interests plays a central role in determining what the future will be like and how well we will work toward common interests. International, governmental, and community institutions, laws, policies, and norms all impact how society manages interactions between cultures and natural resources.

Governing the commons

Garrett Hardin, the late American ecologist, coined the phrase "the tragedy of the commons" to describe what can happen when management of limited resources requires effective decisions by shared users. The "tragedy" to which Hardin refers occurs when the short-term and long-term interests of people are in conflict, or when someone receives benefits at the expense of someone else's access to shared resources.[49] Hardin shows how, in the short term, it is rational and in the best interest of each herdsman in a village to increase the number of cattle he has grazing on the "commons," the open-access, commonly owned lands in the village. The apparent early benefit to an individual herdsman of increasing the number of cattle he has there seems to him greater than the long-term harm resulting from the overgrazing that the additional cattle create; the cost of the overgrazing will be shared by all the herdsmen using the commons, while the individual herdsman will reap the profit that comes from selling additional cattle. Also, if the individual herdsman does not increase his cattle but others increase theirs, he loses out since the overgrazing harms his cattle. Thus the tragedy occurs. Each herdsman, acting rationally and in his own best interest in the short term, increases his stock on the commons. Soon there is so much overgrazing that the grass dies and then the cattle die.

The global commons today are those parts of the planet that are used by many or all nations: the oceans, international river systems, the seabed, the atmosphere, and outer space. Technology can give some nations an advantage over others in exploiting these commons and it is clearly in their short-term interest to do so.

So it is with commercial fishing in the world's oceans. Technology has made possible bigger and more powerful fishing boats, equipped with sonar to locate schools of fish. It has also led to the creation of huge drift nets, some up to 20 kilometers (12 miles) long, which critics claim were used to "strip mine" the seas. These nets allowed a relatively small number of fishermen to catch large quantities of fish. (The United Nations in 1992 banned drift nets over 1.5 miles long but six years later nets much longer than this were still being used in the Mediterranean Sea and parts of the Atlantic Ocean.)[50] New technology also allows trawlers to drag dredges the size of football fields over the sea bottom, scraping it clean. Ninety percent of all large predator fish such as sharks, swordfish and tuna have been caught and there are fewer different kinds of fish in the oceans than before,[51] putting ecosystems at more risk when they are confronted with disruptions such as climate change. There is every indication that many fisheries worldwide are being overfished, or to put it another way, "overgrazed," and are threatened with collapse.[52] If this is not controlled, all nations using the oceans for fishing will be hurt. Not only will their fishing industries be harmed, but unique forms of life on Earth will probably become extinct. This could well be the fate of many species of the fishlike mammal, the whale, unless international efforts to reduce drastically the numbers of whales killed succeed in allowing whale populations to increase.

Fortunately, the tragedy of the commons is not always an inevitable result of shared resources. Elinor Ostrom received a Nobel Prize for her work highlighting the role of communities banding together to manage and regulate pooled resources. Dr Ostrom demonstrated how when communities have long-term control over their resources and have the authority to develop their own rules for how the resources are managed, the resources can be managed sustainably. Other studies have confirmed this model. For example, one study found that lands managed by indigenous peoples could be just as effective as national parks at conserving forest cover.

Global efforts to govern the ozone layer tell a remarkable success story of collective regulation of the commons leading to successful outcomes. Over a period of just a few decades, countries were able to turn around the Earth's protective ozone cover through global efforts to regulate ozone-depleting substances. By 2014, for the first time in recent history, there were indications that the ozone layer had begun recovering, and the hole over Antarctica was shrinking. Please see Chapter 6 for more discussion of ozone.

Finally, possibly one of the most important examples in human history of human beings immersed in a tragedy of the commons situation is occurring today. The world is confronted with a change in its climate caused by human activity, as discussed in Chapter 5, with possibly disastrous consequences for life on the planet. China and the United States, the two largest producers of the main gas causing this change of the climate, CO_2, have only recently pledged to take collective action to limit their emissions. China intends to achieve the peaking of CO_2 emissions around 2030 and the United States intends to reduce its emissions by about 25 percent by 2025. Both countries are reducing the intensity with which they release CO_2, and China has become a global leader in producing new energy technologies such as solar and wind that don't release CO_2, *but* both continue to rely mainly on technologies that use coal, oil, or natural gas to produce energy. Both countries see a short-term advantage for their economies by continuing to use fossil fuels as their main energy source.

By not taking steps to deal effectively with this problem in the face of widespread warnings by scientists of likely long-term dangers, countries continue to see they are involved in a tragedy of the commons situation. Meanwhile the United Nations writ large, other countries (and even some US states and cities) recognize the danger and are beginning to take actions to try to limit this tragedy's impacts.

Inclusive governance and the role of civil society

Inequality can be a big factor in determining the success of governance. As humans, we consume resources very unequally: the richest 25 percent of humans on the planet obtain most of our global consumption.[53] The world has been undergoing rapid globalization, yet is becoming increasingly fragmented. As countries become ever more interconnected, our security depends in large part on effective international institutions to help us manage resources that transcend political borders.[54] These institutions must renew their focus on ensuring that the economy is providing for the basic needs of everyone, especially the poor, something that traditional development efforts have not always succeeded in achieving despite their best intentions. To improve the likelihood of success, as institutions become more powerful, society must ensure that those in power do not abuse their position. This requires more efforts to fight corruption, improve accountability, and strengthen communities.[55]

In the words of a Harvard anthropologist, civil society is "the space between the state and the individual where those habits of the heart flourish that socialize the individual and humanize the state."[56] In simpler terms, it is the activity that people engage in as they interact with other people and it can be seen in neighborhoods, voluntary organizations, and in spontaneous grassroots movements.

Although this activity can be directed toward economic gain, often it is not. It is the activity that makes a community, a connection between people, a realization that each one is dependent upon others and that they share life together. Without a vibrant civil society isolation can result and since human beings are social animals, that isolation can lead to illness, antisocial behavior, and depression.

The civil society approach to development emphasizes social development, how people act toward other people.[57] But the approach can also have important political and economic aspects. The best way to demonstrate this is through examples. In 1973 a group of poor people in India rushed to the forests above their impoverished village and hugged the trees to prevent a timber company from cutting them down. This community action received worldwide publicity and helped to force some governments to reconsider their development policy regarding their nation's forests. The Chipko movement, which grew out of this action, is an example of self-help community action directed against threats and harm to the environment, harm that the local people realize will make their lives more difficult or even impossible.

Civil society can also be seen working in the efforts by some people in poorer countries to raise their low living standards. It is generated by the realization in many poor countries that neither their governments nor the market can be relied on to help their citizens obtain basic needs. Here are two examples. In Latin America after the bishops of the Catholic Church met in 1968 in Colombia and decided that the church should become active in helping the poor, many priests, nuns, and lay Christians helped form Christian Based Communities, self-help groups mainly made up of the poor themselves.

In Bangladesh, economist Muhammad Yunus concluded that the landless poor could never improve their conditions without some extra funds to help them start up an income-producing activity. Since no banks would lend them money, he set up the Grameen Bank.[58] The bank's loans, some starting as small as $35, have been repaid much more reliably than loans from regular banks: over 95 percent of loans have been repaid! By 2011 the bank had lent about $16 billion and served about 8 million borrowers in Bangladesh, 97 percent of whom were poor women.[59] This experience demonstrated that the poor can be good financial risks and has been imitated in 40 other countries, including the United States, where this idea is known as "microcredit" and "microfinance." Worldwide about 130 million people were receiving microcredit loans in 2014.[60]

Civil society can also be directed toward political goals. In Eastern Europe in the 1980s millions of citizens took to the streets to call for the end of their communist governments. This grassroots movement, which spread throughout Eastern Europe, and which was primarily peaceful, led to the end of the Soviet empire and to the collapse of communism in Europe. Western political scientists were amazed that such an occurrence could take place. Few, if any, had imagined that the end of a powerful totalitarian state could come from the nonviolent actions of average citizens. In 2011 peaceful demonstrators overthrew the Egyptian president Mubarak who had ruled the country for 30 years.

A spontaneous grassroots movement also occurred in Argentina in the early 1980s when a group of mothers met daily in one of the main squares in the nation's capital to protest the disappearance of their children (thousands of individuals who were abducted by the military government in its war against subversion and suspected subversion). The silent, nonviolent protest by the mothers helped undermine the internal and external support for the government.

In 2004 the Nobel Peace Prize was given to Wangari Maathai from Kenya who, despite being beaten and jailed by the government, had organized the Green Belt Movement. The movement of mainly very poor rural women planted 30 million trees to help restore the overexploited land of the country.

The internet and its social networking tools can be seen as technology making possible global civil society networks. With the vast amount of information now available to internet users, connections can be fostered among people around the world working for such common goals as monitoring the environment, holding corporations responsible for their actions, and for economic and political purposes. By the early twenty-first century some 650 million people were using the internet, which represented a growth of nearly 600 percent over the previous five years.[61]

Advocates of a robust civil society approach to development and to the relationship between government and the economy say it is easy to show examples of failures by the market and by the state to make people's lives better. It is even easy to show examples where they have made people's lives worse. People have responded to the failures of the market and the state by undertaking self-help activities. Such individuals want to participate in controlling their lives and do not want to let the market or the state be the main determinants of how they should live. They believe that strong reliance on the market or the state can leave the individual stunted.

The advocates of civil society also point to flourishing voluntary efforts in many countries as evidence of the importance of their approach. Although it is impossible to know exactly how many such groups exist today, here are some historical examples:

- In India tens of thousands of groups, many following the self-help tradition established by Mahatma Gandhi, have been involved in promoting social welfare, developing appropriate technology, and planting trees.
- In Indonesia, 600 independent groups worked on environmental protection.[62]
- The Sardovaya organization connects 15,000 Sri Lankan villages to provide humanitarian relief, education, and microcredit lending.[63]
- In Kenya, the Green Belt Movement, described above, seeks to empower women' to improve their communities through planting trees, rendering the land arable and providing resources to the people.[64]
- In Brazil, the Movimento dos Trabalhadores Rurais Sem Terra (Movement of Landless Workers) has provided land to about 370,000 impoverished families by organizing about 2,500 nonviolent occupations of unused farmland.[65]

- The World March of Women, a global nongovernmental organization, endeavors to promote women's equality through coordination of marches, debates, and education in 96 countries.[66]
- The women's self-help movement in the shantytowns surrounding the capital of Lima, Peru, operated 1,500 community kitchens.
- In the United States in the late 1980s an estimated 25 million people were involved in local actions to protect the environment.[67]

Finally, advocates of a robust civil society point to the spread of democracy around the world. In the 1980s many developing nations adopted a democratic form of government and, with the collapse of the Soviet empire, many former communist countries became democratic. An estimated 2.5 billion people lived in fully or partially democratic countries in 1981 whereas in 2001 this number had grown to 3.9 billion people.[68] In 2010 about 45 percent of the world's people lived in countries that were considered free and 20 percent of the people lived in partly free countries.[69] And it is in democracies that voluntary organizations flourish the most.

Some critics have raised concerns that it is impossible to have inclusive governance even with robust civil society participation without addressing structural problems associated with inequality. They point out that while small may be beautiful, it can also be insignificant as compared with multinational and multipolar political and economic forces. Even the admirable Grameen Bank of Bangladesh provided only about 1.9 percent of the credit in the country in 2014.[70] The conclusion of a UN organization sympathetic to the efforts of self-help groups is that while nongovernmental organizations have helped transform the lives of millions of people throughout the world, "What seems clear is that even people helped by successful projects still remain poor."[71]

Efforts at the grassroots level directed toward community-managed economic development often fail. The worker cooperative is often the instrument used, but a majority of these survive only a few years.[72] The members of the cooperatives, where workers come together to purchase and operate a business, are usually inexperienced in management. They are plagued by outside economic forces, and often ill-equipped to deal with complications such as high inflation and uncertain markets.

Critics also point out that oppressive political and economic powers can block the efforts of community groups. One well-publicized example was the assassination of Chico Mendes, the leader of a group of rubber tree harvesters in the Brazilian Amazon region. The large landowners in this region and in other Latin American countries have, with the support of local governments, traditionally used force against civil society activists.

Finally, critics of the civil society approach point to the spread of antidemocratic forces in the world at the same time as democracy is spreading. With the spreading of democracy, the end of the Cold War, and the collapse of communism in Europe, ethnic and regional hatreds surfaced in many countries, hatreds that had been suppressed by the former authoritarian and totalitarian governments. Yugoslavia entered into a cruel civil war and the world saw "ethnic cleansing" reemerge, an idea it had incorrectly believed had been discredited in Europe with the defeat of Nazi Germany. Bitter ethnic hostilities also arose in Africa in the mid-1990s, with thousands slaughtered in horrifying civil wars. Sometimes incited by a few people for political reasons, group hatred toward "others," toward those outside one's group, unfortunately has become fairly common in the post–Cold War world. True civil society, where people have respect and tolerance for those outside their immediate group, does not exist in a number of countries today.[73]

Our political decisions and individual actions have a significant impact on future outcomes. The choices we need to make in order to have a future of sustainable development include creating an economy that does not ignore environmental externalities. It needs to develop technologies to reduce negative environmental impacts and focus on obtaining a better understanding of the relationship between natural resources and society. We must stabilize the human population, reduce inequality, fight corruption, and strengthen international institutions to help us better govern ourselves, and cultivate a stronger sense of community and planetary consciousness.[74]

Finding a development pathway that values our common humanity and reduces conflicts – especially those exacerbated by inequality – can improve the ways in which our resources are used and allocated so that they can be managed sustainably. A shared understanding and respect for our common humanity can also improve our collective governance. The more different cultures perceive others as different from them, the more likely they will not be interested in supporting their survival or sharing resources. As Murray Gell-Mann explains: "Only by acknowledging the interdependence of all people and, indeed, of all life can we hope to broaden our individual outlooks so that they reach out in time and space to embrace vital long-term issues and worldwide problems in addition to immediate concerns close to home."[75]

Conclusion

Leading scholars in many fields increasingly recognize our dependency on natural resources and their respective limits. There seems to be a growing recognition that the size and characteristics of the human population, per capita resource consumption, and how society chooses to govern itself are three of the principal factors that will likely determine our future.

Economic growth – particularly in lower-income countries – can help raise living standards over the long term, but only when it does not exacerbate inequality or lead to diminished supplies of future resources. But does more economic growth make sense in countries with a GDP that is already high? It is unpopular today to suggest that it does not, but this may indeed be the case. The desire to acquire more and more material possessions in wealthy nations has placed a tremendous strain on the planet. This book has been concerned with documenting that strain.

The dangers of collapse are real. Some of them have already taken place in parts of the Earth. Some countries have a population larger than their natural resource base, widespread hunger exists in other countries, and toxic poisoning is increasingly seen in countries with concentrated industrial production. If actions are not taken to reduce greenhouse gases, use water sustainably, stabilize population, and stop widespread environmental deterioration, it is possible that huge loss of life could occur in the future.

The sustainable development future appears to be the one that both rich and poor nations alike should strive for, since unsustainable consumption of resources will broadly lead to increased poverty and political instability. In the language of economics, unsustainable consumption uses up the Earth's natural capital – clean air, water, fertile soil, healthy climate, and so on – for a short-term profit. And a basic principle of economics is that if you expend your capital unwisely (the financial and physical resources needed to produce goods and services), you will eventually go bankrupt. This kind of development compromises the ability of future generations to meet their own needs. One of the basic rules the Native Americans of the Iroquois confederacy followed in North America was the rule of the seventh generation: "consider how your decisions will affect the lives of the seventh generation to come."

Sustainable development is a powerful concept because it is hard to argue against it. A sustainable world would not mean the absence of growth, but the growth that would be emphasized would go beyond an unrelenting desire for more material objects.

The human race seems to be at a critical juncture. Will we realize the destructive things we are doing to life on Earth and pursue a new course before it is too late? Are we as a species meeting our basic physical needs while developing intellectually, morally, and spiritually? Can we live without compromising the ability of future generations to meet their own needs? The uncertainty of these answers is what makes the present day an important and challenging time in which to live.

The stakes are high. We are making both political and individual choices that change our world at an unprecedented rate. For the first time in human history, human beings have the technology to enable them to monitor the planet, to see how our actions are changing the forests, the air, and the water. And we are learning to think of Earth as a single system, a system in which we are just one of the parts. As a species with high intellect and ability to make powerful choices, we have a special responsibility to all of life on the planet. Whether we are learning this fast enough to prevent irreversible destruction and collapse remains uncertain.

There is a growing awareness that human beings need to respect natural limits and move beyond our compulsion to dominate and unsustainably exploit the Earth's resources. We can learn this through reason and experience (such as drinking water that contains cancer-producing chemicals) as well as through expert studies comparing future population and consumption demands with available resources. But either way, we can and do learn – and indeed, our own long-term survival may depend on it. We should remember the wisdom of Joel Cohen:

Until we understand better the interaction between humans and our planetary home, we will not be able to choose how the natural world will treat us. Surprises from the natural world will continue. We are making choices about our future every day. How much we invest in better understanding of those choices and their consequences is also a choice.[76]

Issues or problems have two sides. One side is the task that must be solved. Dealing with this side can be painful since some of these tasks present us with difficult choices. But the other side can light us up, for the issues also present us with opportunities. They give us an opportunity to grow – intellectually, morally, and spiritually. They give us a chance to become more loving, both to our fellow human beings and to the planet itself. And as we grow, so can our society. And as our society grows, we can sharpen our development pathway toward meaningful progress that is truly sustainable for both people and the planet. Not a bad deal.

Notes

1   World Economic Forum, *Global Risks 2011* (Geneva: World Economic Forum, 2011), pp. 29, 31, 38.
2   UN Department of Economic and Social Affairs, *World Economic and Social Survey 2010*, at http://www.un.org/en/development/desa/policy/wess/wess_current/2011wess.pdf (accessed July 2015).
3   Ibid.
4   Ibid.
5   Ibid.
6   World Economic Forum, *Global Risks 2011*.
7   Ibid.
8   Ibid.
9   Ibid.
10 Ibid.
11 United Nations Environment Programme (UNEP), *Modelling Global Green Investment Scenarios: Supporting the Transition to a Green Economy*, 2011, at http://www.unep.org/greeneconomy/Portals/88/documents/ger/GER_13_Modelling.pdf (accessed July 2015). UNEP used a model developed by the Millennium Institute that focuses on future scenarios in the context of sustainable development.
12 Ibid.
13 World Economic Forum, *Global Risks 2011*.
14 Ibid.
15 Ibid.
16 Intergovernmental Panel on Climate Change (IPCC), Fifth Assessment Report, *Climate Change 2014: Synthesis Report* (New York: IPCC, 2014), Summary for Policymakers, p. 9.
17 IPCC, Fourth Assessment Report, *Climate Change 2007: Synthesis Report* (internal citations omitted), at http://www.ipcc.ch/publications_and_data/ar4/syr/en/spms3.html (accessed July 2015).
18 Ibid.
19 UNEP, *Modelling Global Green Investment Scenarios*; IPCC Fifth Assessment Report, *Climate Change 2014: Synthesis Report* (New York: IPCC, 2014).

20 World Economic Forum, *Global Risks 2011*.

21 Ibid.

22 Ibid.

23 Ibid.

24 Ibid.

25 Global Footprint Network, "World Footprint," at http://www.footprintnetwork. org/en/index.php/GFN/page/world_footprint/ (accessed July 2015). See also UNEP, *Modelling Global Green Investment Scenarios*.

26 Rachel Carson, *Silent Spring* (New York: Houghton Mifflin, 1962; anniversary edn 2002).

27 Paul R. Ehrlich, *The Population Bomb*, rev. edn (New York: Avon Books, 1982).

28 Donella Meadows et al., *The Limits to Growth*, 2nd edn (New York: Universe Books, 1974), p. 24.

29 Council on Environmental Quality and the Department of State, *The Global 2000 Report to the President: Entering the Twenty-First Century*, Vol. 1 (New York: Penguin Books, 1982), p. 1.

30 Jared Diamond, *Collapse: How Societies Choose to Fail or Succeed* (New York: Viking, 2005).

31 Joel E. Cohen, "Choosing Future Population" (2009), in TeacherServe, National Humanities Center, *Nature Transformed: The Environment in American History*, at http://nationalhumanitiescenter.org/tserve/nattrans/ntuseland/essays/population.htm (accessed July 2015).

32 World Economic Forum, *Global Risks 2011*.

33 World Commission on Environment and Development, *Our Common Future* (New York: Oxford University Press, 1987).

34 UNEP, *Modelling Global Green Investment Scenarios*.

35 Ibid.

36 Ibid.

37 Ibid.

38 Cohen, "Choosing Future Population."

39 Joel E. Cohen, "How Many People Can the Planet Hold?" *Aspenia* (Aspen Institute Italia, English edn), 43/44 (June 2009), pp. 40–6.

40 World Economic Forum, *Global Risks 2011*.

41 UNEP, *Modelling Global Green Investment Scenarios*.

42 Ibid.

43 World Economic Forum, *Global Risks 2011*.

44 Ibid.

45 Ibid.

46 Stacy VanDeveer, "Consuming Environments: Options and Choices for 21st Century Citizens," in *Beyond Rio+20: Governance for a Green Economy* (Boston: Boston University, 2010), pp. 43–52.

47 Murray Gell-Mann, "Transformations of the Twenty-First Century: Transitions to Greater Sustainability," at http://www.nobel-cause.de/potsdam-2007/book/NobelCause Book_chapter1.pdf (accessed July 2015) (utilizing a scheme modified from a scenario developed by James Gustave Speth, 2008).

48 Wendell Berry, "Out of Your Car, Off Your Horse," *Atlantic Monthly*, 267 (February 1991), p. 63.

49 Garrett Hardin, "The Tragedy of the Commons," *Science*, 162 (December 13, 1968), pp. 1243–8.

50 Marlise Simons, "Boats Plunder Mediterranean with Outlawed Nets," *New York Times*, June 4, 1998, p. A3.

51 Elizabeth Kolbert, "The Scales Fall: Is There Any Hope for Our Overfished Oceans?" *New Yorker*, August 2, 2010.

52 Daniel Pauly and Reg Watson, "Counting the Last Fish," *Scientific American*, 289 (July 2003), pp. 42–7; and Cornelia Dean, "Scientists Warn Fewer Kinds of Fish Are Swimming the Oceans," *New York Times*, July 29, 2005, p. A6.

53 Stacy VanDeveer, "Consuming Environments."

54 Gell-Mann, "Transformations of the Twenty-First Century."

55 Ibid.

56 David Maybury-Lewis, *Millennium: Tribal Wisdom and the Modern World* (New York: Viking, 1992), p. 265.

57 Alan Wolfe, "Three Paths to Development: Market, State, and Civil Society," prepared for the International Meeting of Nongovernmental Organizations and United Nations System Agencies, Rio de Janeiro, 1991.

58 Muhammad Yunus, "The Grameen Bank," *Scientific American*, 281 (November 1999), pp. 114–19. Yunus believes that loans to the poor are best made by private organizations, not by governments. When the new president of Mexico Vicente Fox announced in 2000 that his government was going to begin a small-loan program, Yunus talked him out of the idea, saying "Politicians are interested in the votes of the poor … not in getting the money back." Tim Weiner, "With Little Loans, Mexican Women Overcome", *New York Times*, March 19, 2003, p. A8. See also Celia Dugger, "Debate Stirs over Tiny Loans for World's Poorest," *New York Times*, April 29, 2004, p. A1; Saritha Rai, "Tiny Loans Have Big Impact on Poor," *New York Times*, April 12, 2004, p. C3; and David Armstrong, "Is Bigger Better?" *Forbes Magazine*, June 2, 2008, pp. 66–70.

59 Grameen Bank, "About Us," at http://www.grameen-info.org/about-us/; Grameen Bank, "Monthly Reports 01-2015," at http://www.grameen-info.org/monthly-reports-01-2015/ (both accessed July 2015).

60 International Finance Corporation, "Financial Institutions: Microfinance," Available at http://www.ifc.org/wps/wcm/connect/Industry_EXT_Content/IFC_External_Corporate_Site/Industries/Financial+Markets/MSME+Finance/Microfinance/ (accessed July 2015).

61 United Nations Development Programme (UNDP), UNEP, World Bank, and World Resources Institute, *A Guide to World Resources 2002–2004: Decisions for the Earth* (Washington, DC: World Resources Institute, 2002), p. 21.

62 Worldwatch Institute, "Indonesian Activist Targets Community Waste," at http://www.worldwatch.org/node/6079 (accessed July 2015).

63 Sarvodaya, "About," at http://www.sarvodaya.org/about (accessed July 2015).

64 Green Belt Movement, "Who We Are," at http://www.greenbeltmovement.org/who-we-are (accessed July 2015).

65 Majken Jul Sorensen and Stellan Vinthagen, "Nonviolent Resistance and Culture," *Peace and Change*, 37 (3) (2012), pp. 444, 459; Friends of the MST, "What Is the MST?" at http://www.mstbrazil.org/whatismst (accessed July 2015).

66 World March of Women, "Who We Are," at http://www.marchemondiale.org/qui_nous_sommes/en/ (accessed July 2015).

67 Alan Durning, "Mobilizing at the Grassroots" in *State of the World, 1989* (New York: W. W. Norton, 1989), pp. 157–8. The growth of civil society continued in the 1990s. See David Bornstein, "A Force Now in the World, Citizens Flex Social Muscle," *New York Times*, July 10, 1999, pp. A15, A17.

68 UNDP et al., *A Guide to World Resources 2002–2004*, p. 21.

69 Freedom House, *Freedom in the World 2010* (Washington, DC: Freedom House, 2010).

70 Grameen Bank, Monthly Reports, at http://www.grameen-info.org/monthly-reports/; World Bank, World Development Indicators (2013 revision), "Bangladesh," at http://data.worldbank.org/country/bangladesh; World Bank, World Development Indicators (2013 revision), "Domestic Credit Provided by Financial Sector (% of GDP)," at http://data.worldbank.org/indicator/FS.AST.DOMS.GD.ZS (all accessed July 2015).

71 UNDP, *Human Development Report 1993* (New York: Oxford University Press, 1993), p. 94. See also Barbara Crossette, "UN Report Raises Questions about Small Loans to the Poor," New York Times, September 3, 1998, p. A8; and Dugger, "Debate Stirs over Tiny Loans for World's Poorest."

72 Durning, "Mobilizing at the Grassroots," p. 163.

73 An interesting analysis of the causes of the many ethnic conflicts taking place in the world in the mid-1990s is contained in Daniel Coleman, "Amid Ethnic Wars, Psychiatrists Seek Roots of Conflict," *New York Times*, August 2, 1994, pp. C1, C13.

74 Gell-Mann, "Transformations of the Twenty-First Century."

75 Ibid.

76 Cohen, "Choosing Future Population."

Further Reading

Bossel, Hartmut, *Earth at a Crossroads: Paths to a Sustainable Future* (Cambridge: Cambridge University Press, 1998). Bossel argues that humanity faces a choice between continuing on its present unsustainable path or shifting to a sustainable path that will call for significant changes. He offers his views of what ethical and organizational changes must be made to achieve a sustainable path and gives recommendations of what individuals and organizations can do to aid this transformation.

Boyd, David R., *The Optimistic Environmentalist: Progressing Towards a Greener Future* (Toronto, Canada: ECW Press, 2015). Boyd presents the progress we have made, and are making, to solve many of the environmental problems presented in our book.

Buzan, Barry, and Gerald Segal, *Anticipating the Future: Twenty Millennia of Human Progress* (London: Simon & Schuster, 1998). Even though there have been many setbacks, the authors are optimistic about human progress over the past 20,000 years. The human species has spread over the globe, abolished slavery, and reduced its appetite for large-scale wars. That progress should continue, although there will be ups and downs. They see the world gradually solving its environmental problems and eventually moving into space.

Daly, Herman, *Beyond Growth: The Economics of Sustainable Development* (Boston: Beacon Press, 1996). An unconventional economist, Daly questions the value of economic growth. He believes that traditional economists have a false faith in growth because they do not accurately calculate the cost of depleting resources. While still far from being accepted by the academic mainstream, Daly's ideas have inspired a new academic subdivision called "ecological economics."

Dodds, Felix, Jorge Laguna-Celis, and Liz Thompson, *From Rio+20 to a New Development Agenda: Building a Bridge to a Sustainable Future* (New York: Routledge, 2014). Following up on the 2012 Rio Earth Summit, this book provides policy and practical insight into efforts within and beyond the United Nations to chart a more sustainable pathway for development.

Hertsgaard, Mark, *Hot: Living Through the Next Fifty Years on Earth* (New York: Houghton Mifflin Harcourt, 2011). The author concludes after talking with many scientists that "many, many things have to happen by 2020 if this planet is to remain a livable place." Not only must we stop and reverse our carbon emissions – something we know how to do and have much of the technology to do – but we must prepare for the changes in our world, such as more droughts, which are coming and which can kill millions. American opinion remains the greatest obstacle to doing what needs to be done.

McKibben, Bill, *Eaarth: Making a Life on a Tough New Planet* (New York: Henry Holt, 2010). McKibben believes we have already changed our world because of our carbon-based energy system. But as a "grudging optimist," as one review of this book calls him, McKibben believes we can still voluntarily make necessary changes in our lives before we are forced to make them by the new world, which he calls "Eaarth," we have created.

Musser, George, "The Climax of Humanity," *Scientific American*, 293 (September 2005), pp. 44–7. How we manage the next few decades could lead to sustainability or collapse. This article is part of a special issue of the journal titled "Crossroads for Planet Earth." It contains a series of articles (on population, poverty, biodiversity, energy, food and water, disease, economics, and policy) focused on how we can successfully pass beyond 2050.

Rees, Martin, *Our Final Hour: A Scientist's Warning: How Terror, Error, and Environmental Disaster Threaten Humankind's Future in This Century – on Earth and Beyond* (New York: Basic Books, 2003). Rees is Britain's Astronomer Royal and a professor at Cambridge University. He gives our civilization a 50/50 chance of surviving the twenty-first century. Rees believes the choices we make in the next several decades could decide our fate.

Shi, David, *The Simple Life: Plain Living and High Thinking in American Culture*, new edn (Athens, GA: University of Georgia Press, 2007). Voluntary simplicity is a component of sustainable development. Shi explores the roots of the idea in the lives and writings of Socrates, Plato, Aristotle, Jesus, St Francis, Buddha, Leo Tolstoy, Marcus Aurelius, Gandhi, Confucius, and Thoreau, among others. Its advocates hold that the simple life frees a person for real intellectual, moral, and spiritual growth.

Wilson, Edward O., *The Future of Life* (New York: Knopf, 2002). We still have time and choices we can make to save life on our planet. Here is how Wilson states it: "The race is now on between the technoscientific forces that are destroying the living environment and those that can be harnessed to save it. We are inside a bottleneck of overpopulation and wasteful consumption. If the race is won, humanity can emerge in far better condition than when it entered, and with most of the diversity of life still intact."

Appendix 1

Studying and Teaching Global Issues

For the Student

You may find it useful to learn how the concept "development" can be used to study global issues and to have an overview of the topics covered in this textbook. One way to do this is to examine the structure of a course for which *Global Issues: An Introduction* has been the principal textbook.

Introduction

The first two or three days of the course are spent explaining what "development" means and how development and global issues are related. The book defines development as economic growth plus the social and environmental changes caused by or accompanying that economic growth. In this short introduction we begin to understand some of the main differences in the social and economic conditions of the rich and poor countries.

Population

For two classes we look at the relationship between population and development. The changing population of the world is described, and the causes of the population explosion in the less developed nations are given. Students learn how population growth affects development (rapid population growth hinders development by putting a large stress on resources, health and education facilities, the environment, etc.), and how development affects population growth (development at first makes it greater as it lowers death rates, but later it reduces birth rates as the education

Global Issues: An Introduction, Fifth Edition. Kristen A. Hite and John L. Seitz.
© 2016 John Wiley & Sons, Ltd. Published 2016 by John Wiley & Sons, Ltd.

level of women increases and children become less desirable economically and socially). The demographic transition is explained and students become familiar with the factors that lower birth rates. Some attention during this period is paid to the population policies of major countries, such as China. This segment of the course ends with a consideration of the future – whether a stabilization of the world's population will occur, geographic considerations related to demographic transitions, and whether the carrying capacity of the Earth will be exceeded.

Wealth and poverty

The third week of the course is spent on getting students to consider the extremely difficult question: "Why are some nations rich and some poor?" Students examine conventional approaches or views of economic development: the market approach (also called the neoclassical or capitalist approach) and the state approach (also called the command economy or socialist approach). Globalization, which has greatly expanded international trade, is explained and the uneven effects it is having on poor and rich nations are discussed. Another important consideration raised by this focus is inequality, not just between nations but also within countries, bringing the social dimension of development more acutely into focus.

Food

For two weeks food holds our attention. World food production trends are examined, and a tentative answer is given to the question of how many are hungry in the world today. We investigate the causes of hunger in parts of the South (poverty – the lack of development – is one cause). Students learn how the availability and quality of food affect development (malnourished people are not good producers), and how development affects both the production of food and the type of food consumed (industrialized agriculture produces a large amount of food, but wealthy people often do not have a healthy diet). A short history of the Green Revolution is given. The food policies of the United States and a few other countries are examined. Finally, we think about how changes in the climate, biotechnology, the amount of arable land, and the cost of energy could affect future food supplies.

Energy

One week is not enough time to investigate thoroughly the relationship between energy and development, but it is enough time to introduce students to this vital subject. A description of the energy crisis caused by the developed world's dependency on a polluting and highly insecure energy source – oil – is followed by a summary of the responses to that crisis by the United States, Western Europe, and Japan. The effect of the energy crisis on the South's development plans is explained. As we explore the relationship between energy use and development, students learn about the shift in the types of energy sources that took place as the Industrial Revolution progressed and how there has been a partial decoupling of energy consumption and economic growth – a new ability to produce economic growth with less energy.

Climate change

The subject of climate change (global warming) serves as a good bridge between the environment chapters and the previous discussion of nonrenewable and renewable energy sources. This is an opportunity to explore the limits of the traditional development pathway of economic production and consumption based on the cheap combustion of fossil fuels, which allows for consideration of the ways in which climate change is redefining development. Focusing on the science and impacts of climate change, this chapter explains the global challenges associated with an excess of greenhouse gas emissions in the atmosphere.

The environment

As is the case with energy and climate, one week for each of the two environment chapters is not much time to explore the effects development has on the environment – and the reverse, the effects the environment has on development – but significant information on the subject can be passed to students. (Poor people are hard on the environment as they struggle to survive, but the rich may or may not treat the environment well, often outsourcing their environmental impacts to poorer countries which may not have the same protective level of environmental regulations.) We divide the environment discussion into two parts: Part I considers the impact of economic production based on the extraction of natural resources, and Part II consider the impacts of industrialization associated with pollution and waste.

Part I includes a brief history of the awakening in the United States to threats to the environment caused by industrialization and provides the setting for an examination of the threats to the air, water, and land that have come with development. Airborne lead, the depletion of the ozone layer, and acid rain illustrate some of the main concerns we have at present with air pollution. The current concern with threats to our groundwater by migrating chemicals presents an example of water pollution caused by development. The problem of deforestation in the developing countries is briefly examined so that students become aware of the harm deforestation can bring to the land, its connection to the extinction of species, as well as the changes it can make in the climate. The connection between development and the extinction of cultures is also examined, seeing, for example, how in the name of development the forest homes of numerous indigenous peoples are being destroyed.

Part II considers cancer, chemicals, and pesticides under a section in which we focus on the workplace and the home. Part II also considers the problem of how to handle huge amounts of solid and toxic wastes and demonstrates well to the students the extremely difficult tasks the political system faces as it tries to preserve the land. Recycling and substitution are discussed, as well as environmental politics. The concept of "overdevelopment" (consuming and polluting at a rate that cannot be maintained indefinitely) is also presented, as students consider reducing needs as a possible response to scarcities.

Technology

To many people, technology and development are synonymous. Technology is what makes economic growth and social change happen. Students are reminded of the many benefits that technology has brought to our lives. But because they are more aware of the benefits than the harm technology can produce, the course focuses on the dangers. Students learn that the decision of whether or not to use a certain technology can be a difficult one, especially when considering different levels of economic wealth and capacity. Illustrations of the unanticipated consequences of the use of technology are given, as are examples of the inappropriate uses of technology. Limits to the "technological fix" are illustrated. The issue of war is introduced, with technology making the destructive capacity of weapons greater. The threat of nuclear weapons is presented as a case study under the technology section.

Alternative futures

This book ends by focusing on different possible futures and governance considerations related to the ability to make effective decisions on matters pertaining to global issues. A nice end to the class is to consider the main arguments that advocates make for the possibilities that our present type of development is leading us to "doom," or to continued "growth," or to "sustainable development" in the future and identify the political challenges and options for making effective long-term decisions.

For the Teacher

The problem

Improving and increasing international studies has become a priority on many campuses[1] but as a report for the American Council on Education concludes, "the internationalizing of undergraduate education still has a long way to go."[2] How far it has to go can be easily shown. Reports of the shocking ignorance of people in the United States about other countries are well known, but less well known, and of some embarrassment to the college teaching profession, is that college-age people in the country are the most ignorant of all adults. Adding to the insult is the fact that attending college for four years reduces that ignorance only slightly.[3] Young people aged 18–24 in the United States in the late 1980s possessed *less* information about the world than the same age group had 40 years earlier.[4]

This information is especially surprising given the new emphasis many colleges are placing on international studies. Also surprising is the fact that the average student in a four-year college or university course takes several international studies courses, outside of foreign language instruction, before he or she graduates.[5] But a close look at these international studies courses reveals that most of them still focus on only one country or one region (often Western Europe), and only a few focus on a problem or issue that is found throughout the world. Also, few are interdisciplinary, and *only a minority deal with the world as it is today*.[6]

We indeed seem to be far from achieving what one report called an important characteristic of the truly internationalized university: it is a school where "no student graduates who has never been asked to think about the rights and responsibilities of this country in the world community, or who has never been brought to empathize with people of a different culture."[7]

Preparing students so that they will be able to function in an increasingly complex and interdependent world is a huge task, one that will require a better trained and more committed faculty and college administration. No easy answers, solutions, or quick fixes are possible, but many different methods and approaches are being tried, with varied degrees of success. As the American Council on Education study found, what we do not have now in the United States is a way to know what works, and what does not, and why it does or does not.[8] What we need are reports of successes and failures in the attempts to achieve the important characteristic of the truly internationalized university that the above quotation appropriately identifies.

A solution: perspectives from decades of teaching this course

John L. Seitz

While attending a conference on the developing world, I heard college teachers complain that they could not get their students interested in studying the global South, where most of the world's people live. As I thought about this complaint, I realized that I had discovered an answer to the question: "How do you get American students to want to study the non-Western world?" I know that you don't do it by reminding them that their bananas come from that world. The student's reaction to that statement is: "So what? Who cares?" The way you get them interested is by introducing real global problems and exploring their possible solutions. You demonstrate that global problems are American problems, that our actions help create or solve the problems, and that the problems affect our lives, in the present as well as in the future.

The course for undergraduates I taught is called "Global Issues." Outlined in the section addressed to the student, it focuses on many of the most important global issues today, issues that both the more developed and the less developed nations can no longer ignore.

I believe that one reason many social science teachers do not teach a course on global issues is that they do not know how to deal with these issues in a respectable, scholarly way – in a manner that will prevent the class from becoming just a forum for the discussion of current events. But I have found that there is a concept – "development" – which can serve as the tool we need for treating these issues in a responsible manner. Social scientists commonly use this concept only with reference to the poorer nations, but "development" can also be a powerful tool for analyzing conditions in and actions of the richer nations.

Teaching techniques   How does one teach the above material? I have used a combination of techniques. I have adopted as the basic textbook this book, *Global Issues: An Introduction*. I have also used the latest editions of the Worldwatch Institute's *State of the World*.[9] This book is an excellent annual updating of many of the topics covered in my course, although the large amount of detailed, factual information it contains overwhelms some undergraduates. At times, in place of *State of the World*, I have used the United Nations Development Programme's *Human Development Report*, which covers many development-related subjects.[10] Students read selections from the latest edition of *Annual Editions: Global Issues*, which is a collection of articles from many different sources – some with opposing viewpoints – on many of the issues presented in the course.[11] Students are also required to subscribe to the *New York Times*, which allows them to follow current developments in all of the subjects covered in the course. Weekly quizzes are given on the *Times*.

All possible examination questions are given to the students and we use these questions to guide our discussion of the textbook. I do not give lectures. The questions on the examinations are randomly selected from these questions. I find that students learn the material better when they know what they will be tested on.

Videotapes play an important role in the course. Many excellent programs related to topics in our course appear on public television (see Appendix 2). The experience of seeing an interesting, current portrayal of a topic we are studying is a powerful teaching technique. The tapes reinforce what the students are learning and broaden their knowledge. Also, the tapes serve another important role. Studying global issues can be depressing. The problems are numerous and serious, and at first glance appear to be unsolvable. The tapes help counter that depression by often showing what some individuals are doing to attack these problems. I try to show at least two tapes related to each of the main subtopics in the course.

Students write a five- to eight-page typed research paper. In the paper they focus on an issue in greater depth than we have been able to in the course. The students are required to use at least one, but not more than two, sources from the internet. Appendix 3 gives some relevant internet sources.

A course of instruction following the above outline utilizes three levels of analysis, which contribute to its effectiveness: the individual, the nation, and the international system. To understand the issues one must look at the behavior of individuals, the actions and policies of nations, and the condition of the world's environment as well as of its economic and political systems. Solutions to the global problems require individual efforts, new national policies, and international agreements.

Such a course of instruction has three main goals. The first is to increase student knowledge of some of the most important problems facing the world today, a knowledge that the student learns comes from many different disciplines. The second goal is to help students learn of the complex interrelationships among the issues. The third is to evaluate possible solutions to the problems studied. As the students consider possible solutions, they learn the vital fact that human actions (including their own) can change the world in very different ways.

Can these goals be achieved? Certainly they cannot for every student, nor will every student who achieves one achieve all three. But many can achieve one or more of these goals. Students appreciate an effort that helps them understand the complicated and rapidly changing world in which they live. When we help them acquire this information we are giving them both the knowledge they will need to live in today's world, and more importantly, the knowledge that will enable them, if they so desire, to add their talents to the efforts being made to solve many of these global problems.

Student comments   For many years, at the end of the course, the students were asked to write, in a short unsigned essay, what they felt was the most important thing they learned in the course. These three responses give some common conclusions:

> The most important thing I learned is that problems concerning population, food, energy, etc. are *real*. I feel that most people don't realize the magnitude of these problems. However, by taking this course, I now see that all these problems are greater than I originally thought … This course taught me the first step in combating these problems, and that is to recognize that they are REAL!

> I had … known about the environmental movement and even considered myself an environmentalist. Sure I wanted to take care of my environment; new energy sources sounded cool; pollution was bad and needed to be stopped, etc. However, I never really knew how *interconnected* all of this was until I took this course. … I learned how changes in one area can drastically affect what I previously thought were unrelated things. … I learned that all of these problems are interconnected and must be studied as such if any real (long-term) solution is ever to be found for them.

> The most important thing I learned was to stop thinking like an American and only think about self-interest. Rather now I think about my neighbor be it in Converse Heights or my neighbor in South America. Professor Seitz, you focused my mind to look at the big picture instead of the small one. When I … [threw away an empty] can of Coke previously I would say, "What can I do about recycling?" Now I

see that even a little effort to make a difference does just that, it makes a difference. Now when I get in my car to go to the store, I think twice and now I usually will walk. Before when I said [what's wrong] with one more light on, it's just 20 cents a day lost. Now I think about how [the production of] electricity pollutes the atmosphere, so now I conserve electricity and other fossil fuels as well. To sum it all up, I have learned to be more responsible to this precious world we call Earth. For that, whatever grade I receive, I thank you for opening not just my eyes but my mind.

Notes

1   Ann Kelleher, "One World, Many Voices," *Liberal Education*, 77 (November/December 1991), pp. 2–7.

2   Richard D. Lambert, *International Studies and the Undergraduate* (Washington, DC: American Council on Education, 1989), p. 153. See also "American lack of foreign knowledge 'dangerous,'" *Times Higher Education*, December 2, 2005, at https://www.timeshighereducation.co.uk/news/american-lack-of-foreign-knowledge-dangerous/200107.article (accessed July 2015).

3   Lambert, *International Studies and the Undergraduate*, p. 107.

4   Ibid., p. 106.

5   Ibid., p. 126.

6   Ibid., pp. 115–27.

7   Humphrey Tonkin and Jane Edwards, "Internationalizing the University: The Arduous Road to Euphoria," *Educational Record*, 71 (Spring 1990), p. 15.

8   Lambert, *International Studies and the Undergraduate*, p. 157.

9   Worldwatch Institute, *State of the World* (New York: W. W. Norton, annual).

10 United Nations Development Programme, *Human Development Report* (New York: Oxford University Press, annual).

11 Robert M. Jackson (ed.), *Annual Editions: Global Issues* (New York: McGraw-Hill, annual).

Appendix 2

Relevant Videos

The American Pipe Dream? Eliminating Oil Dependence, produced by the Open University, distributed by Films for the Humanities and Sciences, 2009, 27 minutes.

Arctic Rush: Staking a Claim in the Earth's Uncertain Future (negative and positive effects of the melting of the Arctic ice cover), produced by Canadian Broadcasting Corporation, distributed by Films for the Humanities and Sciences, 2006, 46 minutes.

Arming the Heavens (examines all sides of the space weapons debate), Glenn Baker, writer/producer, distributed by Azimuth Media, 2004, 25 minutes.

Arms for the Poor: The Global Impact of the Weapons Industry, distributed by Films for the Humanities and Sciences, 2006, 30 minutes.

Atmospheric Hole: The History of the Ozone Layer, distributed by Films for the Humanities and Sciences, 2006, 28 minutes.

Baby Crash: Causes and Consequences of Declining Birthrates (why young people in Europe, Japan, and Canada are postponing or deciding not to have children at all), distributed by Films for the Humanities and Sciences, 2002, 46 minutes.

Back to School: The Ongoing Struggle to Educate the World's Children, distributed by Films for the Humanities and Sciences, 2006, 87 minutes.

Be Prepared for Global Warming (although global warming is irreversible, its progress can be slowed, its impacts managed), distributed by Films for the Humanities and Sciences, 2003, 51 minutes.

Global Issues: An Introduction, Fifth Edition. Kristen A. Hite and John L. Seitz
© 2016 John Wiley & Sons, Ltd. Published 2016 by John Wiley & Sons, Ltd.

Becoming Green: Growing Environmental Awareness, a NOVA production, four parts, distributed by Public Broadcasting Service (PBS), 1993, 2000, 2007, 2008, about 75 minutes each.

The Bells of Chernobyl: Ten Years After (cover-up of the effects of the Chernobyl nuclear disaster), a coproduction for Tele Images International, distributed by Filmakers Library, 2000, 52 minutes.

Bhopal: The Search For Justice (after 15,000 people were killed and hundreds of thousands more were permanently maimed by the leak of poisonous gas at a pesticide plant in India, the search for justice for the survivors is still going on), produced by The National Film Board of Canada, 2004, 53 minutes.

Bill Moyers Journal: Farm Subsidies and America's Hungry, distributed by Films for the Humanities and Sciences, 2008, 58 minutes.

Bill Moyers Journal: Global Hunger, distributed by Films for the Humanities and Sciences, 2008, 58 minutes.

The Biofuel Myth: Harsh Realities in the Developing World, distributed by Films for the Humanities and Sciences, 2009, 44 minutes.

Blue Gold: World Water Wars, Purple Turtle Films, Canada, distributed by PBS Broadcasting, 2009, 90 minutes.

The Bottom Line: Privatizing the World (controversy over business's rush to commodify the world's common resources such as drinking water, and human and plant genes), distributed by Films for the Humanities and Sciences, 2002, 53 minutes.

Building the Future – Energy (an upbeat film looks at new, sustainable energy projects in Europe and the United States), directed by Nicolas Brown, UK, 2007, 54 minutes.

Cappuccino Trail: The Global Economy in a Cup, distributed by Films for the Humanities and Sciences, 2001, 50 minutes.

Captive Servants and Child Prostitution, distributed by Films for the Humanities and Sciences, 2008, 45 minutes.

Changing Nature: Population and Environment at a Crossroads (urbanization, industrialization, and agriculture are depleting the earth), distributed by Films for the Humanities and Sciences, 2001, 58 minutes.

Children of Shadows (in Haiti parents are forced by poverty to give away their children to work as unpaid domestic servants or slaves), produced by Karen Kramer, distributed by Filmakers Library, 2003, 54 minutes.

City Life (22-part series examines the effect of globalization on people and cities worldwide), produced by Television Trust for the Environment, distributed by Bullfrog Films, 2001, 27 minutes each.

Clean, Green, and Unseen: Nanotechnology and the Environment (a Fred Friendly Seminar), distributed by Films for the Humanities and Sciences, 2008, 57 minutes.

Climate Change: Hot Times in the City (how climate change will affect urban life), produced by Canadian Broadcasting Corporation, distributed by Films for the Humanities and Sciences, 2007, 44 minutes.

Climate Change: Our Responsibility (examines both ozone depletion and the buildup of greenhouse gasses), distributed by Films for the Humanities and Sciences, 2008, 25 minutes.

Core Meteorology: Atmosphere (dangers of burning fossil fuels), distributed by Public Broadcasting Service (PBS), 2008, 30 minutes.

Core Meteorology: Climates (fundamentals of climate change), distributed by Public Broadcasting Service (PBS), 2008, 30 minutes.

Core Meteorology: Weather (extreme weather events), distributed by Public Broadcasting Service (PBS), 2008, 30 minutes.

Corporate Power in the Age of Globalization (a critical view of the worldwide impact of neoliberal economics), a project of California Newsreel, available at www.newsreel.org.

1   *The Big Sellout* (the implementation of current economic orthodoxy is hurting millions of ordinary people around the world), German film in English and Spanish, 2006, 94 minutes.
2   *The Debt of Dictators* (transnational banks provided large loans to dictators creating debt that is a huge burden to developing nations), Norwegian film in English and Spanish, 2005, 46 minutes.
3   *Black Gold* (unjust conditions under which coffee is produced), UK film, 2006, 78 minutes.
4   *A Killer Bargain* (cheap consumer goods imported by Western companies don't reflect the actual human and environmental costs of their production), Danish film, 2006, 57 minutes.
5   *Maquilapolis* (women who work in the multinational factories in Mexico near the US border), US film, 2006, 69 minutes.

The Corporation (Canadian documentary that examines and criticizes corporate business practices; includes a section on "negative externalities," which can seriously hurt the environment), distributed by Zeitgeist Films, 2003, 145 minutes (divided into separate topics).

Countdown to Hope: Opposing the Threat of Nuclear War (deals with the threat of nuclear war caused by the decline of nuclear security in Russia, the conflict between India and Pakistan, and threats by rogue states and zealot factions), distributed by Films for the Humanities and Sciences, 2001, 57 minutes.

The Curse of Oil (a global history of the oil industry), distributed by Films for the Humanities and Sciences, 2003, 52 minutes.

The Dark Side of Chocolate: Child Trafficking and Illegal Child Labor in the Cocoa Industry, distributed by Films for the Humanities and Sciences, 2010, 47 minutes.

Dying to Leave: The Dark Business of Human Trafficking (illegal immigration and human trafficking), distributed by Films for the Humanities and Sciences, 2004, 57 minutes.

Economic Development: A Global Challenge (introduces the three main determinants of income and expansion – physical capital, human capital, and technology – and examines geographic, historical, and political reasons behind underdevelopment, part of a four-part series titled Global Economics), distributed by Films for the Humanities and Sciences, 2007, 39 minutes.

The Energy Conspiracy (influential organizations have successfully lobbied for the coal, oil, and nuclear power industries against sustainable energy and have convinced the public, with inaccurate information, that global warming is not a problem), produced by Hans Bulow and Poul-Eric Heilburth, distributed by Filmakers Library, 1999, 59 minutes.

The Environment: When Politics and Industry Intersect (two-part series investigates who might be profiting from manipulating environmental laws and who might be molding public opinion and the legislative process), distributed by Films for the Humanities and Sciences, 2000, 30 minutes each.

1   *Scientific Spin Doctors* (on pressing issues such as ozone depletion and global warming, some special interest groups are striving to bend science to their agendas).
2   *Green Pacts and Greenbacks* (to what extent are environmental standards achieving the goal of purifying the air, land, and water in the United States, and are new firms helping some industries meet the legal minimums in environmental protection laws simply to escape penalties?)

Extreme Oil: The Wilderness (search for oil in fragile wilderness areas in Canada and Alaska leads to political controversy), distributed by Films for the Humanities and Sciences, 2004, 57 minutes.

Failed Nation Building: A Case Study of Haiti (one of the world's poorest nations, where US intervention failed), an ABC News program, distributed by Films for the Humanities and Sciences, 2004, 22 minutes.

Fighting the Tide: Developing Nations and Globalization (what globalization means for five developing nations), distributed by Films for the Humanities and Sciences, 2004, 26 minutes each.

1   Malawi: A Nation Going Hungry
2   Ecuador: Divided over Oil
3   Nicaragua: Turning away from Violence
4   India: Working to End Child Labor
5   Guatemala: The Human Price of Coffee

Fighting the Tide 2: Developing Nations and Globalization, distributed by Films for the Humanities and Sciences, 2008, 25 minutes each.

1   Angola: The Curse of Oil (conflict over oil revenues)
2   Bolivia: Partners, Not Masters (natural resources generate wealth and inequality)
3   Tuvalu: Keeping Heads above Water (an island nation threatened by climate change)

Fighting the Tide 3: Developing Nations and Globalization, distributed by Films for the Humanities and Sciences, 2009, 25 minutes each.

1   Colombia: Flowers for the Gringo
2   Mali: Message from the River (climate change, poverty, population growth)
3   Mongolia: Wrestling with Change
4   Niger: In the Shadow of Noma (oral infections that attack malnourished children)
5   Paraguay: Soya and Pesticides
6   Laos: So You Think the War Is Over (unexploded munitions from the Vietnam War still kill innocent civilians)

Free-Market Capitalism Is So 20th-Century: A Debate, distributed by Films for the Humanities and Sciences, 2009, 106 minutes.

Frontline: Missile Wars (explores the US missile defense program), produced by Azimuth Media with PBS's Frontline, distributed by PBS Video, 2002, 60 minutes.

Fueling Our Future: A Fred Friendly Seminar on Alternative Energy, distributed by Films for the Humanities and Sciences, 2008, 58 minutes.

Gimme Green (the ubiquitous American lawn with its negative environmental aspects), available at www.gimmegreen.com, 2006, 27 minutes.

Global Jihad (forces behind Islamic terrorism), an ABC News program, distributed by Films for the Humanities and Sciences, 2004, 20 minutes.

The Global Trade Debate (attempts to offer a balanced look at the realities of globalization and to examine the issues that divide those who support and criticize growing world trade), distributed by Films for the Humanities and Sciences, 2001, 42 minutes.

Global Tribe: Social Transformation Around the World, a three-part series (the struggles of people in developing nations, focusing on the unsung heroes in each country who give inspiration to the rest of the world), distributed by Films for the Humanities and Sciences, 2003, each DVD 28 minutes.

1 *Philippines Journal*: The Spirit of Togetherness
2 *Mexico Journal*: Life in the Earth ("eco-punk" gardeners)
3 *South African Journal*: A Nation's Renewal (rebirth of the country)

Global Warming: The Signs and the Science, produced by Public Broadcasting Service (PBS), distributed by PBS Video, 2005, approx. 60 minutes.

Global Warming: The Rising Storm, distributed by Public Broadcasting Service (PBS), 2007, each disk about 1 hour.

Disk One: Warnings from a Warming Planet (what's happening now)
Disk Two: Predictions for a Warmer Planet (what the future may be like)

Global Warming and the Extinction of Species, distributed by Films for the Humanities and Sciences, 2005, 22 minutes.

Globalization: Winners and Losers, distributed by Films for the Humanities and Sciences, 2000, 40 minutes.

Globalization at a Crossroads, distributed by Films for the Humanities and Sciences, 2010, 29 minutes.

Globalization Is Good (the positive side of the debate), distributed by Films for the Humanities and Sciences, 2003, 50 minutes.

Guns, Germs, and Steel (based on the Pulitzer Prize-winning book with this title by Jared Diamond, a three-part program presents Diamond's controversial theory that geography is the main reason the world is divided into haves and have-nots), produced by Lion Television, London, for National Geographic Television and Films, Washington, DC and distributed by PBS Video, 2005, three 60-minute programs.

Heat: A Global Investigation (this episode of Frontline investigates what powerful companies are really doing to solve climate change), distributed by Public Broadcasting Service (PBS), 2008, 120 minutes.

Home (stunning photographs of earth covering life's journey on the planet and threats by our species to it, especially climate change), a film by Yann Arthus-Bertrand spanning 54 countries, narrated by Glenn Close, distributed by Europa Corp./Elzevir Films, Twentieth Century Fox, 2009, 118 minutes.

Hotspots (extinction of species), distributed by Public Broadcasting Service (PBS), 2008, about 1 hour 45 minutes.

The Hunt for Black Gold: Oil in the 21st Century, a CNBC original documentary, distributed by Films for the Humanities and Sciences, 2008, 45 minutes.

The Hydrogen Age: Energy Solutions for the 21st Century, distributed by Films for the Humanities and Sciences, 2004, 57 minutes.

India Rising: The New Empire, a Canadian National Broadcasting Corporation original program, distributed by Films for the Humanities and Sciences, 2008, 44 minutes.

Journey to Planet Earth, explores the necessity of achieving a balance between the needs of people and the needs of the environment), produced by Emmy Award filmmakers Marilyn and Hal Weiner in association with South Carolina Educational Television (http://www.pbs.org/journeytoplanetearth/home/). Distributed by Screenscope, 25 minutes each (educational cut), or 60 minutes each.

1   *On the Brink* (severe environmental problems can produce political crises and more hostilities. Visits Haiti, Peru, South Africa, Mexico, and United States), 2003.
2   *Seas of Grass* (some grasslands are in grave danger. Visits Kenya, South Africa, Argentina, China, United States), 2003.
3   *Hot Zones* (changes in global and local ecosystems are connected to increased spread of infectious diseases. Visits Kenya, Peru, Bangladesh, United States), 2003.
4   *Future Conditional* (spread of toxic pollution. Visits the Arctic, Mexico, Uzbekistan, United States), 2005.
5   *The State of the Planet: Global Warming*, 2005.
6   *State of the Planet's Wildlife*, 2006.

Kilowatt Ours: A Plan to Re-Energize America (filmmaker Jeff Barrie searches cities, towns and countrysides for solutions to today's energy problems, focusing on energy efficiency and green power), 2007, 55 minutes.

Left Behind: Kenyan AIDS Orphans (award-winning film looks at the lives of children orphaned by AIDS), distributed by Films for the Humanities and Sciences, 2002, 36 minutes.

Legacies of War (focuses on efforts to repair physical, social, and personal damage in several postwar situations around the world), a United Nations Production, distributed by Films for the Humanities and Sciences, 2000, 32 minutes.

Life (30-part series about how globalization is affecting ordinary people; takes us to India, Africa, Asia, Brazil, Mexico, the Pacific Islands, and the United States), produced by Television Trust for the Environment for BBC Worldwide Television, distributed by Bullfrog Films, 2000, 24 minutes each.

Life 3 (12-part series about how globalization is affecting ordinary people; series takes us to Russia, Guatemala, Bangladesh, India, Zambia, Nepal, South Africa, and

Ghana; programs focus on children, health and nutrition, the HIV/AIDS epidemic, poverty, agriculture, trade, sustainable development, women's issues, and human rights), produced by Television Trust for the Environment for BBC Worldwide Television, distributed by Bullfrog Films, 2002, 25 minutes each.

Life 4 (27-part series about global efforts to achieve the UN Millennium Development Goals), produced by Television Trust for the Environment, distributed by Bullfrog Films, 2004, 25 minutes each.

Lives for Sale: Human Trafficking (illegal immigration into the United States from Mexico), distributed by Films for the Humanities and Sciences, 2006, 60 minutes.

Made in China: The People's Republic of Profit (China has become arguably the world's most business-minded country), a Canadian National Broadcasting Corporation original program, distributed by Films for the Humanities and Sciences, 2008, 45 minutes.

The Meatrix, a parody video critical of factory farming, 2006, 5 minutes.

Meltdown: A Global Warming Journey (history of the debate over the theory of global warming, why it remains a highly contentious subject, asks if the global community ever agrees on a concerted plan of action), a BBC production, distributed by Films for the Humanities and Sciences, 2006, 60 minutes.

Mexico City: The Largest City (winners and losers, a city of great contrasts, conditions in a third world megacity), distributed by Films for the Humanities and Sciences, 2004, 26 minutes.

Missing Women: Female-Selective Abortion and Infanticide, distributed by Films for the Humanities and Sciences, 2006, 53 minutes.

Mysterious Poison: The History of PCBs, distributed by Films for the Humanities and Sciences, 2006, 28 minutes.

No Vacancy: Global Responses to the Human Population Explosion, distributed by Films for the Humanities and Sciences, 2005, 92 minutes.

The Nuclear Option: Rethinking Atomic Energy, a Canadian National Broadcasting Corporation original documentary, distributed by Films for the Humanities and Sciences, 2008, 44 minutes.

Ocean Animal Emergency: Troubled Waters for Marine Mammals? (threats by warming seas and pollutants), produced by Public Broadcasting Service (PBS), 2008, approx. 60 minutes.

Of Hopscotch and Little Girls: Stolen Childhood (stories of abuse and neglect of girls around the globe), distributed by Films for the Humanities and Sciences, 2000, 53 minutes.

Oil in Iraq: Curse or Blessing? (the politics of oil in the Middle East), produced by Robert Mugnerot in collaboration with Baudoing Koenig, distributed by Filmakers Library, 2003, 52 minutes.

One Day of War (follows combatants in 16 wars in the same 24-hour period), a BBC production, distributed by Films for the Humanities and Sciences, 2004, 47 minutes.

Our Hiroshima (eyewitness account, archival footage taken before and after the event, and the politics involved in developing and promoting the use of the bomb), distributed by Films for the Humanities and Sciences, 1995, 43 minutes.

Outsmarting Terror, distributed by Films for the Humanities and Sciences, 2006, 52 minutes.

Outsourcing: White Collar Exodus, distributed by Films for the Humanities and Sciences, 2005, 51 minutes.

Overpopulated (documentary that explains demographic trends and their implications for development), BBC, 2014, 59 minutes.

The Peacekeepers (UN peacekeeping force in the Democratic Republic of Congo to quell ethnic fighting), produced by the National Film Board of Canada, 2005, 83 minutes.

Precious Earth: Mapping the Human Condition (eight-part series using global data-mapping to help analyze current issues), distributed by Films for the Humanities and Sciences, 2004, 31 minutes each.

1   *Life Expectancy: Geography as Destiny.*
2   *Infectious Diseases: More Mobility, Greater Danger.*
3   *Decaying Cities: Reclaiming the Rust Belt.*
4   *Empty Oceans: Global Competition for Scarce Resources.*
5   *Crime in the Cities: Public Safety at Risk.*
6   *Birthrate: New Options for Parenthood.*
7   *China's Prosperity: Behind the Scenes of Progress.*
8   *Extinct Species: Red Alert to Humanity.*

Race against Time: The AIDS Crisis in Africa, produced by Canadian Broadcasting Corporation from the Nature of Things Series, distributed by Filmakers Library, 2002, 48 minutes.

Refugees in Africa: Another Quiet Emergency (the plight of people – especially children – displaced and endangered by war), an ABC News program, distributed by Films for the Humanities and Sciences, 2004, 20 minutes.

Religion, War, and Violence: The Ethics of War and Peace (experts, scholars, and religious leaders from a variety of faiths discuss terrorism and its roots, fundamentalism, just war, holy war, pacifism, and the use of violence in the name of God), distributed by Films for the Humanities and Sciences, 2002, 90 minutes.

Renewable Fuels, distributed by Films for the Humanities and Sciences, 2008, 24 minutes.

Scared Scared (people seeking positive ways to react to disasters such as those at the minefields of Cambodia, in post-9/11 New York City, at the toxic wasteland of Bhopal, in war-torn Afghanistan, at Hiroshima, in Bosnia, and in Palestine and Israel), produced and distributed by the National Film Board of Canada, 2004, 104 minutes.

Scarred Lands and Wounded Lives: The Environmental Footprint of War, Video-Takes USA, available at http://www.scarredlandsfilm.org/, 2008, 60 minutes.

Slum Cities (visits Mumbai, India and Rio de Janeiro, Brazil), distributed by Films for the Humanities and Sciences, 2006, 44 minutes.

Star Wars Dreams (missile defense system), produced by Leslie Woodhead, distributed by Filmakers Library, 2003, 50 minutes.

Stealing the Fire: The New Nuclear Weapons Underground (a story of international intrigue in the quest to obtain nuclear weapons), directed by John Friedman and Eric Nadler, distributed by Filmakers Library, 2003, 58 minutes.

Stemming the Flow of Water Pollution, Part 1 (how waters flowing into the seas are being polluted) and *Part 2* (efforts to remediate oceanic "dead zones" in Spain, Brazil, Iran, and Fuji), distributed by Films for the Humanities and Sciences, 2004, 24 minutes each.

Stolen Childhoods (child exploitation), an ABC News program, distributed by Films for the Humanities and Sciences, 2005, 22 minutes.

Story of Stuff (a critical description of conventional development theory and its discontents), video, 2007, 21 minutes.

A Tale of Modern Slavery (caste systems and other archaic traditions perpetuate slavery in some poor countries), an ABC News program, distributed by Films for the Humanities and Sciences, 2005, 20 minutes.

Thinking Globally, Acting Locally about Your Environment (major environmental threats in the United States and positive steps individuals and communities can take to reduce them), distributed by Films for the Humanities and Sciences, 1998, 28 minutes.

Thirsting for War (conflict among Turkey, Syria, and Iraq over the water of the Euphrates River), written and directed by Christopher Mitchell, distributed by Filmakers Library, 2000, 50 minutes.

Time for School: The Global Education Crisis, distributed by Films for the Humanities and Sciences, 2003, 57 minutes.

Too Hot to Handle: Winning the Battle against Global Warming (focuses on perils and solutions), an HBO Production, distributed by Films for the Humanities and Sciences, 2006, 55 minutes.

27 Dollars: Banking for the Poor (Grameen Bank in Bangladesh), produced by Andrea Beretta, distributed by Filmakers Library, 2003, 61 minutes.

Voices of Dissent: Freedom of Speech and Human Rights in China, distributed by Films for the Humanities and Sciences, 2008, 45 minutes.

Waging War against the New Terrorism (how Germany, Italy, and Egypt have combated terrorism in recent decades, and US strategies), an ABC News program, distributed by Films for the Humanities and Sciences, 2002, 23 minutes.

What Are We Doing Here? Why Western Aid Hasn't Helped Africa, distributed by Films for the Humanities and Sciences, 2008, 95 minutes.

Where's the Catch: Pacific Fishing in Crisis, distributed by Films for the Humanities and Sciences, 2005, 26 minutes.

White Light, Black Rain: The Destruction of Hiroshima and Nagasaki, an HBO production, distributed by Films for the Humanities and Science, 2007, 87 minutes.

A Window on a Changing Climate (Antarctic), produced by the National Film Board of Canada, 2009, 52 minutes.

Witness to Hate: Reporting on al Qaeda (report by a BBC correspondent who was shot by al-Qaeda), an ABC News program, distributed by Films for the Humanities and Sciences, 2005, 22 minutes.

Years of Living Dangerously (Emmy-award winning TV series on climate change), produced by The Years Project, 2014, episodes are approx. 60 minutes.

Information on how to rent or purchase available videos is contained in a reference book found in many libraries: *Bowker's Complete Video Directory*, annual, which is published by R. R. Bowker, New Providence, New Jersey.

Appendix 3

Relevant Internet Websites

All these websites were current as of August 2015.

Acid Rain Data and Reports (by US Geological Survey): http://bqs.usgs.gov/acidrain

American Council for an Energy Efficient Economy: http://www.aceee.org

American Water Works Association (international drinking water): http://www.awwa.org

Arms Control Association: http://www.armscontrol.org

Atlas of Global Conservation: http://www.nature.org/atlas

Atomic Archive (development, use and consequence of dropping atomic bomb): http://www.atomicarchive.com

Bank Information Center (World Bank watchdog): http://www.bicusa.org

Biodiversity – Hotspots (by Conservation International): http://www.conservation.org/How/Pages/Hotspots.aspx

Canadian Cryospheric Information Network (ice and snow over Canada including glaciers, polar ice caps, and permafrost): http://www.socc.ca

Canadian Institute for Health Information: http://www.cihi.com

Carbon Dioxide Information Analysis Center (CDIAC) (primary climate change data analysis center of US Department of Energy): http://cdiac.ornl.gov

Carbon Tracker (carbon dioxide measurements from 60 locations around the world) http://www.esrl.noaa.gov/gmd/ccgg/carbontracker

CARE (nongovernmental organization for individuals and families in the world's poorest communities): http://www.care.org

Center for Climate and Energy Solutions (C2ES): http://www.c2es.org/

Center for International Earth Science Information Network (CIESIN) at Columbia University: http://www.ciesin.org

Center for International Environmental Law: http://www.ciel.org

Center for International Forestry Research: http://www.cifor.org

Centers for Disease Control and Prevention: http://www.cdc.gov

Global Issues: An Introduction, Fifth Edition. Kristen A. Hite and John L. Seitz.
© 2016 John Wiley & Sons, Ltd. Published 2016 by John Wiley & Sons, Ltd.

Climate Change (by United Nations Environment Programme): http://www.unep.org/themes/climatechange

Conservation International: http://www.conservation.org

Consultative Group on International Agricultural Research (an alliance of agricultural centers and other organizations that use science to help the poor): http://www.cgiar.org

Coral Health and Monitoring Program (reefs in the United States and Caribbean): http://www.coral.noaa.gov

Corporation for National and Community Service: http://www.nationalservice.gov

Danish Wind Industry Association: http://www.windpower.org/en/

Dot Earth (a blog written by *New York Times* reporter Andrew Revkin examining the growing human impact on earth's health): http://nytimes.com/dotearth

Earth Charter (principles for building a just, sustainable, and peaceful global society): http://www.earthcharter.org

Earth Institute at Columbia University: http://www.earth.columbia.edu

Earth and Moon Viewer: http://www.fourmilab.ch/earthview

Earth Science World Image Bank (6,000 photos from American Geological Institute): http://www.earthscienceworld.org/imagebank

Earth Times: http://www.earthtimes.org

Earthwatch Institute (building a sustainable future, global volunteering): http://www.earthwatch.org

Earthweek: A Diary of the Planet: http://www.earthweek.com

Ecological Footprint, Center for Sustainable Economy (a quiz to measure your demands on nature): http://www.myfootprint.org

EElinked Networks (from the North American Association for Environmental Education): http://eelinked.naaee.net/

El Niño: http://www.pbs.org/wgbh/nova/elnino

Energy Action Coalition (partnership of US youth-led environmental organizations): http://www.energyactoncoalition.org

Energy and Resources Institute: http://www.teriin.org

Energy Star (promoting energy efficiency): http://www.energystar.gov

ENTRI (Environmental Treaties and Resource Indicators, by Columbia University's Center for International Earth Science): http://sedac.ciesin.columbia.edu/entri/

Envirolink: http://www.envirolink.org

Enviromapper (from US Environmental Protection Agency, the site allows you to track down emission sources and other pollution trouble spots): http://www.epa.gov/emcfdata/em4ef.home

Environment 360 (from Yale School of Forestry and Environmental Studies): http://www.e360.yale.edu/

Environmental Data Explorer (more than 500 ecological and economic variables from the United Nations Environment Programme): http://geodata.grid.unep.ch

Environmental Defense Fund: http://www.edf.org

Environmental News Network: http://www.enn.com

Facing the Future: Global Sustainability Curriculum and Teacher PD (tools for educators): http://www.facingthefuture.org

Federation of American Scientists: http://www.fas.org

Food First/Institute for Food and Development Policy: http://www.foodfirst.org

Friends of the Earth: http://www.foe.org

Future of Nuclear Power (an interdisciplinary study by MIT faculty in 2003 with 2009 update): http://web.mit.edu/nuclearpower

Global Forest Watch (an initiative of the World Resources Institute): http://www.globalforestwatch.org

Global Recycling Network: http://grn.com/grn

Global Volunteers: http://www.globalvolunteers.org

Globe Program (Global Learning and Observations to Benefit the Environment): http://www.globe.gov

Globalization101 (a student's guide to globalization): http://www.globalization101.org

Green Burial Council (recycle yourself): http://www.greenburialcouncil.org

Greenpeace International: http://www.greenpeace.org/international.en

HEI Air Quality Database (US data on fine particles and gaseous pollutants, maintained by Atmospheric and Environmental Research): hei.aer.com/login.php

How to Compost: http://www.howtocompost.org

The Hunger Site: http://www.thehungersite.com

Indigenous Peoples' International Centre for Policy Research and Education (Tebtebba): http://www.tebtebba.org

Intergovernmental Panel on Climate Change (IPCC): http://www.ipcc.ch

International Atomic Energy Agency: http://www.iaea.org

International Ecotourism Society: http://www.ecotourism.org

International Energy Association: http://www.iea.org

International Food Policy Research Institute: http://www.ifpri.org

International Institute for Sustainable Development Reporting Services: http://www.iisd.ca

International Renewable Energy Association (IRENA): http://www.irena.org

International Research Institute for Climate and Society at Columbia University: http://iri.columbia.edu

International Solar Energy Society: http://www.ises.org

International Union for the Conservation of Nature (IUCN): http://iucn.org

Izaak Walton League of America (conservation): http://www.iwla.org

Jane Goodall Institute (education and conservation, focusing particularly on the great apes): http://www.janegoodall.org

Job/Volunteer Links (jobs and volunteer opportunities): http://www.igc.org/jobs.html

KOF Index of Globalization (measures the degree of globalization of more than 180 countries): http://globalization.kof.ethz.ch

League of Conservation Voters: http://www.lcv.org

Meatrix (critique of factory farming): http://www.themeatrix.com

NASA World Wind (lets you zoom from satellite altitude into any place on earth): http://worldwind.arc.nasa.gov

The National Academies of Sciences, Engineering, and Medicine (includes the National Research Council): http://www.nationalacademies.org

National Aeronautics and Space Administration (NASA): http://www.nasa.gov/home

National Audubon Society (conservation, focusing particularly on birds): http://www.audubon.org

National Center for Atmospheric Research: http://www.ncar.ucar.edu

National Council for Science and the Environment: http://www.ncseonline.org

National Institutes of Health: http://www.nih.gov

National Oceanic and Atmospheric Administration: http://www.noaa.gov

National Renewable Energy Laboratory: http://www.nrel.gov

National Snow and Ice Data Center: http://www.nsidc.org

National Wildlife Federation: http://www.nwf.org

Natural Resources Defense Council: http://www.nrdc.org

Nature Conservancy (land trusts): http://www.nature.org

Nature Conservancy's Sustainable Waters Program: http://www.nature.org/initiatives/fresh water

Near Earth Objects – Dynamic Site (asteroids etc. by University of Pisa, Italy): http://newton.dm.unipi.it/neodys

North American Association for Environmental Education: http://www.naaee.org

Online Access to Research in the Environment (journals and books made available free to developing countries): http://www.unep.org/oare/

Organisation for Economic Co-operation and Development (OECD): http://www.oecd.org

Ozone Hole Watch (by NASA): http://ozonewatch.gsfc.nasa.gov

Plant Stress (nine environmental stresses on plants and methods for alleviating their impact): http://www.plantstress.com

Population Action International: http://www.populationaction.org

Population Connection (formerly Zero Population Growth): http://www.population connection.org

Population Council: http://www.popcouncil.org

Population Index – on the Web (database of demographic literature published in *Population Index*, 1986–2000): http://popindex.princeton.edu

Population Reference Bureau: http://www.prb.org

Princeton Environmental Institute: http://www.princeton.edu/pei

Public Interest Research Groups (PIRGs): http://uspirg.org

Rainforest Action Network: http://www.ran.org

A Recycling Revolution: http://www.recycling-revolution.com

Reef Check (coral reefs): http://www.reefcheck.org

Renewable Energy World: http://www.renewableenergyworld.com

Resources for the Future: http://www.rff.org

Sci Dev Net (Science and Development Network – scientific information relevant to developing nations to promote North–South and South–South collaboration): http://www.scidev.net

Scientific American (a popular and respected US science magazine): http://www.scientific american.com/

Scorecard: The Pollution Information Site (pollution in individual US communities): http://www.scorecard.org

ServiceLeader.org (volunteering opportunities and community engagement site sponsored by University of Texas at Austin): http://www.serviceleader.org/new

Sierra Club: http://www.sierraclub.org

Silent Spring Institute (researching the environment and women's health, especially breast cancer): http://www. silentspring.org

Smithsonian Environmental Research Center: http://www.serc.si.edu/

Smithsonian National Museum of Natural History: http://www.nmnh.si.edu

Solar News: http://wn.com/solar_news

Story of Stuff: http://www.storyofstuff.org

Student Environmental Action Coalition: http://www.seac.org

Sustainable Agriculture Research and Education: http://www.sare.org

Sustainable Communities Network: http://www.sustainable.org

SustainUS (US Youth for Sustainable Development): http://sustainus.org/

350.org (building a global climate movement): http://www.350.org

Tree of Life Web Project (biodiversity): http://tolweb.org/tree/phylogeny.html

Union of Concerned Scientists (energy, global warming, nuclear arms, environment, food, health): http://www.ucsusa.org

United Kingdom Department for International Development: http://www.dfid.gov.uk

United Nations Children's Fund (UNICEF): http://www.unicef.org

United Nations Development Programme (UNDP): http://www.undp.org

United Nations Educational, Scientific, and Cultural Organization (UNESCO): http://www.unesco.org

United Nations Environment Programme (UNEP): http://www.unep.org

United Nations Food and Agriculture Organization (FAO): http://www.fao.org

United Nations Framework Convention on Climate Change (UNFCCC): http://unfccc.int/2860.php

United Nations Refugee Agency (UNHCR): http://www.unhcr.org

United Nations Population Fund (UNFPA): http://www.unfpa.org

United Nations Population Information Network (POPIN): http://www.un.org/popin

United States Agency for International Development (USAID): http://www.usaid.gov

United States Census Bureau (international database): http://www.census.gov/population/international/

United States Central Intelligence Agency: The World Factbook: https://www.cia.gov/library/publications/the-world-factbook/

United States Department of Agriculture: Natural Resources Conservation Service: http://www.nrcs.usda.gov

United States Department of Energy: http://www.energy.gov/

United States Department of the Interior: http://www.doi.gov

United States Environmental Protection Agency (EPA): http://www.epa.gov

United States Geological Survey: Water Resources of the United States: http://water.usgs.gov

United States National Oceanic and Atmospheric Administration: http://www.noaa.gov

United States Nuclear Regulatory Commission: http://www.nrc.gov

United States Partnership for Education for Sustainable Development: http://www.uspartnership.org

Water Environment Federation: http://www.wef.org

Wildfowl and Wetland Trust: http://www.wwt.org.uk

Wildlife Conservation Society: http://www.wcs.org

World Affairs Council: http://www.world-affairs.org

World Bank: http://www.worldbank.org

World Business Council for Sustainable Development: http://www.wbcsd.org

World Conservation Monitoring Centre/United Nations Environmental Programme: http://www.uncp-wcmc.org

World Food Programme of the United Nations (food aid): http://www.wfp.org

World Glacier Monitoring Service: http://www.geo.unizh.ch/wgms

World Health Organization: http://www.who.int/en

World Resources Institute: http://www.wri.org
World Trade Organization: http://www.wto.org
World Water Assessment Programme (by UNESCO): http://www.unesco.org/water/wwap
Worldwatch Institute: http://www.worldwatch.org
WWF (World Wildlife Fund/World Wide Fund for Nature): http://www.wwf.org

Appendix 4

The United Nations 2030 Agenda for Sustainable Development

During the period between 2000 and 2015, countries banded together through the United Nations to pursue a landmark global initiative to fight poverty and support development. While the sustainable development agenda from the 1992 Rio Earth Summit factored in clearly to some of the individual goals, the overall focus was still on poverty alleviation through the historic paradigm of economic development. During that same period of implementation, countries began to embrace sustainable development as a key pathway to creating an economy that can provide for the population without undercutting the people and planet that form the basis of that very economy.

In 2012, countries met again in Rio for a global summit on sustainable development. By this time, it was clear the development and environment agendas were becoming more aligned. There were questions about how to best integrate economic and social development with environmental considerations, and governments began focusing on high-level efforts to merge development and environment, building from the Millennium Development Goals and Rio summits on Sustainable Dvelopment.

In September 2015, to a standing ovation from many world leaders, 193 nations unanimously adopted the UN Sustainable Development Agenda as a "blueprint for development." UN Secretary-General Ban Ki-moon welcomed the decision, calling it "an agenda for people, to end poverty in all its forms . . . It is an agenda for shared prosperity, peace and partnership (that) conveys the urgency of climate action (and) is rooted in gender equality and respect for the rights of all. Above all, it pledges to leave no one behind."

Global Issues: An Introduction, Fifth Edition. Kristen A. Hite and John L. Seitz.
© 2016 John Wiley & Sons, Ltd. Published 2016 by John Wiley & Sons, Ltd.

This agenda sets forth 169 targets supporting 17 Goals for 2030. As the next step beyond the Millennium Development Goals, these Sustainable Development Goals reflect a concerted global effort to provide for the growing number of people on the planet by alleviating poverty, improving livelihoods, and sustaining the ecosystems necessary to maintain all of the Earth's inhabitants in the coming decades. We have included these goals below, as they are relevant to every chapter in this book. As you think about where "development" is headed, consider what actions governments will need to take to realize all of these goals and how different the world might look if some or all of the goals are achieved.

United Nations Sustainable Development Goals

1 End poverty in all its forms everywhere
2 End hunger, achieve food security and improved nutrition, and promote sustainable agriculture
3 Ensure healthy lives and promote well-being for all at all ages
4 Ensure inclusive and equitable quality education and promote lifelong learning opportunities for all
5 Achieve gender equality and empower all women and girls
6 Ensure availability and sustainable management of water and sanitation for all
7 Ensure access to affordable, reliable, sustainable, and modern energy for all
8 Promote sustained, inclusive, and sustainable economic growth, full and productive employment and decent work for all
9 Build resilient infrastructure, promote inclusive and sustainable industrialization, and foster innovation
10 Reduce inequality within and among countries
11 Make cities and human settlements inclusive, safe, resilient, and sustainable

12   Ensure sustainable consumption and production patterns
13   Take urgent action to combat climate change and its impacts
14   Conserve and sustainably use the oceans, seas, and marine resources for sustainable development
15   Protect, restore, and promote sustainable use of terrestrial ecosystems, sustainably manage forests, combat desertification, halt and reverse land degradation, and halt biodiversity loss
16   Promote peaceful and inclusive societies for sustainable development, provide access to justice for all, and build effective, accountable and inclusive institutions at all levels
17   Strengthen the means of implementation and revitalize the global partnership for sustainable development

Sources

United Nations Sustainable Development Goals Website: www.un.org/sustainabledevelopment/sustainable-development-goals/ (accessed October 13, 2015).

United Nations Sustainable Development Goals website containing the text of all 17 Sustainable Development Goals, expandable by topic: https://sustainabledevelopment.un.org/topics/ (accessed October 13, 2015).

United Nations Press Release, Historic New Sustainable Development Agenda Unanimously Adopted by 193 UN Members, at http://www.un.org/sustainabledevelopment/blog/2015/09/historic-new-sustainable-development-agenda-unanimously-adopted-by-193-un-members/ (accessed October 13, 2015).

Glossary

biotechnology   The technology by which an animal or plant derivative is integrated with a process or tool, such as for medical, industrial, or manufacturing purposes. It can be "low tech" such as yeast for brewing and probiotics found in cheese and yoghurt, or high tech such as cloning and manipulating DNA (genetic engineering) to produce drought-resistant crops or create new a cancer-fighting treatment.

carrying capacity   The total population an ecosystem or other geographic area can sustain without depleting internal resources beyond their rate of replenishment. Human actions can impact carrying capacity such as by cutting down trees and converting to pasture land for livestock.

civil society   Voluntary associations of people that are between the state and the extended family. There are two branches of the use of this concept, one emphasizing economic associations (e.g., Adam Smith) and one emphasizing social and political associations (e.g., Montesquieu, Rousseau, and de Tocqueville). This book uses the latter definition with a focus on social and political organizations such as churches, clubs, interest groups, social movements, and political parties.

climate change (global warming, greenhouse effect)   Variations beyond historic cyclical fluctuations in the Earth's temperature, hydrological cycles, and ocean activity, typically attributed to an atmospheric increase of carbon dioxide and other greenhouse gases.

Global Issues: An Introduction, Fifth Edition. Kristen A. Hite and John L. Seitz.
© 2016 John Wiley & Sons, Ltd. Published 2016 by John Wiley & Sons, Ltd.

demographic transition   The four basic changes the population of a country seems to go through as the country passes from being a traditional, rural and agricultural country to a modern, urban and industrial country. In the first stage, there are high birth and death rates. In the fourth stage there are low birth and death rates. Stages two and three are called the transitional period. In the early part of the transition (second stage) the death rates begin to drop quickly as modern medicine takes hold while birth rates continue to be high. The population begins to increase rapidly, a situation many developing countries recently faced or are still facing. In the third stage of the intermediate period death rates continue to fall and birth rates start to fall also. Population continues to increase but less rapidly than in the second stage. Some developing countries are at present in this state. A few demographers have suggested that there may be a fifth demographic stage where birth rates are so low that the size of the population starts to shrink, a situation that Japan and some European countries appear to be in at present.

developing country   Traditional term referring to a relatively poor nation where agriculture or mineral resources have a large role in the economy while industry has a lesser role. The economic and social infrastructure of the country (transportation, communications, education, health, and other social services) is usually inadequate for its needs. About 80 percent of the world's people live in nations like this, also called **less developed** or **underdeveloped**. These countries are often located in Africa, Latin America, and Asia. (Some of these nations are highly developed in culture and are the homes of ancient civilizations that had great achievements in architecture, religion, and philosophy.) Since many of the less (economically) developed nations are in the southern hemisphere, they are at times referred to as **the South**. During the Cold War these nations were often called the **Third World**, a term still in use. (First World was capitalist, noncommunist nations, and Second World was state socialist countries). Industrialized countries are called **developed** nations. Most of them are located in the northern hemisphere so they are at times called **the North**. The World Bank classifies nations according to their level of income, as measured by per capita gross national income, placing low and middle income countries in the developing category and high income countries in the developed category. The poorest countries such as Bangladesh and Somalia are called the **least developed**. All of these terms are imprecise. There are often many differences among developing nations. Their relative national wealth is often their sole similar quality.

development   Economic growth plus the social and environmental changes caused by or accompanying that economic growth. When the economy expands, more goods (material objects) and services (healthcare, education, etc.) are produced. The economic growth causes or is accompanied by changes in the society – how people live. If pollution results from the economic growth, people may breathe harmful air and drink toxins in their water. If economic growth leads to better education in the country rather than just more consumer goods, a more highly educated society is created which is better able to understand its problems and take appropriate actions to remedy them.

emerging economy   An intermediate category between countries historically classified as "developed" and "developing," often said to include the **BRICS** (Brazil, India, China and South Africa); in the late twentieth and early twenty-first centuries they were also referred to as **newly industrializing economies** (such as South Korea, Taiwan, Hong Kong, Singapore, and Mexico), which became richer by expanding their manufacturing and exporting goods mainly to the United States, Europe, and Japan.

foreign aid (development assistance)   Foreign aid is support from one or more countries (sometime acting through international institutions), typically in the form of favorable loans or grants, intended for a public interest in another country, frequently channeled through national funds. Aid given for economic development is called **development assistance**. Aid given to strengthen the recipient's military forces is called **military assistance**. "From the recipient's perspective, foreign aid adds to the resources available for investment and increases the supply of foreign exchange to finance necessary imports. From the donor's point of view, foreign aid is an instrument of foreign policy, and often comes with implicit or explicit expectations of reciprocity in areas where the recipient can be of assistance. Aid packages frequently restrict the recipient, moreover, to purchases from producers in the donor country." *Source*: "Foreign aid," in Craig Calhoun (ed.), *Dictionary of the Social Sciences* (Oxford University Press, 2002).

Gaia hypothesis   The theory is based on an idea put forward by the British scientist James Lovelock that the Earth operates as a whole system and responds to human activity in a self-regulating manner.

global issues   Issues or problems that affect most nations around the world, that cannot be solved by any single nation, and that show our increasing interdependence. Often interdisciplinary knowledge is required to attack these complex problems, which at times can affect the ability of our planet to support life."

globalization   The increase of global economic, political, environmental, and social activities. Expanding international capitalism, mainly through the reach of multinational corporations; the activities of the more important international political organizations, such as the United Nations, World Bank, International Monetary Fund, and World Trade Organization; and growing global communications and social interactions are leading to a more interdependent world. The emphasis of **antiglobalization** is that the benefits of the new globalization are unevenly shared, with some parts of the world growing wealthier – such as the United States, much of Western Europe, Japan, and sections of China and India – while some nations are not benefiting or being hurt – such as parts of Latin America and Africa. Public protests have been waged over working conditions in many countries, environmental destruction, social justice, and high national debts from development loans, and by anticapitalists who oppose the increasing power of large corporations.

Green Revolution   The bringing of Western agricultural technology to the developing world, including highly productive hybrid seeds and the use of fertilizers, pesticides, and irrigation, which has led to vastly increased yields of rice, wheat, and corn in some countries and during some periods.

Millennium Development Goals   Out of the Millennium Declaration adopted by the 189 nations attending the Millennium Summit in 2000 came eight development goals that nations agreed they would focus on through 2015. They were (1) eradicate extreme poverty and hunger; (2) achieve universal primary education; (3) promote gender equality and empower women; (4) reduce child mortality; (5) improve maternal health; (6) combat HIV/AIDS, malaria, and other diseases; (7) ensure environmental sustainability; (8) develop a global partnership for development.

multinational corporation   Business organization which has its headquarters in one country (often in a developed nation) and branches in other countries (often developing countries) where its production facilities are often located because of cheap labor, access to markets and resources, lower taxes, weaker pollution regulations, and bypassing protectionist barriers. It is the main vehicle in spreading globalization.

negative externality   An economics phrase – the producer and the consumer do not bear all the costs of an economic activity. These costs are passed on to the community at large. For example, many industries in many countries have discharged their wastes into the air, water, and land. Industry generally has considered the atmosphere, rivers, and lakes to be "free goods." The illness and damage to the environment from this pollution was borne by the public. This activity continued until the state or government passed laws stopping or limiting it. Some believe the releasing of carbon dioxide, a major cause of climate change, which is released whenever fossil fuels are burned, is the most dangerous example the world has ever experienced of a negative externality.

pastoralism   A cultural and economic livelihood that involves raising pasture-fed animals, often cattle and sheep, and may include an extensive range of land or even nomadic features. Some indigenous peoples identify as pastoralists.

sustainable   An ability to be maintained at a certain level indefinitely. A widely accepted definition of **sustainable development** is contained in *Our Common Future*, the report of the 1987 World Commission on the Environment and Development (the "Brundtland Report") as "development that meets the needs of the present without compromising the ability of future generations to meet their own needs."

tragedy of the commons   A concept most famously described by Garrett Hardin to point to the incentive for overexploitation when one user absorbs most of the benefits from a choice to use resources beyond their carrying capacity while the costs of that choice are mostly absorbed by other users.

Index

Entries for figures and illustrations are in italics.

3M, 226, 232, 233

acid rain, 164, 196, 200–202
activism *see* civil society
aerosols (soot), 181
Afghanistan War (2001–), 257
Africa
   climate change and environmental
      issues, 98, 179
   energy, 133, 148–149
   food production, 89, 107–108
   hunger and famine, 87, 88, 90, 91
   poverty and inequality, 58
   wars, 257, 282
aging populations, 22–24, 36, 38
agribusiness, 96–97
agriculture, 17, 86–87, 89–91
   and carrying capacity, 39, 112–115
   effect of climate on crop yields, 73,
      178–179, 210
   environmental impact, 94–95, 98–99,
      112–120, 210–211, 226–227,
      246–250, 273
   importance of biodiversity, 213–214

irrigation, 44, 94–95, 98, 105, 107, 203
   and soil quality, 210–211
   sustainable/traditional/organic
      methods, 94–95, 114–115
   technological innovation, 86–87,
      93–97, 105–108, 248–250
aid (development assistance), 2, 59–63,
   109
air pollution, 147–148, 164, 171–173,
   176, 178, 181–184, 192–202,
   277–278
Alvarez, Luis Echeverria, 34
Amazon region, 208, 209, 210–211,
   216–217, 231, 281
American Council on Education, 292,
   293
American Institute of Philanthropy, 59
American Wind Energy Association, 150
Amnesty International, 216–217
animal welfare, 248–250
Annan, Kofi, 77–78, 192
Antarctica, 174
antibiotics, use in factory farms, 249
aquaculture, 118–119

Global Issues: An Introduction, Fifth Edition. Kristen A. Hite and John L. Seitz
© 2016 John Wiley & Sons, Ltd. Published 2016 by John Wiley & Sons, Ltd.

Arab-Israeli War (1973), 130
arable land, 96, 98–99, 109–110, 112–114
Arctic, 173–174, 178, 180, 196, 198, 231
Argentina, 14, 36, 280
Armelagos, George, 94–95
arms race, 254–263
Asia, 58, 88, 89, 90, 98, 116, 208
    climate change and environmental
        issues, 179, 202
    energy, 148, 149–150
    see also individual countries, e.g.
        China, India
Atlantic, 180–181, 231
Australia, 208, 213

Bangladesh
    climate change and environmental
        issues, 176, 205
    economic issues, 140, *141*, 148, 279,
        281
    population growth, 29, *33*
Beijing (China), 194–195
Bennet, James, 166n
Berry, Wendell, 276
Bhutan, 3
biodiversity, 177, 213–214
biofuels, 21, 110, 136, 139, 140–141, *144*,
    148, 151, 181
biotechnology, 115–117
Birch, Charles, 238
Birdsall, Nancy, 5
birth control, 18, 19, 31–36, 42, 47n, 253
birth rates, 9–11, 17–24, 26–31
blended approach, economic
    development, 70–71, 79
Borlaug, Norman, 108
Borneo, 246–247
BP (British Petroleum), 156
Bradsher, Keith, 166n
Brazil
    climate change and environmental
        issues, 14–15, 208, 209, 210–211,
        216–217
    economic issues, 66, 82n, 140, 151,
        162

food, 96, 101, 112, 211
    politics and land use, 280, 281
    population growth, 36–37
breast-feeding, *30*, 90, 103–104
Britain *see* United Kingdom
Brown, Lester, 17, 119
Bucharest World Population Conference
    (Bucharest, 1974), 24–25, 31–32
Buenos Aires (Argentina), 14
Buffett, Warren, 60
Bush, George H. W., 42, 47n, 191
Bush, George W., 42, 47n, 192

Calcutta (India), 12
California, 156, 193–194
Cambodia, 90
Canada, 110, 111, 147, 182, 191, 201
cancer, 224–226
Cantrell, Ronald, 116
capitalism, 63–67, 76
carbon dioxide (CO_2), 147–148, 164,
    171–173, 176, 181–184, 194, 202
carbon footprint, 113, 154–157, 184–185
carrying capacity, 39–43, 112–115
Carson, Rachel, 226, 272
Carter, Jimmy, 134
Catholic Church, 25, 34, 37, 279
cats, parachuting, 246–247
Ceauşescu, Nicolae, 37–38
centralized (state-driven) economies, 66,
    67–71
CFCs (chlorofluorocarbons), 171,
    199–200, 277–278
charities, 58–59, 60
    see also non-governmental
        organizations (NGOs)
chemical pollution, 205–206, 224–227,
    230–232, 235, 273
Chernobyl nuclear accident (1986), 160,
    161
Chicago (IL), 173
children
    effect of air pollution on, 193–194,
        196–198
    effect of chemical pollution on, 227

effects of malnutrition on, 88, 90,
    91–93
poverty, *57*, 58, 88
China (PRC)
    climate change, 181, 182, 183, 270, 278
    economy, 52, 53–55, 58, 66, 80n, 148
    energy issues, 133, 138–139, 148, 157,
        159
        renewable energy, 149–150, 151,
            183
    famine, 90–91
    food production, 90, 96, 108, 109–110,
        115, 118
    forests, 208, 209
    pollution, 106, 138, 142, 148, 181, 193,
        194–195, 202
    population, 10, 11, 19, 23, 35–36
    soil erosion and desertification, 98
    sustainable cities, 13–14
    water use, 105, 203, 205
Chipko movement, 279
chlorofluorocarbons (CFCs), 171,
    199–200, 277–278
cities, 11–15, *16*
civil society, 63, 278–282
Clausewitz, Carl von, 257
Clean Air Act (US, 1970), 193, 202
Clean Water Act (US, 1972), 204
climate change, 44, 170–185
    causes, 66, 79–80, 165, 171–172
    evidence for, 171–181
    and food production, 105, 111, 174
    prevention and mitigation of, 181–185
    regional impacts, 177, 179–180
    tragedy of the commons, 276–278
    see also environment
Clinton, Bill, 218n, 234
Club of Rome, 272
coal, 138–139, *144*, 148
cogeneration, 156
Cohen, Joel, 41, 42–43, 274, 283–284
Cold War, 6n, 254–255, 256
Collapse (Diamond), 273
colonialism, 67
Commoner, Barry, 201, 225–226, 237

commons, governance of, 276–278
communism, 66, 69
Congressional Office of Technology
    Assessment, 232
contraception and birth control, 18, 19,
    31–36, 42, 47n, 253
Convention on Biodiversity (1992), 191
Convention to Combat Desertification
    (1992), 191
coral reefs, 176, 177–178
core-periphery relations, 67–68
corruption, 61
crime, 21–22
Cuban Missile Crisis (1962), 254
culture, 19, 76, 177, 215–217
Curitiba (Brazil), 14
Cuyahoga River (OH), 204

dams, 149, 203
DDT (dichlorodiphenyltrichloroethane),
    246–248
de Grazia, Victoria, 82n
"dead zones" (eutrophication), 106, 250
death rates, 17, 19, 26–28, 173
deforestation, 109, 184, 207–211
democracy, 281–282
Democratic Republic of the Congo, 257
demographic transition, 26–28, 36
dependency theory, 67, 70
desertification, 98
developed nations, 6n
    energy issues, 130–138, 141–146
    international trade, 62, 67–68
    population, 22–24, 36, 38
developing countries, definition, 4, 6n
development
    and culture, 76, 215–217
    definition, 2–5, 80, 82n, 294
    and energy use, 140–146
    and the future, 107–108, 111–120,
        268–284
    and human capital, 70–71, 90, 91–93
    overdevelopment, 238
    and population growth, 20–24, 26–31
    rural development, 108, 109–110

development (*Continued*)
   sustainable development, 4–5, 13–15,
      41, 191–192, 272–276, 283–284
   theoretical models, 269–274
   urbanization, 11–15, *16*, 99, 108–109
development assistance, 2, 59–63, 109
Diamond, Jared, 273
diarrhea, 92
diet, 86, 100–104
Dow Chemical, 155–156
drought, 178
Dubos, René, 268, 275–276
DuPont, 156, 240n
Durning, Alan, 222n

Earth, carrying capacity of, 39–43,
      112–115
Earth Policy Institute, 151
Earth Summit (Rio de Janeiro, 1992), 4,
      25–26, 181, 182, 190–191,
      213–214
Eastern Asia, 58, 88, 89, 98, 149–150
Eastern Europe, 69, 279
Echeverria Alvarez, Luis, 34
economy, 51–80
   and biodiversity, 213–214
   and climate change, 66, 79–80
   development assistance, 59–63
   and energy consumption, 142–146
   food prices, 87, 88, 90, 96–97, 115
   and geography, 72–73
   and globalization, 1–2
   GNP/GDP (gross national/domestic
      product), 3–4, 44–45, 52–53, 60,
      66, 72–73, 80n, 143, 193, 269,
      274, 275, 282–283
   hidden costs, 66
   and human capital, 70–71, 90, 91–93
   knowledge intensive industries, 137
   market-driven vs. state-driven, 63–71,
      76
   multinational corporations, 68, 70
   negative externalities, 66
   oil prices, 1, 130–137
   and population growth, 21

   poverty and inequality, 52–59, 72–73,
      79, 88, 89–93
   recessions, 5, 52–53, 63, 66–67, 76, 79,
      88
   sustainable development, 4–5
     see also sustainable development
   tariffs and trade barriers, 62, 73–74
   theories, 63–73
   unemployment and
      underemployment, 21, 66, 76, 88,
      131
ecosystems, 176, 177–178, 179, 211–214,
      245–248
Ecuador, 231
education, 14–15, 29, 70–71
Egypt, 97, 103, 279
Ehrlich, Paul, 42, 49n, 213, 272
Einstein, Albert, 255
El Salvador, 43, 154
ElBaradei, Mohamed, 263
emerging economies, 13, 28, 182–183,
      194–195
energy, 129–165
   and agricultural systems, 94–95,
      114–115
   biofuels, 21, 110, 136, 139, 140–141,
      144, 148, 151, 181
   and climate change, 66, 79–80, 165
   coal, 138–139, *144*, 148
   cogeneration, 156
   and economic growth, 79–80, 142–146
   efficiency, 136, 137, 143–146, 154–157
   energy transition, 147–155, 156–157
   governmental policies, 133–139,
      164–165
   hydroelectric power, 149
   natural gas, 71, 134, 136, 137, *144*, 147,
      248
   nuclear power, 137–138, 139, *144*, 148,
      157–164
   nuclear weapons, 254–255, 256,
      257–263
   oil, 1, 130–137, 139, *144*, 147
   solar and geothermal energy, 151–154
   wind turbines, 149–150

entrepreneurs, 65
environment, 189–239
  arable land, 112–114
  biodiversity, 177, 213–214
  carrying capacity, 39–43
  deforestation, 109, 184, 207–211
  and economic growth, 3–5, 66
  ecosystems, 176, 177–178, 179,
    211–214, 245–248
  environmental education, 14–15
  environmental footprint, 113,
    154–157, 184–185
  and governmental policy, 41, 225 226,
    227, 232–236
  and meat production, 100–101, 113,
    114, 119, 211, 248–250
  mining, 206–207
  oceans, 176, 180–181, 231
  and politics, 236–238, 279–281,
    283–284
  pollution, 66, 147–148, 164, 171–173,
    176, 178, 181–184, 192–207
    acid rain, 164, 196, 200–202
    aerosols (soot), 181
    CFCs (chlorofluorocarbons), 171,
      199–200, 277–278
    chemicals and minerals, 205–206,
      224–227, 235, 273
    effects on health, 192–194, 196–198,
      199–200, 224–227
    pesticides and fertilizers, 106–107,
      116–117, 226–227, 246–248, 273
    and water quality, 43, 203–206,
      253–254
  radioactive waste, 159, 162, 163–164,
    262–263
  reforestation, 207, 208
  renewable energy, 21, 110, 140–141,
    147–155
  responsible use of resources, 13–15,
    233–236, 240n, 275–278
  rivers and lakes, 43, 203–206, 227,
    253–254
  soil erosion and desertification, 41,
    98–99, 112, 118–119, 208–209

  tragedy of the commons, 276–278
  waste management and disposal,
    228–236
    food waste, 96, 97–98
    plastic waste, 228–230, 235
    recycling, 14, 228, 232, 234–235
    toxic/hazardous waste, 159, 162,
      163–164, 205–207, 230–232, 235,
      262–263
  water quality, 43, 203–206
  water shortages, 43, 203
  see also climate change
Environmental Protection Agency (EPA)
  (US), 98, 134, 193, 199, 202, 204,
  227, 230–231, 249
equality, 277, 278–282
erosion, 41, 98–99, 112, 118–119,
  208–209
ethanol, 110, 140, 151
Ethiopia, 90, 91, 107–108
Europe, climate change in, 179–182
European Union
  climate change, 181–182
  culture, 216
  economy, 66
  energy policy, 136, 145, 146, 147, 149
  environment, 194, 198, 201, 205, 208,
    226, 234–235, 236
  food, 103, 117, 249
  population, 23–24
  technology, 249
eutrophication ("dead zones"), 106, 250
externalities, *see* negative externalities
extinctions, 211–214
extreme weather events, 174–175, 177,
  178, 181

factory farms, 248–250
family planning, 18, 19, 253
famine, 90–91
Farb, Peter, 94–95
fast-breeder nuclear reactors, 137–138,
  158–159
fertilizers, 106
fishing, 117–118, 277

flooding, 208–209
food, 85–120
  and climate change, 105, 111, 174
  diet and lifestyle, 100–104
  fishing and aquaculture, 118–119, 277
  hunger, 87–93
  malnutrition, 90, 91–93
  pesticide residues in, 107, 225–226
  production of, 86–87, 107–108,
    111–120
    future challenges, 119–120
    sustainable/traditional/organic
      methods, 94–95, 114–115
  tragedy of the commons, 276–278
  waste, 96, 97–98
Food and Agriculture Organization
  (FAO), 87–88, 207, 270
Food and Drug Administration (US), 249
Food Policy Research Institute, 270
footprint (environmental footprint), 113,
  154–157, 184–185
foreign aid (development assistance), 2,
  59–63, 109
forests, 109, 184, 207–211
fossil fuels, 79–80, 94–95, 133, 140–142,
  146–148, 153, 171–172
Fox, Vicente, 286n
fracking (gas and oil extraction), 71, 147,
  248
Framework Convention on Climate
  Change (UNFCCC) (1992), 181,
  182, 190–191
free markets, 63–67, 70–71
fuel cells, hydrogen-powered, 154–155
Fukushima nuclear accident (2011), 138,
  142, 161
Fukuyama, Francis, 5
fusion nuclear reactors, 159
future, 268–284
  food production, 107–108, 111–120
  population, 38–44

Gaia hypothesis, 319g
Gandhi, Indira, 35
Gandhi, Mahatma, 280

García Lorca, Federico, 86
gas (natural gas), 71, 134, 136, 137, *144*,
  248
Gates, Bill, 60
Gell-Mann, Murray, 275, 282
General Agreement on Tariffs and Trade
  (GATT), 73–74
genetic engineering, 115–117
geography, and economic development,
  72–73
geothermal energy, 153–154
Germany
  climate change and environmental
    issues, 182, 201, 232, 233
  economy and energy supply, 65,
    152–153
  population, 24
glaciers, 174
global issues
  definition, 1–2
  and the future, 268–284
"global village," 77–78
global warming *see* climate change
globalization, 73–78, 79
GNP/GDP (gross national/domestic
  product), 3–4, 44–45, 52–53, 60,
  66, 72–73, 80n, 143, 193, 269,
  274, 275, 282–283
Goleman, Daniel, 223n
governmental policies, 276–282
  and civil society, 63, 278–282
  climate change, 181–185
  economy, 63–71
  energy, 133–139, 164–165
  environment, 41, 225–226, 227,
    232–236
  food policies, 108–111
  population, 31–38
governmental services, 15
Grameen Bank, 279, 281, 286n
Grant, James, 93
Great Britain *see* United Kingdom
Great Lakes, 204
Green Belt Movement, 280
"Green" Revolution, 105–108, 227, 273

greenhouse gasses, 147–148, 164, 171–173, 176, 181–184, 194, 202

Greenland, 174, 178, 180, 196, 198

Greenspan, Alan, 79

Gulf War (1990–1991), 132, 256, 260

Hardin, Garrett, 253, 276–277

Haryana (India), 18

Hausman, Ricardo, 73

health, 14, 21, 22

  animal welfare, 248–250

  breast-feeding, *30*, 90, 103–104

  costs of healthcare, 22–23

  diet and lifestyle, 100–104

  effects of air pollution on, 192–194, 196–198

  effects of chemical pollution on, 107, 224–227, 246–248

  effects of malnutrition on children, 90, 91–93

  effects of radioactivity on, 159–160

  effects of sunburn on, 199–200

  infectious diseases, 178, 246–247, 249

  obesity, 92, 102

  and productivity, 93

  public health programs, 17

herbicide-resistant crops, 116, 117

Hitler, Adolf, 73

Hooker Chemical Company, 230

Hubbard, Harold M., 242n

human capital, 70–71, 90, 91–93

Hungary, 154

hunger, 87–93, 119–120

Hunger Task Force, 88, 91

hurricanes, 174–175

hydroelectric power, 149

hydrogen-powered fuel cells, 154–155

Iceland, 154

imperialism, 67

India

  civil society, 280

  climate change and environmental issues, 181, 182, 208–209, 279

  economy, 52, 53, 55, 58, 80n

  energy issues, 21, 148, 151, 159, 163

  food, 97, 103, 105, 116

  foreign policy, 261

  population, 18, 19, 29, 35

Indian Ocean, 196

indigenous peoples, 215–217, 277

Indonesia, 208, 280

industrialization, 28, 52, 68–69, 93–97, 105–108

inequality, 52–55, 277, 278–282

infant mortality rates, 17, 19, 29

infectious diseases, 178, 246–247, 249

infrastructure, 6n, 67

interdisciplinary knowledge, 2, 293

Intergovernmental Panel on Climate Change (IPCC), 172, 174, 176–178, 179–180, 185n, 209, 271

intermediate technology, 250–253

International Atomic Energy Agency, 260, 263

International Center for Technology Assessment, 136

International Conference on Population and Development (Cairo, 1994), 26, 33–34

International Conference on Population (Mexico City, 1984), 25

International Energy Agency (IEA), 148, 183, 271

International Labour Organization, 52

International Planned Parenthood Federation, 25, 34

international studies, teaching techniques, 294–296

international trade, 67–68, 72

  knowledge intensive industries, 137

  tariffs and trade barriers, 62, 73–74

Iran, nuclear program, 255, 261–262

Iranian Revolution (1979), 130–131, 250

Iraq War (2003–2011), 133, 256, 257

iron deficiency, 93

Iroquois, 283

Irresistible Empire: America's Advance through 20th Century Europe (de Grazia), 82n

irrigation, 44, 94–95, 98, 105, 107, 203
Italy, 62, 163, 209

Japan
    climate change and environmental
        issues, 44, 182, 230, 234,
        236
    economy and energy supply, 22, 65,
        136–138, 145, 146
    food, 98, 109
    population, 22, 23, 24, 35

Kashmir, 261
Kent, Mary Mederios, 38
Kenya, 280
Kerala (India), 29
Keynes, John Maynard, 63
knowledge intensive industries, 137
Kolkata (Calcutta, India), 12
Kuwait, invasion of, 132
Kyoto Protocol (1997), 181–182

laterite, 211
Latin America
    climate change, 180
    economy, 82n, 279
    energy, 148–149
    environment, 208, 209, 210–211,
        216–217, 231
    food, 89
    sustainable cities, 14–15
lead pollution, 196–198
Lerner, Jaime, 15
Lewis, Simon, 209
Liberia, 251–252
life expectancy, 17
Lima (Peru), 281
List, Friedrich, 70–71
logging, environmental impact of,
    208–211
Los Angeles (CA), 193–194
Lovins, Amory, 157

Maathai, Wangari, 280
malaria, 246–247

Malaysia, 208
malnutrition, 88, 90, 91–93
Malthus, Thomas, 39
Mao, Zedong, 35
market-driven economic development,
    63–67, 70–71, 76
markets, regulation of, 4, 6n, 71, 117
Marx, Karl, 63, 65
May, Robert, 212
McDonald's, 249
measles, 92
meat, environmental cost of, 100–101,
    113, 114, 119, 211, 248–250
Mediterranean diet, 104
megacities, 12–13
Mendes, Chico, 281
Merrill, Dan, 71
methane gas, 139, 149, 151, 171–172,
    181, 184, 248
Mexico, *28*, 34–35, 105, 206, 286n
Mexico City policy, 42, 47n
Middle East, 1, 98, 130–133, 140
migration
    and population growth, 10
    and war, 43
military aid, 60
Millennium Development Goals
    (MDGs), 4–5, 53, 55–57, 59–61,
    79, 81n, 91, 191, 192
Miller, Lynn, 51
Milton, Katharine, 223n
minerals, 206–207, 235
minority ethnic groups, 58, 194, 197,
    215–217
Mississippi River, 273
monoculture, 106
Montreal Protocol on Substances that
    Deplete the Ozone Layer (1987),
    199–200
morality, and foreign aid, 42, 47n, 58–60,
    61
Movimento dos Trabalhadores Rurais
    Sem Terra, 280
Mubarak, Hosni, 279
multinational corporations, 68, 70

NASA (National Aeronautical and Space Administration), 173
National Academy of Sciences (US), 46, 111, 117, 155, 179, 227, 262–263
National Cancer Institute (US), 224–225
National Climate Assessment (US), 181
National Population Council (Mexico), 35
national security, and energy, 132–133
NATO (North Atlantic Treaty Organization), 256–257
natural gas, 71, 134, 136, 137, *144*, 248
natural resources, 8
negative externalities, 66
neo-colonialism, 67–68
New England Journal of Medicine, 197, 249
New Orleans (LA), 174–175
New York City, 174–175
Niagara Falls (NY), 230
Nixon, Richard, 134
non-governmental organizations (NGOs), 58–59, 60
North, the (Global North), 6n
    energy issues, 130–138, 141–146
    international trade, 62, 67–68
    population, 22–24, 36, 38
North America, climate change, 180
North Korea, 91, 255, 261, 262
North Sea oil and gas, 136
Norway, 103, 119, 136, 201
nuclear power, 137–138, 139, *144*, 148, 157–164
nuclear weapons, 161–162, 254–255, 256, 257–263

obesity, 92, 102
Oceania, 88
oil, 1, 130–137, 139, *144*, 147
ONE Campaign, 61
one-child policy (China), 35–36
organic agriculture, 114–115
Organisation for Economic Co-operation and Development (OECD), 62–63

Organization of Petroleum Exporting Countries (OPEC), 130, 131, 140
Ostrom, Elinor, 277
overdevelopment, 238
overpopulation, 43–44
ozone depletion, 171, 198–200, 277–278

Pacific Ocean, 228–229
Pakistan, 21, 105, 148, 261
parachuting cats, 246–247
pastoralism, 88
per capita income, 3, 52–53
Peru, 281
pesticides, 106–107, 116–117, 226–227, 246–248, 273
Pimentel, David, 98
plastic waste, 228–230, 235–236
polar regions, 173–174, 178, 180, 196, 198, 231
policing, 68–69
politics
    and civil society, 63, 278–282
    colonialism and neo-colonialism, 67–68
    communism, 66, 69
    democracy, 281–282
    environmental politics, 236–238, 279–281
    and nuclear power, 157–158, 161–164, 254–255, 256, 257–263
    and oil, 1, 130–138
    suppression of dissent, 68–69
    terrorism, 162, 163, 263
    wars, 130–131, 132–133, 254–263
pollution, 66, 147–148, 164, 171–173, 176, 178, 181–184, 192–207
    acid rain, 164, 196, 200–202
    aerosols (soot), 181
    CFCs (chlorofluorocarbons), 171, 199–200, 277–278
    chemicals and minerals, 205–206, 224–227, 230–232, 235, 273
    effects on health, 192–194, 196–198, 199–200, 224–227

pollution (*Continued*)
  pesticides and fertilizers, 106–107,
      116–117, 226–227, 246–248, 273
  and water quality, 43, 203–206,
      253–254
population, 7–46, 119
  aging, 22–24, 36, 38
  birth control, 18, 19, 31–36, 42, 47n,
      253
  birth rates, 9–11, 17–24, 26–31
  death rates, 17, 19, 26–28, 173
  and development, 20–24, 26–31
  and the future, 38–44
  governmental policies, 31–38
  life expectancy, 17, 22
  optimum size of, 42–43
  overpopulation, 43–44
  'population explosion,' 3, 8–22, 38–39
  sex ratio, 18–19, 35–36
Population Bomb, The (Ehrlich), 272
postharvest waste, 96, 97–98
poverty, 52–55, 194, 197
  extreme poverty, 53, *54*, 55, 56–59,
      61–62, 79
productivity, and health, 93
public transportation, 14
PV (solar photovoltaic) cells, 151–153

quality of life, 41

radioactive waste, 159, 162, 163–164,
      262–263
Reagan, Ronald, 42, 47n, 254
recessions, 5, 52–53, 63, 66–67, 76, 79, 88
recycling, 14, 228, 232, 234–235
reforestation, 207, 208
religion, and family planning, 19, 25, 34,
      37
renewable energy, 21, 110, 140–141, *144*,
      148–155
Repetto, Robert, 242n
resource efficiency, 13–15, 233–234,
      240n, 275–278
Rhine (river), 205
Ricardo, David, 65

rice, 108, 116
Rifkin, Jeremy, 130, 165n
Rio Earth Summit (1992), 4, 25–26, 181,
      182, 190–191, 213–214
Rio+20 (2012), 192
Romania, 37–38, 234
Royal Society of London, 46
rural development, 108, 109–110
Russian Federation, 24, 111, 147–148,
      154, 159, 207
  foreign policy, 255, 257
  see also Soviet Union

Sahel region (Africa), 58, 90, 98, 179
San Francisco (CA), 227
Sardovaya organization (Sri Lanka), 280
Saudi Arabia, 132, 133, 147, 191
SC Johnson Wax, 233
Schell, Jonathan, 259–260
Scheper-Hughes, Nancy, 61–62
Schumacher, E. F., 250–251
Scotchgard, 226, 231, 232
sea levels, and climate change, 175–176
Seattle (WA), 227
Seitz, John L., 21–22, 155
sex ratio, 18–19, 35–36
Shenzhen (China), 13–14
Silent Spring (Carson), 226, 272
Simon, Julian, 42, 49n, 269
slums, 11–12
*Small Is Beautiful: Economics as if
      People Mattered* (Schumacher),
      250–251
Smil, Vaclav, 114
Smith, Adam, 63–65, 72
smog, 192–196
  see also air pollution
soil erosion, 41, 98–99, 112, 118–119,
      208–209
solar power, 151–153
Somalia, 91
soot (aerosols), 181
South, the (Global South), 4, 6n,
      140–141, 293
  see also development

South Asia, 58, 88, 89, 148
South Korea, 71, 109, 202
Southeast Asia, 88, 89, 90, 98, 116, 208
Soviet Union
    arms race, 254–255, 258–260, 262
    economic issues and energy use, 67,
        69, 70, 160
    food, 87, 90, 110
    see also Russian Federation
Spain, 52, 149
Sprout, Harold, 236–237
Sprout, Margaret, 236–237
Sri Lanka, 280
"Star Wars," 254–255
state-driven economic development,
    67–71
Stevenson, Adlai E., 189
Stockholm Conference (1972), 190
strip mining, 206–207
stunted growth, children, 88, 90, 91–93
substitution, of non-renewable resources,
    235–236, 240n
Sudan, 91, 257
Superfund, 232
Survival International, 217
sustainable agriculture, 114–115
sustainable development, 4–5, 13–15, 41,
    191–192, 272–276, 283–284
Sweden, 28, 201

Taiwan, 109, 151
tar sands, 147
taxation, 156, 184
technology, 244–264
    agriculture, 86–87, 93–97, 105–108,
        248–250
    biotechnology, 115–117
    energy transition, 147–155
    impact on ecosystems, 245–248
    intermediate technology, 250–253
    nuclear weapons, 161–162, 254–255,
        256, 257–263
    regulation of, 71, 117, 199–200,
        225–226, 227, 248, 249–250
Teitelbaum, Michael S., 47n

temperate zone, agricultural production,
    73
terrorism, 162, 163, 263
Thailand, 32, 118–119, 202
Third World *see* South, the (Global
    South)
Three Mile Island nuclear accident
    (1979), 159–160, 161, 163
Thurow, Lester, 237
Toxic Release Inventory, 230–231
toxic/hazardous waste, 159, 162,
    163–164, 205–207, 230–232,
    262–263
Toynbee, Arnold J., 244
trade, 67–68, 72
    knowledge intensive industries, 137
    tariffs and trade barriers, 62, 73–74
traditional agriculture, 94–95, 114–115
tragedy of the commons, 276–278
    see also climate change
transportation, 6n, 14, 67, 72, 73
    and energy efficiency, 145–146,
        154–155
trash collection and disposal, 14, 151
    plastic waste, 228–230, 235–236
    recycling, 14, 228, 232, 234–235
    toxic/hazardous waste, 159, 162,
        163–164, 205–207, 228–236,
        262–263
tribal cultures, 215–217, 277
tropical zone, agricultural production, 73
Tuvalu, 176

Ultimate Resource, The (Simon), 42
UN Security Council, 261–262
UNDP (United Nations Development
    Programme), 3, 55, 79
unemployment, 21, 66, 76, 88, 131
UNICEF (United Nations Children's
    Fund), 103
United Kingdom
    climate change and environmental
        issues, 182, 192–193, 194, 201
    energy, 136, 142
    food, 97–98, 103

United Nations Conference on
   Environment and Development
   (UNCED, Rio de Janeiro, 1992),
   4, 25–26, 181, 182, 190–191,
   213–214
United Nations Conference on
   Sustainable Development (Rio de
   Janeiro, 2012), 192
United Nations Conference on the
   Human Environment
   (Stockholm, 1972), 190
United Nations Development
   Programme (UNDP), 3, 55, 79
United Nations Environmental
   Programme (UNEP), 176, 198,
   270–271, 274, 275, 284n
United Nations Food and Agriculture
   Organization (FAO), 87–88, 207,
   270
United Nations Framework Convention
   on Climate Change (UNFCCC),
   181, 182, 190–191
United Nations Fund for Population
   Activities, 25
United Nations Millennium Declaration,
   4–5, 59
United Nations Millennium
   Development Goals (MDGs),
   4–5, 53, 55–57, 59–61, 79, 81n,
   91, 191, 192
United Nations Sustainable Development
   Agenda and Goals (SDGs), 5, 192
United States
   aquaculture, 118
   climate change, 180, 181, 182,
      183–184, 191–192, 278
   cultural imperialism, 76, 215–216
   diet and lifestyle, 100, 101–103
   economic growth, 71, 75–76, 142–146,
      165n
   energy efficiency, 156–157, 167n
   energy policy, 147, 148
   environmental politics, 236–238
   food production, 93–96, 97, 115
   foreign aid, 62, 109

   foreign policy, 130, 131, 132–133
   governmental policies, 134–136,
      225–226, 227
   nuclear power, 159–160, 162
   oil, 130–131, 132–133
   pollution
      air pollution, 193–194, 201, 202
      lead pollution, 196–198
      pesticides and fertilizers, 226–227
      water pollution, 204–205
   population, 95
   poverty and inequality, 52, 194, 197
   recessions, 66–67, 88
   reforestation, 207, 208
   renewable energy, 110–111, 149, 150,
      151, 154
   soil erosion and desertification, 98, 99
   technological innovation, 71, 251–255
   waste collection and disposal, 228,
      230–231, 232, 234, 262–263
   water use, 203
urbanization, 11–15, *16*, 99, 108–109
US Environmental Protection Agency,
   98, 134, 193, 199, 202, 204, 227,
   230–231, 249
US Food and Drug Administration, 249
US National Academy of Sciences, 46,
   111, 117, 155, 179, 227, 262–263
US National Cancer Institute, 224–225

VanDeveer, Stacy, 275
Venezuela, 139, 216, 217
vitamin deficiencies, 92
von Clausewitz, Carl, 257

Wallerstein, Immanuel, 67
Waltz, Kenneth, 255
Ward, Barbara, 101–102, 109, 232
wars, 43, 130–131, 132–133, 254–263
Washington Consensus, 4–5
waste, 228–236
   chemicals and minerals, 205–207,
      230–232, 235
   food waste, 96, 97–98
   plastic waste, 228–230, 235–236

radioactive waste, 159, 162, 163–164, 262–263

recycling, 14, 228, 232, 234–235

water

acid rain, 164, 196, 200–202

and climate change, 174, 175–178

hydroelectric power, 149

irrigation, 43–44, 94–95, 98, 105, 107, 203

oceans, 176, 180–181, 231

rivers and lakes, 43, 203–206, 227, 253–254

wealth and poverty, 51–80

weather, and climate change, 174–175, 177, 178, 181

West Germany *see* Germany

Western Europe *see* European Union

wheat, 108

Wilson, Edward O., 212, 214

wind turbines, 149–150

Wolfe, Alan, 82n

women

education, 29

poverty, 58, 88

use of contraception, 19, 29, 32–33

World Bank, 6n, 53, 58, 88, 195, 203, 251

World Economic Forum, 269, 270, 271, 273, 275

World Health Organization, 88, 90, 93, 104, 107, 193, 194, 205, 227, 247, 249

World March of Women, 281

World Population Conference (Bucharest, 1974), 24–25, 31–32

World Resources Institute, 99, 107, 114–115, 118

World Summit on Sustainable Development (Johannesburg, 2002), 191–192

World Trade Organization (WTO), 74–75

Yanomami, 216–217

Yergin, Daniel, 131–132

Yugoslavia, 281–282

Yunus, Muhammad, 279, 286n